A Multimodal Analysis of Picture Books for Children

Discussions in Functional Approaches to Language

Series Editor: Robin Fawcett, Cardiff University

The books in this series are mainly addressed to teachers, researchers and postgraduate students of language in universities and colleges, though some will be equally suitable for bright undergraduate readers. The books will be readable but scholarly.

Books in the series present and discuss a new or established topic in linguistic theory, or a new description of an area of language, or both. They may also offer a critique of a previously published work of either theory or description. Any relevant alternative approaches will also be discussed.

Published

The Development of Scientific Writing: Linguistic Features and Historical Context
David Banks

English Tense and Aspect in Halliday's Systemic Functional Grammar: A Critical Appraisal and an Alternative
Carl Bache

The Structure of Modern Irish: A Functional Account
Brian Nolan

A Multimodal Analysis of Picture Books for Children

A Systemic Functional Approach

Arsenio Jesús Moya Guijarro

SHEFFIELD UK BRISTOL CT

Published by Equinox Publishing Ltd.

UK: Office 415, The Workstation, 15 Paternoster Row, Sheffield, South Yorkshire S1 2BX
USA: ISD, 70 Enterprise Drive, Bristol, CT 06010

www.equinoxpub.com

First published 2014

British Library Cataloguing-in-Publication Data

A catalogue record for this book is available from the British Library.

ISBN 978 1 908049 77 3 (hardback)
978 1 908049 78 0 (paperback)

Library of Congress Cataloging-in-Publication Data

Moya Guijarro, Arsenio Jesús. A multimodal analysis of picture books for children: a systemic functional approach / Arsenio Jesús Moya Guijarro.
pages cm. – (Discussions in Functional Approaches to Language)
Includes bibliographical references and index.
ISBN 978-1-908049-77-3 (hb) – ISBN 978-1-908049-78-0 (pb)
1. Modality (Linguistics) 2. Children's literature–History and criticism. 3. Children–Books and reading–English-speaking countries. 4. Children–Books and reading. 5. Narration (Rhetoric) 6. Discourse analysis, Literary. I. Title.
P99.4.M6M68 2014
302.2–dc23
2014011967

Typeset by S.J.I. Services, New Delhi
Printed and bound by Lightning Source Inc. (La Vergne, TN), Lighting Source UK Ltd. (Milton Keynes), Lightning Source AU Pty. (Scoresby, Victoria).

To my beloved son,
Abraham Prince.

Contents

List of tables

List of figures

Acknowledgements

I would like to express my gratitude to Chris Butler for his invaluable input and encouraging remarks throughout the research and writing stages of this book. His kind dedication and generosity, along with his unquestionable expertise, have proven indispensable for the structuring and creative development of this study, and have certainly perfected its potential as a useful tool for strategically approaching children's picture books. I am particularly grateful to him for dedicating his time to clarifying some of the analytical aspects and for helping with the statistical analysis presented in Chapters 6, 7 and 8. I am solely responsible for any errors which remain.

I would also like to thank Claudia Alonso, Christine Harris and Maria Baldereli for their stylistic suggestions and helpful advice for the finishing touches of the book.

Last but not least, the author wishes to thank the following publishing houses for granting permission to reproduce both written and visual material:

Text and Illustrations © 1984 John Burningham. From *Granpa* by John Burningham, published by Jonathan Cape. Reprinted by permission of The Random House Group Limited.

Text © 1994 Sam McBratney. Illustrations © 1994 Anita Jeram. From *Guess How Much I Love You* written by Sam McBratney and illustrated by Anita Jeram. Reproduced by permission of Walker Books Ltd, London SE11 5HJ. www.walker.co.uk

Copyright © 1983 Anthony Browne. From *Gorilla* by Anthony Browne. Reproduced by permission of Walker Books Ltd, London SE11 5HJ. www.walker.co.uk

Text and Illustrations © 1992 by North-South Books Inc.. From *The Rainbow Fish* by Marcus Pfister. Reproduced by permission of NorthSüd.

Photo of the cover image made by David Segovia Llanos.

1 Introduction

The study that is proposed here goes beyond the relation between the representation of reality and language alone; instead, it aims to analyse the intersemiosis between verbal and visual elements in a sample of nine picture books. The chapters included in this book take the most relevant systemic-functional and visual social semiotic theories a step further from previous studies and apply them to the genre of children's tales. Within the frameworks of Halliday's Systemic Functional Grammar (SFG) and Kress and van Leeuwen's Visual Social Semiotics, I attempt to identify the verbal and visual strategies available to the writer and illustrator: (i) to convey representational meanings; (ii) to set up interpersonal relationships within the tale itself, as well as external relationships between writer and reader; and, finally (iii) to create coherent tales. This is achieved by analysing and identifying the ideational, interpersonal and textual choices available to the writer to create meaning in picture books, and comparing them with the corresponding representational, interactive and compositional choices made by the illustrator. The analysis reveals how the verbal and visual modalities contribute to each other's meaning and illuminates the multiple semiotic possibilities inherent to the combining of verbal and non-verbal language in picture books.

The current study offers an innovative aspect in relation to previous analyses of picture books. These children's stories have been approached primarily from a literary perspective according to their themes (Feaver 1977) and also in connection with cognitive development (Spitz 1999; Moya and Ávila 2009). However, in these analyses, the intersemiosis between verbal and visual aspects has been neglected. Indeed, only a few researchers, among them Moebius (1986) and Nikolajeva and Scott (2000), have studied the alliance between language and illustrations in this genre through a fundamentally literary framework that, although revealing, unfortunately disregards the meaningful exegetical possibilities afforded by a purely linguistic analysis. Other researchers such as Lewis (2006), Unsworth (2006, 2008 a and b), Painter (2007), Martin (2008) and Painter *et al.* (2013) have also analysed picture books in some of their studies from a multimodal perspective. However, their works do not consider the age of the children for whom the tales are intended as a key factor in the verbal and visual organizations of the stories. The study of this factor is important, since the cognitive development of the children for whom the tales are intended may play a key role in the verbal and visual choices available to writers and illustrators to create stories that are both coherently organized and appropriate for their potential readers.

1.1 Aims and scope of the book

The primary aim of this book is to explore the choices available to the writer/illustrator in conveying representational, interpersonal and textual meanings in both the verbal and non-verbal components of nine picture books designed for children of three different stages of cognitive development (Piaget, 1981, 1984): sensory-motor stage (0–2 years old), pre-operational stage (3–6 years old) and concrete operations stage (7–9 years old). After analysing three representative picture books from each age group, I have also tried to determine the extent to which the age factor influences the verbal and visual choices actually made by writers and illustrators of children's tales to create stories that are appropriate and sufficiently interesting for their potential readers. The potential readership's age is of chief relevance, and the wide spectrum that children's literature absorbs cannot and should not be easily dismissed. Reynolds (2005: 2) attests to the impossibility of downplaying this factor when claiming that the age group of the young children 'encompasses everything from the earliest literature such as myths, legends, folk and fairy tales to the latest work for teenage readers. Its audience ranges in age from newborns to those who are preparing to leave school.' Considering the multitude of genres and psycho-social cognitive developments at play, there is little wonder in the fact that sometimes it is difficult to ascertain to what age group a specific tale is aimed at. In the editorial world, for strictly commercial reasons, recommendations are usually made about the appropriate age to read a story, which usually extends the period for which, initially, a certain work had been created. It is not unusual to find reviews of picture books in which the age range that the story is aimed towards is significantly expanded. At times, as as was the case in the following recommendations made for the picture book, *Where's Spot?* by Eric Hill, the tale is even promoted as an attractive story for children up to six years old, when in reality it is appropriate for children up to two years old:

> This is a great book for all ages and although it was given to me for a 2 year old, it could be used before this age and beyond; ... Five and six year olds eagerly anticipate the opening of each flap and are overjoyed when they can 'guess' the hidden object.
> (http://www.ciao.co.uk/Wheres_Spot_Eric_Hill__Review_5751574)

Thus, the public range that can consume the literary product described is amplified. This, however, can lead mediators (those who recommend books to parents and preschool and primary school teachers) to make erroneous recommendations when the time comes to select the most appropriate readings for the infantile public. Sometimes the selection and recommendation of stories are motivated more by purely commercial motives than by objective criteria and reasoning that take into account the cognitive development of the reader and linguistic and visual factors.

For this reason, some researchers on children's literature have devoted their studies to the appropriate classification of children's stories according to the reading comprehension level and cognitive development of their prospective readers. These studies are based on literary analysis and also on Piagetian developmental psychology. Using Piaget's (1981, 1984) framework as the basis of their studies, Cerrillo (1996) and Cerrillo and Yubero (2007) classify storybooks by taking the difference in the cognitive stages of the intended audiences as an explanatory variable. These researchers categorize children's tales on the basis of four Piagetian-based stages of cognitive development: the sensory-motor stage, which includes children from 0 to 2 years of age, the pre-operational stage (3–7 years) and two stages of concrete operations (from 7–9 years and from 9–11 years). The child readership or audience is by no means homogeneous and the cognitive and linguistic abilities of the youngest children vary substantially by age. A suitable selection of storybooks according to age needs to consider the cognitive ability of the child at each stage of development, as it is essential that stories are tailored to meet the linguistic and psychological maturity of the children for which they are written and illustrated.

The study carried out in this book attempts to contribute in the specific task of providing more empirical clues to classify picture books according to the age group of the children for whom they are initially intended. Utilizing

SFG and Kress and van Leeuwen's social semiotics, I have attempted to expand the information that is shown on the tales' covers, on web pages, public brochures or literary reviews that state the age range for which a specific tale has been written and illustrated.[1] The analytical tools offered by SFG and Visual Social Semiotics have been applied to the sample books in order to identify the verbal and visual strategies used and preferred by writers and illustrators in the tales intended for the children of each stage of cognitive development. I have performed an analysis to find out whether there is a statistically-significant positive correlation between the types of strategies used to represent the narrative reality in the tales included in each age group and the age of the children for whom the tales were initially created. This way I have tried to determine the extent to which the age factor exerts an influence on the verbal and visual strategies used by writers and illustrators to create tales that are appealing to young readers. The acquired results, based on linguistic and visual analysis, give mediators specific clues to help them choose appropriate tales that are adequate for the cognitive development of young readers.

This book also aims to contribute to the critical analysis of Halliday's Systemic Functional Grammar and Kress and van Leuwen's Visual Social Semiotics. The application of the Systemic Functional Linguistics and Visual Social Semiotics categories to the empirical analysis of the tales has at times generated difficulties. These problems, as well as the ways in which they have been resolved, are described and exemplified with extracts taken from text

1. In a recent publication on visual narratives Painter *et al.* (2013: 3) state that, although Kress and van Leeuwen's visual semiotics provides an invaluable tool to approach the visual word, their grammar is 'insufficiently developed for addressing key aspects of picture books'. They essentially refer to the lack of systems available in Kress and van Leeuwen's grammar to deal with relations between images in sequence and to express emotional engagement. The study that is carried out here is fundamentally based on Kress and van Leeuwen's grammar, since it seeks to offer a general semiotic model for analysing a broad range of images. I have also taken some of Painter (2007) and Painter *et al.*'s (2013) theories (focalization, character appearance through metonymy, etc.) which, building on Kress and van Leeuwen's visual grammar, extend and develop the principles to understand the relation between verbal and visual modes in picture books. The applications of the new systems they propose, with their different levels of delicacy, offer relevant information for research on aspects of pathos and affect, ambience, graduation, etc. which are beyond the scope of this book. Unfortunately, this book was published only after the research for the present volume had been completed.

samples. A critical vision of the theoretical models used and their practical applications is thus offered. In the sections on 'troubleshooting' included in Chapters 3, 4 and 5, I discuss some of the problems encountered while trying to apply the categories of SFG and Social Semiotics to the sample texts. When necessary, these troubleshooting sections are also contemplated to suggest what possible revisions to the theoretical frames would improve the theories' applicability to the analysis of picture books.

1.2 Structure of the book

Chapter 1 is an introduction which outlines the scope of the book, its structure and its overall motivation (sections 1.1 and 1.2). Section 1.3 relates the appropriateness of the children's picture books that form the sample texts to child development and cognition. The last section of this chapter describes the main characteristics of picture books as a genre devoted to young readers and specifies the features of the tales which have been selected for analysis.

Chapter 2 offers a justification of why Systemic Functional Linguistics and Visual Social Semiotics are coherent frameworks for carrying out a textual and visual study of picture books. I give reasons for preferring SFG-theory to other existing alternatives such as Functional Discourse Grammar or the Cardiff Grammar, which are also used to analyse language through metafunctional domains. In this chapter, reference is also made to the Multimodal Discourse Analysis by O'Halloran (2004, 2005) and the Multimodal Interactional Analysis by Norris (2004) as they are, together with Kress and van Leeuwen's (2006) Social Semiotics, the three main approaches within multimodal studies (Jewitt 2009c: 28–29). The final section of the chapter offers a definition of the notion of mode, a controversial term which has been approached from different multimodal perspectives.

Following the first two chapters outlining the aims of the book and the data subjected to analysis, Chapters 3, 4 and 5 examine the theoretical perspectives instrumental to the study: the categories used by Halliday (2004) and Kress and van Leeuwen (2006) within the representational, interpersonal and textual metafunctions. Basic system networks that show the semiotic and simultaneous choices available in a given domain are used in the theoretical sections to present the different verbal and visual resources available to the user of the language within SFG-theory and Visual Social Semiotics to create meaning. In these three chapters, I discuss each of the three metafunctions separately and exemplify each one by focusing on one representative case study. In the three of them, a section called *troubleshooting* is devoted to those aspects of the representational, interpersonal and textual metafunctions of the language whose application to the analysis of picture books may cause some problems to the analyst. Examples extracted from the tales are provided and commented on in order to describe the difficulties encountered. The decisions made to sort them out are illustrated, thus contributing to the critical analysis of the systemic functional and social semiotic approaches and their applications to real texts. The chapters finish with the analysis of the intersemiosis of verbal and visual elements in three specific tales intended for young children: *The Very Hungry Caterpillar, Where the Wild Things Are* and *Gorilla*. This part incorporates an intermodal perspective on the study of the tales, as it includes not only the meanings created by the verbal and the visual modes as independent texts, but also the resulting meaning conveyed by the interplay and combination of their verbal and visual modalities. Among other approaches, the theories developed by Gill (2002), Unsworth (2006, 2008 a and b) and Unsworth and Cléirigh (2009) are considered to describe the resources available to the analyst for defining the intermodal construction of representational, interpersonal and textual meanings.

In Chapters 6, 7 and 8 I consider all the tales of the analytical corpus in an effort to identify the choices afforded to the writer/illustrator in conveying representational, interpersonal and textual meanings in the sample texts. This way, I show how the three metafunctions operate in relation to the issue of age-appropriateness. The verbal and visual strategies used by the writers and illustrators of the tales to: (i) represent the narrative reality (Chapter 6); (ii) enable the engagement between the child-reader and the characters of fiction (Chapter 7); and (iii) create coherent wholes of communication (Chapter 8), are identified and exemplified. The comparison between the choices available to writers and illustrators to convey representational, interpersonal and textual meanings reveals the extent to which age is a key factor in the intersemiosis of verbal and visual modes in the sample texts. A chi-square analysis using SPSS is carried out to prove whether the differences in distribution are statistically significant.[2]

2. The SPSS (Statistical Package for Social Sciences) is an adequate statistical package to investigate the association between the variables under research as it exposes the contrast between the observed values of frequency and those which would be expected if there were no association between frequency of linguistic features and age stage.

Chapter 9, divided into three sections, summarizes the main points made in the book and the main results obtained. The first section recapitulates and reflects on the way in which the verbal and visual modalities correlate through their construction of representational, interactive and textual meanings in the tales intended for the youngest children (0–2 years). The other two sections deal with the strategies used by writers and illustrators to combine verbal and visual modes in picture books aimed at 3–6 and 7–9 year-old children. Special emphasis is made on the influence that the age factor has on a picture book's creation. The results of the analysis may also help teachers and mediators recommend more appropriate readings for children of different evolutionary periods.

1.3 Picture books, child development and the age factor

In this section I introduce a description of the common characteristics that define the stories that have been included in each stage of cognitive development. Along with design and format, the major criteria of selection of storybooks underlying the different developmental stages are conceptual and linguistic difficulty, which naturally increase as the child gets older and has a more developed cognitive capacity. Each stage is slotted into age groups and is defined by different cognitive structures, which signify a specific way of comprehending reality and expressing it linguistically (Piaget 1981, 1984). The theory of the developmental stages by Piaget provides an adequate framework to carry out this study, since the degree of development of the child, psychologically as well as linguistically, at different ages, conditions his or her capacity to understand the illustrated stories created for him/her.

I am aware that other psychological theories do not consider Piaget's philosophy as a sensible choice, especially those that follow Vygotsky (1978), and emphasize the importance of social factors in children's development (Donalson 1978; Light *et al.* 1979).[3] However, as the main aim of this book is to identify the verbal and visual strategies available to writers and illustrators of picture books intended for children in different age groups,

3. Piaget (1981, 1984) defends the idea that children's development is self-constructed and is not dependent on social factors. However, Vygotsky (1978) considers that knowledge is fostered from social interaction with others. Development is therefore seen as a consequence of social and cultural learning experience and not as the result of cognitive biological stages.

Piaget's framework, also adapted by other specialists in children's literature, seems to be the most suitable for our purposes. It helps to categorize literary works according to the developmental stage and reading capability of the prospective children. Furthermore, the fact that the selected works have been recommended for some specific age groups in different studies, some of them widely recognized, supports our choice in favour of this particular framework. Classic studies on children's literature with sound psycholinguistic basis defend this perspective and classify literary works according to the features mentioned before (Tucker 1984; Townsend 1990; Cerrillo and Yubero 2007; Strachan 2008; Moya and Ávila 2009).

Following essentially Cerrillo and Yubero's (2007: 287–289) classification of children's tales, I will allude to the topics, literary structure and format of the tales intended for the children of each cognitive stage of development. The first is the sensory-motor stage and comprises children from birth to 2 years. In this phase the child experiences sensory-motor actions with his body and, therefore, feels especially attracted to the musicality of rhymes and verses accompanied by movements and gestures (lullabies, mimicry games). Thus, for children of normal development in this period, understanding the storybooks requires that they are capable of learning about themselves and their environment through motor and simple reflex activity. The topics tend to be closely related to the child's environment (the home, toys) and the animal world. The tales are characterized by a very simple structure and simple content with basic expressions. In terms of their design, full-page, colour illustrations with simplified images are predominant as they help the child decode the content that is being transmitted. The format and the font are large. The books are made of resistant materials so that children can manipulate them freely without breaking them.

The stories intended for children in the pre-operational stage, from 3 to 6 years of age, expand the range of topics dealt with, and revolve around the home, nature and school; fables and short stories with daily anecdotes and personified animals are also included. Regarding literary structure, the storybooks are characterized by their expressive simplicity and sparse conceptual content. The temporal sequence of events is made clear to the child and, consequently, there are no digressions or detailed descriptions that could interfere with the temporal development of the plot. While large format design is still preferred with many illustrations, all in colour, with brief, large-print text, at this stage the amount of the verbal language increases considerably. As a result, repetition and syntactic parallelism are more predominant. In turn, the illustrations are less schematic than in the previous stage and pay more attention to detail. The understanding of the tales included in this period requires that the child can associate symbols with objects or represent objects through images and words. The child also needs to be capable of thinking about objects that are not in the immediate context.

The tales assumed to belong to the first two stages of cognitive development are more likely to be written with the intention of being read to young children by adults. However, the stories included in stages 3 and 4 are written to be read by the child. In these stages, they have a high enough literacy level and are capable of reading storybooks by themselves. At the age of 7 most children have reached the capacity to read tales on their own (Cerrillo and Yubero 2007). The themes of the tales included in the concrete operations stage I (from 7–9 years of age) are more complex and belong to fantastic stories and extraordinary legends. The literary structure is brief, with clear orientation, quick development and brief conclusion, and much action. The structures are less simple and do not utilize as much repetition or syntactic parallelism as in the previous period. As for the design, although the illustration still fulfils a key role, the text gains relevance in the tales intended for children in this cognitive stage. The illustrations are more complex and more realistic than in the previous phases. To understand the stories of this stage, children need to be able to conceptualize time and develop an ability to make rational judgements about concrete phenomena without manipulating them physically.

Finally, in the tales intended for children in the concrete operations stage II, from 9–11 years of age, subject matter deals with realistic stories (biographies, sport), adventures, detective and mystery stories, animal life, humoristic elements, explorations of other countries and fantastic literature. The plot is clear but more elaborate, most frequently involving a resolution to the problem structuring the storyline. The syntactic structures are more complex than in the previous stages. The description of characters is still brief. The stories are longer and occasionally require subdivision into chapters, each one introducing a new adventure. The tales contain an average of 120 pages. In terms of design, illustrations are less important (one or two per chapter). The typography is normalized, the format is conventional. To understand the stories in this stage, children need to be capable of conceptualizing and ordering objects in a logical and temporal sequence. These tales have not been considered in this study since they contain a predominance of language over illustrations.

The stories intended for children of 11 years of age and over deal with more varied topics (realistic adventures, personal conflicts, social topics, sport, humour, biographies of well-known people, mystery, etc.) The literary structure of the stories is more complex and sometimes different plots intersect within the same tale. The description of characters and their environment is less stereotyped and more individualized. Overall, the stories are designed to give heed to the personal conflicts of the child. The presence of illustrations is scarce and the development of the plot lies essentially in the written language. The books intended for children over 11 years of age, in the concrete operations stage II, are more similar to books written for adults. From 15 years of age and over, the topics are amplified and the limitations previously mentioned concerning topics, literary structure and design disappear. At the age of 15, the children reach the cognitive maturity to read what is considered to be proper literature for adults (Cerrillo and Yubero 2007).

It is important to point out that the developmental stages that I have referred to are for guidance, for there are numerous factors of different types (social, cultural and familiar environments) that can accelerate or decelerate the psychological and linguistic development of the child (Piaget 1981: 197). In the same manner, depending on their cognitive development, children can continue to enjoy tales that correspond to a previous stage. This usually occurs when they re-read the stories that they had been told in previous years (Cerrillo and Yubero 2007).

An additional clarification must be made in this sense. Following Cerrillo (1996: 52–53) and Cerrillo and Yubero (2007: 288–289), Piaget's concrete operations stage has been divided into two groups: concrete operations stage I (7–9 years old) and concrete operations stage II (9–11 years old). These four years constitute a period during which the children's capacity and the interest in reading are dramatically developed. Generally speaking, at 7 years old, children begin to acquire the capacity to read on their own, and this ability develops throughout the four years referred to above until they finally reach full autonomy for reading. In this study, I will only deal with the stories intended for children from the sensory-motor stage until the concrete operations stage I, from 0 to 9 years of age, as the illustrations play an important role in the tales included in these three stages of cognitive development. In the tales intended for children over 9 years old, the illustrations are kept to a minimum and, therefore, the tales lack the visual material that is essential to carry out the study that is proposed here. In addition, the period of adolescence has been excluded due to the fact that, following the conventional evolvement of literacy, at this stage readers are likely to favour novels over children's literature.

1.4 Selection of sample texts

The selection of the sample texts covers nine children's picture books written throughout the twentieth century. All of them are well-known and have garnered extensive readership, as the literary studies carried out by Hürlimann (1968), Townsend (1990), Hunt (1991, 2004), Zaparaín and González (2010), among others, as well as journals specialized in children's literature (CLIJ, Children's Literature in Education) have clearly stated. So, '[...] a standard of literary merit (has been) required' (Townsend 1990: 64). Among the main sources consulted in order to contrast the literary quality of the selected stories, I have turned to traditional studies on children's literature, such as those by Hazard (1964), Hürlimann (1968) or Soriano (1995). As expected, there are no references to more current stories in this type of works, which is why I have also consulted more recent publications on children's stories praised by critics in the last decades. Studies by Townsend (1983), Colomer (1998, 2001), Hunt (2004), Gamble and Yates (2002) and Ávila (2007) are examples of these. Dictionaries and encyclopedias on children's literature, such as those by Carpenter and Prichard (1984), Bravo-Villasante (1985) or Cullinan and Person (2001), not only include references to the great classics of children's literature, but also to the works of great authors, who although less known, have contributed pieces of great literary value. Finally, given the developmental nature of the focus of this multimodal study, Bortolussi's (1985: 121), Tucker's (1984: 1–2; 2002a and b), Cerillo's (1996: 50–53) and Cerrillo and Yubero's (2007: 287–289) reviews of children's storybooks have also been considered as they specify the age, the cognitive stage of development and the reading capabilities of the target readers. Tucker (1984: 1–2, 2000a, b) also considers of invaluable importance selection of tales in accordance to age; he affirms that storybooks are designed to offer the child solutions to the psychological needs of each developmental stage. The studies carried out by Townsend (1990), Hunt

(2004), and Moya and Ávila (2009) also specify the age of the intended child for whom the tales are created.

Nine stories written by authors of children's books throughout the twentieth century and directed towards children between the ages of 0 and 9 have been chosen. The text, as well as the illustrations, plays a fundamental function in the construction of the plot, as is usually the case of tales intended for the children in these age groups. The tales are not adaptations; they are original stories which stand out for their literary richness and quality, an opinion that has been shared by critics and is clearly reinforced by the popularity of the books among the young public. Each work has been written by a different author so that the conclusions cannot be attributed to the individual style and particular language used by each specific creator.

The sample texts contemplate stories published in English that have won literary awards, regardless of their original language. I have not limited myself to the British or North American scope. However, I have also included works written in other countries in the Commonwealth. I have tried to choose works that have received awards of great professional prestige, for example, the Caldecott Medal or the universally known Andersen Award. My aim is not to delve into the particularities inherent to national forms of literature, but rather to insist on the universality of artistic manifestations, especially in such a globalized world like the one we currently live in, where English seems to be a language of reference.

The Very Hungry Caterpillar, for example, first appeared in 1969 and since then it has been translated into over 50 languages and has sold more than thirty million copies. It is the winner of awards such as the American Institute of Graphics Arts Award in 1970 and the Nakamori Reader's Prize in Japan in 1975. In 1969, the book received a citation from *The New York Times* as one of the ten best picture books, and in 2003, after a poll conducted by the BBC, it was declared one of the United Kingdom's most beloved books. Another example of the recognition gained by picture books that make up the sample text is *Where the Wild Things Are,* Sendak's signature work. It was first published by Harper Collins in 1963, and since then more than 19 million copies have been sold worldwide. The book was awarded the Caldecott Medal as the most distinguished book of the year in 1964. In 1970 it also received the Hans Christian Andersen International Medal. Sendak has received many awards for his work as writer and illustrator of picture books. Among them, in 1983 he received the Laura Ingalls Wilder Award for devotion to children's literature. In 1996, he was also honoured by the

President of the United States with the National Medal of Arts. Finally, in 2003, he shared with the Austrian author Christine Noestlinger the Astrid Lindgren Memorial Award for Literature. As an example of a story intended for children belonging to the third stage of cognitive development, I refer to *The Rainbow Fish,* Pfister's best known picture book. It has remained a bestseller in the United States since 1992. So far, the tale has been published in more than thirty languages. Pfister has received various awards for this tale: The American Booksellers Association award in 1995, the prestigious Critici in Erba Prize at the Bologna Children's Book Fair and also the Christopher Award in 1993 for writing and designing books which teach moral values to children.

Among the nine selected books, I have also chosen some contemporary classics, that is, works that can be considered models to imitate due to their notable literary quality. They are known to have persevered as a success among children for generations after they were created or written. These are works that, during different time periods, have provided different exegeses and admitted successive re-readings, while their validity and acceptation remain intact. *The Tale of Peter Rabbit* (1902) by Beatrix Potter, *Where the Wild Things Are* (1963) by Maurice Sendak or *The Very Hungry Caterpillar* by Eric Carle (1969) show clear evidence of this. Picture books have changed considerably since the early twentieth century as they belong to a genre that is constantly evolving. However, traditional picture books that have become contemporary classic literary works are also part of this study. These books are still published and translated into many languages all over the world, have won different awards and nowadays still enjoy a wide readership. In addition, in the case of the three classic picture books referred to here, the same person acts as both writer and illustrator, which guarantees an appropriate interrelation between the verbal and visual components of the tales when deciding which strategies are the most adequate to represent meaning. My selection therefore includes works that have defied time. Because of this, among the most recent books that I have chosen are the ones that continued being published for at least one generation after their author and that are still popular years after their first publication. In this sense, I have followed Jordan's maxim (1973: 39): 'Until a book has weathered at least one generation and is accepted in the next, it can hardly be given the rank of a classic [...]'.

Although a data set of three books per age group may seem, at first sight, small as a basis for drawing broader conclusions about the verbal and visual strategies available to create texts that are adequate for the cognitive level of their potential readers, the analyses carried out reveal that, with certain exceptions that will be commented on in Chapters 6 and 7, the three books included in each specific age group follow similar strategies to reflect the narrative reality in the verbal and visual modes. For this reason, I have not considered it necessary to increment the number of books analysed to study the tales belonging to the three age groups under study. The detailed analysis executed for each book provides interesting findings concerning the verbal and visual organization of the picture books and reveals the meaning potential that is born of the intersemiosis of verbal and non-verbal modalities in the genre of children's stories.

I conclude this section by expounding the plots of the nine picture books that form the sample texts. As a genre, children's stories basically consist of a plot which develops from an initial complication towards a final resolution by passing through a range of intermediate stages (Fabb 1997: 165). As stories, their main characteristics are their condensed style and brevity. All this implies that the texts are basically formed by short sentences, usually in the past, which contribute to the plot's development of the action: there are neither digressions nor detailed descriptions which can interfere with the narrative tension. These characteristics are especially evident in the tales intended for the children in the first cognitive stage, the sensory-motor stage. The picture books *Where's Spot?* by Eric Hill ([1980] 2009), *The Very Hungry Caterpillar* by Eric Carle ([1969] 2002) and *Dear Zoo* by Rod Campbell ([1982] 2007) have been chosen as tales prototypically intended for children between 0 and 2 years of age. In *Where's Spot?* the story line is simple and is developed quickly and dynamically. The little dog, Spot, has temporarily disappeared. His mother starts searching the entire house but, unexpectedly, only other animals turn up (a snake, a hippo, a lion, a monkey, an alligator, a turtle, etc.). Finally, the daring puppy comes out of his hiding place and, along with his mother, has dinner. Equally simple and quickly developed plots are found in the other two stories of the sensory-motor stage. In *The Very Hungry Caterpillar*, a little caterpillar comes out of his cocoon one Sunday morning when the sun comes up. The caterpillar, just having been newly-born, is hungry and he devours all the food he comes across for a week until he turns into a very large and fat caterpillar. Then, he makes a cocoon and, after two weeks, he turns into a beautiful and colourful butterfly. Lastly, in *Dear Zoo*, a child writes the zoo asking them to send him a pet. The zoo sends him one wild animal after another, each in their respective cages (an elephant, a giraffe, a lion, a camel, a snake, etc.). However, the protagonist child sends them back to their origin given that they are not what he is looking for in a pet. Finally, after much thinking, the zoo decides to send him a little dog that they boy keeps and adopts as his pet.

The tales *Grandpa* by John Burningham ([1984] 2003*), Guess How Much I Love You* written by Sam McBartney and illustrated by Anita Jeram ([1994] 2006) and *Where the Wild Things Are* by Maurice Sendak ([1963] 2000) are studied as picture books intended for children in the pre-operational stage (3–6 years). These stories, though all equally simple, present a story line that is a bit more elaborate. *Granpa,* for example, is a moving account, regarding the relationship between a little girl and her grandfather. The main characters in *Granpa* carry out different activities together: they plant seeds in a greenhouse, play different games, go fishing, make an imaginary plan to travel to Africa, etc. There is a moment when Granpa becomes ill and passes away. However, the message of the author is not one of sadness: the memories of the grandfather continue in the mind of the little girl, who pensively contemplates the empty armchair of the old man after his death. In the last illustration, the little girl is pushing a baby carriage within a sunny and colourful background. There is a predominance of green and yellow colours, typically associated with hope and happiness. Life goes on.

The following story included in the pre-operational stage is *Guess How Much I Love You*, which also deals with family relations, but this time the relationship is established between a father and his son. Bedtime has come but before going to bed, the little hare wants to show his father just how much he loves him in quantitative terms. Little Nutbrown Hare uses an ample repertoire of gestures and pirouettes to symbolize the love he feels for his father, Big Nutbrown Hare. The little hare extends and raises his arms as much as he can, does a handstand, jumps, etc., but when his father repeats the same actions, given his greater size, he always surpasses his son. Sleepiness soon takes hold of Little Nutbrown Hare when he looks up at the sky and points to the moon as the furthest distance that marks the limit of his love for his father. Big Nutbrown Hare puts his son to bed, gives him a goodnight kiss and lies down beside him, whispering that the love can be even greater. The fatherly love does not only reach the moon but also makes its way back to Earth. The fatherly love appears to be infinite.

A plot just as interesting for young readers that also touches on mother-child relationships is that of *Where the Wild Things Are*. In this tale, Max, the protagonist, dresses up as a wolf and plays pranks (pounding a nail into the wall and bothering his dog). Discovered by his mother, she scolds him and calls him *wild thing*, which infuriates Max so much that he threatens to eat her. As a consequence, his mother sends him to his room without dinner. Max does not resign himself to solitude; rather he transforms it into a magic forest that leads him to an ocean that the protagonist crosses in a little boat until reaching Wild Land, where monsters live. In spite of their threatening appearance, Max manages to tame them using his penetrating stare and they end up making him their king. Everyone has a phenomenal time in Wild Land wreaking havoc, following their wild instincts. However, whilst the monsters sleep, Max experiences feelings of loneliness and the need to return to his loved ones. He has regretted his bad behaviour and once his childish temper tantrums have been tamed, he decides to return home, despite the monsters' protests, who implore him to stay with them. Once back in the reality of his room, he finds dinner waiting for him, still warm.

Finally, within the concrete operations stage (from 7 to 9 years), the three picture books examined are *The Tale of Peter Rabbit* by Beatrix Potter ([1902] 2002), *Gorilla* by Anthony Browne ([1983] 2002) and *The Rainbow Fish* by Marcus Pfister ([1992] 2010), all following a well-devised plot of great interest to the young reader. *The Tale of Peter Rabbit* is Beatrix Potter's first book and, as Taylor (1987) suggests, probably her best. Regarding the plot, Peter is forbidden by his mother to enter Mr McGregor's garden and she reminds him of his father's fatal end for trespassing this property. However, following his natural instinct, he disobeys her and stuffs himself with vegetables until he gets sick. There is a point when he encounters Mr McGregor and is almost caught. Finally, he manages to escape from the peasant and comes back home with a stomachache. While he has some camomile tea for dinner, his obedient sisters have bread, milk and blackberries. Certainly, some moralistic values predominate in the verbal narrative, but, despite Peter's disobedience, the narrator seems to be on the side of the transgressor (Scott 2001: 19). The protagonist is a burglar that trespasses Mr McGregor's property and steals his vegetables, disobeying his mother without hesitation. However, he gets his reward: eating some lettuce, French beans and radishes. In spite of this, the punishment imposed seems to be limited to a dose of camomile tea to heal his physical pain.

The other two books included in the concrete operations stage are *Gorilla* and *The Rainbow Fish*. *Gorilla* deals with a solitary girl, Hannah, who loves gorillas. Her greatest dream is to see a live gorilla. However, her father always seems to be too busy to take her to the zoo. The night before her birthday, Hannah discovers that the gorilla that she asked her father for as a gift for her birthday is no more than a stuffed toy. Whilst she sleeps, something surprising happens: the toy gorilla turns into a real one. He invites her to the zoo and they spend a magical night together full of adventures and fun. Finally, Hannah wakes up on her birthday and feels happy next to her stuffed animal toy. When she goes downstairs quickly to tell her father what she had experienced in her dream, she encounters another surprise: her father has found the time to take her to the zoo to visit the primates, which has her overrun with joy. It seems that in Hannah's world, dreams come true.

Lastly, *The Rainbow Fish* tells the story of the most beautiful fish in the ocean. His golden scales are admired by all the rest of the fish, who long for his presence in games. However, the Rainbow Fish is too proud and constantly rejects the invitations of his peers to play. One day, a little fish asks for one of his shining scales, but the Rainbow Fish angrily refuses, which wins him the antipathy of the others, who turn their back on him in that moment. Rainbow Fish ends up feeling lonely. His beauty is not good for anything now that no one admires it. He sadly approaches a wise octopus who advises him to give a shining scale to each fish in the sea. Finally, Rainbow Fish gives in and shares his scales. Though now he is no longer the most beautiful fish in the sea, he has made new friends with whom he spends his time playing, as well as learning the value of friendship.

2 Systemic Functional Grammar and Visual Social Semiotics

Now that the aims and scope of this book have been explained in Chapter 1, I will attempt to offer a justification of the theoretical models selected to carry out the multimodal analysis of the sample texts. To do this, I will analyse the main premises of Halliday's Systemic Functional Grammar (2004) and Kress and van Leeuwen's Visual Social Semiotics (1996, 2006) since, without ignoring the contributions brought by other theoretical models, these are the two frameworks on which the essential aspects of this study rest. I intend, therefore, to clarify the reasons that have led me to adopt Halliday's Systemic Functional Grammar as the theoretical framework used to identify the verbal options that are at a picture book writer's disposal to represent a narrative reality, establish interaction with the young reader and, finally, create coherent texts. To justify the choice of the theoretical framework, I compare Halliday's version of SFG with other structural-functional grammars such as Functional Discourse Grammar (Hengeveld and Mackenzie 2008, 2009) and Role and Reference Grammar[1] (Van Valin 1995, 2005; Van Valin and LaPolla 1997). Reference is also made to the approaches that have had the most repercussion within the current multimodal studies: O'Halloran's Multimodal Discourse Analysis (2004, 2005, 2008) and Norris' Interactive Approach (2004) to multimodality. These two frameworks, together with Kress and van Leeuwen's (2006) Systemic-Functional Semiotics, are the three main lines of research that have studied the meaning-making resources of multimodal ensembles (Jewitt 2009).

1. Structural-functional approaches pay attention to both the structural and functional aspects of the study of language and aim to reveal the nature of the relationship that exists between the two. Structural-functional approaches provide an explicit framework of principles through which the structures and interpretation of expressions can be described.

Consequently, this chapter aims to explain: (i) why the functionalist approaches are better adapted for the study at hand as opposed to the non-functionalist models (sections 2.1 and 2.2); and (ii), in more detail, why Halliday's version of Systemic Functional Linguistics and Visual Social Semiotics are more appropriate than other functional and multimodal accounts to carry out a study of the verbal and visual features of picture books (sections 2.3 and 2.4). Finally, in section 2.5 I attempt to offer a definition of the notion *mode*, a controversial term that has been dealt with from different perspectives by the different theories that have approached the analysis of multimodal texts.

Up until the end of the twentieth century, the more conservative definitions of text referred to its essentially linguistic nature. However, at present text is preferentially defined as a semiotic object wherein different modes and resources of a non-purely verbal nature co-occur (Fowler, 1986, cited by Martínez-Cabeza, 2002: 38; Kress 2010: 133). Fairclough (1995a: 4) falls in with this line of thought when he speaks of the existence of *multi-semiotic texts* and states:

> I think it is necessary to move further towards this view than I have done in these papers, where a text is mainly understood as written or spoken language. A strong argument for doing so is that texts in contemporary society are increasingly multi-semiotic; texts whose primary semiotic form is language increasingly combine language with other semiotic forms. Television is the most obvious example, combining language with visual images, music and sound effects. But written (printed) texts are also increasingly becoming multisemiotic texts, not only because they incorporate photographs and diagrams, but also because the graphic design of the page is becoming an ever more salient factor in evaluation of written texts.

The truth is that any communicative phenomenon is composed of a variety of modes, and all of them contribute, depending on their affordances and constraints, to the creation of meaning[2] (Kress and van Leeuwen 2006; Kress 2010).

2. The term *affordance*, or semiotic possibility, emanates from Gibson's work (1977). According to this psychologist, each object permits certain things to be done according to its characteristics and perceptible properties, in exactly the way van Leeuwen (2005a: 273) explains: 'Affordances are the potential uses of a given object, stemming from the perceivable properties of the object. Because perception is selective, depending on the needs and interests of the perceivers, different perceivers will notice different affordances. But those that

Taking this premise as a starting point, I agree with the definition that Kress and van Leeuwen (2001: 40) offer of text as a semiotic object in which various modes and resources of a verbal and non-verbal nature intervene in order to create meaning in a determined communicative context. For them, a text is: '[...] that phenomenon which is the result of the articulation in one or more semiotic modes of a discourse, or (we think, inevitably, always) a number of discourses.' This idea is also shared by Lim (2007: 195), who assumes that the process of meaning making in text is necessarily multimodal, and points out that: '[...] in order to understand meaning making, it is no longer sufficient to deconstruct and analyse the use of verbal language in a text. Instead, the operation of other semiotic resources must also be factored in as contributing to the total meaning made in the text.' These words from Lim (2007) clearly summarize the complex phenomenon of meaning in exactly the way in which it is seen in the present study.

Picture books are composite wholes in which the representation of reality is essentially expressed through both verbal and visual modes. In them, words and images reinforce each other without necessarily offering the same information. Good picture books are a richer experience than the sum of their independent components (Nodelman 1988; Moya and Pinar 2008; Moya 2011). Thus, an appropriate approach to them requires the adaptation of a multimodal perspective that provides the tools to study their verbal and visual components, as well as the meaning that emanates from the combination of both semiotic modes.

2.1 Functional versus formal approaches to language

Before briefly presenting some of the basic premises of Halliday's SFG, I will now make reference to the convenience of adopting functionalist models as opposed to formalist models to conduct the analysis presented here. Formal approaches aim to identify 'the formal properties which underlie the architecture of grammar' (Mendikoetxea 2011: 362). Formalist approaches essentially focus on formal aspects of a phonological, morphological, and syntactic nature and also on semantic aspects. However, for formalists the study of language in use is not a priority, since formalism is concerned

remain unnoticed continue to exist objectively, latent in the object, waiting to be discovered.' The term *constraints*, on the contrary, refers to the limitations of a specific semiotic mode to create meaning in a specific context of communication.

largely with abstract competence. For them, language is considered to be self-contained and is independent from external factors (Butler 2003: 5–10).

Even though the generativist paradigm lost importance at the end of the 1960s and in the 1970s in favour of functionalist approaches, one cannot deny that Generative Grammar (GG) has existed for more than half a century and continues to be, in some fields, the approach par excellence to undertake formal studies. Since the 1950s, Noam Chomsky's GG (1957, 1965, 1986, 1995, 2005) has been the formal approach that has brought the most advances in the study of the structure of language (Maendikoetxea 2011: 363).

By adopting a mentalist approach to the study of grammar, Chomsky aims to explain what a native speaker knows about his language in order to understand and be able to generate an infinite number of well-formed sentences without having encountered them before. The internal knowledge of the structures that rule the speaker's native language (grammatical competence) is implicit, innate and unconscious. Chomsky assumes that each individual is biologically endowed with an innate language capability which enables him or her to acquire the grammar of any natural language. Unlike earlier approaches such as structuralism or traditional grammar, Chomskyan linguistics approaches grammar from a mentalist perspective, conceiving it as a system of abstract principles that govern the internal structure of a language.

The speaker's linguistic competence, that is, the innate knowledge he or she has of his or her language, is different from linguistic performance, the use the speaker makes of the language in specific situations. The aim of Generative Linguistics focuses exclusively on linguistic competence since, as Chomsky (1965: 18) points out, '[l]ike most facts of interest and importance [...] information about the speaker-hearer's competence [...] is neither presented for direct observation nor extractable from data by inductive procedures or any known sort.' In fact, for Chomsky (1965: 4–5), real language in use 'cannot constitute the actual subject matter of linguistics, if this is to be a serious discipline.'[3]

This idea contrasts with the philosophy underlying functional approaches, which study the relation between grammar and meaning in context. While formal grammars are autonomous and semantically arbitrary, a functional grammar is semantically motivated (Halliday and Matthiessen 1999: 3–4). Functional approaches are interested in the way language

3. Noam Chomsky is 'less interested in language as communication than in the abstract properties which are claimed to be valid for all human languages' (Butler 2011: 365).

functions as a tool to interact with others. Representatives of the different functional schools (Halliday (2004), Dik (1989, 1997a and b), Hengeveld and Mackenzie (2008), Givón (1993, 1995, 2001 a and b), Hopper and Thompson (1980, 1993), etc.) seem to agree that the main aim of language is 'the establishment of inter-human communication; other aims are either secondary or derived' (Dik 1989: 21). Dik (1997a: 3) insists on the idea that language is used to establish interaction with others and points out:

> In the functional paradigm, [...] a language is in the first place conceptualized as an instrument for social interaction among human beings, used with the intention of establishing communicative relationships. Within this paradigm one attempts to reveal the instrumentality of language with respect to what people do and achieve with it in social interaction.

Halliday (1985: xiii) also shares this philosophy and states:

> Language has evolved to satisfy human needs; and the way it is organized is functional with respect to these needs – it is not arbitrary. A functional grammar is essentially a 'natural' grammar, in the sense that everything in it can be explained, ultimately, by reference to how language is used.

In fact, Halliday (1978: 192) argues that the grammar of a language is not just a set of rules which can be applied to produce correct sentences, but a meaning-making resource that must be studied in relation to its role in human communication.

Contrasting with formal approaches, which view language as 'an infinite set of structural descriptions of sentences' (Foley and van Valin 1984: 7), functional approaches share the point of view that language can only be understood in relation to its function in human communication and interaction. This implies a change of focus from linguistic competence to communicative competence or, in the case of Halliday (2004), to language potential.[4] FDG is also interested in social context but only to the extent that

4. Halliday (1978: 109) defines the meaning potential in two different ways: 'The meaning potential, which is the paradigmatic range of semantic choice that is present in the system, and to which the members of a culture have access in their language, can be characterized in two ways, corresponding to Malinowski's distinction between the "context of situation" and "the context of culture" (1923, 1935). Interpreted in the context of culture, it is the entire semantic system of a language. [...] Interpreted in the context of situation, it is the particular semantic system, or set of subsystems, which is associated with a particular type of situation or social context.'

it is needed in order to explain obligatory grammatical choices. In turn, RRG, however, is not interested in the social side of language. What functional approaches seem to share is the principle that language is essentially a tool to establish communication between human beings. Therefore, the philosophy underlying functional approaches seems to be more appropriate than the ideas defended by formalist approaches to carry out this study, where I analyse how picture book writers and illustrators use verbal and visual language to create meaning within a genre and a specific communicative reality.

Although the differences between functionalism and formalism are evident, the work of Culicover and Jackendoff (2005) on Simpler Syntax shows there may be some degree of partial rapprochement between them. Certaintly, Culicover and Jackendoff's (2005) model is still formalist since it retains the main principles of generative grammar.[5] In fact, they admit the validity of a mentalist approach to language and distinguish between the user's competence of the language and his or her specific performance. They also maintain that syntax, as well as semantics and phonology, has its own autonomy, since there is no asymmetric dependency between any of these language components. Nevertheless, they reject some central tenets of orthodox generative grammar. For example, they see syntax and lexicon as a continuum (Culicover and Jackendoff 2005: 25) and propose a monostratal model of syntax, without hidden layers. They also abandon the syntactocentric architecture of grammar in favour of a parallel architecture. Moreover, they replace the derivation rules of generative grammar by constraint satisfaction processes. Finally, while in Generative Grammar, the surface structure is differentiated from the logical form, that is, the underlying or hidden level of syntax, in Simpler Syntax, Culicover and Jackendoff (2005: 7) recognize only a surface structure and deny the need for a deep structure. They assume that the syntax-semantic interface, in line with the semantic and pragmatic structure of utterances, provides the required details for the interpretation of a given syntactic structure. In this way, the proper names, Chomsky and *Plato*, in the utterance, 'Chomsky is next to Plato up there on the top shelf', are interpreted as the books by Chomsky and Plato. According to Simpler Syntax, this information is supplied exclusively

5. Simpler Syntax is a model which defends a 'theory of syntax with the minimum structure necessary to map between phonology and meaning' (Culicover and Jackendoff 2005: 22).

by semantic and pragmatic principles where syntax does not fulfil a role (Culicover and Jackendoff 2006: 416).

The basic idea of Culicover and Jackendoff's approach can be summarized as follows: '[...] given some phenomenon that has provided putative evidence for elaborate syntactic structure, there nevertheless exist numerous examples which demonstrably involve semantic or pragmatic factors [...] [and thus] given a suitable account of the syntax-semantics interface, all cases of the phenomenon in question are [to be] accounted for in terms of relevant properties of semantics/pragmatics' (Culicover and Jackendoff 2005: 5). Culicover and Jackendoff (2005) argue for more comparative studies of linguistic theories, since these may bring different linguistic perspectives much closer together. The works carried out by Butler (2003) and later by Gonzálvez-García and Butler (2006) have contributed greatly to the development of this task. Reference will be made to them in the following sections.

2.2 Functional approaches

In this section I will comment upon the main characteristics that functional models share, independently of the specific theoretical principles that govern them. Unlike formalist approaches, essentially centred on structural aspects, as has been stated in section 2.1 the central tenet of Functionalism is that language is essentially a means of human communication in social and psychological contexts (Butler 2003, 2011). Thus, language is not an arbitrary or a self-contained system, which is autonomous from external factors of a social, psychological, or cognitive nature, but shaped and motivated by them (Croft 1995, 2001; Butler 2003: 33). Syntax, for instance, is assumed to be at least partially motivated by semantic and pragmatic factors and is regarded as a means to express semantic and pragmatic meanings. Functional approaches reject the autonomy of the linguistic system in favour of functional explanations and aim to explain how people communicate with one another.

Just as there are different formal approaches to the study of language, there are also different functional approaches (Butler 2011). Nichols (1984: 102–103), quoted in Butler (2003: 28), classified them into three large groups: i. conservative or generative functionalism; ii. moderate functionalism; and iii. extreme functionalism.

i. The first group, conservative or generative functionalism, is represented by the works of Prince (1981) and Kuno (1980), and adds functional notions to formalism. As Kuno (1980: 117–118) points out, theories of grammar 'must have a place or places where various functional constraints on the well-formedness of sentences or sequences of sentences can be stated, and each theory of grammar can benefit from utilizing a functional perspective in analysis of concrete syntactic phenomena'. In essence Generative Functionalism (GF) accepts functional explanations to deal with some formal aspects. Anaphoric relations and information structural patterns, for example, are analysed in some of Prince's works 1978, 1981). However, GF does not challenge the essential tenets of formal approaches to language, as it admits the autonomous nature of grammar from external factors. In addition, the study of language as communication is not one of its central aims (Butler 2003: 34–36; Croft 1995: 496–497). These facts have led linguists such as van Valin and Newmeyer to assess GF just as an extension of formal theories rather than an alternative to them (van Valin 2000: 330).

ii. The second group, moderate functionalism, is concerned with the study of both the function and the forms of the language, and the relationship between the two. Within this group, Nichols (1984) includes the following approaches: Dik's Functional Grammar (FG), Halliday's Systemic Functional Grammar (SFG), Van Valin (2005) and his colleagues' Role and Reference Grammar (RRG), and the works of Givón (1995) and Croft (1995). At the most formal end of moderate functionalism, approaches such as RRG (van Valin and LaPolla 1997; van Valin 1995, 2005), FG and Functional Discourse Grammar (FDG) (Hengeveld and Mackenzie 2008), appear together. SFG and Givón's and Croft's Functionalisms, however, are located at the most functional end of the spectrum.

Moderate approaches to functionalism reject the claim that the language system is independent from external phenomena. Among other factors, they all accept the importance of grammatical forms and their specific functions in communication and can be defined as structural-functional accounts of language (Butler 2003). However, they are located in different positions within the functional spectrum, since they also differ in aspects concerning their commitment to cognition, typological adequacy and, finally, the point that is of most interest to us here, their commitment to textual relations (Butler 2003, 2005; Gonzálvez-García and Butler 2006). SFG, together with the work of Givón, have the strongest commitment to the study of textual factors. FDG shows, however, lower interest in text analysis. Finally, RRG has the lowest levels of commitment with text structure as it is not interested in the relationships between text and social contexts. Although RRG pays attention to aspects such as information structure in the clause, types of clause linkage, topical chains and reference tracking in discourse, it has no model of discourse and pays no attention to socio-cultural aspects (Butler 2003: 43).

iii. Finally, the third group, extreme functionalism, located at the most radically functionalist end of the spectrum, considers grammar as an epiphenomenon of discourse (Butler 2003; Gonzálvez-García and Butler 2006). Grammar is denied any independent existence of its own, and is seen as emerging from the requirements and dictates of discourse interaction. In this most radical extreme of functionalism is Emergent Grammar (EG)/ Interactional Linguistics (IL), represented by Hopper (1987, 1998), Hopper and Thompson (1980, 1993, 2008), Fox (2007), Bybee (2010, 2012). In this approach although structure is not disregarded, the focus falls essentially on the study of patterns of usage in everyday spoken interactions. As Hopper (1998: 160) points out: 'The grammar of a language, then, consists not of a single delimited system, but rather, of an open-ended collection of forms that are constantly being restructured and resemanticised during actual use.' This idea differs from moderate functionalism where grammars are seen as entities in their own right and both forms and functions are considered to be essential parts of the study of language. Unlike Generative Linguistics, where the features of the grammar are considered to be innate in the mind of the individual, EG claims that the grammar emerges only from language in use and is acquired through experience.

Gonzálvez-Garcia and Butler (2006) and Butler (2006) compare 11 models (SFG, FDG, RRG, EG/IL, Functional Grammar (FG), Cognitive Grammar (CG), Cognitive Construction Grammar (CConG), Givón's approach, Radical Construction Grammar, the approach of Fillmore *et al.* and, finally, the approach of Golberg) on a set of 36 criteria to analyse the closeness of relationships between Functional theories and Cognitive Linguistics. The results are visualized by means of a dendrogram and show how closely or distantly related the models are to each other in terms of their basic properties.[6] Concerning descriptive and explanatory adequacy, they analyse features such as the use of naturally-occurring data, the importance

6. A dendrogam is diagram which is used to illustrate the arrangement of data into clusters which share similar properties.

of studying texts/discourses, not only the sentences in them, typological adequacy, diachronic adequacy, cognitive adequacy, sociocultural adequacy and, among others, acquisitional adequacy. Their study shows that functional theories and Cognitive Linguistics share a substantial number of features, but that there are other features which distinguish the two main groups within a space which might be characterized as 'functional-cognitive space' (Gonzálvez-García and Butler 2006: 82). Approaches such as FDG, RRG, EG/IL, SFG and Givón's Functionalism reject both the autonomy of the linguistic system and the autonomy of syntax in favour of functional explanations. The approaches referred to above agree that language is primarily a means of communication and that this has important consequences for the structuring of language systems. FDG and RRG take the less radical stance that some, but not all grammatical phenomena, are motivated by meaning/function. Other features, centrality of text and context, cognition and typological orientation, however, make explicit important differences between the specific accounts.[7]

The approach that has been adopted to carry out the study that is proposed here, SFG (Halliday 2004), lies between the two extremes just referred to, although it is closer to the radical functional extreme models (Butler 2003, 2005, 2006; Gonzálvez-García and Butler 2006).

2.3 Systemic Functional Grammar: Main tenets

At this point I outline the theoretical principles of the SFG as developed by Halliday and his associates in the Sydney School. Hallidayan SFG is discussed in relation to other functional approaches to language, explaining how this functional theory is similar to and, in turn, differs from the Cardiff Grammar, FDG and other functional accounts. The purpose of this chapter is not to delve into the similarities and differences that exist between the functionalist approaches, or between these and cognitive linguistics. Butler's (2003, 2005, 2006, 2009, 2011), Butler and Gonzálvez-García's (2005) and Gonzálvez-García and Butler's (2006) studies on systemic-functional approaches present these aspects in great detail and have provided a deep theoretical basis to

7. For further information about the relationship between functional models, and between these and cognitive approaches, see Butler (2003, 2005, 2006) and Gonzálvez-Garcia and Butler (2006).

determine the similarities and differences that exist between the different models that approach language from a functional perspective. I will now refer to a few of their reflections and conclusions that will help us justify the selection of the functional model chosen to develop the study proposed here.

2.3.1 Attention to natural data and text structure

The comparison of the linguistic models carried out by Butler (2003, 2005, 2006, 2009), and Gonzálvez-García and Butler (2006) shows that SFG stands out as having a unique combination of features that make it an appropriate model to identify the verbal choices made by writers of picture books to create meaning, interact with the young reader and form coherent wholes of communication. The first aspect that makes SFG an appropriate model to carry out this study is that it works with naturally occurring linguistic data and text collections as analytical samples, not just isolated sentences. In addition, SFG pays detailed attention to the structure of texts in their contexts of production and reception. Although in Halliday's (2004) SFG, the unit of analysis *par excellence* is the clause, SFG is primarily concerned with the structure and function of texts. In fact, Halliday (1994: xxvii) states that:

> the current preoccupation is with discourse analysis, or 'text linguistics'; and it is sometimes assumed that this can be carried out without grammar – or even that is somehow an alternative to grammar. But this is an illusion. A discourse analysis that is not based on grammar is not an analysis at all, but simply a running commentary on a text [...].

This interest in analysing authentic samples of language and texts makes SFG different from other functional approaches such as FDG or RRG. FDG, for instance, uses naturally-occurring data occasionally for examples and has no model of discourse structure above the move (Hengeveld and Mackenzie 2006, 2008).[8] Although FDG adopts a top-down rather than a bottom-up approach and is a theory with concessions to processing, Hengeveld and Mackenzie (2008) admit that it is not a grammar of discourse. As Hengeveld

8. The move consists exclusively of one or more temporally ordered acts of discourse, as in shown in the following example where two acts, marked by a slash, can be distinguished: "'Watch out,/ because there may be trick questions in the exam'" (Hengeveld and Mackenzie 2006: 671). FDG does not recognize any unit beyond the move, but it does model discourse acts and moves and indeed regards the discourse act as the basic linguistic unit.

and Mackenzie (2008: 29) point out: 'FDG [...] is not a "discourse grammar" in the sense of a grammar of discourse [...] deriving from text-linguistic analysis. Rather, FDG wishes to understand those systematic properties of the Discourse Act (the *minimal* unit of communication) that require reference to its being situated within an interactive Move by the language user.' They also immediately go on to say that 'FDG also differs from SFG in concentrating on the individual-psychological rather than the social dimension of the language user, although the two aspects are of course closely connected in that social interaction is mediated through individual psychologies' (Hengeveld and Mackenzie 2008: 29). The conceptual and the contextual components of FDG are developed only to the extent necessary to account for grammatical phenomena. FDG does not attempt to offer a complete description of discourse precisely because it proposes a discourse unit only if some reflex can be found in grammatical organization. This is the reason why, for example, it is assumed that English does not have the pragmatic function of topic (Moya 2005). Unlike in Japanese, where the particle *wa* is a mark for topicality, in English there are no specific markings or positions for topic status. A new unit is set up in FDG only if it proves to have some strictly grammatical repercussion. Moya (2005) points out that this may be a disadvantage for FDG and states that only if we drop the requirement that a theory should deal exclusively with those aspects of discourse which are reflected in the grammar, will we be able to explain how discourses are structured and how they are built up during communication. A functional theory which takes as its object of study 'how the language user works' must recognize the higher units which have been established by discourse analysts, as well as the lower ones which are reflected in the grammar. However, FDG does not seem to consider them of primary interest.

Finally, RRG, as its name suggests, is more a theory of grammar than a theory of discourse structure and function, and in it the use of naturally occurring data is not a major priority either. However, the part of theory that deals with information structure and switch reference is well developed, as the works of van Valin and LaPolla (1997: 199–236, 417–430, 484–492) demonstrate (Gonzálvez-Garcia and Butler 2006: 54).

2.3.2 Commitment to socio-cultural aspects

Another feature typically associated with the Sydney Grammar that is of interest to us here is that it places a strong emphasis on socio-cultural factors.

SFG is strong on sociocultural adequacy, since it has a highly developed model of social context and its relationship with linguistic choices. The social orientation of Halliday's Grammar stems from the works by Firth (1957) and Malinowski (1923, 1935). Language cannot be studied separately from the functions it fulfils in a specific context of communication and has essentially evolved to perform social functions. Firth (1957) insists on the connection that needs to be established between theoretical constructs and textual data, and affirms: 'Each function will be defined as the use of some language form or element in relation to some context' (Firth 1957: 6). Malinowski also highlights the connection between texts and their cultural environments and the assumption that language is primarily 'a mode of action and not an instrument of reflection' (Malinowski 1923: 312). SFG is very much concerned with the relationships between language and the social-cultural context in which it is produced and understood. Language is assumed to be part of a social situation and as such it cannot be separated from it. As Malinowski (1923: 306) states:

> A verbal utterance becomes only intelligible when it is placed within its context of situation [...] an expression which indicates on the one hand that the concept of context has to be broadened and on the other that the situation in which words are uttered can never be passed over as irrelevant to the linguistic expression.

Influenced by Malinowski, Firth (1957: 195) acknowledges that the meaning of an utterance 'is the functional relation of the sentence as a whole to the processes of a context of situation in the context of culture'. Later on, Halliday adopts these ideas and points out that language essentially fulfils social needs. As a result, any structural aspect of the language needs to be explained on the basis of its function in communication (Halliday 1985: xiii).

As members of a culture the speakers of a language take part in different communicative activities such as casual conversations, service encounters, discussions, etc., which can be identified by their communicative purposes in a specific context and by their specific structural organizations. These social activities are modelled in SFG as genres, defined as 'staged, purposed, goal-oriented activit(ies) in which speakers engage as members of our culture' (Martin, 2001: 155) or as 'recurrent configuration(s) of meaning' which are used to develop social practices (Martin and Rose, 2008: 6). The context of culture is seen as linked to a set of specific contexts of situation, which is one level down from the context of culture and has three different variables (Gregory 1978, 1988; Eggins 2004; Martin and Rose 2007): field, tenor and mode, each of which is hypothesized to correlate respectively with one of the three metafunctions distinguished by Halliday (2004): experiential, interpersonal and textual, discussed in section 2.3.3.

The contextual notion of field refers to the activity that is being developed. In turn, the contextual notion of tenor describes the set of relationships that are established between the participants involved in a specific communicative interaction. These relations are defined on the basis of three variables: power relations (equal or unequal), social distance (intimate or distant) and emotional involvement (detached or emotionally involved). Finally, the contextual notion of mode is concerned with the form by which the message is transmitted, e.g. written or spoken (though see Gregory (1967) for more delicate distinctions). These differences in the context of situation (register) are meaningful and lead to linguistic variations in texts. The communicative purpose involved in a social activity and the contexts of culture and situation determine the linguistic choices made by the speaker at different levels: above the clause in discourse-semantics, also in the lexicogrammar of clauses and, finally, at the expression level in phonology and graphology.[9] In this sense, as Butler (2003: 44) states:

9. SFG is stratified or ranked into two types of level of language: content and expression. There are two content levels: semantics, which acts as the interface between the physical and social context and language itself, and lexico-grammar, which takes us from meaning to wording. SFG claims that grammar and lexis are not separate, but form the two poles of a single continuum. Within the expression level, we distinguish between phonology/graphology, on the one hand, and phonetics/graphetics, on the other. Phonology is concerned with the organization of the sound patterns of spoken language into formal structures and systems. Graphology deals with the organization of the orthographic patterns of written language into formal structures and systems. In turn, phonetics, which is the lowest level, is the stratum where the actual sounds produced are described. Finally, graphetics is the stratum at which actual letters, punctuation marks, etc. are explained. The relation between the strata is one of realization. Semantics is realized by lexico-grammar, which in turn it is realized by phonology/graphology, which in turn is realized by phonetics and graphetics. At any given stratum/level there is a scale of rank on which units are arranged hierarchically in a 'consist of' relationship (Halliday 2004). For the lexico-grammar, we have clause, group/phrase, word and morpheme. A clause consists of one or more groups/phrases, a group consists of one or more words, a word of one or more morphemes.

> It is noteworthy that Halliday's focus here is on the social and cultural functions of communication: indeed, we shall see that this a major characteristic of Halliday's approach, and is much more fully developed in SFG than in the other functional approaches considered here.

This characteristic makes SFG different from other functional accounts such as FDG and RRG, where the use of language in context is not a priority. The interest of SFG in contextual factors makes this approach useful for our analysis, as the aim is of this book is to identify the verbal and visual choices made by writers and illustrators of nine different picture books, intended for children belonging to three different age groups and distinct contextual characteristics (see Chapter 1, sections 1.3 and 1.4 for a description of the picture books that form the sample texts).

2.3.3 Metafunctional orientation

Linked to the openness of SFG to social matters are the three metafunctions distinguished by Halliday,[10] which are understood as general functions which language serves. As Butler indicates (2011: 365), functionalists do not only take the premise that language is an instrument for communication as a starting point, but they also assume that the forms that languages take are closely associated with the functions that communication serves in our everyday lives. In this sense, Halliday (1985, 1994, 2004), Halliday and Hasan (1989 [1985]) and Martin (1992) distinguish three broad functions that language performs, each, as has been stated in section 2.3.2, associated

10. The idea of metafunction was introduced before the term was used. Earlier in 1968, Halliday writes of 'functional components' and later in 1970 of 'macrofunctions' (Halliday 1970b). In Part 3 of 'Notes on Transitivity and Theme in English' Halliday (1968) talks of *components of grammar* representing the four functions that the language is required to carry out as a communication system: the experiential, the logical, the discoursal and the speech-functional or interpersonal. By 1970, specifically in Halliday (1970b), the reader can see that *ideational, interpersonal* and *textual* are terms which are used for these 'generalized uses of language'. The concept of a metafunction probably emerges in Halliday (1968), in particular in Part 3 of 'Notes on transitivity and theme in English' and then it is completely clear in Halliday (1970a) (Fawcett, 2011, comment on Syfling List). Martin (2011, Syfling List) complements this information in a subsequent comment and affirms that the term *metafunction* appears for the first time in 1974 in *Language and Social Man* (vol. 10).

with a specific contextual variable. The three main metafunctions are the following. First, through language we construe human experience, that is, represent and express our experience of reality, internal as well as external, and reflect on who is doing what to whom, and under what circumstances (experiential metafunction). This metafunction is complemented by the logical metafunction, which is concerned with constructing the logical relations of language by means of conjunction, coordination, subordination, modification, etc. The experiential, which deals with the construction of a model of experience, and the logical metafunctions are sometimes considered together as ideational. Second, through language we can also develop interaction. Sometimes we establish communicative exchanges with others, where the speaker adopts a role (giving or asking for information, for example), and the receiver acquires a complementary function (answering the formulated questions, agreeing, refusing information, etc.). At other times we evaluate or comment on the content of the situations or events surrounding us. This is also part of the interpersonal metafunction. Finally, language enables us to create coherent messages whose elements are joined to form a coherent whole in a specific context (textual metafunction).

The three metafunctions are realized independently and simultaneously in the clause structure (Halliday 2004). This way, in a clause such as 'Could we float away in this house, [...]?', taken from the picture book, *Granpa* (2003), the ideational meaning is constructed by means of the participants, 'we' and 'this house', the material process, 'float', and the circumstances 'away' and 'in this house'. At the same time, interpersonal meaning is construed by the mood element of the clause, in this case the finite (*could*) precedes the subject (*we*), making the clause interrogative. Finally, textual meaning is construed by locating the mood element, 'could we' in thematic position. These are the lexico-grammatical choices made by the writer of the tale to represent this event, to create interaction and to make a coherent clause. From the different choices available within the system networks to convey meaning, the writer of the tale has selected simultaneously a material process from the system of transitivity, an interrogative structure from the mood system and, finally, a multiple theme (interpersonal + topical) from the theme system. Notice that the writer had also the possibility of locating the circumstance, in this house, in thematic position and, therefore, choosing a marked thematic option. The resulting clause would be: 'In this house could we float away?' However, as tends to be the most frequent choice in stories for young children, the writer has preferred to place the subject and the finite form of the verb in the thematic slot of the clause. This way it is easier for child-readers to identify the main characters in the story as they are established as topical entities from the beginning of the clause without any further ado.

The metafunctional orientation of SFG is of interest to us here as in this study I aim to identify the options available to the writers and illustrators of picture books to represent the narrative reality reflected in the tales through: (i) the processes involved in the representation of the narrative world; (ii) the participants associated with them; as well as (iii) the circumstances attendant on the processes themselves (ideational (experiential) metafunction). My aim is also to identify the relationships set up by the young child and the represented participants involved in the stories (interpersonal metafunction). Finally, I attempt to identify the choices made at the textual level in order to determine how the tales are organized as coherent wholes from a thematic, compositional and informational perspective through the combination of verbal and visual strategies (textual metafunction).

FDG also recognizes two types of metafunctional meaning: 'representational' and 'interpersonal.' As Hengeveld and Mackenzie (2006: 671) point out: 'The interpersonal level accounts for all the formal aspects of a linguistic unit that reflect its role in the interaction between speaker and addressee.' The interpersonal level, which roughly corresponds to Halliday's textual and interpersonal metafunctions, includes information structuring as well as speech act functions. The interpersonal level deals with the structure of discourse acts in terms of subacts of ascription and reference. In addition it deals with the integration of acts into moves and, among other factors, it also discusses the operators and modifiers for all levels in the interpersonal hierarchy. However, the approach does not concentrate on the study of the clause as a communicative element in a specific context of communication. In turn, the representational level, as Hengeveld and Mackenzie (2006: 673) state: 'accounts for all the formal aspects of a linguistic unit that reflect its role in establishing a relationship with the real or imagined world it describes [...]. The representational level thus takes care of the semantics of a linguistic unit.' Finally, FDG does not incorporate a textual component. What Halliday (2004) treats as textual is handled, only in part, at the interpersonal level in FDG, which is seen as discourse-pragmatic in nature.

The functionalist approach that most approximates the Sydney school model is Fawcett's (2008) Cardiff Grammar. The Cardiff Grammar, whose origins are in Halliday's work in the 1970s, is concerned with both language and its use in the generation and understanding of texts. As Fawcett (2011 Syflying List) points out: 'It has an overall architecture that explains how language is used, and it provides components and procedures for both the "cognitive-interactive" and the "socio-cultural" aspects of SFL.' Both the Sydney and the Cardiff approaches are concerned with building a theory of language and describing texts (Fawcett 2000: 78–81). In addition, both approaches are centrally structural-functional, as they are concerned both with form and function and with the relationship between the two (Butler: 2003, 2005). Like Halliday's version of SFG, Fawcett's approach treats paradigmatic relations as the generative heart of the model and formalizes them in terms of system networks. Finally, both SFG and the Cardiff grammar use realization rules (Cardiff) or realization statements (Sydney) to map systemic choices on to formal realizations. It is assumed that the selection of each option within the system contributes to the formation of a specific structure.[11] However, while the Sydney Grammar is primarily socio-cultural in orientation, the Cardiff model claims to be essentially cognitive-interactive (Butler 2003; Gonzálvez-Garcia and Butler 2006). It is cognitive in the sense that it models the planning and execution of texts and it is interactive in that it also gives some attention to the role of society and culture in understanding language in use. Another important difference between the two models is concerned with their different levels of networks. The Sydney Grammar has two levels of networks: at the semantic level, in the ideation, interaction and text bases; and at the lexico-grammatical level, in the networks of transitivity, mood and modality, theme, etc. The relationship between the two levels is one of realization as higher levels are realized by lower levels. However, the Cardiff grammar has only one level of networks, and these are explicitly semantic. This way, realization rules take us straight from semantics into syntactic form. The Cardiff model is thus simpler in its basic architecture than the Sydney model, though realization rules can be quite complex.

Finally, the last difference between both grammars that is of most interest to us here is related to their metafunctional orientations. While eight major (experiential, logical relations, interpersonal, negativity, validity, affective, thematic, and information) and two minor (discoursal and inferential) strands of meaning are distinguished in the Cardiff account at the semantic

11. The semiotic choice, information giver, in the Cardiff grammar, for example is realized by the rule: Subject Op (Operator) or Subject Main Verb or if [being] Subject Op/Main verb.

level (Fawcett 2008: 167), only three metafunctional domains are differentiated in the Sydney school, and they are important in both the semantics and the lexico-grammar: ideational (experiential and logical), interpersonal and textual (Halliday 2004). Thus, the number of metafunctional domains differs considerably between the two models and there is no one-to-one correspondence between the eight strands of meaning distinguished by Fawcett and the three Hallidayan metafunctions. The fact that the Hallidayan metafunctions directly correspond to the three types of meaning, which I attempt to study throughout the chapters of this book, makes Halliday's grammar an appropriate framework to identify the verbal strategies used by writers of picture books to create coherent meaning and attract the child's attention to their stories. In turn, these three types of meaning – ideational, interpersonal and textual – maintain a one-to-one correspondence with the metafunctional domains (representational, interactive and compositional) distinguished by Kress and van Leeuwen (2006) in their grammar of visual design to study the meaning potential of images in multimodal products.

2.3.4 Use of systems and system networks

Regarding the form of the grammar, in addition to being a functional, contextual and social theory, SFG is, as has been stated in the previous section, also a systemic theory. It uses systems, combined into networks (transitivity, mood, theme, etc.) which operate at a number of levels and model paradigmatic relations.[12] The systems formalize the paradigmatic choices or abstract features which are available to the speaker of a language to make meaning and are basically defined by their opposition to each other. They are combined in system networks which, in principle, are able to generate and differentiate the linguistic structures of a given language. Halliday (1994: 15–16) puts it this way:

12. A system is understood as a closed set of options which are available to the user of the language and from which just one may be selected. The real usage of the system in a specific communicative context is the instantiation which allows us to differentiate between the theoretical system itself and its practical realization. In turn, a system network is a set of systems linked in relations of simultaneity (choices can be made from two or more systems independently) and/or dependency (one system depends on a choice from another system).

> One of the things that distinguishes SFL is that it gives priority to paradigmatic relations; it interprets language not as a set of structures but as a network of systems, or interrelated sets of options for making meaning. Such options are not defined by reference to structure; they are purely abstract features, and structure comes in as the means whereby they are put in effect, or 'realized'.

Meaning is thus conveyed through the choices made within the features available in the system and the system networks that are established within the semantic and lexico-grammatical strata of a specific language. This paradigmatic perspective enables the approach to offer a model which contrasts the abstract choices available in a language to convey meaning with the real instantiations made by the user of the language in a given stretch of discourse. Thus, SFG is concerned both with the whole system of the language and with individual texts. The former, the underlying language system, is the potential of a language as a resource for making meaning. The latter, the text itself, however, is an individual instance of that abstract potential at work.

The correlation between the system of the language and the specific text makes SFG different from other functional accounts to language such as FDG or RRG. SFG prioritizes paradigmatic relations, whereas FDG and RRG are essentially structural grammars, though units in the structures have operators associated with them, which offer a number of different choices (e.g. in tense, illocution, etc.). The fact that SFG prioritizes paradigmatic relations, as formalized in system networks, is another aspect that makes it appropriate for the study that is carried out here, as I aim to identify the verbal and visual choices actually made by writers and illustrators to convey representational, interpersonal and textual meanings in a sample of nine picture books written in the English language and intended for young children.

Up until now we have seen that, unlike formal approaches to language, functional models pay considerable attention to language as a tool for human communication, are in favour of functional explanations and give primacy to semantics and pragmatics over syntax. Some of them also show a strong commitment to textual and contextual aspects, interpersonal phenomena (e.g. speech acts) and information structural factors (topic, focus, etc.). However, the way they deal with these issues varies considerably from one approach to another (Butler 2003, 2005, 2006, 2009). SFG is the approach that seems to be the most appropriate for the purposes of our study, as it is the most text-oriented approach to language and it is strongly concerned with the relationships that are established between texts and the socio-cultural contexts in which they are produced and understood (Butler 2003: 15). As Halliday points out (1994: xxvii):

> In general, [...] the approach leans towards the applied rather than the pure, the rhetorical rather than the logical, the actual rather than the ideal, the functional rather than the formal, the text rather than the sentence. The emphasis is on text analysis as a mode of action, a theory of language as a means of getting things done.

Another reason that has led me to adopt Hallidayan SFG-theory over other functional approaches lies in its metafunctional orientation, by which three different types of meanings are distinguished at the semantic and lexico-grammatical strata of the language: ideational, interpersonal and textual. Since one of my aims is to identify the choices actually made by writers: (i) to represent the narrative reality of nine children's stories; (ii) to create engagement between their fictional characters and the young child; and (iii) to identify the textual patterns adopted by writers to form coherent and appealing picture books, SFG and its metafunctional orientation offers the tools to carry out this type of analysis. In addition, Halliday's SFG is the only approach which claims a strong commitment to paradigmatic organization or system networks to model choice relations. This makes it a useful account to identify the choices actually made by writers to construct the narrative reality without going beyond the cognitive capabilities of their prospective readers.

These specific features make the Sydney Grammar different from other approaches such as FDG or RRG. Although these approaches reject the autonomy of linguistic systems and syntax in favour of functional explanations, they do not give so much attention to the structuring of text and to textual/contextual relations as SFG-theory does.

2.4 Approaches to multimodality

Having justified the choice of SFG as the appropriate model to carry out the analysis of the verbal language of the sample texts, in this section I now attempt to explain why Kress and van Leeuwen's Visual Social Semiotics is the model that has been fundamentally adopted to carry out the analysis of the visual component of children's tales.

Jewitt (2009c: 28–29), in her handbook of multimodal analysis, distinguishes three main approaches to multimodality. These are: Hallidayan social semiotic multimodal theory of communication, extended and elaborated by Kress and Van Leeuwen (2001, 2006), van Leeuwen (2005a) and Kress (2010); systemic-functional grammar multimodal discourse analysis, associated with O'Toole (2011 [1994], 2004), Baldry and Thibault (2006), and O'Halloran (2003, 2004, 2005, 2007, 2008); and multimodal interactional analysis, exemplified by the works by Scollon (1998, 2001), Scollon and Scollon 2003, 2009) and Norris (2004, 2009). Each approach attends to different features of multimodality and different aspects of research. This is, to a certain extent, due to their different historical influences and the different emphasis they give to contextual factors and the sign-maker (Jewitt 2009).

2.4.1 Visual social semiotics

Kress and van Leeuwen's (2001, 2006) Social Semiotic approach emerges essentially from Halliday's (1978) theories of social semiotics, Barthes's Semiotics (1977) and Interactional Sociology (Goffman 1983; Hall 1992; Bateson, 2000; Jewitt 2009). Using Halliday's semiotics and SFL as the basis of their studies, Kress and van Leeuwen (2001, 2006) develop a grammar of visual language to account for types of semiotic meanings other than those encoded by language. They argue that visual compositions are also assumed to convey representational meaning, to establish interaction between the Represented Participants and the viewer and, finally, to form coherent messages. In the past, representational, interpersonal and textual meanings, as developed in Halliday's account, tended to be organized through the traditional modes of speaking and writing. However, nowadays, both verbal and non-verbal components are considered to be crucial tools for the construction of meaning (Baldry and Thibault 2006; Ventola and Moya 2009; Kress 2010). Halliday's recognition (1978: 4) that '[...] There are many other modes of meaning, in any culture, which are outside the realm of language' implies that the understanding of meaning not only requires the analysis of language in text, but also the study of other semiotic resources, such as images, gestures, sounds, etc., which are not necessarily verbal in nature.

In *Reading Images*, Kress and van Leeuwen provide the analyst with a series of semiotic system networks or taxonomic diagrams that display the visual semiotic resources available in a given domain. The systems map the choices available to the members of a community to create representational, interactive and compositional meaning as well as their different meaning potential when they are used in a specific context of communication.[13]

In fact, Kress and van Leeuwen (2006) explicitly distinguish a number of systemic oppositions which are realized by different visual structures. They contrast, for example, narrative processes which contain vectors of motion in which one participant is presented as doing something to another, with conceptual processes. The latter do not connect participants by means of vectors and represent entities in their more general and abstract essence. In turn, Kress and van Leewen (2006) differentiate between two types of narrative representations: action and reaction processes. Action images involve vectors of motion that are typically formed by diagonal arrows. These connect two participants in a unidirectional or bidirectional transactional action. Reaction Images, however, involve eye lines which may connect a reactor with another participant, the phenomenon, in a transactional reaction. Sometimes the reactor is not connected to any other participant involved in a visual process. The system of representational meaning is further developed in Chapter 3.

Moving to interaction, Kress and van Leeuwen (1996, 2006) distinguish different systems: image act and gaze, social distance and intimacy, horizontal angle and involvement and, lastly, vertical angle and power, each of them with their own sub-classifications. The producer has different systematic choices and will select one from the whole range of options to make his/her message clear to the viewer. Focusing on the system of image act and gaze and its two alternatives, demands and offers, the choice of a demand image implies that the producer attempts to establish a direct contact between the Represented Participants and the viewer. In contrast, the choice of an

13. Van Leeuwen (2009: 68) also admits that there are semiotic practices that can be explained as system networks or modes, which include both binary and simultaneous choices within the system. However, after studying the meaning potential of voice and the quality of voice, he argues that there are also resources that are better described in terms of parametric systems, that is, as 'systems which articulate meaning directly in or with the material characteristics of the signifier, or "media"'. In this second type of systems, there are only simultaneous choices; the choices they offer are graded and are open to intermediate positions (van Leeuwen 2009: 74–75). Parametric systems articulate meaning directly with the material characteristics of the signifier. Taxonomic systems, however, are taxonomic diagrams that offer all the semiotic, binary and simultaneous, choices which are available in a given domain (Van Leeuwen (2009: 68).

offer suggests that there is an absence of direct gaze between the depicted participants and the viewer. The choices in relation to the interpersonal metafunction are further explained and referred to in Chapter 4 of this book.

Finally, Kress and van Leeuwen (1996, 2006) also distinguish different options in relation to compositional meaning. The variables of information value, framing and salience complete the set of choices that are differentiated in the semioticians' visual grammar. As an example, it seems evident that the placement of elements within a visual composition is associated with specific information values. The contrasts top/bottom, left/right and centre/margin involve important differences in meaning potential. While the top zone is associated with the ideal and generalized essence of information, the bottom zone is related to real and more specific information. In turn, while the centre of a composition is presented as the nucleus of information, the margin is associated with subservient information. Finally, the left and right zones of a visual composition correspond to the given and new information positions, respectively. In the case of framing there are also choices, which include connection and disconnection between elements in an image. Finally, regarding salience, choices between maximum and minimum salience can also be, to a certain extent, identified, and these are essentially affected by the relative size of the pictorial elements, their location in the foreground or background of the composition, and colour and tonal contrasts, among other features. These aspects are further developed in Chapter 5 of this book.

Forceville (2010a and b) and Machin (2007: 184) have shown scepticism about the possibility of generating reliable quantitative data on some of the visual systems that Kress and van Leeuwen (2006) establish in relation to categories such as distance, angle and modality. In Forceville's (1999) review of Kress and van Leeuwen's visual grammar, he points out that these categories are sometimes fuzzy and describe a continuum between extremes rather than clear binary oppositions. A feature which seems to be problematic is that of modality. The problem is that the modality choices available within the system are simultaneous and graded. Consequently, the categories are not easily subject to quantitative analysis as there are no systematic scales or rules to distinguish the eight codes that can be applied to the types of modalities established by Kress and van Leeuwen (2006): naturalistic, scientific and sensory modality. Modality markers or scales (colour differentiation, illumination, etc.), through which it is determined whether an image is more or less real or unreal, are not clear-cut and may work independently of each other. This makes it difficult to establish clear binary oppositions between the possible choices available to assess the true value of an image. Certainly, although the categories of modality may create some problems providing quantitative data, other features within the interactive metafunction such as image act and gaze, distance and angle lend themselves more easily to quantitative analysis and objective distinctions.

Although initially Systemic Functional Grammar was the basis for Kress and van Leeuwen's (2006) approach to multimodality, Kress has, as Jewitt (2009: 29) points out: 'moved towards a more flexible notion of grammar, with a focus on people's situated choices of resources rather than emphasizing the system of available resources.' This means Systemic Functional Grammar and its network systems, although still relevant in many respects for the Social Semiotic approach, have now lost part of their grammatical influence on the Social Semiotic framework to multimodality. In fact, when studying the visual features of a multimodal ensemble, attention is given not only to the pre-defined modal network systems, but essentially to the communicative resources available to people in a specific social and cultural context. In addition, the system is seen as a resource with rules and regularities and is considered to have a dynamic character (Jewitt 2009: 34, 36). The choice of a semiotic resource from the system implies meaning, but this selection is regulated by social conventions. The cultural and social contexts shape the specific choices made by the users of the language from all the resources available to them to express meaning. As the modal systems are shaped by the context and their specific use, they are not seen as fixed or prescriptive elements, but as elements in constant change. Consequently, new semiotic resources are continuously created as potential options to respond to the interest of sign-makers when communicating. It is precisely the interest and purposes of individuals in communication that determines the choice of one semiotic resource over another. Each individual chooses the semiotic resource that is considered to be more appropriate to create meaning and establish interactions with the other members of his/her social and cultural community (Jewitt 2009).

Therefore, Social Semiotic Multimodality focuses on the rules, regularities and patterns that are made socially and that emerge from the modal systems of representation and communication in use. The researchers involved in social semiotics aim to analyse how the modal resources available are used by the members of a community to create meaning in a specific social context. Sign-making and the use of modal resources are seen as social processes. Together with Kress and van Leeuwen (2006), authors such as Jewitt (2009), Ventola *et al.* (2004), Ventola and Moya (2009), and Machin (2007), among others, could be identified within the social semiotic approach to multimodality.

2.4.2 Multimodal Discourse Analysis

The second approach to multimodal studies is known as Multimodal Discourse Analysis. SFG is the main theoretical framework of Multimodal Discourse Analysis which is, as has been stated, typically associated with the works by O'Halloran (2004, 2005) and O'Toole (2011 [1994]). Unlike Kress and van Leeuwen (2001: 4), who approach discourse from a macro-textual perspective and define discourses as: 'socially constructed knowledge of some aspect of reality [...] developed in specific social contexts', O'Halloran (2004, 2005) and O'Toole (2011 [1994]) focus on the analysis of discourse at the micro-textual level (Jewitt 2009).[14] Influenced by a systemic perspective, O'Toole (2011, 2004, 1994) adopts a constituent structural model with different ranks and differentiates between four ranked units to describe the meaning potential of pictures and art. Evidence of this is O'Toole's (2004) study of the Sydney Opera House building through a hierarchical organization of elements that go from the smallest or lower rank (the element) to the higher ranks (rooms, floors and the whole building). The basic ranked units distinguished by O'Toole (2011, 1994) in artwork are: work, episode, figure and member. Within the feature of work, for example, he establishes different systemic oppositions: narrative scene (+story) versus scene (+depiction). In turn, the feature of scene is divided into portrayal (+human) and non-human (O'Toole 1994: 12). Each rank has its own systems at representational, modal and compositional levels.[15] Semiotic resources are, therefore, considered as metafunctionally orientated systems of meaning.

14. Through the macroanalytic approach, the aim is to capture the process of meaning making of the text in its totality regarding the relations between the distinct units of which it consists. A microanalysis, on the other hand, focuses on a detailed description of the semiotic resources used in the creation of the text.
15. Machin (2009: 187) criticizes O'Toole's (1994, 2004) approach to the multimodal analysis of art. He argues that his analysis of visual art relies essentially on contextual and cultural knowledge and that knowledge about Greek mythology is required to interpret the work of *Privamera* by Botticelli. In addition, as Dillon (2006) also argues, images are not always easily divided into definable

This approach to the visual analysis of art is later adopted by O'Halloran (2004, 2005) to describe the metafunctional-based systems of semiotic resources and their meaning potential, along with the mechanisms through which semiotic resources are integrated and combined in multimodal discourses. Using SF-MDA O'Halloran (2004, 2005) analyses visual semiosis in films (O'Halloran 2004), and the intersemiosis of images and mathematical symbolism in mathematical texts (O'Halloran 2005) and mathematical classroom discourse (O'Halloran 2000). Baldry (2004: 84) also adopts the concept of rank to analyse a car advertisement from an approach that he labels: 'Systemic-functional tradition of multimodality'. He establishes a series of functional units and distinguishes between sub-phases, phases and macrophases, minigenres and genres.

Like Kress and van Leeuwen's (1996) model, O'Toole's (1994) also incorporates systemic and paradigmatic oppositions. He identifies a set of ranks and systems to describe the meaning potential of images. However, unlike Kress and van Leeuwen (2006), O'Toole (2011, 2004) does not extend the description of the model to system networks.[16] In addition, as Knox

components. Grammar in verbal language connects syntactic elements to form coherent clauses. But it is difficult to admit that images are made of signs that can be combined according to specific rules. Providing that these rules exist, they are not like language. In addition, in fact, it is not also always possible and worthy to break an image down into a specific visual system, since most of the meaning potentials of visual elements come from their association with other cultural or contextual constructs.

16. Kress and van Leeuwen (2006) and O'Toole (1994) use equivalent terms to the ones employed by Halliday (2004) to refer to the representational, interactive and textual meanings of images. However, some differences in terminology can also be identified when they describe their approaches to multimodality (Martin 2002: 311). Kress and van Leeuwen (1996, 2006), for instance, identify systems for representational, interactional and compositional meanings, which correlate with the three metafunctions distinguished in SFG, respectively: ideational, interpersonal and textual. In turn, OToole (1994) also differentiates three metafunctional domains in his analysis of art compositions and, like Kress and van Leewuen (1996), uses the terms representational and compositional to describe the representational and textual metafunctions of the language. In addition he uses the term, modal to refer to Halliday's interpersonal metafunction. Finally, Lemke (1998b) utilizes a different terminology and coins the terms, presentational, orientational and organizational to make reference to Halliday's three metafunctional domains (Painter *et al.* 2013: 7).

(2009: 112–113) indicates, the systemic oppositions established within the systems are not always exposed in an explicit manner in the discussion that O'Toole (1994: 9) offers in his multimodal model. It is the reader who must implicitly infer and identify the different systemic oppositions from the theoretical discussion (narrative themes, scenes, portrayals) and their corresponding structural realizations. This fact differentiates his approach to multimodality from Kress and van Leeuwen's approach, which shows a stronger commitment with paradigmatic oppositions and system networks. O'Toole's approach, however, seems to show a stronger interest in the concept of rank and stratification on three planes: the expression plane (phonology, graphology and typography), the content plane (grammar and discourse semantics) and the context plane (genre, register and ideology).

The aim of scholars working within the MDA approach is to identify the semiotic resources available to the user of the language to create meaning in a specific social and cultural context, their functionality and meaning potential and, finally, their combination and integration in multimodal artefacts. As Jewitt (2009: 33) points out: 'The emphasis is placed on understanding and describing semiotic resources and principles of their systems of meaning in order to understand how people use these resources in social contexts for specific purposes.' Together with O'Halloran (2004, 2005) and O'Toole (2011, 2004), authors such as Baldry (2004), Baldry and Thibualt (2006), Lim Fei (2007) and Stenglin (2009) work within this approach to multimodality.

2.4.3 Multimodal Interaction Analysis

The Interaction Analysis is the third multimodal approach referred to in Jewitt's (2009) Handbook on multimodality. Due to its historical influences, Scollon and Scollon's (2003) mediated discourse analysis, Goffman's (1983) interactional sociology and Kress and van Leeuwen's multimodality (1996, 2001, 2006), this approach gives great importance to the notions of context and interaction in use (Jewitt 2009). Using the Multimodal Interactional Analysis, Norris (2004, 2009) analyses the actions carried out by a social actor to express meaning interactively. She analyses both the messages expressed and sent by the users of the language and the other individuals' reactions to these messages in a specific situation of communication.

The unit of analysis of the multimodal interactional approach is the action(s) carried out by an individual in interaction with others. Two main types of actions are distinguished: lower level and higher level actions.

While the former are the smallest meaningful interactional units, the latter consist of a series of chained lower-level actions or multiple actions, which are bracketed by an opening and a closing part. A meeting among three friends, for example, can be considered as a higher-level action that consists of a series of lower-level actions. The gestures used by the individuals in the encounter, the intonations units of each individual in interaction; shifts in posture, gaze changes, etc. ... all are chains of lower-level actions (Norris 2004: 13).

Norris (2004: 79; 2009: 78) proposes two concepts that are linked to the actions that social actors perform at a specific time and place by using different communicative modes: modal density and modal configuration. Modal density is determined by the modal intensity or modal complexity that is involved in the construction of a higher-level action. A higher level action such as sending an SMS requires high modal density if we consider the modes of gaze, language and object handling that are directly related to the SMS. However, the modal density involved in this action is medium when the same social actor is simultaneously conversing with another individual at a specific place while s/he is sending the SMS and using other modes such as posture, gaze, language, gesture, layout, etc. (Norris 2009: 78). Thus, modal density enables the analyst to deal with the multiple actions that social actors may carry out simultaneously in interaction. The amount of attention paid to each action, that is, the degree of awareness required from the actor to perform a given action is a crucial factor in the determination of its modal complexity. From this notion, it can be deduced that in interactional multimodality the modes utilized while performing an action play different roles and functions. Through the concept of modal configuration, Norris (2009: 78, 90) refers to the hierarchical position of all the modes that are at play in a specific moment of a higher level action and the way they are structured in relation to one another; this is basically established on the basis of the meaning that is being constructed.

As Jewitt (2009: 34) points out: 'This perspective shifts attention from representation and communication (the focus of Kress, van Leeuwen and O'Halloran) to interaction.' Communication in Norris's framework is essentially understood as on-going interaction between individuals and as a multimodal process in which different communicative modes (gestures, gaze, posture, movement, space and material objects), also referred to by Norris (2009: 90) as mediational means, are combined to convey meaning. Thus, the focus of Norris's analysis falls essentially on interaction. Norris (2009) acknowledges that there is not a predetermined modal system outside the interaction established by individuals in a specific context. In Kress and van Leeuwen's approach, as well as that of other authors associated with social semiotic multimodality, the interest is on the paradigmatic oppositions that emerge from modal systems of communication in use. In turn, in O'Halloran's multimodal discourse analysis, attention is essentially paid to the semiotic systems of representation and the way they interact with each other. However, in Norris's (2004, 2009) account of multimodality, the focus is on the rules and regularities that emerge when social actors interact and use the systems of representation in on-going interactions. Other aspects related to representational or compositional matters, however, are outside the focus of Norris's Interactive Approach to multimodality. Together with Norris *et al.* (2003, 2009), Jones (2005, 2009) and Norris and Jones (2005) are references that could be situated within this approach to multimodality (Jewitt 2009).

Of the three multimodal approaches referred to in this section, Visual Social Semiotics, Multimodal Discourse Analysis and Norris's Interactive Analysis, the one that best adapts to the needs of the present analysis is Kress and van Leeuwen's (2006) Social Semiotics. As previously mentioned, this approach is essentially an extension of the postulates defended by Halliday (1978, 2004) and in which three levels of meaning are distinguished – representational, interactional and compositional – which correspond to the three macrofunctions of SFG – representational, interpersonal and textual, respectively – that we analyse in the present study. The fact that the three metafunctions established by Halliday maintain a one-to-one correspondence with the three levels of meaning distinguished by Kress and van Leeuwen has led me to adopt these two approaches as the basic theoretical frameworks to carry out the analysis of the sample texts. As O'Halloran (2009: 2) highlights in the following quote, social semiotics expands on systemic-functional theory in order to apply it to semiotic resources other than language and, in this way, covers the range of semiotic resources and modes, verbal and non-verbal, which intervene in a communicative exchange:

> The multimodal social semiotic approach draws upon Michael Halliday's (1978, 1994 [1985]; Halliday and Matthiessen, 2004) systemic functional (SF) theory to provide frameworks for conceptualizing the complex array of semiotic resources which are used to create meaning (e.g. language, visual imagery, gesture, sound, music, three dimensional objects and architecture) and detailed practices for analysing the meaning arising from the integrated use of those resources in communication artefacts (i.e. texts) and events.

In addition, both approaches, SFG and Visual Social Semiotics, have a strong commitment to social and contextual factors and study the meaning of texts in a specific context of communication and within a specific culture. Like SFG-theory, Kress and van Leeuwen's Visual Semiotics is social in orientation. In fact, in Systemic Social Semiotics, social activities are also modelled as genres, which are understood as configurations of meanings (Martin and Rose 2008: 44–45). These are realized by different modalities (images, language, sound, etc.) which perform a social function in a specific context of communication.

Finally, influenced by SFG-theory, Visual Social Semiotics builds in paradigmatic oppositions and system networks. The choices within the systems provide the analyst with the range of abstract options which are available to the user of the language to make meaning. The adoption of Kress and van Leeuwen's approach to multimodality and its paradigmatic orientation will allow us to identify the choices actually made by illustrators of picture books to represent the narrative reality, to create interaction with the young reader and to construct coherent wholes of communication.

Although the proposed analysis essentially adopts Social Semiotic Multimodality as the framework that provides the tools to study the sample of picture books, I start from the premise that considering different well established paradigms in the analysis of multimodal discourse is beneficial and can lead to a better understanding of communication in contemporary society. For this reason, in this analysis of picture books, the notion of metonymy (Forceville 2009), which is proposed by scholars working within other multimodal frameworks, is also taken into consideration in Chapter 6 of this book. Forceville has demonstrated the applicability and usefulness of this concept in analysing how images and words interact with each other in the construction of representational meaning. Finally, the works by Barthes (1977), Golden (1990), Agosto (1999), Nikolajeva and Scott (2000, 2001), Gill 2002, Unworth (2006) and Unsworth and Cléirigh (2009) on words and images complementarity in multimodal ensembles will also be considered to analyse how images and words are co-deployed in picture books.

2.4.4 Assumptions within Multimodal Social Semiotics

As Visual Social Semiotics is the approach essentially adopted in this book to carry out a multimodal analysis of picture books from a systemic-functional perspective, at this point I will refer to some of its basic premises and to the general assumptions that are commonly held among the followers of this approach. Some of these assumptions are also shared by scholars who work within other multimodal frameworks such as Multimodal Discourse Analysis and Multimodal Interaction. The first assumption that is accepted by academics and scholars working on multimodality is that communication is multimodal and often involves more than one semiotic mode. Jewitt (2009: 14) assumes that in multimodal approaches meaning is made through the combination of different communicative modes, not only written or spoken language. Multimodal researchers cast doubt on the traditional belief that semiotic resources such as gaze, gesture, posture or image function merely as support to language and are not able to create meaning on their own (Kress 2010). Indeed, in multimodal approaches language is no longer considered the central mode of communication; language is just one semiotic resource, among others, for making meaning (Kress 2009: 54, 58). As Jewitt (2009: 3) acknowledges:

> Indeed it has been argued that the modern world has become a visual phenomenon that conflates looking, seeing and knowing (Jenks 1995) – a kind of 'vision machine' created through new visualizing technologies in which people are caught. (Virilio 1994)

Evidently, Jewitt (2009) and Kress (2010) adopt a social semiotic approach to communication and understand language as the 'result of people's constant social and cultural work' (Jewitt 2009: 3). Norris (2004: 1), who heads the research on interactive multimodality, also states that 'all interactions are multimodal.' In turn, Scollon and Scollon, sharing a similar perspective, emphasize the multimodal nature of communication by pointing out that:

> In the present we would argue that language is no longer taken as an independent and prototypical model of all modes of communication. It does continue to be an influence on researchers in the field of multimodality, largely as a resource for ideas about how to begin to analyse separate communication modes … it is fatal to the research endeavor to simply transport linguistic analysis over into the analysis of other modes. The question of modality must necessarily be developed within each mode. (Scollon and Scollon 2009: 180)

Since language is no longer the exclusive mode in contemporary communication, we cannot apply its traditional models and methods to analyse all types of meaning. This may conceal the nature of non-verbal modes and limit the understanding of multimodal artefacts. The 'linguistic imperialism' (Machin 2009: 189) of verbal modes, which have been the focus of linguists and scholars for centuries, is now coming to an end. Since the last decade an interest in multimodality and the meaning potential of non-verbal modes has increased among academics and researchers. New approaches for analysing language need to be applied to understand the way communication is created in our technological society. This does not mean, however, that language and linguistic modes cannot offer interesting ideas to delve into the study of the multimodal products created today. As Scollon and Scollon (2009: 175) point out by referring to systemic functional approaches, linguistic models may be useful for analysing communication, providing that they do not impose their own methods as the only way to deal with other non-verbal modes:

> While the older structural models of linguistics have largely failed to be productive in nonverbal communication and multimodality studies, languages remain rich resources of ideas for the study of multimodality as Kress and van Leeuwen (1996, 2001) and others have amply demonstrated. This is particularly the case of functional linguistics or systemic functional grammar (Halliday 1978, 1985). (Scollon and Scollon 2009: 175)

Theories and concepts used in linguistics may not belong solely to the study of language and could be productive in their applications to other semiotic resources (Lim Fei 2004: 221). In fact, the application of SFL to other semiotic resources has proven to be useful as demonstrated in the work of O'Toole (2011), Kress and van Leeuwen (1996), Lemke (2000, 2002), O'Halloran (1999, 2000), Baldry and Thibault (2006) and Ventola and Moya (2009), among others. It may be argued that the adoption of a linguistic theory for other semiotic resources is not the most appropriate solution. Lim Fei (2004) considers that there should be a balance between the adoption and rejection of linguistic theories for visual analysis and intersemiotic processes.

The second assumption within social semiotics multimodality is that modes are 'inextricably shaped and constructed by social, cultural, and historical factors' (Jewitt 2009: 22). Kress (2010: 81) emphasizes this idea by stating that 'modes are the product jointly of potentials inherent in the material and of a culture's selection from the bundle of aspects of these potentials and the shaping over time by members of a society of the features selected.' As human beings we use the semiotic resources available to us to communicate and create codes which are known to all the members of our community. A symbol, an object or a sign becomes a semiotic system only if the members of the community accept it and are able to decode it and interpret its meaning.[17] Indeed, Kress (2009: 58–59) acknowledges that a mode is 'what a community takes to be a mode and demonstrates that in its practices ...'. Modes are therefore constructed on the bases of 'the daily social interaction of people' (Jewitt 2009: 21). Similarly, Baldry and Thibault (2006), O'Toole (2004) and O'Halloran (2004) share Kress's view and acknowledge that the semiotic resources of modes are shaped by their use in a particular social context.

Third, scholars on multimodality also assumed that that each mode has its own affordances (meaning potentials, following Gibson's (1977) and van Leeuwen's (2005a) terminology) and constraints to create meaning and, therefore they carry out different semiotic jobs through their semiotic resources.[18] The choice of a mode to represent meaning is essentially determined by its specific semiotic resources and materialities, which make it represent the world in a particular way (Kress 2009: 54, 58; Jewitt 2009: 15). As Kress (2010: 96) affirms: '[...] modes offer distinct ways of engaging with the world and distinctive ways of representing the world. They offer different and distinct potentials for presenting the world; distinct possibilities of transcription; [...]'. Images, for example, use different resources than written language. Writing has words, clauses, sentences, which are organized through grammatical and syntactic rules. It also has graphic resources such as font, size, colour, frames, etc., the latter realized by graphic resources such as punctuation marks, spacing between words and paragraphs, etc. (Kress 2009: 55).[19] However, images lack these resources and they do not contain

17. 'A semiotic resource system is thus a system of semiotic forms that we can use for the purpose of making texts' (Baldry and Thibualt 2006: 18).
18. Semiotic resources are understood as the materials and artefacts people use to communicate (Jewitt 2009: 17).
19. Frame is another semiotic resource to make meaning. In line with Bateson (2000), Kress (2009: 66) points out that 'frames and means of framing are essential to all meaning-making, in all modes'. Not only do images have frames, writing is also framed. Punctuation (full stop, commas, etc.), for instance, is a device for framing in writing. White space, colour bands, silence, etc. are other framing devices used in verbal and visual modes. The function of framing is either linking or separating an entity from others in surrounding context. The entities inside a frame are given unity and coherence and are shown as belonging to the same class of entities. In turn, frames can also segment and separate entities. They determine what is outside the frame defining it as different, as disconnected from what is inside.

words, clauses or sentences which are organized through syntactic principles. Unlike words, which respond to the logic of time, images are based on the logic of display. In turn, like writing, speech contains lexis and grammar. However, the material of speech, sound, is different from graphics, the material of writing. In addition, while sound is received through the sense of hearing, writing is perceived by the sense of sight. Although speech and writing are subsumed under the same level, language, their differences in affordances and materiality justify that they are conceived as two different modes. In fact, Kress (2009: 58) classifies them as two separate modes and explains his decision as follows:

> Unifying speech with writing – with their different materiality; the distinct logics of time and space, or sequence and simultaneity – exposes the impossibility of a mode called 'language'. From a multimodal perspective it becomes difficult to see what principles of coherence might unify them. As a consequence, I take speech and writing to be distinct modes.

Images, speech and words have different affordances, that is, different potentials and limitations to express and represent reality in a specific social and cultural context. Consequently, they fulfil different semiotic works and offer distinct representations of the world (Kress 2010: 84).

The last assumption within the approaches to multimodality referred to in this chapter is that the intersemiosis of two or more modes in a multimodal production generates meanings which are beyond the information transmitted by each mode in isolation. Through their 'resource integration principle', Baldry and Tibault (2006: 4) point out that modes are combined in multimodal artefacts and that this interaction is significant in the process of making meaning. When several modes are co-deployed in a communicative event, each contributes in different ways to the construction of meaning and adopts specific organization principles. This depends, to a certain extent, on their different affordances and constraints. Therefore, their contribution is always 'partial to the whole of the meaning' (Jewitt 2009: 25) that is transmitted in a multimodal ensemble. Sometimes, they express almost symmetrical meanings; at others they complement one another. They may even offer contradictory meanings and generate tension, which is also meaningful. Independently of the way they complement each other, makers of meaning have different choices at their disposal, both within and across modes, to create meaning.

2.5 Towards a definition of mode

At this point I will address the concept of mode, a controversial term that has been defined from several perspectives and that has generated different interpretations within the three multimodal approaches referred to in the previous section. I will address the issue of mode by referring to Jewitt's (2009) and Kress and van Leeuwen's (2006) and Kress's (2009, 2010) definitions of this concept. O'Halloran's (2004, 2005) and Norris's (2004, 2009) approaches to modality are also considered in an attempt to specify how the concept of mode is defined within other important multimodal approaches, such as Multimodal Discourse Analysis and Multimodal Interactional Analysis. Finally, Forceville's (2009) and Elleström's (2010) perspectives on multimodality and their corresponding definitions of mode are commented on to complete and show the different positions adopted by researchers on the field of multimodal studies. After referring to some of the disputed aspects that generate boundaries among the different approaches to multimodality, I will take a practical stand while analysing the different definitions of mode and their possible realizations.

Defining mode is a slippery task as there is no agreement upon what constitutes a mode and it is often difficult to separate the analysis of different modes in interaction. In face-to-face-conversation, for example, different dimensions of meaning such as gaze, gesture, movement, etc. may occur at the same time, which makes it difficult to establish the boundaries between them when they are combined to construct meaning (Norris 2004; Elleström 2010; Forceville 2010a, 2011). For as long as there is no clear agreement about when a (potential) dimension of meaning earns the right to be promoted to mode-status, the number of candidates for mode can grow to enormous proportions.

Starting with the social semiotic approach to multimodality, Kress and van Leeuwen (2006) and Jewitt (2009) consider mode from a similar perspective, essentially as a dimension shaped by social, cultural and historical factors. In her introduction, Jewitt (2009: 1) defines modes or modalities as semiotic resources used for making meaning in a culture and distinguishes between modes such as image, writing, gesture, gaze, speech or posture. Kress (2009: 54) defines mode as: 'a socially and culturally given resource for making meaning' and differentiates between image, writing, layout, music, gesture, speech, moving images and soundtrack as examples of modes used to represent meaning and establish communication. Kress (2009) also refers to phenomena such as furniture, clothes, food, etc., and points out that they are also capable of generating meaning. As these phenomena usually communicate in a specific social and cultural context, Kress launches the question of whether they should also be considered as modes. Other aspects such as layout, colour and font are also defined as modes in Kress's approach (2010: 79) when he states: 'Image, writing, layout, music, gesture, speech, moving image, soundtrack and 3D objects are examples of modes used in representation and communication.' The semiotician also asserts:

> The digital media of representation/production/communication facilitate the use of many such technologies of transcription: modes such as speech, moving image or still image, writing, colour, layout all appear and are available to be used. (Kress 2010: 97)

Therefore, he also seems to raise layout, font and colour to the status of mode, increasing this way the controversy around the semiotic dimensions of this concept. Font, colour and layout are culturally-specific and socially-agreed by the society where they are produced. Thus, they may create meaning and act as semiotic resources within a specific cultural and social situation.

In line with Kress and van Leeuwen's approach, Jewitt (2009: 22) acknowledges that:

> [...] in order for something to 'be a mode' there needs to be a shared cultural sense of a set of resources and how these can be organized to realize meaning [...] What is considered a mode and interaction between modes is inextricably shaped and construed by social, cultural and historical factors.

An individual can establish that an object, symbol or sign possesses a determined significance, but this does not make it a semiotic system or a communicative sign until the members of the community accept, interpret and satisfactorily decode its significance. Some uses may have lost their original meaning or may have simply disappeared entirely. These uses would be part of the theoretical semiotic potential of a sign but not of its real semiotic potential. See, for example, the use made of fans in Spain from the sixteenth until the nineteenth century, where they were used in public events to express a great number of related meanings within the art of courtship. This resource has been lost in present times and, therefore, does not form part of the real semiotic potential of the fan, but rather of its theoretical semiotic potential. This implies that modes are transformed by the people who use them through social interaction in a specific context of communication and that new modes are constantly being created.[20] As Jewitt (2009: 26) states, this flexibility and contextual dependence make 'the task of building stable analytical inventories of multimodal semiotic resources complex.'

Within a Multimodal Discourse Analysis perspective, O'Halloran (2005: 20, 2008, 2009) and O'Toole (2004) seem to approach mode from a different view than that adopted in Social Semiotics. They consider dimensions such as language, images, architecture and mathematical symbolism as semiotic resources rather than modes (Jewitt 2009: 21). For them, while modes are the channels of communication (e.g. visual, aural, olfactory, tactile), semiotic resources are systems of meaning that are available to the user of a community to fulfil different communicative functions. Within semiotic resources, O'Halloran (2011: 2) includes:

> aspects of speech such as intonation and other vocal characteristics, the semiotic action of other bodily resources such as gesture (face, hand and body) and proximics, as well as products of human technology such as carving, painting, writing, architecture, image and sound recording, and in more contemporary times, interactive computing resources (digital media hardware and software).

The system provides choices which, in turn, are meaningful when they are selected and combined by the sign-maker in multimodal artefacts. Language, as a semiotic resource, can then be realized either by written text (visual mode) or by spoken language (oral mode). O'Halloran (2009) argues that the meaning potential of the semiotic resource of mathematical symbolism changes considerably when it is realized by either a written mode or a visual mode. Note that in opposition to O'Toole's (2004) and O'Halloran's (2005, 2009) approach, van Leeuwen (2005a) and Kress and van Leeuwen (2006) define semiotic resources not as systems of meanings, but 'as the actions, materials and artefacts we use for communicative purposes, whether produced physiologically, for example with our vocal apparatus, the muscles we use to make facial expressions and gestures – or technologically – for example, with pen and ink, or computer hardware

20. In social semiotics the rules are socially made and are not resistant to the modifications imposed by social interaction. Signs are the result of social interaction in a communicational context and are socially and culturally regulated by the people who use them (Van Leeuwen 2005a). In contrast, in traditional semiotics, rules or codes are fixed and unable to suffer transformations (Barthes 1977).

and software – together with the ways in which these resources can be organized' (van Leeuwen, 2005a: 285).

The human being in his interaction with the world that surrounds him uses the resources within reach in order to communicate and, consequently, create codes that are recognized and recognizable to him and his community. These resources possess a semiotic potential thanks to which meaning may be built and, additionally, they are based on some type of physical materiality which allows for their recognition by a linguistic community (Van Leeuwen, 2005a: 4). They are not abstract entities, but rather communicative systems that, through the variable of mode, are perceived by one of the senses.

The distinction between semiotic resource and mode leads O'Halloran (2005: 20) to differentiate between multisemiotic and multimodal texts.[21] Multisemiotic texts combine different semiotic resources such as images, language or music. Multimodal texts, however, combine different modes or communication channels (visual, aural, tactile, etc.) in a situation of communication. These two different approaches to mode and semiotic resources make it even more difficult to decide which communicational dimensions deserve the status of mode.

Within a Multimodal Interactional approach, Norris (2004: 11–12; 2009: 79–80) defines communicative modes as semiotic systems of representation which have rules and regularities; these are constructed on the basis of the actions performed by social actors in a specific time and place. Norris (2004) acknowledges that interaction is always multimodal, since in social interaction different means of communication are combined to express meaning. In line with Kress and van Leeuwen (2001), Norris (2004) distinguishes between proxemics, posture, head movement, gesture, gaze, spoken language, layout, print, and music, among others, as the main modes of communication when participants are interacting. Norris assumes (2004) that modes have no clear boundaries and that there is not a specific definition for this concept. In fact, she (2004: 11) states that mode is:

21. Matthiessen (2009: 15–22) recognizes the existence of multisemiotic systems that integrate with each other in differing degrees, from maximum integration (there is a dominant semiotic system and the other systems of expression with their distinct *modalities* are integrated into the same strata of content) to minimum integration (two or more semiotic systems are presented as separate regarding content and mode of expression and they are only integrated and coordinated through the superior strata of the context).

> A heuristic unit that can be defined in various ways. We can say that layout is a mode, which would include furniture, pictures on a wall, walls, rooms, houses, streets, and so on. But we can also say that furniture is a mode. The precise definition of a mode should be useful for the analysis.

Thus, any communicative means that plays a part in a specific interaction is regarded as a mode, independently of its materiality or importance in the communicative exchange. This approach opens up the range of candidates for mode-status and shifts the focus from representation and communication (as is the case of Kress and van Leeuwen's and O'Halloran's proposals for modality) to interaction (Jewitt 2009: 34).

Finally, from a totally different standpoint, Elleström (2010) offers a new perspective to modality. When he establishes what should be counted as mode, he distinguishes between four different types of modalities, the material, the sensorial, the spatiotemporal, and the semiotic modality, which are applicable to discussions of all media or messages. Material modality is the physical interface of the message and it involves three modes: animate bodies, inanimate objects and manifestations of non-material phenomena such as light or sound-waves. Sensorial modality deals with physical and mental perception and comprises the modes of sense-data, that is, bodily receptors that register these data and transfer them to the nervous system. The spatiotemporal modality deals with movement in space and temporal changes, while the semiotic modality governs the processes of attributing meaning to things and events and the interpretation of signs. Peirce's symbol, index and icons are the three most important modes of the semiotic modality. Indexes point to the nature of the entities they represent; an animal footprint, for example. Symbols are arbitrary: words, emblems, brands are evidence of this. Finally, icons are represented through resemblance or similarity. A photograph or a picture of a lion provides a good example of an icon. Thus, text, music, gesture and image, traditionally considered by Kress and van Leeuwen (2006) and Kress (2010) as modalities, are not analysed as such in Elleström's approach (Forceville 2011).

It is evident then that serious scholars on multimodality do not always agree on the definition and characterization of mode, which makes it difficult to determine what dimensions of communication should be given the status of mode (Forceville 2006, 2010b: 58; Bateman 2008). As author of this work on multimodality and picture books, these intricacies lead me to adopt a practical stand and state my perspective in this field before starting the analysis of the sample texts and their different modalities. Avoiding the intricacies referred to before and in line with Forceville (2009, 2010b) I postulate six different modes or semiotic resources for making meaning: written language, spoken language, visuals, music, sound and gestures. In the case of layout, colour, font, etc., I assume, as does Kress (2010: 87), that there is not a straight-forward answer as to whether these features should be considered as modes or not. Kress (2010) states that questions such as 'Is layout/font/ colour a mode?' need to be tackled from both a socially and formally oriented perspective.

From a formal perspective, font, colour and layout are considered as modes provided that a group of people use them with a degree of regularity and assume that they have meaning potential in a specific social and cultural context. Shared practices and understanding within a community are essential features for a communicational dimension to become a mode (Kress 2010: 87). It is therefore the community that decides what is and what is not regarded as mode in a specific context of communication.[22] The social perspective of the previous questions focuses on the requirements or functions that a communicational resource has to fulfil in the three metafunctions distinguished within SF-theory: representing reality, interacting with others and forming coherent messages. Layout, colour and font are modes only if they meet these requirements. This is the test that Kress (2009, 2010) proposes for a communicational resource to reach the status of mode. Kress (2009: 59) affirms that layout, colour and font are a mode because they meet the three requirements referred to before. They may be representative of the actions, states and events that go on in the world; they may also establish social relations between the participants involved in communication. Finally, these dimensions may also create internally coherent texts. Thus, Kress's response to the question 'Is layout/colour/font a mode?' is affirmative.

I also accept that colour and font are features that fulfil a role in the compositional, interactive and even representational metafunctions of the language. Font and colour are frequently used in visual compositions to give salience or prominence to some specific elements in a multimodal ensemble. In addition, colour and font also fulfil a function in framing elements

22. Forceville (2011) criticizes this perspective based on social parameters. In fact, although he considers that Kress's view is a practical solution for the definition of mode, he also points out that the definition given by the semiologist allows mode to be applied to any meaning-making resource.

together, showing that they have something in common, or framing them as separate entities belonging to different groups. Elements can be grouped together or separated from each other by continuity or discontinuity of colour and shape. Thus, these modal dimensions also seem to fulfil a role in the interpersonal and compositional metafunctions of the language. Finally, by association, colour and font may also generate meaning for a specific social and cultural group and, therefore, represent our experience of the world. Kress and van Leeuwen (2002) support this argument and affirm that while saturated colours are associated with emotional intensity, pale colours, in contrast, are related to moderation. Through colour and font entities, processes and circumstances are often represented in abstract art compositions. Even in realistic compositions Represented Participants and their corresponding processes may be depicted through colour. Evidence of this is the 29th illustration of the picture book *Gorilla* (2003) by Anthony Browne. By association with the red clothes that Hannah, the protagonist in the story, frequently wears, she is represented by a dash of red that accentuates the sensation of speed when she rushes downstairs to tell her father what had happened during her dream. A flash of what may be interpreted to be Hannah's red robe speeding down the stairs is enough to represent the girl metonymically. In the case of font, van Leeuwen (2005b) and Machin (2009) also acknowledge that metaphorical associations play a key role in the meaning potential of visual communication. Machin (2009: 186) explains this fact in the following way.

> Heavier fonts can be seen as bolder, stronger and more stable than lighter slimmer fonts, although this can also suggest something overbearing and immovable as opposed to something more subtle. Here qualities of stronger and more stable things in the world are transferred to fonts and therefore to the things they describe. The meaning is transported from one domain to another.

However, in the case of layout, I can't help wondering whether this communicative dimension is able to represent reality by itself and without the presence of other visual elements. There is no doubt that layout conveys meaning. A photograph of a politician at the top of the front page of a newspaper generates meaning related to relevance and salience. The arrangement of elements on the printed page is meaningful and culture-specific. The positions, left/right and top/bottom of the page, for example, are associated with givenness/newness and ideal/real, respectively (Kress and van Leeuwen 2006). But the meaning of the visual composition referred to comes essentially from the represented participants that are depicted in a particular background and involved in certain visual processes. Layout is a feature that affects the elements of the mode of image. However, layout does not name or depict elements or (represented) participants in a semiotic space. So, its primary function is not to communicate or to represent reality. In addition, by itself, it seems to be unable to represent processes and their participants and circumstances in a specific context. What layout does is basically to organize information in space, to determine the information status of the visual components of a multimodal artefact, and, finally, to orient readers or viewers towards categories such as central or marginal, given or new, or real or unreal (Kress, 2009: 64; 2010: 92). These facts lead me to consider it as more of a semiotic dimension than as a mode.

Kress (personal communication, May 2011) does not share this line of argumentation and affirms that whatever a community decides upon as a mode is a mode (Kress and van Leeuwen 2001, 2006; Kress 2010). Kress assumes that not all modes perform the same kind of activities in each of the three metafunctions distinguished by Halliday, but, as long as they do something that may plausibly belong to the domain of a metafunction, they deserve to have the status of mode. For this reason, Kress defines layout as a mode since it assigns entities to specific parts of a framed space, which is somehow ideational in essence. Similarly, for Kress, although gesture does not have, for instance, colour, it is a mode. In gesture, quite often something that is afterwards articulated as a word is realized by some facial or body movement. Certainly, this is not a word, but it does indicate that some entity, not named, not shown, is at issue.

In any case, and in an attempt to adopt a practical perspective, as the picture books that form our sample texts are bimodal composite wholes essentially made of illustrations and words, I analyse their verbal and visual components as their main semiotic modes, each one with their own semiotic resources and affordances to construct meaning in the three metafunctional domains distinguished within Systemic Functional Linguistics and Visual Social Semiotics. In addition, and without negating the meaning potential of colour, font or layout, these aspects will be dealt with as dimensions that support the main verbal and visual modes of these illustrated stories and thus contribute to the construction of their meaning.

3 Representational Meaning: Characters, Narrative Events and Settings

In Chapter 2 SFG was considered a linguistic approach that provides a model to describe how verbal language is used to create experiential, interpersonal and textual meanings simultaneously (Halliday 1978, 2004). In addition, Kress and van Leeuwen's (2006 [1996]) Visual Social Semiotics is regarded as an approach that offers an appropriate framework to analyse other non-verbal semiotic modes which can also be assigned representational, interactive and compositional meanings. Both SFG and Visual Social Semiotics deal mainly with the study of the verbal and visual aspects of language in context. Regardless of the mode chosen to communicate, the forms taken by the written and visual modes of a message are closely related to the social functions the language is required to fulfil and to the social situation in which it is used (Halliday 2004; Bowcher 2007; Martin 2008; Kress 2010).

Halliday's SFG account and specifically its representational meaning potential are described first in section 3.1. After this, an outline of the main representational features of Kress and van Leuwen's semiotic account is provided in section 3.2. The third part of this chapter is a review of the models used in the literature to label the intersemiotic relations established between words and images in multimodal artefacts and their possible applications to the picture books selected for analysis. After commenting on some troubleshooting aspects related to the representational metafunction of language, the last part of this chapter delves into the way images and words complement each other as interdependent components of the picture book, *The Very Hungry Caterpillar*, written and illustrated by Carle (2002 [1969]).

3.1 Representing and visualizing the narrative reality

As pointed out in Chapter 2, Halliday (2004) develops a Systemic Functional approach in relation to verbal language and establishes a set of grammatical systems which realize the three metafunctions of language. Within the SFG framework, every text is assumed to express three types of meanings simultaneously: (i) ideational, which represents our experience of the world inside and around us; (ii) interpersonal, which enacts social relationships and reflects the speaker's attitudes towards the content of communication; and (iii) textual, which coordinates and organizes the other two meanings in order to form a coherent text.[1]

Of the three metafunctions, the one that is concerned with the ability of language to convey some information about reality at the lexico-grammatical

Table 3.1 Types of processes

Process Type	*Type of meaning*	*Example*[2]	*Typical participants*
Material	Doing Happening	Max wore his wolf suit. A forest grew and grew.	Actor, Goal Actor
Mental	Affection Cognition Perception	We love you so! He smelled good things to eat	Senser, Phenomenon
Relational	Attributive Identifying	They were frightened His mother called him wild thing	Carrier, Attribute Identified, Identifier
Behavioural	Bodily happenings Volitional processes Social processes	They roared their terrible roars...	Behaver
Verbal	Communication	And Max said "I'll eat you up!"	Sayer, Receiver, Verbiage
Existential	Existence	There was a high wall all around	Existent

1. The ideational metafunction embodies experiential (participants, processes and circumstances) and logical (connections between different structures) meanings. The study carried out here focuses essentially on the former.
2. Examples taken from *Where the Wild Things Are* and *Gorilla*. Table adapted from Halliday (2004: 173).

stratum is the ideational. The conceptualization of patterns of experience is conveyed in language by choices in the system of transitivity. As shown in Table 3.1, these involve primarily the type of process selected (realized by a verb), and also the number and type of participants involved in it (typically persons, things or abstract entities), the attributes or qualities ascribed to them (which typically characterize, identify or locate them) and, finally, the circumstances of place, time and manner, etc. relative to the process itself. These are less centrally involved in the process than the participants themselves (Downing and Locke 2006: 122–123).

The ability of language to conceptualize and describe patterns of experience through the participants and circumstances associated with a particular verbal process leads to a first and basic distinction between three main types of processes: material, mental and relational. The first type, material, reflect the processes of the external world, while the second, mental, refer to the processes of consciousness. While material processes are typically processes of doing, happening, causing and transferring, mental processes are processes of perception (experiencing or sensing), of cognition, of desideration and of emotion and affection. The typical participants associated with material processes are *actor* (usually a human entity acting intentionally) and *goal* (a participant affected by the action).[3] As far as the prototypical participants in a mental process clause are concerned, these are *sensor* and *phenomenon*, or a projected clause. Added to material and mental processes are those of classifying and identifying, known as relational, which are processes of having, being or becoming in which a participant is identified or situated circumstantially (Halliday 2004). They express intensive (being), circumstantial or possessive relations, and are typically associated with the participants *carrier / identified* and *attribute / identifier*. Attributive relational processes have a *carrier* and an *attribute*, while identifying relational process have a *token* and *value*.

Finally, although not clearly set apart, further categories located at the three boundaries can be distinguished: behavioural, verbal and existential processes (Halliday 2004). Behavioural processes reflect outer manifestations of inner aspects of our experience and include volitional processes, bodily experiences and psychological behaviour. Verbal processes are processes of

3. The participants in a picture book are the narrator and essentially the characters, which are typically realized by nominal or pronominal forms and fulfil the grammatical functions of subject or object (Sunderland 2011: 65).

saying and communicating in which one participant is the *sayer*, typically human, and what is communicated is the *verbiage*.[4] By means of existential processes, phenomena of all kinds are recognized to exist, or to happen. The participant associated with them is the *existent*.

In the same way SFG offers an account of the linguistic choices that are available to the language speaker in order to create meaning through oral or written words, Kress and van Leeuwen's Visual Grammar expands upon the SFG model to establish a systematic account of semiotic options that may be applied to any image. The adaptation of both approaches requires the use of both linguistic and visual labels. Following Halliday, the linguistic labels adopted for the analysis of the meanings transmitted by the verbal mode are ideational, interpersonal and textual. These have their corresponding terminology when applied to the study of images: representational, interactive and compositional (Kress and van Leewen 2006).

Like linguistic structures, visual structures are also assigned visual processes, which depict actions or relations and, in turn, are associated with Represented Participants (the entities depicted) and specific settings (circumstances of time, place, manner and accompaniment). Within the visual system, Kress and van Leeuwen (2006) distinguish between narrative and conceptual images (see Figure 3.1). The former are associated with both (i) action processes, which are similar, although by no means identical, to material and behavioural processes in language, and (ii) reaction processes, equivalent, to a certain extent, to mental processes of perception in the linguistic system of transitivity (Kress and van Leeuwen 2006; Astorga 2009). Although not necessarily identical in function, conceptual images are related to relational and existential processes in language and their associated participants. In addition to narrative (be it action or reaction) and conceptual processes, Kress and van Leeuwen (2006) distinguish other types: speech and mental processes, which can be represented in the visual mode by speech and thought bubbles. Along with the visual processes, the representational meaning in images is also concerned with participant roles and with specific circumstances.

Thus, representational meaning involves the key processes: narrative and conceptual, which are differentiated by the presence of vectors, defined as diagonals that connect objects in a visual composition. While narrative

4. SFG uses the term *verbiage* to refer to a type of participants in verbal processes. Throughout this book I also use the term *verbiage* in a different sense, to mean the verbal, textual part of a multimodal discourse.

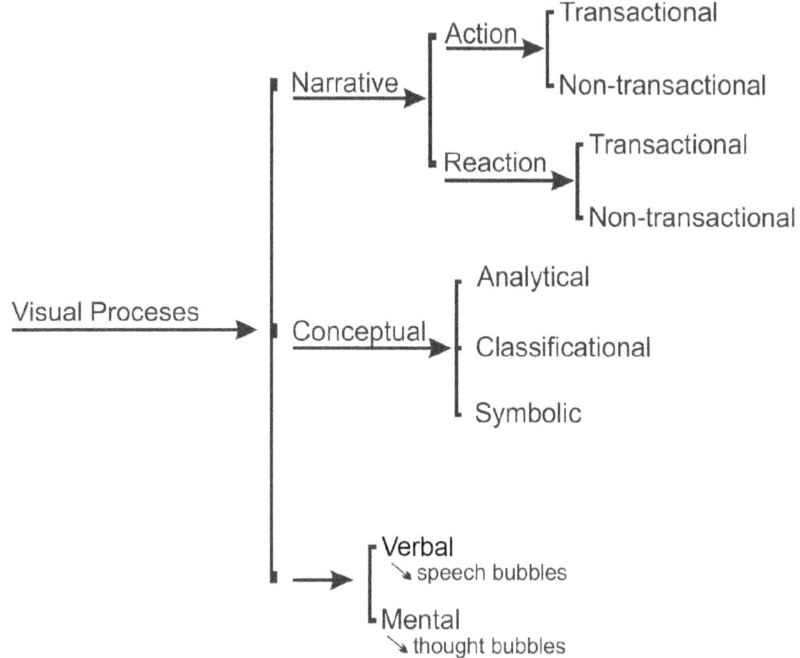

Figure 3.1: Visual processes (adapted from Kress and van Leeuwen (2006))

processes are characterized by vectors of motion which allow viewers to create a story about the Represented Participants (RPs), conceptual images are more static and do not include vectors, but rather, they represent participants in their more generalized and timeless essence (Kress and van Leeuwen 1996: 79). Painter *et al.* (2013: 56–67) assign three main functions to conceptual images. As they lack vectors and favour the observation of the participants in a visual composition, they are sometimes included at the beginning of the stories to introduce the characters. Other times they are also used in narrative stages that require a pause or a reflective moment rather than the representation of movement and action. Another function associated with conceptual images is 'to guide the child in reading for significance' (Painter *et al.* 2006: 56), that is, to facilitate the reader's identification and understanding of symbolic values and meanings hidden in the story.

Conceptual images define a participant as a member of a class, illustrating its features and qualities. So, they are entity-oriented, as they are seen as carriers that possess attributes. Kress and van Leeuwen (1996, 2006) distinguish three types of conceptual processes: analytical, classificational and symbolic. Although not frequently found in picture books, analytical images are sometimes embedded within more complex images in this genre (Lewis 2006: 151). The structure *carrier with attributes* is categorized as an analytical conceptual process, which relates participants to each other in terms of a part-whole relation (Kress and van Leeuwen 1996: 93). As for classificational images, they bring different entities together to show that they have something in common. Classification is typically characterized by two features: compositional symmetry and taxonomic structure. In these, a superordinate element (a tree, for example) is frequently shown in relation to other subordinate components (orange tree, oak tree, apple tree). Sometimes, however, only the subordinate participants are represented visually. Symbolic images are conventionally associated with symbolic values. They are somehow made salient in the visual composition as their components are represented in great detail through colour (Kress and van Leeuwen 2006). In *Guess How Much I Love You*, written by McBratney and illustrated by Anita Jeram (1994), for example, double spread 1 offers a typical symbolic image. The large, green tree that casts a shadow over Big and Little Nutbrown Hares symbolizes the protection and warmth associated with home.

In turn, narrative processes show unfolding actions and events carried out at a particular moment in time and surrounded by a specific setting, which is typically absent in conceptual images. Unlike conceptual processes, narrative images are process-oriented as they are similar to clauses containing material, mental, and behavioural processes and their related participants and circumstances. Kress and van Leeuwen (2006) distinguish two types: action and reaction. While the former create the narrative with vectors of motion and show an actor doing something in a transactional or non-transactional situation, the latter, in contrast, build the narrative by eyelines acting as vectors between the RPs. A further aspect to be noticed is that action processes may have a transactional or a nontransactional character, which is similar to the transitive and intransitive features of processes in language. In transactional processes there is a goal or phenomenon represented at the end of the vector that shows directionality from an actor to a goal. However, in non-transactional processes there is no represented goal or phenomenon. This frequently creates an air of mystery or tension in picture books (Lewis 2006).

As in language, where there are different types of circumstantial information (manner, location in place and time, cause, accompaniment, etc.), in the visual mode the processes and the participants involved in them appear within settings and are frequently accompanied by tools and other figures that complete their meanings. Three kinds of circumstances can be distinguished in pictures: circumstances of means, of accompaniment and of setting (Kress and van Leeuwen 2006: 72). Circumstances of means are realized by various tools and are frequently present in action processes; they can also be realized by parts of the body and by non-discrete objects. Circumstances of accompaniment are minor characters in an image and can be found in illustrations where participants are clearly connected by colour or other means, but not by any vector or by eye lines. These are not typical of pictures depicting action or reaction processes but are more likely to appear in analytical images. The last type is the most common in this genre. The setting usually establishes the situation and the nature of the world in which the events take place and is drawn with less detail than the major participants. In the creation of visual setting there is a variety of combinations that range from no setting at all to a fully depicted background (Lewis 2006).

In addition, the analysis of the variations of setting, that is, the differences and similarities in context and location that may be identified between successive images, are likely to reveal interesting details about circumstantial information and time progression (Painter *et al.* 2013: 78–80). On some occasions the degree of details in setting varies from image to image. In others, the same level of detail is maintained between two successive images. When the setting is *decontextualized*, that is, reduced in comparison to a previous depiction, the characters are brought into focal position and gain the prominence that enables them to transmit and provoke emotions. However, when the opposite occurs and the setting is *recontextualized* and gains in contextual details, the viewer is moved from a specific depicted participant to a different emotional mood or atmosphere. If the same circumstantial context is maintained between two images, a change in perspective or orientation may suggest that the timeline is advancing in the story or even that a new activity sequence is starting.[5]

5. The change in perspective is achieved through different visual techniques: panning horizontally, dolling-up or down vertically, zooming in on or out of a character, extending a frame, etc. (Painter *et al.* 2013: 80–81). For further information about the system of intercircumstance relations, see Painter *et al.* (2013: 78–83).

3.2 Words and images: Intersemiosis

The models of SFG and Visual Social Semiotics, described in the previous section, offer the tools to analyse the verbal and visual modalities of multimodal products. However, they do not seem to consider the effect and potentiality of synergizing both modes in the process of creating meaning (Sipe 2008, 2012). As Unsworth (2006: 55) points out: 'current research indicates that articulating discrete visual and verbal grammars is not sufficient to account for meanings made at the intersection of language and image.' He also states that a theoretical description and a specific metalanguage need to be developed to deal with the meaning potential of the interplay of images and words in multimodal products. This section aims to outline some of the contributions made in this area and generate a coding scheme of representational intersemiosis that will be applied to our sample texts in subsection 3.4.3 and later, in more detail, in Chapter 6. The discussion will be limited to the function of verbal and visual intersemiosis at the representational level of analysis. The interdependence of images and words to construct interpersonal and textual meanings will be dealt with in Chapters 7 and 8 of this book.

Since Barthes (1977) distinguished two image-text relations, elaboration and relay,[6] to define the interanimation between verbal and visual codes, other visual communication researchers have also proposed further categories to delimit how visual and verbal modes complement each other in the transmission of meaning and how this co-deployment is achieved. Schwarcz (1982), Golden (1990), Agosto (1999) and Nikolajeva and Scott (2000, 2001), among others, have applied their theories to the genre of picture books. They offer different taxonomies to define the relationship established between images and words in picture books, most of them grouped within the two main categories distinguished by Barthes (1977). Among the models, the most elaborate one is that proposed by Nikolajeva and Scott (2000), who provide five categories to describe word and image interactions, ranging

6. While in elaboration the textual component restates the meanings of the image or *vice versa* in such a way that both the verbal and the visual codes express the same meaning, in relay, the verbal component expands the meanings transmitted by the images or *vice versa*. In relay each code adds new meanings to complete the message going beyond the information transmitted in one of the two components (Barthes 1977).

from symmetrical relationship at one extreme of the scale to contradictory interaction at the other. Between these two poles they distinguish three other types of interaction: enhancement, complementarity and counterpointing.[7] However, these terms are not absolute and the boundaries drawn between them are not always clear-cut especially in the cases of enhancing and complementarity, as the only feature used to distinguish them is the amount of information (minor versus significant) that one of the two modes provides in a specific picture book (Moya and Pinar 2008).

Lewis (2006: 59) positions himself against the approach defended by Nikolajeva and Scott, which he describes as limited. Lewis (2006) assumes that picture books may admit more than one type of interactive relationship, as they may show more than one effect. Thus, the word/picture relationship is not necessarily the same throughout the whole story, it might change from composition to composition and, therefore, there might be different types of visual and textual interanimations across and within images. In line with Lewis's philosophy, Gill (2002) states that an intermodal analysis requires a detailed and systematic description of the way each image coheres with the verbal text accompanying it. Juxtaposed images and words are related to each other during the process of reading and this relationship is established by the reader's intention and determination to find a connection between them. This process often requires inferences on the part of the reader, which will be more or less direct depending on the cognitive effort that is necessary to recognize an intermodal link between verbal and visual components. In this sense, following Gill's (2002) work on picture books for young children, Unsworth (2006: 60) distinguishes three types of inter-modal relationships within the ideational/representational metafunction: ideational concurrence, ideational complementarity and connection (see Figure 3.2).

Ideational concurrence takes place when the verbal and the visual modalities are equivalent in ideational meaning and, thus, the inference required from the viewer to understand the coherence established between words and images is minimal. Moya and Pinar (2009: 112) label this type of

7. In the case of enhancement, there seems to be little difference between what the words say and what the pictures show, but in complementary relationships, one strand within the text appears to expand upon the other in ways which seem to affect the overall meaning. Therefore, text and image are essential to forge a true understanding of the content of the story (Nikolajeva and Scott 2000: 230; Nikolajeva 2010: 32). The term counterpointing will be referred to later in this section.

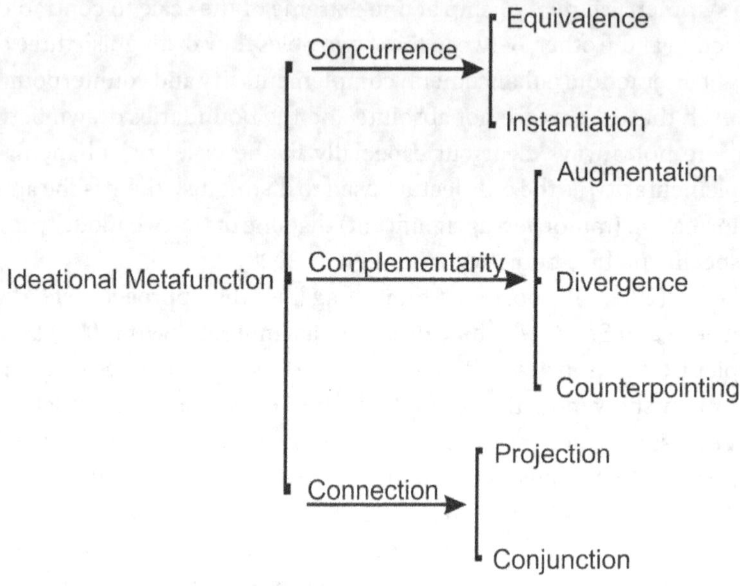

Figure 3.2: Intersemiotic systems within the ideational metafunction (adapted from Unsworth 2006, 2008a, b)

coherence as *symmetrical interaction.* The similarity in meaning often implies equivalence in the participant-process-phenomenon (and circumstantial) configuration of the reality represented via verbal and visual elements. Unlike Gill (2002) and Unsworth (2006, 2008a, b), who restrict the analysis of verbal and visual intersemiosis to nuclear constituents, participants and processes, I have also included circumstances like semantic elements that determine the degree of equivalence which may be established between verbiage and images. After comparing picture books intended for very young children with those meant for older children I have noticed that the representation of the setting varies considerably between the tales written and illustrated for children at different stages of cognitive development. This has led me to bear circumstantial elements in mind when discussing the contribution of verbal and visual modalities to the process of making meaning in picture books.

An example of equivalent ideational concurrence is provided in the first double spread of *The Very Hungry Caterpillar*, where the participant, *a little egg*, the process, *lay*, and the circumstances, *in the light of the moon* and *on a leaf*, are faithfully echoed in the visual composition: 'In the light of the moon a little egg lay on a leaf'. Clearly, this type of intersemiosis involves certain similarities in the meanings expressed by verbal and visual modalities. However, as the *functional specialization* of images and words is different (Kress 1997, 2000, 2003a, b; Lemke 1998b; Golden 1990), the equivalence between verbal language and illustrations does not necessarily imply a simple duplication of meaning (Schwarcz 1982; Nodelman 1989; Silva-Díaz 2006; Hanán-Díaz (2007), Unsworth 2006, 2008a, b). Each modality specializes in the transmission of specific meanings and has, as Bezemer and Kress (2008: 176) point out, its own *epistemological commitment* or *unavoidable affordances*, which are inherently linked to it. In fact, while the resources of language are essential for representing sequential relations and making categorical distinctions, the resources of images are better for the representation of spatial aspects and non-linear relationships (Lemke 1998a, b; Graham 2000; Unsworth 2006).

In ideational concurrence the image-text interplay usually responds to a relation of instantiation or specification of some kind where either the verbal or the visual component provides an example of the activity described or shown through another modality (Gill 2002: 79; Unsworth 2006: 60). Double spread 2 of *Gorilla* by Browne (1983) is evidence of this fact. In it the text reads: 'He went to work every day ...' and in the visual mode a man, Hannah's father, is depicted walking and carrying a briefcase. Although the processes of *going to work* and *walking with a briefcase* are different, they offer similar information here as the image shows the father is on his way to work. The text acts as a useful tool to interpret the image and specify that the father is walking to work and not to his house or somewhere else. Here the meaning offered by the words is essential to interpret the visual information depicted in the illustration. In turn, the picture adds specificity to the verbal text as it provides an instantiation of the text and attaches additional meaning referring to the type of work the man does.[8]

The second type of interplay distinguished by Unsworth (2006: 62) is *Ideational Complementarity*. While in ideational concurrence there is a certain equivalence in the meanings transmitted by words and images, in this verbal and visual intersection either words or images provide information that is missing in the other semiotic component. Unsworth (2006: 60) states

8. Thus, it seems evident that *ideational concurrence* can also be achieved without a one-to-one equivalence of participants-processes configuration necessarily existing between the two modalities. The level of redundancy that is necessary to categorize a link between words and images is variable and depends on contextual factors.

that this type of intersemiosis takes place when 'what is represented in images and what is represented in language may be different but complementary and joint contributors to an overall meaning that is more than the meanings conveyed by the separate modes.' In relationships of complementarity the written mode and the images do not necessarily have an equivalent circumstantial participant-process-phenomenon configuration, and the visual component often shows new information elements which are missing in the textual mode (Moya and Pinar 2009: 112). In fact, the links between words and images are created here via the distribution of meaning across the two different modalities as they co-operate intersemiotically in the construction of reality. In line with Gill (2002) and Unsworth (2006), Moya and Pinar (2009) assume that relationships of ideational complementarity occur in three main cases:

i. When significant segments of the narrative are provided in pages that consist of images or text alone. In *Where the Wild Things Are* by Sendak (1962), for example, the dance of the *wild rumpus* is represented in three double spreads without words. The *wild rumpus* is a metaphor of Max's tantrum after the quarrel with his mother. Max, the protagonist in the tale, blends in with the monsters and behaves like one of them, giving free rein to his wild instincts.
ii. When significant passages of the plot are shown by images alone, even though the text is also co-present in them. *Dear Zoo* by Campbell offers a clear instance of this verbal and visual intersemiosis. The suspense points of the recurrent sentence, 'So they sent me a(n) ...' cannot be understood without the pictures. They become essential resources to fill the gap and identify the different animals sent to the child-protagonist from the zoo.
iii. Finally, when juxtaposed images and text jointly construct activity sequences. This happens, for example, when the images show the end result of a process referred to in the verbal text and reveal the temporal sequence of different aspects within the same process.[9]

9. Gill (2002) calls this type of interplay *distribution* and distinguishes two types: intra-process distribution, the one described and exemplified here, and extra-process distribution. While in the former text and images portray different aspects of the same shared process, in the latter words and images offer different aspects of two different processes that are related through an activity sequence. In this way images fill a gap missing in the ideational representation of the verbiage (Unsworth 2008b).

> *Gorilla* by Anthony Browne also provides an example of this intersection. In the sixth double spread the text announces that Hannah, the main character of the tale, and the gorilla, her stand-in father, crept downstairs and that she put her coat on while the gorilla put on her father's hat and coat. The illustration just shows them completely dressed up, showing the result of the process announced in the verbiage. This helps to establish an equivalence or resemblance between the gorilla and the real father (Gill 2002).

Unsworth (2006: 63–64) differentiates between two subtypes of ideational complementarity: *augmentation* and *divergence*. While in augmentation each modality provides additional information which is consistent with the other mode, in divergence text and images 'follow different courses without intersecting' (McCloud 1994: 154). Although this divergence is not frequently used in picture books intended for young children, it can be found in some tales. In divergent (Unsworth 2006) or contradictory interactions (Nikolajeva and Scott 2000, 2001; Lewis 2006) images and words express entirely different things. This contradiction is a challenge for the reader who has to mediate between words and images to correctly interpret the story that is being narrated. Once again the penultimate illustration of *Gorilla* sets an example. The text reads that 'Hannah looked at him (her father)'. However, the illustration shows that she is looking at a picture of a gorilla printed on a birthday card she is holding in her hands. As Stevenson (1998) suggests, the images tend to depict what really happens while the verbiage embodies the concept of contrast.

Added to these types of intersemiotic coherence is what Nikolajeva and Scott (2000: 232) have named *counterpointing interaction*. A counterpointing dynamic occurs when words and images provide alternative information and collaborate to express meanings which are beyond the scope of either modality standing alone. In counterpointing interaction, the writer and the illustrator may show an intentional lack of coherence between the verbal and the visual modes, opening the storyline up to multiple interpretations (Sikorska 2005). This term deals with those cases where words and pictures provide different kinds of information and the reader must make some effort to integrate the two. Two types of counterpointing interaction are distinguished by Nikolajeva and Scott (2000): (i) ironic counterpoint, which takes place when the story is told from an ironic point of view and words and images do not duplicate each other but seem to show a low level of coherence; and (ii) perspectival counterpointing, which occurs when the story is told from a different perspective and what the characters in the tale and the viewers perceive is different. For example, the monsters in the tale *Where the Wild Things Are* by Sendak (1963) are described in the text as terrifying and frightening beings. However, the illustrations show that they are not such scary creatures, presenting a story of a different nature. Therefore, in counterpointing the link that is created between verbal and visual modalities is more indirect than in the previous categories and, therefore, a greater degree of inference is required from the reader to understand the coherence of juxtaposed images and words.

Following Halliday's terminology on logical relations of expansion (addition, time, cause, purpose, comparison, etc.) or projection (direct or indirect speech and thought), Unsworth (2006: 66) also distinguishes another type of intersection between words and images: connection. This is, in turn, subdivided into two further categories: projection, which involves quoting speech and reporting thoughts, and conjunction, subdivided into causal, temporal and spatial relations. Projection is typically realized in images by speech or thought bubbles. It also occurs when a verbal or mental quotation in a text is realized by images rather than language. There may also be a juxtaposition of quoted speech in verbal language and a participant in the visual mode that represents the source of the quotation (Unsworth 2006: 64). However, these types of intersemiosis are not frequently used in picture books intended for 0–9 year-old children and therefore they will not be considered in our analysis. They are more typical of magazine advertisements which contain demand images and close-up shots or of comics which contain speech or thought bubbles.

In the case of conjunction, temporal and causal relations between verbal and visual modes have been identified in picture books by Gill (2002), Unsworth (2008, b) and Painter *et al.* (2013) in successive images. In the picture books that form the sample texts the connective relation between images is essentially temporal, as the events depicted in them are necessarily articulated by temporal relations of succession. These successive relations are realized either by the repetition of the same character from image to image or by the depiction of different characters and settings in facing images. One way or another, children's stories, regardless of the age group for which they are initially intended, are articulated by temporal relations of succession and simultaneity. Through them the stories progress in a brief span of time from an initial complication until the final resolution of the conflicts that construct their different plot lines.[10]

Some examples of the types of intersemiotic relations referred to in this section will be given in section 3.4 of this chapter, where I deal with the combination of images and words and their contribution to the construction of representational meaning in *The Very Hungry Caterpillar*. In addition, in Chapter 6 additional examples of verbal and visual intersections are commented upon.

3.3 Troubleshooting

Now, I will consider those aspects related to the representational metafunction of the language that may cause a problem to the analyst when applying the Hallidayan categories to the sample of picture books. To deal with them, examples taken from specific tales are analysed in detail. The same procedure will be followed when applying Kress and van Leeuwen's representational visual semiotic categories to the nine picture books selected for analysis. First, I will focus the study on the tale chosen to exemplify the ideational metafunction of language and its potentiality to represent reality, *The Very Hungry Caterpillar*. Later, the analysis is extended to the other picture books, essentially those that are included in the second and third stages of cognitive development, as they contain more complex transitive components that may lead the analyst to some troubleshooting situations.

The Very Hungry Caterpillar starts this way: 'In the light of the moon a little egg lay on a leaf'. In this clause, the verb *lay* is described in the grammar as a prototypical existential process with a circumstantial tinge, typically used in English to introduce new entities into the discourse (Halliday 2004: 258). However, *lay* has been classified here as a relational process since, in this specific context, it carries circumstantial information about the location of the entity, *egg*. Relational processes create clauses fundamentally expressing

10. Painter *et al.* (2013: 71) propose a system to identify inter-event connections in successive images. However, they recognize that the set of choices offered delimit the relations that need to be inferred to make sense of a sequence of connected images. For further information about connection and other cohesive ties between images and text both in single and successive images, see Lemke (2000, 2002), Martinec and Salway (2005), Unsworth (2006, 2008a and b), Royce (2007) and Painter *et al.* (2013).

states of being and having and they can be intensive, possessive or, as is the case here, circumstantial. The participant, *egg*, does not carry a topical function. The reader has to wait until the second double spread of the picture book to encounter the actual topic of the story, a caterpillar: 'One Sunday morning the warm sun came up and – pop! – out of the egg came a tiny and very hungry caterpillar'. Once the caterpillar becomes topical (Moya 2006), he and his insatiable appetite will be referenced continuously through the use of the personal pronoun, *he*, and a definite expression.

Now we go on to examine problematic examples extracted from other tales, essentially *Granpa, Where the Wild Things Are* and *The Rainbow Fish*. Some of the problems have to do with the number of processes that can be counted in a specific clause. In *Granpa*, for example, the sentence, 'That was not a nice thing to say to Granpa', has been analysed as containing only a relational process, *be*. However, *say*, a prototypical verbal process, has not been considered for the purposes of transitivity. The element, *to say to Granpa* is rankshifted as a qualifier of *thing* and, therefore, in line with Halliday's grammar (2004), its verbal process and its elliptical *sayer* do not need to be counted.

In *Where the Wild Things Are* the sentence, 'They roared their terrible roars and gnashed their terrible teeth and rolled their terrible eyes', poses some difficulties when the analyst tries to classify the process contained in it as either material or behavioural. *Roar* is rather like *snarl* or *hiss*, which are classified as behavioural processes in Halliday (2004: 251). The grammar, however, does not seem to provide examples to categorize *gnash* and *roll* as either behavioural or material. Both material and behavioural processes respond to the question: *what did X do?* and their unmarked tense is the progressive. Thus, SFG does not seem to provide a definite and clear test to put these two processes within a specific category. However, for the purposes of this analysis, I have analysed these last two processes as material since they appear in transitive relations, typically associated with action processes. Although behavioural processes may be candidates for more than one entity, most of them typically involve only one participant role: the *behaver*. Furthermore, the meaning of *gnashing their teeth* and *rolling their eyes* convey external actions that do not necessarily reflect inner aspects of our experience, or typically human-physiological or psychological behaviour (Halliday 2004: 248).

Another sentence that is of interest to us in *Where the Wild Things Are* is: 'He found his supper waiting for him', uttered by the narrator in the final stage of the story. Here, the transitivity of two separate clauses needs to be analysed in detail. *He found his supper* answers the question *what happened?* so it can be classified as material. In addition, the idea of supper waiting for someone seems to be an example of personification. If the subject of the clause was animate, then it would clearly be a material clause. Although *wait* is preceded by an inanimate entity, *supper*, the personification has led me to count this process as material in this specific context.

My last comment concerning this tale is associated once again with the number of processes that can be identified in a sentence as 'He wanted to be where someone loved him best of all'. Following Halliday (2004: 516), *want to be* is a verbal group complex and represents just one relational process. So, for the purposes of transitivity, and in an attempt to adhere to what Halliday's SFG says, the verb, *want* has not been counted as a mental process of affection. A different view has been adopted in the analysis of the following sentence, this time taken from a different picture book, *The Rainbow Fish*: 'He swam off to join his friends'. In it, two different verbal groups have been distinguished; the second belonging to a separate subordinate clause of purpose. As both processes answer the question, *what did the Fish do?* they both have been classified as material. Similarly, in the sentence, 'A rather peculiar feeling came over the Rainbow Fish', *come over* responds to the question *what happened to the Fish?* suggesting the presence of a material process. However, this process is semantically very similar to *experience* in: 'He experienced a rather peculiar feeling', which is clearly mental. In fact, the verbal complex, *come over* is rather similar to *assail*, which is given in Halliday (2004: 210) as an example of the *please* type rather than the *like* type process in mental clauses. The last troubleshooting examples are provided by the sentences: '[...] but you will discover how to be happy' and 'The Rainbow Fish wavered [...]'. Although at first sight they may contain a material flavour, the processes *discove*r and *waver* have been categorized as mental. Although *waver* can surely answer the question 'what happened to the Fish?' it is in the same family of verbs as *decide*, which Halliday (2004: 201) classifies as mental-desiderative. Finally, *discover* means *come to know*, as does *realize*, which is prototypically mental in nature.

Now that I have made reference to a selection of examples that have created some difficulty in the analysis of verbal language from a representational perspective, I will deal with the study of the visual components of the tales selected. In this respect, two different aspects will be commented on. The first is related to the narrative or conceptual character of most of the pictures in *The Very Hungry Caterpillar*. Most of the illustrations show the foods that the tiny animal wolfs down until he becomes a beautiful butterfly. In fact, if it was not for the hole that goes through them, most of the images would lack vectors and would be categorized as conceptual and analytical. Their main function would be to show the young child what the fruits and other foods the caterpillar devours are like. However, the presence of holes activates the vectors of motion that turn these apparently conceptual images into narrative illustrations, containing movement and dynamism. For this reason, the majority of the illustrations in the tale by Carle have been counted as narrative-action rather than conceptual images.

The second aspect to be dealt with is related to the semiotic choices Kress and van Leeuwen (2006: 74) distinguish in their grammar of visual design. They classify narrative images into action and reaction processes and their corresponding subtypes. As Gill (2002: 10) points out, although Kress and van Leeuwen differentiate between unidirectional and bidirectional transactional action processes, they do not provide these two distinct categories when they refer to transactional reaction processes. However, in picture books such as *Gorilla* the distinction between unidirectional and bidirectional reaction images turns out to be essential to understand the relationship that Hannah, the protagonist, establishes with both her real and substitute fathers. To resolve this, following Gill (2002) I will extend Kress and van Leeuwen's framework by adding to the category of transactional reaction processes two further sub-choices: unidirectional and bidirectional, which establish a difference between reciprocated and non-reciprocated eye contact images.

In *Gorilla* reaction processes are essentially constructed depending on the crossing gazes between the characters of the tale, especially Hannah and the primate. In fact, they are engaged in bidirectional or reciprocated reaction processes in which Hannah acts as the reactor and the gorilla as the phenomenon which establishes eye contact with the other represented participant. This reaction link gives a sense of companionship to the relationship that is kept between Hannah and her substitute father. However, the images where Hannah and her real father are depicted together show a lack of eye contact between the two represented participants. Although Hannah makes various attempts to establish interaction with her father, he never makes eye contact with her daughter. It seems evident that the use of unidirectionality and bidirectionality in reaction processes also contributes greatly to the creation of meaning in this picture book as a whole: the real father cannot be reached and the eye contact is necessarily transferred to a substitute father, the gorilla. This picture book will be analysed in more detail in Chapter 8, which deals with textual/compositional meaning.

3.4 *The Very Hungry Caterpillar*. Analysis and exemplification

Having commented on some troubleshooting analytical aspects, the aim of this section is to exemplify the theoretical notions introduced in the previous sections and, in turn, analyse the intersemiosis of verbal and visual components in the picture book *The Very Hungry Caterpillar* by Carle. The interplay between verbal and visual components will be studied by comparing the circumstantial participant-process configuration of the verbal component with the corresponding RPs, visual processes and settings shown in the pictures. This comparison will serve to determine the types of interaction that all the visual and the verbal elements exhibit individually in each double spread.

The edition used for this analysis was published by Puffin Books in 2002. Eleven double spreads have been distinguished. They have been numbered from the first to the last page and references will be made to those numbers. The images have not been included in the present chapter, as Eric Carle does not grant permission for his illustrations to be used in academic publications. The study is structured as follows. First, I will identify the verbal choices made by the writer of *The Very Hungry Caterpillar* to convey representational meaning. Later, the way the artist represents reality in the illustrations is analysed. Finally, the intersemiosis of words and images to jointly construct reality is studied in the picture book in question.

3.4.1 The representation of reality in the verbiage

In this tale reality is essentially represented through material and relational processes and their associated participants. As shown in Table 3.2, material and relational processes reach 96% of the tokens identified. Only one mental process has been found, and it represents 4% of the cases counted. The 13 material processes used by the author (46%), *look for, eat, build, stay, nibble* and *push*, etc., construct the plot development of the story. The material process, *come*, in 'the warm sun came up' expresses action and movement and, due to its presentational function, also acquires an introductory flavour. Once the main character has been introduced, the hungry caterpillar starts to look for some food and, on the first day, Monday, he eats through a red apple. As he is still hungry, on the second day, Tuesday, he wolfs down two green pears. On Wednesday, he devours three purple plums. On Thursday, still hungry, he eats through four red strawberries and on Friday through five oranges. On Saturday, the sixth day, he devours ten different food items including a piece of chocolate cake, an ice-cream, a pickle, a slice of Swiss cheese, a slice of salami, a lollipop, a cherry pie, a sausage, a cupcake and a slice of watermelon. That night he has a stomach ache; however, on the seventh day, Sunday, still unsatisfied, he eats through a nice green leaf. At this point he is not hungry anymore and has become a big, fat caterpillar. He builds a cocoon around himself and after two weeks the final transformation takes place. The processes contained in these sentences are all material and give movement and dynamism to the story.

Table 3.2 Textual processes in *The Very Hungry Caterpillar*

Process type	*Absolute values*	*Values in percentages*
Material	13	46
Mental	1	4
Verbal	0	0
Relational	14	50
Behavioural	0	0
Existential	0	0
Total	28	100

The reality represented by these material processes is complemented with 14 relational processes that describe the different states of the protagonist. The most frequently used are: be, have, feel and become. They express both positive and negative polarity. After eating through the different foods, he is said to be *still hungry*; an expression that is repeated a total of five times. He is also said to have a stomach ache. After eating a green leaf, he feels much better, he is not hungry anymore and is described as a big, fat caterpillar. And finally, he becomes a butterfly.

In addition, as Table 3.3 reveals, most of the processes accounted for are of an intransitive type (82% of the cases identified), since these are usually associated with one entity. Excerpt 1 sets an example. In it, a syntactic pattern is followed and repeated throughout the entire story: an actor, the caterpillar, the processes in which he is involved and the adjuncts of place, represented by the different foods that are devoured by the hungry and tiny animal. This pattern favours syntactic parallelism and repetition, two elements typically present in children's stories. The intransitive inclination just referred to contrasts with the transactional nature of most of the illustrations where the caterpillar acts as actor and the food items he goes through are the goals which are affected by the material process of eating. This aspect will be further commented on in section 3.4.2

> [...] On Monday he ate through one apple. But he was still hungry. On Tuesday he ate through two pears, but he was still hungry [...] On Saturday he ate through one piece of chocolate cake, one ice-cream cone, one pickle, one slice of Swiss cheese, one slice of salami, one lollipop, one piece of cherry pie, one sausage, one cupcake, and one slice of watermelon. That night he had a stomach ache! (*The Very Hungry Caterpillar*, Carle [1969] 2002).[11]

Table 3.3 Textual processes: Transitivity

Process type	*Absolute values*	*Values in percentages*
Transitive	5	18
Non-transitive	23	82
Total	28	100

The processes and their participants are developed within a specific circumstantial framework, as most sentences start with an adjunct of time: on Monday, on Tuesday, on Wednesday, etc., which marks the temporal sequence of events. In this picture book, the presence of adverbial components in thematic position is quite frequent, and they move the topical element, the caterpillar, towards the rheme of the clause. In this way the theme coincides with the adverbial group that specifies the temporal frames in which the actions carried out by the main character are developed. Possibly, through repetitive and accumulative structures, the author of the story intends to familiarize the young child with the names of the days of the week, numbers, foods and some habitual concepts of daily life.

11. Note that the number of pages of the storybooks has not been specified. The reason is that most stories belonging to the early developmental stages are not paginated due to their brevity. The only exception is *The Tale of Peter Rabbit* as it appears published within the Century Edition of Potter's *The Complete Tales*, 2002.

3.4.2 The representation of reality in the visual mode

As picture books are composite wholes consisting of both verbal and visual components, at this point I will study how the visual mode complements the information that the verbal component presents. In order to do so, I will follow the model proposed by Kress and van Leeuwen (2006). As reflected in Table 3.4, there is a predominance of action images over conceptual and embedded processes. Action images constitute 82% of the tokens identified. Reaction images only reach 9% of the cases accounted for, the same percentage that embedded images reach. These are characterized by the presence of both narrative (action plus reaction) and conceptual features in the same illustration.

Table 3.4 Visual processes in *The Very Hungry Caterpillar*

Process type	*Absolute values*	*Values in percentages*
Action	9	82
Reaction	1	9
Embedded	1	9
Total	11	100

Action images bring dynamics to the narration and show the activities carried out by the story's protagonist, the very hungry caterpillar, until transforming into a beautiful butterfly after having wolfed down lots of edibles. In order to serve as an example, the sixth double spread is cited, in which the little caterpillar is preparing to eat four strawberries after having previously eaten through three plums.[12] The holes made in the above mentioned fruit are evident proof of the vectors of motion that give these images a narrative character. This fact is emphasized on the verso of the double spread, where the child-viewer perceives the small creature emerging from the heart of the third plum. These narrative images correspond to the material process, ate, which makes constant reference to the little caterpillar's capacity to devour, and always describes the little creature as hungry and represented in motion.

Another narrative action image is localized in double spread 8 where the caterpillar eats from one piece of chocolate cake, moving on to an ice-cream, then a pickle, etc., until finishing with a slice of watermelon.

12. http://cuentosinfantiles.biz/wp-content/uploads/2013/09/IMG_20130912_181755.jpg (accessed 29 November 2013).

Once again the holes in the fruit give the illustration a narrative character, given the vectors of motion that generate and represent the trajectory made by the hungry caterpillar. The caterpillar is then in turn represented by a sad face and a curved body, showing the stomach ache referenced in the verbal component: 'That night he had a stomach ache!' Like the pictures of the different food items, the image of the hurting caterpillar is also of a narrative nature, since it shows the state that he is in after passing so much food through his curvaceous body.

The last double spread, which reproduces a flying and colourful butterfly in movement, also offers another example of an action image. In it one can see the beautiful attributes of a butterfly with big, colourful wings. The richness of colours and the size of the represented participant attract the young reader's attention towards the character in the illustration, which brings the story to an end. In the verbiage there is a relational process, *was*, which corresponds, in part, to the conceptual nature of the image depicted as it shows what a colourful butterfly in movement is like.

The narrative character of the illustrations is also shown in the first double spread. Here, one can see a little egg on a leaf on a moonlit night, a reaction image in which the moon makes eye contact with the child-viewer inviting him to become part of the story. The illustrator introduces the participant, a little egg, on the narrative scene here. Afterwards, a small and hungry caterpillar emerges from the egg, who is the real protagonist of the story. After the moment of its birth, the caterpillar begins to search for food (double spread 3). In the illustration the young animal appears with tones of green and red lifting itself up on two legs to scan the horizon on a sunny morning in search of food. The text, in turn, references this action through a material process: 'He started to look for some food.' There exists, therefore, a correspondence between the utilization of material processes in the verbal component and their visual representation through narrative images. As indicated in section 3.2, material processes are equivalent, although not necessarily identical, to narrative images, concretely to the so-called action images (Kress and van Leeuwen 2006). Right from the beginning of the story, the narrative character of the images is made explicit.

Lastly, in this picture book an embedded image has been identified in which narrative and conceptual processes combine to convey a representation of reality. The caterpillar is shown to us on the verso (left hand side of the double spread) in a walking posture and is depicted as a corpulent animal after having devoured the food shown in the previous illustrations. The legs of the animal act as vectors that generate movement and make this part of the double spread narrative in nature. However, on the recto (right hand side) of this double spread appears a cocoon, built by the caterpillar. Even though material processes predominate in this double spread in the verbal mode (build, stay, nibble and push), the image is essentially conceptual and analytical as it shows what a cocoon is like.[13] The dynamic character of the process in the verbiage contrasts with the static nature of the illustration, whose brown colour and big size attract the young child's attention.

Concerning the transactional character of the illustrations, I previously stated that the processes in the verbiage were mostly intransitive due to the fact that they were usually associated to one entity, the doer, the hungry caterpillar, and the different adjuncts of place represented by the food items. This fact contrasts with the transactional character of the images drawn in the different double spreads of the tale. In the visual component the caterpillar is shown to be involved in transactional processes associated with a minimum of two RPs: he, himself, and the different foods he eats through until he finally has his fill. As can be seen in Table 3.5, transactional visual processes predominate in the illustrations (73% of the cases counted). Double spread 6, already cited, is a good example. The caterpillar has devoured three plums and is getting ready to eat four strawberries. This pattern is repetitive throughout the entire story, as the caterpillar tends to be shown in association with the food items he eats. The transactionality of these images gives the tale a dynamic character, as the protagonist is always engaged with the entities that help him grow in order to face his final transformation.

Table 3.5 Types of visual processes. Transactionality

Process Type	*Absolute values*	*Values in percentages*
Transactional	8	73
Non-transactional	3	27
Total	11	100

3.4.3 The synergy of images and words. Concluding remarks

My aim has been to discover the motivations behind some of the choices that were made in rendering information in *The Very Hungry Caterpillar*

13. http://cuentosinfantiles.biz/wp-content/uploads/2013/09/IMG_20130912_181956.jpg (accessed 29 November 2013).

by analysing representational meaning in the visual and linguistic semiotic modes and, in this way, to determine the extent to which the verbiage and the visual complement one another. The analysis of the representational meaning shows that the reality narrated in the story is shown in the verbiage through material and relational processes. The material processes identified generally make reference to the eating habits of the tiny caterpillar. The relational ones, in turn, play a descriptive role, defining the changes that the protagonist goes through during the different phases of growth. These linguistic patterns have, to a certain extent, a clear correspondence in the visual mode where there is a predominance of narrative images, mainly action images, as the narrative is basically created by vectors of motion. The tiny caterpillar is constantly coming out of the core of the different fruits to continue eating. The finger-sized holes that appear in the food accentuate the vectors of movement that characterize most of the illustrations of the story. Conceptual images, however, have been kept to a minimum as most of the double spreads contain vectors of motion. In fact, only one conceptual picture, included in an embedded image, has been identified in the recto of double spread 10.

The material and relational processes and the participants associated with them, the caterpillar and the foods, tend to be faithfully represented in the visual mode. In this sense, both modes seem to support each other in order to offer the child the most relevant information in the story. However, circumstantial information of time is not usually reflected in the illustrations, only in the linguistic component. Except for the three first double spreads, where one sees the moon (to make reference to the night) and the sun (which introduces a sunny, Sunday morning) the rest of the double spreads are missing a setting or background information. This way, the author/illustrator centres the child's attention on the main participants of the story and avoids reflecting secondary elements in the visual mode that would have made the comprehension of the message more difficult.[14]

At first, given the simplicity of the plot and structure of the tale, it seems logical to think that the relationship that is established between the verbal and visual components would respond to the verbal and visual juxtaposition of *ideational concurrence* (Gill 2002; Unsworth 2006, 2008a and b). Text

14. In other picture books, such as *Granpa, Gorilla* or *The Tale of Peter Rabbit,* the illustrations are provided with a setting, which is not mentioned at all in the linguistic mode. The only exception is *The Tale of Peter Rabbit,* published in the centenary edition of *The Complete Tales* by Potter, 2002.

and image should contribute similar information in such a way that a child under two years of age, without the capacity to decipher written language, is able to understand the plot of the story by interpreting the information given through the illustrations. However, after comparing the participants and processes present in both semiotic modes, verbal and visual, it has been confirmed that the relation between image and word in *The Very Hungry Caterpillar* is essentially defined by relationships of ideational complementarity where either text or illustration offers information that is missing in the other mode.

Of the 11 double spreads that make up the story, nine of them are of a complementary nature, and in only two (the first and the last double spreads) do words and images express similar information through different modes, thus facilitating the comprehension of the message for the child-reader. The visual proximity of the pictures to the objects they represent helps young children when they decode the message, especially at such a young age when they cannot identify verbal graphemes. For example, in the last double spread the text and image offer the same information. The caterpillar is now a beautiful butterfly, a reality that is reflected in the full-coloured illustration. In the first double spread, there is a similar case. The image offers the same information that the text anticipates: 'In the light of the moon a little egg lay on a leaf'.

The number of cases in which the text and image complement each other in order to offer different information to the viewer is larger. In the fourth double spread, for example, the circumstantial element, realized linguistically as *on Tuesday,* is not reflected in the image, the one in which one perceives one apple, two pears, and a tiny caterpillar coming out of an apple. This pattern is repeated throughout the story, since most illustrations lack a setting or background information that might have otherwise marked the timeline of events. In addition, the fact that the tiny animal is still hungry is not reflected in the current illustration.

In the penultimate double spread, the intersemiosis between text and image also responds to verbal and visual relations of ideational complementarity. The verso shows a big, fat caterpillar, faithfully echoed in the verbiage that corresponds to this image. In turn the verbal mode adds that the caterpillar is no longer hungry and that it is no longer a tiny being. On the recto a cocoon, the house that the big caterpillar has constructed, is also faithfully presented in the image. However, the verbal mode adds relevant information, essentially realized through material processes that are not reflected in the image: the caterpillar has built a small house and has stayed inside for more than two weeks. Later he nibbles a hole in the cocoon and pushed his way out.

The results of the analysis confirm that, although two illustrations are a faithful echo of the meanings transmitted by the verbal text, the word/image interaction that is used in *The Very Hungry Caterpillar* to transmit meaning is essentially one of ideational complementarity. Through complementarity the reader's attention and the narrative tension are kept alive since images and words contribute differently to the story line: either the images expand the meaning of the words, or the words provide information that is missing in the visual mode, as is often the case in this picture book. Certainly the most relevant information, that which brings dynamism to the narration (the caterpillar eating food until transforming into a beautiful butterfly), is reflected reiteratively in both semiotic modes. This ideational concurrence facilitates the comprehension of the message on the part of the child, who can listen and, all the while, see in the illustration the information that is read by the mediator who narrates the story. Other aspects of a circumstantial nature (temporal adjuncts referring to the different days of the week), or specific features related to the main character (state of health, construction of a cocoon, insatiable appetite, etc.) are represented only in the verbal component.

The young age of the children for whom this tale was written and illustrated seems to determine the verbal and visual intersemiosis of ideational concurrence and complementarity that predominate in the picture book. These seem to be useful techniques to create a tale that is both easily accessible for young children to understand and, in turn, interesting enough to grab and maintain their attention. No relations of counterpointing or contradiction have been identified in this tale as, in them, the link between verbal and visual modalities is more indirect and more inference is required to understand the cohesion that is established between images and words. These intersemiotic relations escape the cognitive ability of the two-year-olds for whom the tale is written and illustrated. Verbal/visual interplays of these types would have made the plot much more difficult for young children to follow. In chapter 6, when I delve into the representation of reality in tales intended for older children, I will determine the extent to which juxtapositions of indirect coherence turn out to be essential to understanding the meaning writers and illustrators desire to convey to their potential readers.

4 The writer/illustrator and the child-viewer's interaction

Language is not only used to represent reality and our perception of the internal and external aspects of world. It essentially fulfils a role in communication and offers a range of resources to speakers/writers to establish interaction with the other members of their community. This chapter focuses on the theoretical tools proposed by Halliday (2004) and Kress and van Leeuwen (2006) within the interpersonal/interactive metafunction to analyse how words and illustrations contribute to the creation of interaction in multimodal texts. SFG has proved to be a powerful account to describe interpersonal patterns reflected in the verbiage. In turn, the Grammar of Visual Design proposed by Kress and van Leeuwen provides a descriptive framework for the interpretation of interactive features in the visual mode. The theoretical tools will be applied and exemplified this time through the analysis of the picture book, *Where the Wild Things Are*, the most known work by Sendak. I will analyse the aspects of engagement, involvement, power and intimacy which establish relationships between the illustrator/writer, the prospective readers, and the represented participants in the picture book at hand. Later, in Chapter 7, the analysis will be extended to the other picture books that form the sample texts.

The current chapter is structured as follows: first, the frameworks upon which the analysis is based are referred to in section 4.1. Special attention is paid to the interpersonal and interactive aspects of Systemic Functional Linguistics and Visual Social Semiotics, respectively. In section 4.2, the methodology is outlined and some troubleshooting aspects that arise from the application of the theoretical frameworks to the analysis of picture books are commented on. This section continues with the study of the interpersonal and interactive features of the tale in order to determine how verbal and visual modalities contribute to the establishment of engagement between the RPs themselves, and between these and the child-reader.

4.1 SFG and Visual Social Semiotics: Interpersonal/ Interactive meanings

As stated in Chapter 2, SFG approaches texts as communicative interactions in cultural and situational contexts and assumes that language expresses three types of meanings: representing our experience of the world inside and around us (ideational metafuction), enacting social relationships (interpersonal metafunction) and finally, creating coherent wholes of communication (textual metafunction).

In SFG language is essentially used to establish social interaction with others. Of the three metafunctions that are distinguished by Halliday (2004), representational, interpersonal and textual, the one that is concerned with enacting social relationships between the speaker and the listener in a specific context of communication is the interpersonal. The interpersonal metafunction deals with the clause as an exchange of information and as an exchange of goods and services. Within the SFG account, at the lexicogrammatical stratum, interpersonal meaning includes, along with the expression of opinion and attitude, the mood of the clause, expressed in English by the presence/absence and ordering of subject and finite verb.[1] As shown in Figure 4.1, major English clauses, those with a predicator, can be either indicative (having a mood element consisting of subject and finite) or imperative (with no subject). In turn, indicative clauses can be declarative (when the subject precedes the finite), or interrogative (if the finite precedes the subject) (Halliday 2004).

In addition, in the semantics, interpersonal meaning includes the type of speech act chosen (statement, offer, question and directive), realized by grammatical options and encoded by means of three syntactic moods (declarative, interrogative and imperative). As shown in Table 4.1, the system

1. Mood and Residue are the major functions of the clause when viewed interpersonally. The mood element makes the clause 'negotiable' and consists of Finite (positive and negative polarity included), Subject and sometimes Modal Adjuncts (probability, etc.). The Residue, the part of the clause that does not belong to the mood element, consists of Predicator, sometimes also of Complements and Adjuncts.

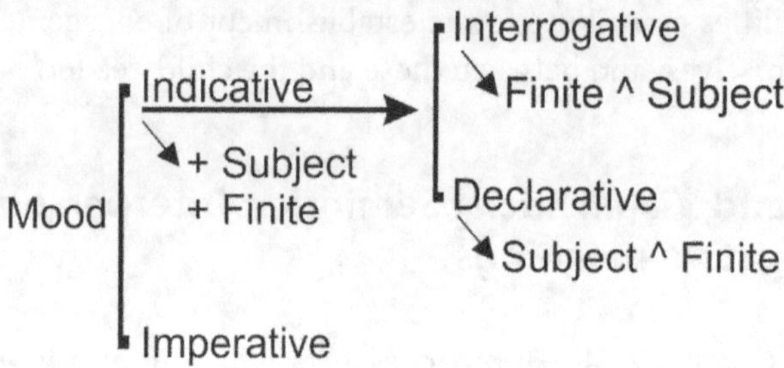

Figure 4.1: Basic system of mood (adapted from Halliday 2004)

of mood organizes the clause as an interactive event in which the speaker adopts a speech role, essentially: (i) giving or demanding information (by means of statements and questions); or (ii) exchanging goods and services (be the commodity an offer or a command), and assigns a complementary role to the listener which he wishes him to adopt (Halliday 2004). Each speech act has its expected social response and its discretionary alternative. A statement, for example, offers information that can be either acknowledged or contradicted. A question usually seeks information but may also admit a disclaimer (I don't know). In turn, in an offer of goods and services the expected response is an acceptance, but a rejection is also possible. Finally, a demand of goods and services constitute some kind of command that can be either undertaken or rejected.

The interpersonal function not only includes interaction, but also implies evaluative meaning. In language, evaluative meaning is realized through the system of polarity (positive or negative), and essentially through the system of modality, which includes mood and comment adjuncts. Mood adjuncts are closely associated with the meanings of the mood system and are concerned with temporality, modality and intensity. In turn, comment adjuncts are less

Table 4.1: Speech functions and their congruent realizations

Commodity exchanged > *and Role in exchange* V	*Information*	*Goods and services*
Giving	Statement Declarative mood	Offer Various realizations
Demanding	Question Interrogative mood	Command Imperative mood

tied to the grammar than mood adjuncts and are restricted to indicative clauses. They essentially reflect the speaker's or writer's attitude to propositions as a whole (declaratives clauses only) or to particular speech functions. They introduce elements of doubt (degrees of certainty and probability and degrees of usuality and frequency). The attitudes and judgements embodied in a text can also be expressed by the use of lexis and attitudinal subjective epithets within nominal group and copular structures (Halliday 2004: Table 10 [6]; Royce 2007: 69).

'Language which had been seen as a full means of expression; as the foundation of rationality; sufficient for all that could be spoken or written, thought, felt and dreamt (Eco, 1979), is now seen as a partial means of doing these' (Kress, 2010: 84). Interaction is not only created through language; images also play a key role in the process of making interpersonal meaning. Artists and illustrators use the specific resources available in the visual mode to establish communication with their viewers. Among the visual options available to create interpersonal meaning are gestures, which make commands, offers of information, or offers of goods and services, and the absence or presence of facial expressions towards the viewer. The interactive function (also called the engagement or modal function in O'Toole's terms (1994, 1999)) is reflected in the way images attract the viewer's attention and is concerned with the type of relationship established between three types of participants: (i) the producers of the image, the artists and designers; (ii) the readers of the image, in this case children under nine; and finally (iii) the RPs, which may be related to one another through vectors of motion, or eye lines (Kress and van Leeuwen 2006).[2]

In this sense, Kress and van Leeuwen (2006) distinguish four types of systems associated with the interpersonal function: those of (i) image act and gaze; (ii) social distance and intimacy; and (iii) horizontal angle and involvement; and, finally, (iv) vertical angle and power (see Figure 4.2). The four systems work interpersonally, as they show the way in which what is represented in a visual composition interacts with the viewer (Matthiessen 2007: 20). Within the system of image act and gaze Kress and van Leeuwen (2006) differentiate between: (i) images in which something is required of

2. In the case of tales devoted to the youngest audiences, another participant comes into play since between author and the young child, who is still unable to interpret the written word, the figure of an adult mediates (normally a parent or a teacher at a nursery school) that tells (not just reads) the story while the young child sees the images depicted.

the reader through visual contact or search for some kind of engagement (demands); and (ii) images that solely present information (offers), but lack eye contact vectors between the viewer and the characters depicted.[3] Those visuals which present information do not require the viewer to react to anything nor do they demand from him/her a particular behaviour or reaction; they simply offer information that can be either acknowledged or contradicted. In offers, the RP becomes an object of contemplation and presents itself for inspection to an observer without being involved in a quasi-personal relationship. However, in demand images, the RP looks out directly at the viewer, requiring a strong engagement with him (Kress and van Leeuwen 1996, 2006).[4]

Related to the system of image act and gaze, focalization is another factor to be considered in the visual mode. It analyses the eyes through which the narrative world is seen. The reader/viewer can contemplate the actions or thoughts of the RPs that make up the narration vicariously through the point of view of a character, be it main or secondary, and not through his own eyes (Moebius 1986; Painter 2007). Sometimes, the utilization of only one image offers the possibility of simultaneously having a reader's perspective and a character focalization. This technique is known as, *viewing along with the focalizing character* (Painter 2007: 47–48). In it, the reader is usually positioned behind the character's back and sees *over the shoulder* what is happening within the narrated world through both his own eyes and the focalizing character's eyes. At other times a character's hands, feet or shadow are depicted at the bottom edge of the illustration suggesting that the viewer contemplates the RPs and their settings through the eyes of the metonymically represented character.

Indirect or character focalization may also be achieved across successive images in a two-picture sequence. This technique is known as *viewing across*

3. While Kress and van Leeuwen use the terms *offer* and *demand* to describe the system of image, act and gaze, Painter (2007: 42) and Painter *et al.* (2013: 20) adopt the options *contact* (+ eye contact) and *observe* (- eye contact), to indicate if the viewer is looking for a certain engagement with the RPs or, on the contrary, if they only wish to observe them.
4. Painter *et al.* (2013: 18–30) reinterpret Kress and van Leeuwen's (2006) systems of contact and propose additional systems that focus on affectual dimensions of meaning: *Focalization, Affect, Pathos.* These systems are essentially concerned with the representation of characters. For further details on these interpersonal systems, see Painter *et al.* (2013: chapter 2).

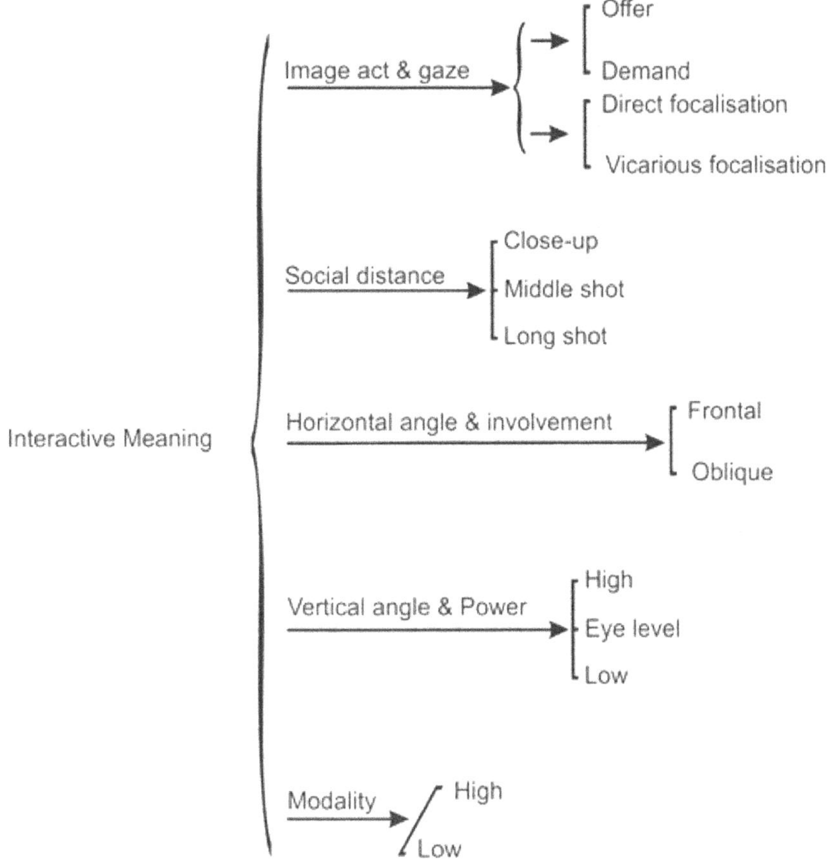

Figure 4.2: Interactive function in images. Basic features (adapted from Kress and van Leeuwen (2006) and Painter (2007)

two images (Painter *et al.* 2013: 24). This happens when the first illustration offers a character either in an offer or in a demand image and the subsequent illustration shows what the character sees or is looking at that first image (Painter *et al.* 2013: 29). It may also be encoded by placing us, as readers, in a character's viewing position, as is the case of the eleventh double spread of Browne's *Piggybook* (2008). Here, we see Mr Piggott and his two sons, already transformed into pigs, from the perspective of Mrs Piggott, who has just returned home after having left her family because of their chauvinistic attitudes. On the left-hand side of this illustration Mrs Piggott is facing us and looking down at the male characters, who are depicted from a rear view.

On the right-hand side of the double spread, the three males can be seen looking up directly at us and placing us, as readers, in the same viewing position the mother enjoys in the preceding illustration (Painter *et al.* 2013: 26). By using character's focalization, the illustrator encourages the reader to be more involved in the character's fictional world. Further examples of focalization taken from our sample texts will be provided in section 4.2.3 of this chapter and in Chapter 7.

The degrees of social distance and intimacy, the level of involvement by the viewer and, finally, the power relations between the viewer and the represented participants complement the information transmitted by the visual mode (Kress and van Leeuwen, 2006 [1996]). The system of social distance relates to the degree of intimacy established between the viewer and the RPs depicted in a composition, determined by how close they appear to the viewer in an image (Kress and van Leeuwen 2006: 124–129). The scale, resulting in feelings of intimacy or distance, varies between close-up shots, which create intimacy between reader and the RP, as the image is in close proximity to the viewer, and long-shots, which express distance, objectivity and an impersonal relationship. Close-ups generate involvement with the characters by showing us their facial expressions and, presumably communicating the way they feel. An intermediate level of intimacy is realized by middle-shots. While in long shots participants are portrayed full length and, 'there is an invisible barrier between the viewer and the object', in close-ups 'the object is shown as if the viewer is engaged with it. Unless the object is very small, it is shown only in part'; sometimes only the head and shoulders or even the face are made visible. In turn, in middle shots, 'the object is shown in full but without much space around it. It is represented as within the viewer's reach' (Kress and van Leeuwen 2006: 127–128).

In the visual mode attitude is established by perspective techniques, that is, by the way the viewer and the RPs are located in relation to the vertical and horizontal planes (Kress and van Leeuwen 2006: 129–143). The choice of a particular point of view greatly affects the way we understand the situation depicted. While the horizontal angle determines our emotional involvement with the RPs (frontal angle), or detachment (oblique angle) from them, the vertical angle reflects relationships of power and vulnerability, depending on whether the RPs are looked at from a low or a high angle respectively. The horizontal angle is concerned with the relationship between the position of the RPs and the viewer and determines the level of involvement between the image-producer, the viewers and the represented participants in a visual composition. When we are positioned to view participants frontally (they are presented facing us) we are persuaded to feel a sense of involvement or similarity to them. We sense that these people (or characters) are like us and are part of our world. The oblique angle, however, implies that the RP is one of them, not one of us; they are presented so as to be detached from us (Kress and van Leeuwen 2006).

The vertical angle, in turn, transmits two types of power relationships, that between the RPs and the viewer, and that between the RPs within an image (Kress and van Leeuwen 2006). As shown in Figure 4.2, we can be positioned from a high, low or eye-level angle. When the point of view is arranged upwards or downwards along a vertical axis, an increase or a decrease of power over the RPs can be experienced. The viewer has power over the RP if it is projected from a high angle. However, the RP has power over the viewer if seen from a low angle. Finally, RPs aligned at eye level angles have equal power status with their viewers (Kress and van Leeuwen 2006). Similarly, these power relationships can also be recognized between the RPs depicted in a visual composition. Two characters may be depicted facing each other, suggesting an equal power relationship between them, or even solidarity if they are close to one another However, if a RP is looking up to or down on another, they are presented as having a different power relationship (Painter *et al.* 2003: 17). The distinct choices determine the interactive effect, that is, the degree of engagement the visual artist intends to create when constructing the multimodal text (Unsworth 2007; Kress 2010).

In language, evaluative meaning is realized through the system of polarity and essentially through the system of modality, which reflects the speaker's or writer's stance towards the content of communication. Images also possess degrees of modality ranging from high to low levels of credibility. It is important to note here that, unlike the other interpersonal systems referred to in this chapter, the system of modality does not offer opposed choices with clear boundaries, but rather different degrees of credibility or realism within a scale that moves from minimalist to naturalistic representations. In the case of naturalistic modality, the more an image resembles whatever it is in the real world in a specific setting, the higher degree of modality it is likely to have (Kress and van Leeuwen 2006).

Adopting a similar perspective, Painter *et al.* (2013: 30–35) differentiate three broad styles to determine the degree of realism of a drawing: minimalist, generic and naturalistic. The minimalist style is the most iconic and the least naturalistic of all and, in terms of affect or emotion, it essentially encodes happiness or unhappiness. Regarding encouragement, the minimalist style generates some emotional detachment from the character. In characters depicted in a minimalist style circles or ovals are used for people's heads, dots or small circles for eyes, and there is usually a lack of accurate facial and body proportions in their representations. The generic style, however, is characterized by the greater amount of details in terms of the musculature of the human face. The mouths of the characters are more expressive and consequently the range of emotions and kinds of behaviour that can be expressed increase considerably. Common humanity is recognized and, therefore, it encourages a higher degree of emotional engagement between the participants and the viewer than the minimalist style. The naturalistic style encourages the readers' identification with the characters even more, since they are presented as real individuals who are capable of expressing a full range of emotions. The six tales of our sample texts intended for the first and second age groups (0–2 and 3–6 year-olds) are essentially minimalist in style. The tales included within the third age group (7–9 year-olds) follow a generic style, sometimes combined with certain features typically associated with the naturalistic style. The representation of the gorilla and the chimpanzee behind bars in *Gorilla* by Browne is evidence of this. The apes' facial expressions and gazes and the wrinkles around their eyes are features that are close to a naturalistic style, which provides the characters with the potential to express emotions such as solitude and unhappiness.

The modality of an image is not only established in terms of its resemblance to reality; it is also motivated by the cultural standards of what is real and unreal within a specific social group (Kress and van Leeuwen 2006: 160–163). Kress and van Leeuwen differentiate between four coding orientations of visual modality: naturalistic modality, scientific modality, abstract modality and sensory modality. Nowadays, naturalism is the leading standard by which visual realism is determined. The resemblance of an image to the objects or participants it represents in the real world is, in turn, defined by eight different modality markers which help us to describe different degrees of accuracy or abstraction in images: colour saturation, colour modulation and colour differentiation, articulation of background and articulation of detail, depth, illumination and brightness.[5]

5. For further information about the types of visual modality and modality makers, see Kress and van Leeuwen (2006: 161–163, 165–166), Machin (2007: 57–59) and Moya (2010: 137–138).

4.2 The Analysis. Interpersonal and interactive meanings: *Where the Wild Things Are*

So far the basic tools available to study the interpersonal/interactive meanings transmitted by the verbal and non-verbal modes in *Where the Wild Things Are* have been referred to. As stated in section 1, my aim is to identify the choices made by the writer and the illustrator of *Where the Wild Things Are* for the creation of interpersonal/interactive meaning. In order to carry this out, I will explore the correlation between verbal and non-verbal components in the narrative by comparing the interpersonal meaning of the verbal component with the corresponding interactive meaning transmitted by the illustrations. This analysis will shed light on the way the interplay of visual and verbal resources contributes to creating engagement.

The edition of *Where the Wild Things Are* used in this study is that published by Red Fox in 2007 [1963]. Eighteen double spreads plus a single page have been distinguished and will be referred to following this order in the analysis of the tale. Except the last page, which contains only a short text, in the majority of the double spreads text and images are intertwined in the verso and the recto of the page. From the first to the eighth double spreads, and in double spreads 17 and 18, the same pattern of structure and design is employed since in all of them the text appears on the verso, while the images are depicted on the recto. This pattern changes from double spread 9 to 11, and from double spread 15 to 16, where text and images are intertwined in both the verso and the recto of the pages: the images occupy the middle and higher parts of the page while the text is located at the bottom part. In addition, there are three double spreads (12–14) which consist of images alone. The 18 double spreads have been numbered from the first to the last page and references will be made to those numbers.

4.2.1 Troubleshooting

Before dealing with the analysis of the verbal and visual strategies available to the writer / illustrator to create interpersonal meaning, I will refer to some aspects related to the interpersonal metafunction that may cause a problem for the analyst when applying the Hallidayan SF-theory to the study of the verbal component of picture books. To deal with them, examples taken from specific tales are analysed in detail. First, I will focus the study on the tale chosen to exemplify the interpersonal metafunction of the language, *Where the Wild Things Are.* Later, the analysis is extended to the other picture books included in the sample texts.

One of the difficulties is associated with the identification and counting of the mood structures in the verbal mode. Within the SFG framework, only independent clauses are capable of distinguishing mood (Halliday 2004: 135, Figure 4.15). This implies that major, free clauses can have a mood-residue structure and, in turn, can be established as either declarative, interrogative or imperative. However, dependent clauses, if finite, can have a mood structure in terms of Subject + Finite. But whether finite or not, they do not determine mood type, as is made clear in Figure 4.15 (Halliday 2004: 135), where only major, free clauses select between indicative and imperative, and if indicative, then declarative or interrogative. Therefore, dependent clauses, although they may have a mood structure (S / F) when they are finite, have not been considered for the analysis of mood. Examples of these clauses can be found in excerpt 1, where only the main clause, 'a forest grew and grew', which contains a verbal group complex (paratactic extending, Halliday 2004: 491), is capable of being selected for mood type. After this, we appear to have a paratactic clause complex which follows the subordinating conjunction, 'until'. Since this complex is subordinated, there is no possibility of mood selection. On the contrary, the four independent clauses included in excerpt 2 have been counted as declaratives, as they are related in a paratactic relationship with one another. Note that, 'so he went to bed' is paratactic elaboration (Halliday 2004: 414) and that the direct quotation, 'I'll eat you up!' is also in a paratactic relation with the verb 'say'. The only clause that cannot choose for mood type in the second excerpt is the non-finite clause, 'without eating anything', which is hypotactically related to the previous structure, 'so he went to bed'.

1. That night in Max's room a forest grew and grew until the ceiling hung with vines and the walls become the world all around and an ocean tumble by with a private boat for Max and he sailed off through night and day [...] to where the wild things are. (*Where the Wild Things Are,* Sendak [1963] 2000)

2. His mother called him 'Wild Thing!' and Max said: 'I'll eat you up!' so he was sent to bed without eating anything. (*Where the Wild Things Are,* Sendak [1963] 2000)

In the case of ellipsis, the situation needs further clarification and the analyst has to make a decision as to whether or not s/he is going to distinguish a mood structure in a clause with some ellipsed components. Examples taken from *The Rainbow Fish* and *Granpa* will be provided to deal with this troubleshooting aspect. In the case of clausal structures such as: 'Give away my scales? My beautiful shining scales?' (*The Rainbow Fish*), the analyst has to reconstruct both of the two components of the mood element to make the clauses available for mood choice. In the examples given, what is probably ellipsed is *should I*, with *I* as the subject and *should* as the finite of these ellipsed clauses. As with so many issues in linguistics, modality is a question of gradation. If an independent clause has both a subject and a finite verb, then there is clearly a structure that can be classified as either declarative, interrogative or imperative. If there is only one of these, then the situation is less clear, and it is even less clear if we have to reconstruct both, subject and finite. To solve this problem and make a decision as to where to put the cut-off point I will refer to the notions of anaphoric and exophoric ellipsis described by Halliday (2004: 100). An ellipsed subject or finite verb can be recoverable or presupposed from either the preceding discourse (anaphoric ellipsis) or from the rhetorical structure of the situation (exophoric ellipsis). Thus, if either the Subject or the Finite are recoverable from either the discourse or the rhetorical situation, the clause will be reconstructed and be assigned a modal structure. However, if there is neither an overt subject nor an overt finite in a clause, I will classify it as moodless, even though both the subject and the finite could be reconstructed from the rhetorical situation. So, a complex nominal group such as 'Not just an ordinary fish, but the most beautiful fish in the entire ocean' (*The Rainbow Fish*) will be analysed as just that and will not be assigned a modal structure. I am not keen on postulating a mood element that is entirely ellipsed. Those cases where the analyst has to supply the entire mood implicit element are not going to be counted for modality purposes in the analysis. They will be treated as minor clauses.

However, if either the subject or the finite is present in a clause and only one of them is omitted, the clause will be reconstructed from the discourse or from the rhetorical structure and will be counted for the purposes of modality. An ellipsed clause such as 'What if you catch a Whale, Granpa?' (*Granpa*) will be reconstructed as: 'What (S) would (F) happen if you catch a whale, Granpa?' Although from a purely formal perspective it does not have an explicit mood element, the subject is present and only the finite has to be supplied (would). Therefore, the structure will be counted as an ellipsed interrogative for the purposes of the analysis.

Now I will deal with another troubleshooting aspect that also deserves a comment. It is related to Kress and van Leeuwen's concept of visual modality

(2006: 163) which, as the authors of *Reading Images* also agree, is more complex than simply its realization in language. According to their model, a diagram is understood as having low modality on the basis of its lack of realistic representation, but, in scientific contexts, it can also be considered as having high modality on account of its potentiality to represent content in a highly accurate manner. Indeed, the applications of the modality markers used by Kress and van Leeuwen (1996, 2006) to determine the credibility of a visual instance are not clear, and the categories they offer (colour modulation, colour differentiation, background representation, detail representation, tonality, etc.) are more a continuum between high and low modality than clear binary oppositions (Machin 2007: 180). In this sense, Forceville (1999: 168) also points out that Kress and van Leeuwen give little information about the way modality markers can be applied to different genres.

Characters in picture books are depicted, not photographed; therefore, they are not lifelike. In theory, within a naturalistic code, this would imply that the illustrations would have a low level of modality. Nevertheless, the main characters in the tales, essentially in those intended for 7–9 year-olds, are usually depicted in detail and with a certain degree of realism. The gorilla and the orang-utan in *Gorilla* by Browne are evidence of this. Similarly, Peter in *The Tale of Peter Rabbit* shows movements and poses which give Potter's illustrations a high level of realism. Kress and van Leeuwen (2006: 164) state that within the naturalistic criterion the degree of modality of an image is determined by its resemblance to reality and also by the culture and social group in which it is produced and intended to be understood. In addition, there is another factor that deserves to be mentioned here. The modality of images could also be affected by genre-related issues. Illustrations in picture books such as *The Tale of Peter Rabbit*, *Gorilla* or *Where the Wild Things Are* are real pieces of art, and reflect the objects depicted with a high level of resemblance to reality (Peter, the gorilla and the orang-utan, the wild things), especially if we consider that they are part of stories intended for children. Characters turn into real participants in the literary and imaginary world of the children for whom the tales are written and illustrated. When an image is observed, the viewer understands its meaning and what it represents through his knowledge of the genre conventions of representation, in this case the representational standards of children's picture books. Thus, along with the features distinguished by Kress and van Leeuwen (2006) to determine the degree of modality of an image, genre conventions may also have a direct influence on what can be considered as real or unreal in a specific visual instance, and also on the way images are observed and interpreted by the child-viewer (Moya 2010: 137–138). This aspect will be developed further and exemplified in Chapter 7.

4.2.2 Interpersonal choices in the verbiage

In this section I will study the mood structures and the attitudinal lexis used by the writer to transmit interpersonal meaning to the reader. After this, the relations of contact, distance and attitude will be dealt with within the visual component, and compared with the information that the verbiage offers regarding interpersonal features. As can be seen in Table 4.2, most clauses are declarative throughout and reach 88% of the cases counted. Thus, in the verbiage there is little that is of stylistic importance which is signalled through the grammar, since declarative mood structures do not encourage much engagement. The explanation for this lies in the fact that, while the utilization of imperative and interrogative modes interrupts the thread of the story, declaratives generally contribute directly to the continuity of the plot. Through them, Sendak gives information about the different actions and states in which Max is involved: (i) from the beginning of the tale, when he makes mischief at home and his mother sends him to bed without supper; (ii) to the intermediate and final stages, when he starts an imaginary trip from his room to the place where the wild things live. His room turns into a forest without boundaries and restrictions. From it, an ocean leads the protagonist to a wild land where Max is appointed king of all the wild things. There he gives free rein to his wildest instincts while he dances the wild rumpus with the creatures created by his imagination.

From a semantic perspective, out of the 29 declarative clauses identified, two are exclamations. They are used by Sendak to highlight two relevant passages of the narrative plot and make the story progress. In double spread 3, for example, through an exclamation, 'I'LL EAT YOU UP!', Max is

Table 4.2: Mood structures in *Where the Wild Things Are*

Mood structures	*Absolute values*	*Values in percentages*
Declarative	29	88
Imperative	4	12
Interrogative	0	0
Total	33	100

threateningly confronting his mother, which leads to a punishment that later activates an imaginary journey in the story. In the solitude of his room, Max uses his imagination to escape from the restrictions imposed on him by his mother and enters the world of magic and fantasy. The arrival to the place where the wild things live brings him all the freedom that the maternal figure has taken away. He starts to behave wildly, even ending up dominating the monsters that inhabit the wild land. There is another exclamation in double spread 16 that is worthy of mention and that marks another important moment in the story: 'we love you so!', stated by the wild things, who seem not to want to let the protagonist leave. The initial rage gone, Max again misses the warmth of his home and, in spite of the monsters' pleading him to stay where they are, Max decides to return home. Maternal love is more powerful than his desire for freedom. When he arrives once again in his room, he finds a plate of hot soup, which may well symbolize the maternal love and care that children need from their parents

Only four commands, realized through imperative clauses, have been found in double spreads 10, 11, 15 and 16, which reach the rate of 12% of the tokens identified. They are of special interest to us here, as they create an interactive relationship between the main character, Max, and the wild things: 'BE STILL!' (double spread 10), 'let the wild rumpus start!' (double spread 11), 'Now stop!' (double spread 15), 'Oh please don't go- ...' (double spread 16). The first three are uttered by Max who tells the wild things to be still in order to tame them by staring into their eyes. He also commands that they start the wild rumpus, a wild dance in which everyone gives free rein to his wild instincts. Finally, when Max is tired, he imitates his mother by ordering the monsters to stop the wild rumpus and go to bed without their supper. These commands are all taken into account by the wild things, who follow their king's desires. They are so much in love with him that they plead with him to stay in wild land. Three out of the four imperative clauses used act, at the discourse level, as exclamations. Indicated as such by punctuation, they are signals to adults reading aloud to children that Sendak is highlighting important passages in the narrative plot: Max has become king of the wild land and the wild things love him and respect him. In spite of this, there is a moment when he gets angry with them and sends them to bed. Then he starts to miss maternal love, which arouses his desire to come back home again.

The tale does not make use of interrogative clauses, which might have created engagement between the characters or between the writer and the child-reader. Thus, so far it seems that the narrative voice reflects the events from an objective and distant perspective, as the lack of interrogative clauses, the scarce use of imperative clauses, and the high presence of declarative mood structures may suggest.

The attitudes and judgements embodied in the text, realized by the system of modal assessment and by choice of lexis, are also part of the interpersonal metafunction of the language (Halliday 2004: Table 10 (6). Modal adjuncts are not present in this tale to express the writer's attitude to the content of communication. However, attitudinal lexis within nominal group and copular structures is used by Sendak to express evaluative meaning and to describe Max and the wild things' personalities. Within a lexicogrammatical framework, Max is described as wild (his mother called him 'WILD THING!', double spread 3) and also as lonely (And Max the king of all wild things was lonely, double spread 15) when he starts missing home. The wild things, in turn, are also associated with the quality of being wild, a modifier that constantly precedes the head of the noun phrase, thing, which makes reference to the creatures that live in the wild land. On some occasions, they are also related to the adjective, frightened, when Max arrives to wild land and manages to subjugate all the wild creatures. Thus, both Max and the monsters are constantly associated with the adjective, wild, which is recurrently used in the verbal mode as a quality that defines their main features. The visual mode, however, does not seem to correlate with the verbal description invoked by the writer of the tale, referring specifically to the characteristics attributed to the wild things. This aspect will be further developed in the following section.

4.2.3 Interactive choices in the illustrations

In this section I shall attempt to determine how the visual elements create interpersonal meanings throughout the tale by focusing the analysis on the interactive features that Kress and Van Leeuwen (1996, 2006) distinguish in their Grammar of Visual Design: (i) image act and gaze; (ii) social distance and intimacy; (iii) horizontal angle and involvement; and finally (iv) vertical angle and power, with their respective classifications. The aim is to find out whether the illustrations suggest relations of intimacy or whether they imply a certain level of detachment, similar to that achieved by the high utilization of declarative clauses in the verbal component. The analysis of the images, exposed in Table 4.3, sheds light on the visual techniques used by Sendak to

Table 4.3: Interactive features. Absolute and relative values

Categories		*Absolute values*	*Values in percentage*
Image act and gaze	Offer	17	96
	Demand	1	4
Social distance and intimacy	Close-up	2	11
	Middle-shot	13	72
	Long-shot	3	17
Horizontal angle and involvement	Frontal	1	4
	Oblique	17	96
Vertical angle and power	High	0	0
	Eye-level	18	100
	Low	0	0

create engagement and possibly forge the identification of the young child with the main character in the story. Offers, middle-shots, oblique and eye-level angles are prominent in the majority of the illustrations.

Concerning Image act and gaze, the analysis proves that there is a predominance of offers (96%) over demand images, which only count for 4% of the analysed cases. Through offers, the RPs are presented as items of information for the child, but without creating an affinity with him. They simply reflect the sequence of actions carried out by the main characters of the story, as shown in double spread 9, when Max arrives to the place where the wild things live and receives the wild greetings and threats from the monsters.[6] In the next double spreads, the 10th and 11th, the story progresses and Max tames the wild things with the magic trick of staring into their eyes. They appoint him king of wild land. In these illustrations the RPs continually look at each other, exchanging their gazes. In these cases, there is no eye contact with the viewer and, consequently, there is no demand on the child-reader to be involved in any way beyond accepting or rejecting the offers of information made by the illustrator.

However, one demand image has been identified in double spread 7 and it fulfils the narrative purpose of encouraging us to empathize with the main character. In this double spread, Max looks directly at the recipient of the story demonstrating happiness in his smile. He has just started his trip to the place where the wild things live after his room has transformed into a forest

6. http://www.trazosdetinta.com/wp-content/uploads/2009/10/Maurice-Sendak30.png (accessed 30 November 2013).

and a turbulent ocean. Max's smile and direct gaze at the child-reader may be interpreted as an invitation to be involved in his adventure and become part of the imaginary story he is starting to live.[7] In picture books this type of reaction image is not common as its utilization usually interrupts the development of the narrative plot. The illustration exhibits the moment in which the protagonist finds himself in a state of happiness. In turn, it also contributes to the development of the story. The text accompanying the images announces that Max has sailed off to wild land, a fact that is also reflected in the visual mode, as Max is depicted on his private boat moving towards the right of the double spread. This demand image achieves a strong engagement between Max and the child, and forges the identification of the latter with the hero of the tale.

Perspective techniques also perform a role in the achievement of engagement and affinity between the RPs and the viewer. In double spread 6, for example, when Max is walking into the forest that his room has been transformed into, the forest itself is focalized on from Max's gaze.[8] This is a case of double focalization (Painter 2007): Max has his back to the viewer, who can see the wild vegetation both from his own eyes and also from the protagonist's eyes or a perspective close to it. This way, the child sees the same setting as the protagonist, and this favours the identification between the child-reader and the child-protagonist in the story.

With regards to the second feature of interactive meaning, social distance and intimacy, middle-shots dominate (72% of the cases counted). Characters are portrayed as full figures surrounded by their settings, but within the reach of the child-viewer, which accentuates the involvement between him and the RPs. Double spread 7, already cited, provides a good example of a middle shot with frontal and eye-level angles. In it, Max is surrounded by exterior elements, the ocean and a big tree, but he is depicted with a certain proximity to the child-reader: on board his private boat, the viewer can observe him from head to waist. The boat and the big tree are shown from the exterior setting at full-length, but close enough to the child-reader to appreciate certain aspects of their detailed features: the tree shows the cuts in the bark that surrounds its trunk, the different tonalities of the leaves that populate its crown are also perceived, Max's shadow is projected on the sails

7. http://www.trazosdetinta.com/wp-content/uploads/2009/10/Maurice-Sendak21.png (accessed 30 November 2013).
8. http://www.trazosdetinta.com/wp-content/uploads/2009/10/Maurice-Sendak20.png (accessed 30 November 2013).

of the boat; all of these details that can only be seen from a middle-shot view, relatively close to the viewer.

Out of the 18 double spreads identified, there are also three long shots and two close-ups which only total 17% and 11% of the tokens counted, respectively. In long shots characters are shown full-length and surrounded by a setting, although they are not necessarily located in the very far distance.[9] The three long-shots found display characters surrounded by the interior and exterior settings where Max and the wild things develop their actions. The background elements, as Scott (2001) states, usually provide a high degree of contextual detail as evidenced in double spreads 1 and 2 when Max is making mischief either by hammering a nail into the wall or annoying his dog. Long shots give the tale a sense objectivity and distance from the reader (Nodelman 1988: 151; Kress and van Leeuwen 1996, 2006). In spite of this, in the long-shots identified in *Where the Wild Things Are* Max is depicted within the child-reader's reach. A possible reason why picture books have more middle and long-shots than close-ups may be genre related. In long or middle-shots there is more for the child to see, which is an important tool for interaction between the mediator (reading parent, teacher, grandparents ...) and the child who is following along. Questions like, 'Where is Max in the picture?' or 'What things do you see in Max's room?' prompt interaction between the young reader and the adult.

Finally, although close-ups are usually infrequent in picture books (Nodelman 1988), the two identified in *Where the Wild Things Are* generate involvement with the main character and the wild things by presenting to the child-reader their facial expressions and also communicating the way they feel. As evidenced in double spreads 12 and 14, where Max and the wild creatures are dancing the wild rumpus, there are looks of happiness in the protagonists' faces. In addition, the illustrator depicts their physical features in great detail (horns, combs, claws, teeth, yellow eyes, etc.), their funny gestures, their smiles and the knowing looks that they give each other. The great presence of middle-shots and the utilization of close-ups suggest involvement between the RPs depicted in the tale and the viewer.

As for the third feature of interactive meaning, horizontal angle and involvement, most of the angles are oblique (96% of the tokens counted).

9. Note that Kress and van Leeuwen's notion of long shots differs from the non-technical sense, where the shots in which characters are located in the distance are considered to be long.

Only one frontal angle has been recognized in the tale. Double spreads 7 and 9, already described, provide examples of frontal and oblique angles, respectively. In double spread 7, the plane of the represented objects and the plane of the illustrator run parallel (Kress and van Leeuwen 2006: 134). However, in double spread 9, the subjects of the illustration (Max and the wild things) are not situated in front of the viewer, but shown from the side lines. They are marginal, at 90 degrees, which makes this illustration an oblique angle. Thus, as most of the illustrations in the picture book are oblique angles, the viwer contemplates the actions and events narrated with a certain detachment, as if the child was not directly involved in Max's adventure. Perhaps the explanation for this lies in the illustrator's attempt to demonstrate to the child-reader that in most parts of the narration Max lives in the world of dreams and imagination, far away from reality. Unlike oblique angles, which show the participants from the side lines and create a sense of detachment (Kress and van Leeuwen 2006: 134), frontal angles generate involvement with the child-reader, since the viewer stands facing the RPs so that their facial expressions, or at least their eyes, are gazing at him. The frontal angle used in double spread 7 is, as has been previously stated, an invitation on the part of the illustrator to the young child to become part of the adventure that the protagonist in the story is going to partake in. Max smiles at the viewer confirming his happiness after leaving home and directing himself to the place where the wild things are. This is also the only demand image identified in the tale.

Finally, regarding vertical angle and power, the fourth feature of interactive meaning, all the images identified are eye-level angles; no high or low angles have been used by Sendak. Eye-level angles imply that the viewer is at the same level as the main characters, and therefore feels identified with them. In this way, the author successfully encourages the reader to identify with the protagonist in the story; he is treated as if he has the same condition and status as the characters of fiction.

Concerning modality in *Where the Wild Things Are,* there is a combination of indicators of high and low modality, which, as Lewis (2006: 164) points out, seems to be often the case in picture books. Max is illustrated with the basic features of a child: the mouth, for instance is represented by a line, with the edges up or down depending on the state of happiness or anger of the protagonist. Sendak's illustrations are not photographs, and the protagonist's characterization is not very detailed, but sufficient enough for a child to identify the visual representation of the human figure. According to the visual perspective defined by Kress and van Leeuwen (1996, 2006), within the naturalistic interpretation this would imply a low level of modality. However, as previously stated, within the genre conventions of children's picture books, fictional characters are interpreted as real beings by children and, consequently, this increases the level of modality of the illustrations in the tale. In addition, the wild things, with a half lion, half horse-like nature, although belonging to the imaginary world of the protagonist, are wonderfully illustrated. Their movements and poses are very detailed and naturalistic, achieving a high level of modality, especially if we assume that they are the protagonists of a tale intended for young children.

4.2.4 Intersemiosis of images and words

So far the verbal and the visual modes of *Where the Wild Things Are* have been approached as independent texts, each conveying specific meanings. At this point, I will reflect on the way words and images inter-relate as interdependent components to create interpersonal meaning. SFG and Visual Social Semiotics describe how verbal and visual modalities work independently of one another. However, as Unsworth (2006: 56) states, they do not provide the resources to describe the meaning that is made from the synergy or intersection of language and images in combination. This is, in Unsworth's (2006, 2009) words, the current challenge that researchers on multimodality face.

In line with this challenging task, Royce's systems of complementarity (2007) will be applied to analyse the interpersonal meanings that are created through the interaction of verbal and visual modes in *Where the Wild Things Are*. Royce argues that attitude is a key semantic feature within the interpersonal metafunction and develops intersemiotic systems for interpersonal meaning according to the SFG choices of mood and modality. Hence he distinguishes between two basic types of intersemiotic relations within the interpersonal metafunction: *attitudinal congruence* and *attitudinal dissonance*. *Attitudinal congruence* takes place when both images and verbal language cooperate to construct parallel interpersonal content and a similar kind of attitude. This occurs, for example, when the characters do not direct eye contact towards the viewer in the visual mode and the verbal narrative is presented from an external narrator's point of view. Both modalities co-operate to create social distance between the RPs and the viewer. In turn, Royce classifies interpersonal interaction as *attitudinal dissonance* when the intersemiosis of image and word leads to opposite or ironic attitudinal meanings (Royce 2007: 68–69). Dissonance is produced, for example, if there are choices or signs of engagement in the visual mode which converge with expressions showing lack of intimacy in language.

The analysis of the combination of words and images in the picture book in question reveals that images and words sometimes express different attitudinal meanings. Certainly, as stated earlier, most of the clauses in the text are declarative and realize the unmarked speech function of making a statement. In turn, the visual part of the tale also addresses the viewer from a distance perspective without demanding anything from him, as offers and oblique angles are the most predominant features of the visual component. So there are no direct attempts to involve the reader specifically in the verbal and visual information presented in the tale. The viewer is not asked to react or give a positive response apart from agreeing or disagreeing with the information presented. However, there are other features in the illustrations which create engagement and involvement between the RPs and the child-viewer, suggesting a dissonance in the attitude reflected by the verbal and visual modes of this picture book. For example, the declarative clauses of the verbal mode present the information as fact and emphasize in an objective tone the scary nature of the wild monsters. When Max arrives to the wild land on his private boat and tames the wild things, the first creatures he comes across adopt a threatening attitude towards him: roaring, gnashing their teeth, showing their claws, etc. The attitude expressed in the verbal mode contrasts with the attitude achieved by the eye-level and middle-shot images used by Sendak to show the RPs with a certain proximity to the young child. The images reveal that the monsters do not seem to be as aggressive as the verbal component may suggest and that they can also form part of the child-viewer's world. Although the monsters display threatening poses and carry out scary actions, their faces and features are softened by their warm and funny appearances. In fact, in double spreads 9 and 10, for example, the protagonist's facial signs of dissatisfaction are even stronger than those depicted in the faces of the monsters. There is even a moment when they become scared of Max after confronting him. In double spread 15, even though the wild things roar, gnash their teeth and show their claws to Max, he is depicted smiling at them while saying goodbye. So it seems that words and images offer two alternative perspectives and collaborate to communicate meanings which are beyond the scope of either one alone. While the words present the monster in an objective and distant tone, the images depict them from a more touching perspective bringing them closer to the child's world.

The dissonance between words and images reflects the two different emotions that Max, any young child, may experiment with: anger and love. Max's anger is represented by the fierce behaviour of the wild things and their threatening actions. Their humorous and tender sides, however, are evidence of Max's need for parental love and home warmth and affection. Through his imagination Max transforms his bedroom into an extraordinary ocean and forest inhabited by wild creatures, where he gives free rein to his anger. Although the monsters he encounters in his adventure are described as threatening creatures, the illustrations reveal a different attitude. In fact, Max succeeds in taming them with a single glance, becoming the wildest thing of all and their king. Once Max's anger vanishes, he realizes he misses parental love and decides to come back home where he finds a hot supper waiting for him. This fact leads him to reality again and makes him realize that his anger is just a passing stage that can be controlled.

Together with attitudinal congruence and dissonance, Royce (2007: 68–69) also distinguishes another system of intersemiosis within the interpersonal metafunction: positive and negative *reinforcement of address*. *Positive reinforcement* implies an identical form of address in the verbal and visual modes. For example, the depiction of demand images in the visual mode is a direct form of address which is, to a certain extent, equivalent to the utilization of the second person pronoun, you, or the inclusive first person plural pronoun, we, in the linguistic mode. As the analysis carried out in section 4.2.3 demonstrates, although most illustrations are oblique angles and the presence of demand images is low, most pictures in *Where the Wild Things Are* let the reader observe Max and the wild things in the foreground from a close and almost touching proximity, a limited perspective that favours the observer's identification with the RPs in the story (Scott 2001: 22). This identification with the main character, forged from the illustrations, contrasts with the narrative voice adopted in the verbal text. For example, in the ultimate double spread where Max has just arrived back home, the external narrator's words in the third person emphasize the remoteness of the action: '([he sailed back over a year ...] and into the night of his very own room where he found his supper waiting for him [and it was still hot]'. However, the illustration that accompanies this text is a middle and eye-level angle in which Max and the elements that form the interior setting are depicted in the foreground, relatively close to the viewer. If we contrast this image with another similar view of Max's room in double spread 3, we will realize that there are important differences in the locations of the elements in the visual compositions. Although both illustrations are middle and eye-level angles, they forge the identification between the child-reader and the protagonist in different ways. In the third double spread, Max reveals dissatisfaction in his face after being sent to his room, where the pieces of furniture (a table and a bed) are depicted in a relatively distant background. In contrast, in the 18th double spread Max is shown just after coming back from wild land. A smile lights up his face, and the furniture in his room is portrayed in the foreground, in a closer proximity to the visual reach of the child-reader, which encourages more the identification between him and the main character. These two examples show that there is not reinforcement of address in the verbal and visual modes of *Where the Wild Things Are.* While the writer presents the story from an objective tone, guaranteed by the utilization of the third narrative person, the middle and eye-level angles used by the illustrator, together with the depiction of elements in the foreground, generate engagement between the fictional characters and the viewer, favouring his involvement in the story.

4.2.5 Conclusion

The comparison of the verbal and visual choices made within the interpersonal metafunction in the bi-modal text, *Where the Wild Things Are,* reveals that both the verbiage and the illustrations combine to reinforce the identification of the reader/viewer with the main character in the story. However, the visual mode seems to contribute more to the creation of engagement between the RPs and the child than the verbal mode. In the verbiage there is a predominance of declarative mood structures over imperatives, of which only four cases have been identified. The latter demonstrate the interactive nature established between Max and the wild things, as they refer either to the commands made by Max or to the wild creatures' request for Max to stay where they live. The tale does not make use of interrogative clauses, as their utilization would have interrupted the natural flow of the story. The high presence of declarative clauses throughout demonstrates that the verbal component accompanying the pictures does not seem to encourage much interaction. This lack of interaction is sometimes also reflected, to a certain extent, in the visual part, in correspondence with the declarative mood structures chosen by Sendak, as there is a predominance of offers and oblique angles. Most illustrations are offers since Max and the wild creatures keep looking at each other or at the exterior elements that form the background, without making any demand apart from acceptance or rejection of suggested information. In addition, the illustrations are mainly oblique angles, which do not generate involvement between the child-protagonist and the child-reader (Kress and van Leeuwen 2006).

Although the utilization of offers and oblique angles may imply distance and detachment from the viewer, other devices related to distance and perspective reveal that the illustrator makes choices which do create affinity with him. In contrast to the horizontal axis, which reflects involvement or detachment by means of frontal and oblique angles, the vertical angle usually expresses power (Kress and van Leeuwen 2006 [1966]: 146–147). As Max and the monsters are seen neither from above nor below, there is no power difference established between them and the observer. All the images are represented from an eye-level angle, which implies that the child (and probably the adult) is at the same level as Max and therefore feels identified with him. Finally, from the perspective of distance, most of the shots utilized in the tale are middle shots and they show the RPs at a certain proximity to the viewer, which forges an identification between him and the imaginary character. According to Kress and van Leeuwen's approach (1996, 2006), middle shots seem to imply some social relationships between the characters in the story and the young child as in them the visual elements are depicted within the viewer's reach.

These features are reinforced by the use of two close-ups, where the RPs are in an intimate relationship with the viewer, by the depiction of RPs in the foreground (relatively close to the child-reader), and by one demand image. Unlike offers of information, in demand images eye contact is established between the RPs and the child-reader, creating involvement by direct gazing. Finally, the effect of detachment achieved by the utilization of three long-shots is diminished by the use of focalization techniques, which gives the child-viewer the feeling of being involved in Max's world.

With regards to interpersonal attitude, the intersemiosis of images and words shows that the threatening actions carried out by the monsters in the images do not turn out to be as wild and terrible as is suggested in the verbiage. The text presents the monsters from a distance perspective through the almost exclusive utilization of declarative clauses. The illustrations, however, offer a closer perspective of the wild things as if they were part of the young child's world, and reflect wild creatures that are almost friendly and caring. Their traits do not seem to show the harshness of expressivity that the adjectives *wild* and *terrible*, used repeatedly in the text, may imply. The text and the artwork offer two different perspectives of the monsters and complement one another to explore the contradictory emotions of love and anger the protagonist experiments with after his mischief at home and during his adventure in the wild land.

Writers and illustrators need to master and be familiar with the verbal and visual strategies which may be exploited and combined to create interaction between the young reader and the protagonists in children's picture books. The use of demand images and frontal, closed, middle and eye-level angles may contribute to bring the child-reader and the fictional characters much closer together. This way, the child will find it easier to identify with the protagonists of the tale and to understand the message the author intends to transmit.

5 Creating textuality and compositional meaning

With the study of the representational and interpersonal metafunctions complete, in this chapter, the focus is on the textual and compositional aspects of Systemic Functional Linguistics and Visual Social Semiotics to analyse how the verbal and the visual modes contribute to the coherence of picture books. In language textual strategies (reference, ellipsis, thematic progression, information flow, etc.) can be used to create coherent wholes of communication and direct the reader or listener towards the most relevant information of a communicative exchange. Similarly, in the visual mode, artists and illustrators use different visual strategies (information value, framing and salience) to arrange visual (and also verbal) material into accessible units of information. The placement of verbal and visual material in different positions within a visual composition determines the way the reader's attention is directed through the narrative, as well as giving prominence to some elements over others.

In this chapter I will use *Gorilla,* a picture book written and illustrated by Anthony Browne, and intended for nine-year-olds and under, to analyse how verbal and visual components complement each other in order to transmit textual and compositional meaning. A comparison of the two elements will shed light on the way the visual and verbal resources contribute to the construction of compositional meaning in this visual narrative. Later, in Chapter 8, the analysis is extended to the other picture books that form the sample texts.

5.1 Theoretical framework: SFG and Visual Social Semiotics

The theoretical foundation for this analysis is mainly extrapolated from the SFG approach to language as a social semiotic process (Halliday 1978, 2004), and from Kress and van Leeuwen's Visual Social Semiotics (2006), and these frameworks for the study are referred to first of all. Special attention is paid to the textual and compositional aspects of Halliday's (2004) Systemic Functional Linguistics and Kress and van Leeuwen's (2006) Visual Social Semiotics, respectively. Once the methodology is outlined, the textual and compositional features of *Gorilla* are analysed in order to determine how verbal and visual modalities contribute to the organization and understanding of the story.

5.1.1 The textual metafunction

The textual metafunction is concerned with the resources language has for creating coherent texts with relevance to the contexts in which they are produced and understood.[1] Within these, the thematic structure gives the clause its character as a message, as a communicative event, analysed as a two-part structure with thematic and rhematic elements. Within SFG, theme is considered a predication-internal entity (Halliday, 2004) and is defined on the basis of two criteria: 'the theme is the starting-point of the message; it is what the clause is going to be about' (Halliday, 1985: 39). The rest of the message is where the clause moves after the point of departure and is called the rheme, which in English always follows the initial position.

Theme is considered to be a meaningful choice that specifies the angle from which the speaker/writer projects their message: 'It is what sets the scene for the clause itself and positions it in relation to the unfolding text' (Halliday, 2004: 66). In fact, Halliday distinguishes between marked and unmarked themes in order to analyse the communicative intentions that lead the speaker/writer to move a clause constituent from its typical place to the initial position of the clause. A theme is unmarked when it coincides

1. Kress (2010), Martin (2008: 114) and O'Halloran (2008) are of the opinion that the complementarity of images and words in multimodal texts can only be understood in relation to the function they fulfil within a specific genre and context of situation.

with the subject of a declarative clause, the finite form or the *wh*-element of an interrogative modal clause or the predicate of an imperative structure. However, the speaker/writer does not always use a prototypical pattern; on many occasions the realization of his message requires a marked option with some specific informative connotations. Marked themes either provide some kind of setting for the clause or express a feature of contrast or emphasis. Unmarked themes are much less likely to involve a deliberate choice than marked themes, as the latter are more significant and 'more truly thematic than non-marked themes' (Goatly, 2008: 61).

Eggins' query 'how much of what comes first in a clause counts as theme' (Eggins 1994: 275–276) is of interest to us here. Although in many cases the theme is simple and is realized by a sole constituent, there are also clauses that present a more complex initial structure. In fact, Halliday admits the possibility that within the thematic part of a clause complex, three different types of theme can be included: ideational, interpersonal and textual themes. Halliday affirms that the theme of a clause extends from its beginning up to the first element that fulfils a function in transitivity and that this thematic constituent, mainly if it is a participant, tends to be topical (Halliday, 1994: 52).[2]

The theme is primarily concerned with the organization of information within individual clauses. However, linguistic studies over the past decades have assessed the theme also as a function that transcends the limits of the clause in order to contribute decisively to the global articulation of a text, establishing its method of development (Fries 1981; Moya and Ávila 2009). This is probably the greatest merit that Daneš has added to studies on Functional Sentence Perspective and textual organization (Downing and Locke, 1991, 2006). Through his thematic progression theory, he demonstrates the importance of the thematic clause structure, with its two elements, theme and rheme, in the organization and cohesion of the message. Daneš (1974: 118–120) distinguishes three basic thematic progression patterns:

2. Thus a theme can have textual, interpersonal and ideational components. The last, and the only obligatory, element of a theme is the ideational part. When speaking of multiple themes, Halliday states that only ideational themes are, in principle, referential and can be assigned a topical status. In contrast, textual and interpersonal components, structural elements (and, but, that, when ...), conjunctives (anyway, besides ...), continuatives (oh, well ...), modal adjuncts (probably, frankly ...), vocatives and finite operators which are typically located before ideational elements do not exhaust the thematic potential of the clause and do not fulfil a topical function.

1. Simple linear thematic progression or TP with linear thematization of rhemes. In this progression, the rheme of a clause becomes the thematic constituent of the following clause, giving the text a dynamic character; 2. TP with a continuous or constant theme. In this progression the same theme, although not necessarily carried out by the same clausal element, is shared by a series of utterances, each of which adds new information about it; 3. TP with derived theme. In this model, a broad spectrum theme, which Daneš calls hypertheme, gives rise to the themes of the clauses which follow to form a chain of subthemes deriving from the general theme.[3] Although often texts do not conform to these models strictly, Daneš' thematic progression theory was and continues to be a necessary point of reference for many later studies on textual organization, and is worth bearing in mind.

5.1.2 Composition in images

Equivalent to textuality in verbal language is composition in images. Here the theme and rheme realizations of the textual metafunction are applied to pictures to find out how a visual composition is organized and structured. The analysis of compositional features of a multimodal text determines the extent to which some elements within a visual information unit are given more information value and relative salience than others.[4] In addition to the analysis of the visual in relation to the verbal elements, the intersemiosis in compositional terms also involves the study of the visual components in

3. The potential of thematic progression is not exhausted by these three patterns. Daneš himself proposes other more complex textual structures that comply with a combination of the three described models. Among the possible combinations, Daneš highlights the split rheme pattern in which the rheme of a clause can be divided into two or more elements, generally coordinated, each of which is taken up as a theme in following clauses.
4. Extrapolating from verbal language, Painter *et al.* (2013: 91–92) refer to the units of information in visual texts as *focus groups*, defined as units which contain 'material that is grouped together compositionally as some kind of unity or "eyeful" to which we are guided to attend'. In turn, each focus group may contain 'a single focus of attention or else two or more visual elements arranged in compositional pattern that encourages us to hold them in view simultaneously'. For further information about the focus network they propose for describing the main compositional patterns found in picture books, see Painter *et al.* (2013: 109–120).

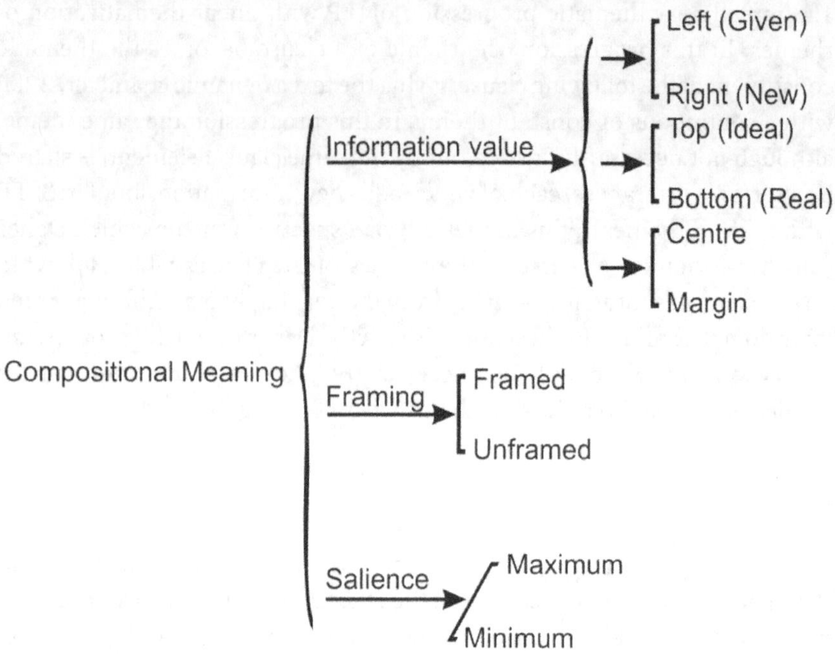

Figure 5.1: Compositional meaning. Basic features (adapted from Kress and van Leeuwen 2006)

relation to each other through the main principles of composition, that is, information value, visual salience and visual framing (see Figure 5.1). The challenge is to see how the textual and the compositional work together in the different passages of a picture book by using different modes of realization.

Information value, the first feature of compositional meaning, varies according to the placement of visual elements within the page. They can be placed in the centre or margin. Another possibility is for them to be positioned on the right or left, which is called given/new structure. The final placement is on the top or lower half of the page, which is referred to as ideal/real. Information value is related to Moebius' code of position (1986: 139). According to this conventional and graphic code, it often matters whether the main character is depicted high or low on the page (ideal/real), in the centre or on the fringe (centre/margin), on the left-hand side or the right (given/new).

Visual Information makes significant use of the centre, placing one or more elements in the middle and others around it in the margin. In the structure centre/margin, the RPs in the centre provide the nucleus of information to which surrounding and marginal elements are subservient (Kress and van Leeuwen 1996: 206). If there is only a single element in the centre and is not surrounded by additional components, the viewer's gaze is unambiguously attracted towards this character. Apart from giving this component the most visual prominence, the option of placing a single element in the centre is typically used in picture books to fulfil different functions: i. to create a moment of stasis at a particular stage of the narrative; ii. to introduce a character; or iii. to create an effective closure on the final page (Painter *et al.* 2013: 113). At other times, the centre is not filled and the participants are located either around it or around the edges of the image, usually achieving a centred and balanced composition. If there is eye contact between two human participants or they are placed face to face, a relationship of intimacy is created. However, if there is no eye contact between them or two characters are depicted back to back, a disconnection or a conflict is generated. Sometimes, the visual components of a composition do not follow a centred organization and consist of similar ideational elements displayed in a series. This visual technique is used both to create an effect of dynamism and to show a group of characters together, sometimes carrying out the same activity (Painter *et al.* 2013: 111). The illustration where Little NutBrown Hare, one of the characters of *Guess How Much I Love You,* is jumping up and down provides an example of the same character depicted in a series of movements.

With regard to the given/new distinction, in written texts *given* is presented as something the receiver already knows, as a familiar and agreed-upon point of departure for the message to commence. *New* is presented as something not yet known (Halliday 2004). Following Halliday (2004), Kress and van Leeuwen (2006) associate the right and left zones of an image with the new and given states of information respectively. Being on the left-hand side or on the right are locations that have significance. Participants and events on the left-hand side of a visual display are considered as something already known, as a familiar point of departure for reading the picture. However, this does not imply that those visual elements located on the left are necessarily known to the viewer; they are merely presented as such (Kress and van Leeuwen, 1996: 187; Hoperabundo and Ventola, 2009). Contrastingly, the right hand-side presents new information, something or somebody the viewer must pay special attention to (Kress and van Leeuwen, 1996: 186). A different, but complementary, perspective is presented by

Moebius (1986), Nodelman (1988) and Nikolajeva and Scott (2001). They consider that the left-hand side of a picture is a position of relative security while the right-hand side is a position of relative risk or adventure.

Another way of organizing the elements in an image is provided by the division between ideal and real. The ideal is presented on the top of the picture and is normally emotive and imaginary. It is the idealized or generalized essence of the information. Real, however, is more specific information (details), and more practical, oriented information (consequences, directions for action). Kress and van Leeuwen (1996: 191–206; 2006: 186–187) consider the top and bottom of an image as the realms of the ideal and the real respectively. Adopting a different approach, Moebius (1986) associates the positions of top/bottom with a sense of high/low self-esteem or social status respectively. Low self-esteem, low spirits or low social status are related to the bottom position. However, height on the page may be an indication of an ecstatic condition or dream vision, a mark of social status or power, or of a positive self-image. Nodelman (1988: 131; 1999: 136) reinforces Moebius' point of view, as he states that an object of the same size has more weight in the top half of a picture than in the bottom half. Generally a character that is in the margin, distanced or reduced in size on the page, and near the bottom, will be understood to possess fewer advantages than the one that is large and centred. This fact may be strengthened or weakened depending on whether the character is centred or in the margin, large or small, or presented in one or more scenes on the same page (the code of diminishing returns).[5]

Framing is the second feature of compositional meaning and determines whether the elements of a composition are either given separate identities, or are represented as belonging together. While framing stresses the individuality and differentiation of an element, the absence of framing makes it part of a group. The lack of frame lines and empty spaces between the RPs may also join elements together. Elements can be grouped together by connecting vectors and by continuity of colour and shape.

Colour is one of the key features of framing. Besides building up the basic image, colour fulfils another two visual functions in multimodal texts: i. bringing a character into the focus of attention; and ii. connecting or

5. According to this code, the more frequently the same character is depicted on the same page, the less likely the character is to be in control of a situation, even if in the centre.

separating important objects both within simple pictures and across whole sequences (Lewis 2006: 105; Kress and van Leeuwen 2006: 203). In *Angry Man* by Dahle and Nyhus (2003), for example, the red colour of Daddy's hands, face and left ear announces the violent tendencies of the father, who beats both Boj, his son, and his wife at home. Boj and Daddy are the main characters in this tale where the problems of a dysfunctional family are dealt with. The colour red forms a kind of unity among the characters in this book: Daddy, Boj, Boj's mother and even Granddad. Daddy's red hands and knuckles strike Mummy; Mummy's red face is evidence of the violent situation at home; even Boj's face is sometimes red. But the situation that is being depicted in this tale is more complex than that. The viewer can conclude that Daddy has also grown up in a violent family environment (Bjorvand (2010: 229–230). In one of the final illustrations the viewer can see an old man, probably Granddad, who is pinching Daddy on his left leg. Granddad is depicted with a red hand and a big red mouth. So, the colour red also creates a link between Daddy and his father. Red symbolizes the anger and violence that Daddy has probably inherited from his father in the past and, in turn, is developing towards his wife and his son, Boj. In addition, the colour red is also present in Boj's hands and in part of his face. Perhaps the child has also inherited Daddy's violent behaviour. All these meanings and connections between the characters of this tale are exclusively expressed in the visual mode through the use of colour.[6]

The lack of framing stresses group identity and, in turn, generates involvement and a reduction of social distance between the RPs and the viewer (Moebius, 1986: 141; Nodelman, 1988: 51; Nikolajeva and Scott, 2001: 62). The fact that an illustration is unframed (that is, a picture that covers

6. Colours have a lot of symbolism and are used to transmit some basic codes, taken predominantly from culture (Zaparaín and González 2010: 238). In western cultures for example, green is associated with optimism and hope while reds are used to create intensity, passion and violent emotions. Colours are also associated with variables of temperature and space. Yellows, reds, and oranges give a feeling of warmth. Greens and blues, on the other hand, are linked to coldness. Cold tones communicate distance in the shot; warm tones communicate closeness; clear tones: spaciousness; dark tones, however, reduce space and limit the perception of the surroundings (Díaz 2007: 131). In addition, colours have connotations that associate emotions or personality traits to them. Saturated colours can express aggressiveness or bravery, while pastel colours can indicate shyness and inhibition (Colomer 2005: 29).

the whole area of a page or a double spread) without margins constitutes an invitation to view the story from within and makes it easy for the viewer to identify with the depicted characters. As Painter *et al.* (2013: 103–104) state: 'Where an image is unbound (unframed), there is in effect no boundary (other than the page edge) between the world of the child reader and the depicted story world.' However, the use of frames normally creates a sense of detachment between the picture and the reader, enabling him to observe the events depicted in a visual composition from an objective and unemotional perspective (Nikolajeva and Scott 2001: 62; Nodelman 1988: 51). The use of frames may also create an effect of confinement for the characters within a specific setting. *Where the Wild Things Are* provides a good example. The illustrations where Max, the main character, is framed limit his freedom. Once he escapes from the boundaries of his room, he is allowed to give free rein to his wildest instincts, breaking out of the confinement imposed at home.

Lastly, salience, the remaining feature of composition, refers to the ability of an RP to capture the viewer's attention. Salience establishes a hierarchy of importance among the elements in an image; the most important RP is that which normally gets the greater salience. Salience is determined by a variety of features such as: i. size (the larger the RP, the greater its salience); ii. sharpness of focus (RPs have less salience when they are out of focus); iii. tonal contrast (areas of high tonal contrast have greater salience); iv. colour contrast[7] (strongly saturated colours have greater salience than soft colours); and finally, v. the placement of an object in the foreground and background of a composition (an RP in the foreground has greater salience than an RP in the background). However, none of these criteria alone is sufficient to measure visual relevance, which is always dependent on the complex interaction between all the elements referred to before (Kress and van Leeuwen, 2006). The features of size and location, for instance, are closely associated with each other. Moebius (1986) and Nikolajeva and Scott (2001) consider size a key feature in the analysis of picture books. They affirm that

7. Although colour is analysed here as a feature of compositional meaning that determines the salience of an entity and fulfils a textual function, I share van Leeuwen's (2011) point of view when he states that colour fulfils a role in the three metafunctions of the language. Colour may also be used to represent entities and settings (ideational metafunction) and to create emotions in the viewer (interpersonal metafunction).

a character depicted as large and centred has more significance and maybe more power than a character who is small. However, large size alone is not a sufficient criterion for the reading of an advantage; as Moebius (1986: 148–149) suggests, 'it may be a figure of an overblown ego'.

5.2 *Gorilla*. Analysis and exemplification

So far, the tools available from SFG and Visual Social Semiotics to analyse the meanings transmitted by the verbal and non-verbal modes in multimodal texts have been dealt with in section 5.1. After commenting on some aspects that may give rise to troubleshooting interpretations within the analysis, this section delves into the verbal study of *Gorilla* and then deals with its compositional features. The analysis of the interaction of these semiotic resources will shed light on the way verbal and visual components complement each other to create textuality in tales.

5.2.1 Methodology: Some troubleshooting aspects

All independent major clauses have a thematic constituent located in initial position. In the case of compound sentences, '... the point to bear in mind is that there will be two thematic domains – that of the clause nexus and that of the clause' (Halliday, 2004: 394). Thus, a in a clause complex such as 'Don't be frightened, Hannah, said the gorilla' (*Gorilla*, Browne [1983] 2002, double spread 6), in which the direct speech clause is projected by the reporting clause as a separate paratactically-related clause, two thematic constituents have been identified: the first, *don't be*, and the second, *said*. In addition, in line with Halliday's grammar (2004) a theme-rheme structure is also allocated to the hypotactically related clauses of a clause complex. Therefore, in a dependent clause such as 'if you would like to go to the zoo', which forms part of the clause complex: 'I just wondered if you would like to go to the zoo' (*Gorilla*, Browne [1983] 2002, double spread 6), *if you* has been analysed as a thematic constituent. *If* is a structural theme, followed by *you*, a topical theme. In turn, the theme of the main clause is *I* and the rest, *just wondered* is the rheme.

With regard to embedded clauses such as *what had happened* in 'Hannah rushed downstairs to tell her father what had happened' (*Gorilla*, Browne [1983] 2002, double spread 14), it has been considered that they are not full constituents in the clause complex structure as they function either as part of a group element (qualifiers in nominal groups or post-modifiers in adverbial groups) or as constituents or nominal elements in their own right (Martin and Rose 2003: 173). Thus, as they do not have the same status as independent or dependent clauses, they have not been assigned a proper thematic/rhematic structure, but are assessed as elements inserted in the structure of another clause or clause complex. Halliday (2004: 100) also admits that the contribution of embedded clauses to the thematic structure of the text is minimal and can, for practical reasons, be ignored.

Ellipsed clauses are also frequently found in the sample texts. Halliday (2004: 100) is keen to denote a thematic structure within a clause with ellipsed elements providing that they are presupposed from the preceding context (anaphoric ellipsis) or from the rhetorical situation (exophoric ellipsis). In the case of anaphoric ellipsis, I will treat the ellipsed subject (they) in a clause such as: 'So they thought very hard, and sent me a … (illustration of a kitten)' (*Dear Zoo*, Campbell [2007] 1982, double spread 8), as being understood from the previous clause (they thought very hard) and therefore, the subject, although ellipsed, contributes to the thematic progression of the tale. When two clauses are linked by coordination – in a paratactic structure – the subject of the second clause may be ellipsed, but it counts as a topical theme in a constant thematic progression.

The situation changes when both Subject and Finite are omitted and have to be reconstructed from the rhetorical situation (exophoric ellipsis). The reconstructed elements do not seem to play a relevant role in thematic progression. An utterance such as *Happy birthday, love* in '"Happy birthday, love," he said' (*Gorilla*, Browne [1983] 2002, double spread 14), has been analysed as consisting only of rheme in an elliptical version of *I wish you a happy birthday*. A similar case is offered in '"Time for home?" asked the gorilla' (*Gorilla*, Browne [1983] 2002, double spread 12) where the reported clause is a separate paratactic clause which functions as rheme, rather than theme, in an exophoric elliptical clause with the expanded version: Is it time for home? Finally, 'up and over' (*Gorilla*, Browne [1983] 2002, double spread 8) might conceivably be put in the exophoric ellipsis category, on the basis of a fuller version such as *Let's put it up and over*, in which case it would be a minor clause consisting of only a rheme. These examples respond to the type of exophoric ellipsis (Halliday, 2004) and show how the subject and the finite are filled in from the rhetorical structure rather than from the discourse itself. 'Such clauses have, in fact, a thematic structure;

but it consists of Rheme only. The Theme is (part of) what is omitted in the ellipsis' (Halliday 2004: 100). Therefore, as there is neither an overt subject nor an overt finite, their contribution to the thematic progression of the text is minimal and, like embedded clauses, they have also been ignored for the purposes of thematicity. Neither idiomatic expressions such as 'never mind' (*Gorilla*, Browne [1983] 2002, double spread 8) that presumably belongs to the anaphoric ellipsis category (Halliday 2004: 100), or minor clauses such as 'Maybe tomorrow' (*Gorilla*, Browne [1983] 2002, double spread 2) have been assigned a thematic structure. Finally, '*See you tomorrow*' (*Gorilla*, Browne [1983] 2002, double spread 13) has not been analysed as a minor clause, since it has the verb *see*. The subject, I, and the future form, will, are ellipsed, so it has been assumed that the whole clause constitutes a rheme.

There is another troubleshooting aspect that deserves a comment. It is related to the visual grammar developed by Kress and van Leeuwen (2006) when describing the distribution of information in visual compositions. Although Kress and van Leuwen (2006) associate the left and right locations of an image with given and new information, respectively, this aspect requires further clarification when dealing with the practical analysis of multimodal texts. Examples, which will be commented on in Chapter 8 of this book, demonstrate that the typical distribution proposed by Kress and van Leeuwen is not always fulfilled in the picture books that form the sample texts.[8] The left or right position of participants in motion turns out to be very relevant in picturebooks. The fact that pictorial compositions are read from left to right makes us perceive movement from left to right across an illustration as the natural way. This habit is so much established that when altered, the inversion frequently carries a significance for the represented participants in the story (Lewis 2006: 113).

5.2.2 Textual analysis of the tale

Let's start now with the verbal analysis of *Gorilla*, specifically the typology of themes that predominate in the verbiage in order to see how this visual narrative is structurally organized. As is shown in Table 5.1, both simple and multiple structures have been identified, but the simple type occurs more frequently (74.4%).

8. For a critical discussion on the association between given and left position and new and right position, see Bateman (2008).

Table 5.1: Simple and multiple themes in *Gorilla*

Theme	*Absolute values*	*Values in percentages*
Simple theme	67	74.4
Multiple theme	23	25.6
Total	90	100

Evidence of this fact is shown in excerpts 1 and 2 where the thematic slots of the clauses tend to be realized by sole ideational elements that make reference to one of the protagonists in the story, Hannah and the gorilla, together with her father. The first clause of the tale introduces Hannah as the protagonist as she is located in thematic position and continues in this slot in the following three clauses. The rhematic parts of these inform the reader about her interest and passion for gorillas as well as the activities she is engaged in with relation to the primates: she reads books on gorillas, she watches television programmes on gorillas and she also draws pictures of gorillas. This rhythm, as Gill (2002: 48) states, is broken in the last clause of the first paragraph: 'But she had never seen a real gorilla', which leads to the disruption of the balance achieved in the first four clauses of the tale, introducing a problem in the story. Consequently, Hannah's father is activated as theme of the following clauses, connecting him to the problem his daughter has in relation to her interest in gorillas. He is always busy and does not seem to have time to take her to the zoo to see a real gorilla. The last sentence of double spread 3, for example, summarizes Hannah's unhappiness and blames her father for her loneliness: 'They never did anything together.' This fact, expressed from the perspective of the omniscient narrator, is faithfully reflected in the visual mode, where Hannah is depicted alone having a sandwich while watching television. I will come back to this aspect later in section 5.2.3. In turn, the gorilla himself starts to reach the status of protagonist when he turns into a real animal in the dream world of the girl-protagonist. Then he shares the thematic position of the clause with Hannah, who is always kept in the status of main character. During this stage either Hannah or the gorilla, or sometimes both together, occupy the thematic positions of the clause. The rhemes, however, are reserved for the activities that both protagonists carry out together and also for expressing Hannah's emotions and thoughts.

(1) Hannah loved gorillas. She read books about Gorillas, she watched gorillas on television, and she drew pictures of gorillas [...] Hannah

threw the gorilla into a corner with the other toys and [...] went back to sleep. (*Gorilla*, Browne [1983] 2002)

(2) [...] Her father didn't have time to take her to see one at the zoo. He didn't have time for anything. He went to work every day before Hannah went to school [...]. (*Gorilla*, Browne [1983] 2002)

There are also 23 instances of multiple themes, formed by textual (mainly structural conjunctions such as *and, but, when, if,* etc.) and experiential components. Sometimes the textual themes function as markers of temporal continuity in the narrative structure. Particularly interesting is the use of the adverbial elements, *then* and *afterwards,* placed at the beginning of clauses reproduced in excerpt 3. These elements are part of multiple themes in their respective clauses and their effect is to mark the temporal sequence of the actions carried out in the story. After these textual and structural components, the ideational themes make reference to the main characters, Hannah and the gorilla.

(3) [...] and he (Gorilla) gently lifted her up. Then they were off, swinging through the trees towards the zoo[9] [...] Afterwards they walked down the street together. "That was wonderful," said Hannah, "but I'm hungry now." (*Gorilla*, Browne [1983] 2002).

In other cases (see excerpt 4), the multiple themes introduce a certain touch of disappointment in relation to Hannah, either because her real father does not take her to visit the gorillas at the zoo or because she is given a toy gorilla for her birthday rather than a real primate. These facts position the father as the entity that is responsible for the girl's dissatisfaction. He is potentially able to make Hannah happy, although in the initial and intermediate stages of the tale he fails in the attempt to do so (Gill, 2002: 49).

(4) It was a gorilla, but it was just a toy. Hannah threw the gorilla into a corner with her other toys and went back to sleep. (*Gorilla*, Browne [1983] 2002)

In the thematic structure only three interpersonal elements have been found as there are no vocatives and there is only one modal adjunct expressing probability, *maybe*, in 'Maybe at the weekend, he would say' (*Gorilla*, Browne [1983] 2002, double spread 3). In addition, there is only a finite operator

9. The non-finite clause has been treated as a separate clause hypotactically related to the main clause. It, therefore, has its theme (swinging) and rheme components (through the trees towards the zoo).

(*Do you want to go to the zoo?*, double spread 14) and a sole *wh-* interrogative (*What would you like to do now?,* double spread 10).

Regarding the marked or unmarked typology of themes, as can be seen in Table 5.2, most themes (80%) are unmarked or prototypical realizations. Themes tend to be realized by clause constituents that fulfil the syntactic function of subject in a declarative mood structure (see excerpt 1). However, 20% of the cases counted are marked themes and they are realized by structural and ideational components that fulfil a syntactic function other than subject. These marked themes typically fulfil two different functions in discourse: they either mark the sequential time progressions or activate new stages in the development of the plot.

Table 5.2: Unmarked and marked themes in *Gorilla*

Theme	*Absolute values*	*Values in percentages*
Unmarked theme	72	80
Marked theme	18	20
Total	90	100

In many cases, as is shown in 5 and 6, the initial slot of the clause is filled by experiential themes which mark the temporal sequence of the actions carried out by the main participants in the story. These marked themes are typically realized by circumstances of time (*the next day, at the weekend, the night before her birthday, in the night*) and are followed by other experiential components which carry out a topical function, mainly Hannah, her father and the gorilla. In excerpt 6, the marked theme, *the night before her birthday* fulfils a different function and introduces a new stage in discourse. The narration tells us that Hannah is excited before her birthday because she has asked her father for a gorilla. Soon the reader finds out that her expectations will not be met. Her excitement is soon deflated when her father fails once again to make her dreams come true: the gorilla that she is given for her birthday is just a toy gorilla. In addition, the marked theme, *in the night,* marks the activation of a new stage in the narration, shifting the text to a more fantastical dimension and giving the gorilla the status of main character. Both images and words are essential here to understand what the text is about (the toy gorilla has become real) and to introduce the gorilla as a prominent character in the visual mode. This aspect will be further developed in section 5.2.3.

(5) But the next day (textual + ideational themes) he was always too busy. 'Not now. Maybe at the weekend,' he would say. But at the weekend he was always too tired [...]. (*Gorilla*, Browne [1983] 2002)

(6) The night before her birthday, Hannah went to bed tingling with excitement – she had asked her father for a gorilla! In the middle of the night, Hannah woke up and saw a very small parcel at the foot of the bed. [...] In the night something amazing happened [...]. (*Gorilla*, Browne [1983] 2002)

Another marked theme, *the next morning* (see excerpt 7), repositions the temporal sequencing of the story and introduces a new stage in the narration, shifting from the world of magic and dreams to everyday reality. Hannah has just woken up and sees her toy gorilla again. Her dream is over and the gorilla of her dreams is replaced by the figure of the real father. This time, however, the reality reflected in the verbal mode connotes positive affect: the father, exhibiting tenderness and engagement, invites Hannah to go to the zoo as a birthday present. This contrasts with the lack of interaction and contact between Hannah and her father in the first stages of the tale, where he was the cause of Hannah's loneliness and dissatisfaction (Gill 2002). Now, the father is shown as responsible for the protagonist's happiness.

(7) The next morning Hannah woke up and saw the toy gorilla. She smiled. Hannah rushed downstairs to tell her father what had happened. 'Happy birthday, love,' she said. 'Do you want to go to the zoo?' Hannah looked at him. (*Gorilla*, Browne [1983] 2002)

Added to these thematic features is the notable coincidence throughout the text of the grammatical function of subject, the textual function of theme, and the pragmatic-discourse function of topic carried out by the main characters (Hannah, the gorilla, and the real father). In fact, theme and topic overlap in 73.3% of the cases counted (see Table 5.3). By following this strategy, the entities about which information is given are activated from the beginning of the clause, usually in subject position. The analysis verifies that the correlation between theme and main characters is notable. Even

Table 5.3: Theme and topic overlapping in *Gorilla*

	Absolute values	*Values in percentages*
Theme and topic overlap	66	73.3
Theme and topic do not overlap	24	26.7
Total	90	100

the new topic that introduces the main character in the first paragraph of the story is placed in the initial slot of the clause: '*Hannah loved gorillas*' (*Gorilla*, Browne [1983] 2002, double spread 1).

The simple arrangement of the structure and content of this storybook seems to be determined by the writer's desire to make the understanding of the plot easy for the young child. The book is intended for nine-year-olds and under and therefore the story should be easy for them to decode. In only 24 cases are theme and topic not realized by the same clause constituent. This lack of correlation usually happens either when: (i) the topical entity (Hannah) is part of an imperative structure that postpones its activation in discourse as in: 'Don't be frightened, Hannah' (*Gorilla*, Browne [1983] 2002, double spread 6); or (ii) when the theme is realized by a verbal process (said) in a reporting clause: '"You'd better go in now, Hannah," said the gorilla' (*Gorilla*, Browne [1983] 2002, double spread 13). By placing the experiential elements that carry out a topical function in the final slot of the clause the writer creates expectations and attracts the child's attention to the topical entities in a special way. In other occasions: (iii) the theme is omitted and the clause has only a rhematic component as in: '*up and over*!' (*Gorilla*, Browne [1983] 2002, double spread 8) or '*So many gorillas*!' (*Gorilla*, Browne [1983] 2002, double spread 8) , where the thematic slots *let's go* and *there were* are left out.

The analysis of the thematic structure of the tale would be incomplete without the study of the thematic progression of its clauses and how these are thematically organized to achieve coherence. As shown in Table 5.4, an overall view of the thematic progression of *Gorilla* confirms that part of it (34,5%) follows a constant theme pattern (Daneš, 1974), realized by the repetition of Hannah and Gorilla/She/He throughout the story (see examples 1–3). There is no doubt that constant theme is a very appropriate pattern for children's narratives, for in this way, given information is reiterated so that the young child does not lose the thread of the plot. Following the constant thematic progression, the linear theme also presents an important relevance in the final percentage, reaching 22.2% of the cases counted. In excerpts 8 and 9, the model of linear theme is maintained, as the themes of the second clause, *he* and *she*, come from the rhemes of the preceding clauses: *asking him a question* and *took Hannah to see the orang-utan, and a chimpanzee*. Throughout the story, at different intervals, the writer also produces sequences of linear thematic progression. These chains give the tale

Table 5.4: Patterns of thematic progression in *Gorilla*

Thematic Progression	*Absolute values*	*Values in percentages*
Constant TP	31	34.5
Linear TP	20	22.2
Derived TP	1	1.1
No TP	38	42.2
Total	90	100

a sense of dynamism as they allow Browne to place the three main characters about which information is transmitted in alternative thematic positions.

(8) When Hannah asked him a question, he (her father) would say, 'Not now. I'm busy. Maybe tomorrow.' (*Gorilla*, Browne [1983] 2002)

(9) The gorilla took Hannah to see the orang-utan, and a chimpanzee. She thought they were beautiful. But sad. (*Gorilla,* Browne [1983] 2002)

There is only one example of derived TP in this tale, Hannah/her father (see excerpt 10). The reason for this absence in favour of linear and constant TPs is that the latter organize the text in a way that makes it easier for the young child to understand the thread of the story. Even the linear TP, whose dynamic character might cause certain difficulty for the young child, turns out to be an appropriate structural tool in this picture book since the plot is centred on only three heroes, Hannah, her father and the gorilla. The pattern of derived thematic progression may require inferences and associations that go beyond the cognitive ability of children at such an early age:

(10) [...] But she (Hannah, the parenthesis is mine) had never seen a real gorilla. Her father (derived theme) didn't have time to take her to see one at the zoo. (*Gorilla,* Browne [1983] 2002)

The constant and linear thematic progressions identified are frequently altered throughout the tale: (i) by the insertion of statements by the omniscient narrator, which controls the characters and the development of the story *('In the night something amazing happened,'* double spread 5); (ii) by the presence of two imperative clauses with mental and material processes in the initial slot of the clause ('Don't be frightened, Hannah,' double spread 6); 'Come on then, Hannah,' double spread 7); (iii) by the presence of circumstances of time such as, *the night before her birthday, in the middle of the night,* etc., which mark the temporal sequence of the plot without carrying a topical function; (iv) by the activation of presentative there-constructions that occupy the initial position of the clause ('When they arrived at the zoo, it was closed, and there was a high wall all around,' double spread 8); (v) by the presence of reporting verbs located at the beginning of reporting clauses (*said the gorilla*); and finally (iv) by the utilization of thematic clauses consisting of rhematic components solely. Therefore, as is shown in excerpt 11, although some fragments that follow a constant or linear progression are found, in its totality the tale does not follow a defined thematic pattern due to the alternating nature of the structural elements that occupy the initial position of the clause (*Hannah, don't be, said, the gorilla, they, a perfect fit,* etc.). This alternation of thematic constituents lends dynamism to the story:

> (11) Hannah was frightened. 'Don't be frightened, Hannah,' said the gorilla, 'I won't hurt you. I just wondered if you'd like to go to the zoo.' The gorilla had such a nice smile that Hannah wasn't afraid. 'I'd love to,' she said. They both crept downstairs, and Hannah put on her coat. The gorilla put on her father's hat and coat. 'A perfect fit,' he whispered. (Gorilla, Browne [1983] 2002)

5.2.3 Compositional features

After analysing the textual aspects of *Gorilla,* I will now focus the attention of the study on its compositional characteristics. Concerning the visual elements of the tale, 31 illustrations and 14 double spreads have been distinguished. The majority of the double spreads contain two framed illustrations. The exceptions are double spread 5, which contains four plates, and the last spread, which consists of only one illustration and, unlike the others, it is unframed. Due to space restrictions, only three plates have been reproduced here as Figures 5.2, 5.3 and 5.4.

As stated in section 5.1, compositional meaning is concerned with the organization of the RPs within an image and involves features such as the distribution of information, framing and salience. With regard to the distribution of information, Hannah, the gorilla and her father are given a prominent information status as they are usually in the centre of the illustrations. However, the number of times that they are found in this position varies depending on their importance in the development of the plot. So, Hannah, who appears a total of 23 times in the illustrations, is located in the centre 18 times and only five at the margin. Gorilla, on the other hand, appears a total of 19 times, with 13 of those in the centre and the remaining six in the margin. Finally, the real father is depicted in the centre three times and in the margin only twice. The elements that compose the background, garments, the food Hannah and Gorilla eat (pudding, cakes, bananas, strawberries ...), the pair of gorillas dancing on the lawn, the pictures on the wall with inter-textual elements, etc., which are usually of lesser relevance to the plot, are subservient and tend to be found in the margins.

The drawings that decorate the walls of the house are attributed to Hannah. Although most pictures contain gorillas, the drawing in the penultimate illustration depicts two human figures that could presumably represent Hannah and her father. As Gill (2002: 56) points out this introduces 'a shift in the protagonist's internal state from complete absorption in gorillas to an interest in her relationship with her father'. In turn, this parallels the father's greater involvement with Hannah, as it is at this stage that he invites her to go to the zoo and, consequently, allows himself to be distracted from continuous work. In the visual mode this is represented by a sign of engagement as the father is touching and embracing Hannah's shoulders showing a positive feeling. However, although the text announces that Hannah looks at her father, the images still fail to reciprocate direct eye contact between the two characters.

Regarding the distribution of given and new elements, the tale is divided into 14 double spreads and a final illustration. The text guarantees the connection between the images shown in the 14 double spreads. As shown in Figure 5.2, the page opens with the visual part on the left-hand side, which usually sets the situation. Beneath it there is verbiage. On the right-hand side of the double spread, a wordless plate is depicted. The illustrations on the left-hand side present information that could be considered familiar to the reader (Kress and van Leeuwen 2006) and this is somehow demonstrated in the text. The illustrations on the right-hand side, however, introduce new information, corresponding, to some extent, to the visual element of greater size. Hannah has thrown the toy gorilla into a corner with the other toys and has gone back to sleep, a scene depicted in three small illustrations in the verso. The second part of the text, 'In the night something amazing happened', refers to a fact that is presented as something new and can only be understood if the illustration on the right of this double spread is contemplated: the gorilla has become real. The textual ellipsis is filled by the pictures. In this way, the image contextualizes the verbiage, adding definitiveness to the representation. In the double spread referred to, a clearly defined temporal sequence is followed through a given-new polarization of

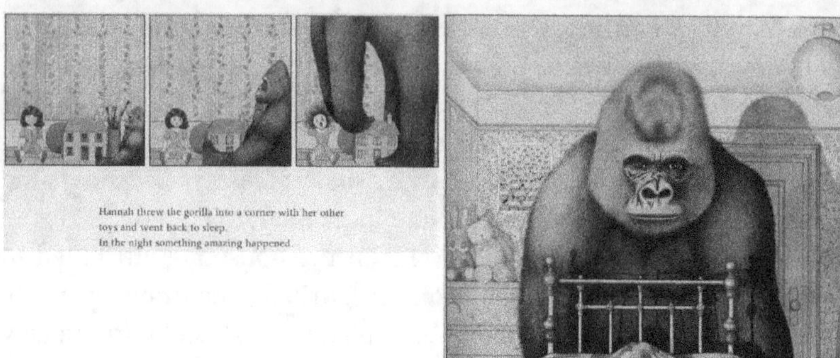

Figure 5.2: Something amazing happened.[10]

elements. However, this sequential distribution of images in time is not a constant pattern found throughout the story. At other times, as is the case with double spread 9, included here as Figure 5.4, both the illustrations on the right and left-hand sides contain new information. Hannah is contemplating an orang-utan and a chimpanzee, introduced for the first time in the story. The former is located on the verso of the double spread, the latter on the recto. The given / new distribution of information of the tales that form the sample texts is discussed further in Chapter 8.

As for the feature, ideal and real, the bottom of the visual composition, the real, is frequently occupied by Hannah and her toys. In the ideal, the top, the pictures that decorate the rooms and the figure of Super-gorilla in the motion picture are found. In the image of Super-gorilla (double spread 10), for example, the picture on the screen clearly represents the idealized version of reality while the people watching the film are located below. In this story, the figure of the gorilla is associated with the protagonist's dreams and wishes and belongs to the fantasy world. The picture of La Gioconda, represented with the face of a gorilla, appears on the top in double spread 4, just like King Kong in double spread 5, the moon in double spreads 6, 7 and 12, and Chaplin in double spread 10. However, Hannah appears in the bottom of double spread 14, represented through a metonymy that accentuates the sensation of speed: a flash of her red robe speeding down the stairs is enough to refer to Hannah in her totality (Forceville 2009). In

10. Copyright © 1983 Anthony Browne. Double spread 5. From *Gorilla* by Anthony Browne. Reproduced by permission of Walker Books Ltd, London SE11 5HJ. www.walker.co.uk

general terms, while Hannah and her toys are positioned within reality, the gorilla tends to be featured within an ideal zone.

Framing is another aspect of the compositional metafunction. In *Gorilla,* there are frames, which are an indication of social distance between the RPs and the young child. The use of frames suggests that the RPs and the young child belong to different worlds, the imaginary world of the characters in the story against the world of reality which the child belongs to. Besides, the frames around the visual elements create detachment between the visual and verbal modes, which do not mesh with each other. This way the two modalities are treated as separate identities. Only the last illustration deviates from this pattern, as in it there are no frame lines that separate the represented participants (Hannah and her real father) from the child-viewer, and the verbal from the visual elements. Indeed the shadow reflected from their bodies connects the image to the brief and final sentence of the tale: 'She was very happy', announcing the resolution of the initial conflict and the re-establishment of balance.[11]

Framing devices such as eye line vectors also fulfil a connecting or disconnecting function in this tale. Hannah and the gorilla are portrayed as connected elements in all the visual compositions as there is eye contact

11. Painter *et al.* (2013: 92–102) analyse how verbal and visual elements are integrated into the page, considering the verbal text as a purely visual unit or graphic phenomenon. The system they propose for studying the *intermodal integration* of verbiage and images distinguishes two main options: *integrated* and *complementary* layouts. While in the former the verbiage is incorporated as part of the visual image, in the latter, words and images occupy different spaces within the layout of the page. They are placed either on separate pages or in clearly demarcated sections of a single page. Both layouts have been identified in our sample texts. The three tales intended for the youngest children (*The Very Hungry Caterpillar, Dear Zoo, Where's Spot?*), follow an integrated layout where words and images share the same white space background. However, the tales aimed at 3–6- year-olds use both complementary (*Where the Wild Things Are*) and integrated (*Granpa, Guess How Much I Love You*) layouts. Finally, the tales intended for 7–9 year-olds also adopt both types of layouts, sometimes even combining them in the same book (*The Rainbow Fish* and *Gorilla*). *The Tale of Peter Rabbit* adapts itself to the complementary layout. So, it seems that there is no one-to-one relationship between the choice of layout and the age span for which a specific picture book may have been illustrated. For further information on the system of layout and its sets of choices, see Painter *et al.* (2013: chapter 4).

between the two represented participants. However, there is no bidirectionality in the eye line vectors drawn between Hannah and her father at the initial stages of the story. Although Hannah tries to connect with her father visually, there is no reciprocity from the father's gaze. She is, therefore, involved in unidirectional eye line vectors as reactor of the visual process. Similarly, dividing lines within the setting are used as disconnecting vectors between the girl-protagonist and her father. In Figure 5.3, for example, the lines created by the horizontal lines of the table where they are having breakfast and the boundary established by the newspaper the father is holding separate him from Hannah, frustrating her desire for interaction with the paternal figure. A disconnecting device akin to the one just referred to is also found in double spread 2 where the horizontal lines of the carpet that Hannah is stepping on and the vertical line that arises from the chair where his father is seated separate the two represented participants. These compositional features emphasize the lack of companionship that characterizes the relationship between Hannah and her real father and, in contrast, highlight the idea of togetherness that defines the relationship between Hannah and the primate (Gill, 2002).

As previously stated, the only illustration that is not inserted inside a frame is the last. In it Hannah strolls happily with her father towards the zoo holding a toy gorilla in a setting that lacks contextualization and attribution. Hannah and her father have their backs turned and there are no background

Figure 5.3: Having breakfast.[12]

12. Copyright © 1983 Anthony Browne. Double spread 1. From *Gorilla* by Anthony Browne. Reproduced by permission of Walker Books Ltd, London SE11 5HJ. www.walker.co.uk

elements surrounding them. Hannah is depicted within framed enclosures in 30 illustrations, until she finally gets the attention of her real father. Even when the toy gorilla becomes real at night and they start their imaginary trip to the zoo, Hannah is surrounded by a series of rectangular enclosures. These may suggest that she feels imprisoned and uncomfortable with the situation happening at home. However, when her dream becomes reality and she is taken to the zoo by her father, the visual elements are rid of the frames that restrict them and limit their space.[13]

Although the majority of the illustrations are framed, there are two that deserve special comment (see Figure 5.4). They are those that reflect the sadness of the orang-utan and the chimpanzee in the zoo. They are two close-ups, as they only show the faces of the primates, letting their sentiments and sad eyes be made out, perhaps a reflection of their lack of freedom. In these cases, Browne has used frames within frames as he presents the RPs inside square and rectangular enclosures covered by bars. In the previous

Figure 5.4: The orang-utan and the chimpanzee in the zoo.[14]

13. Moebius also relates framing to what he calls the code of round versus rectilinear shapes. Following this code, a character framed in a series of circular enclosures is more likely to be secure and content than one framed in a series of rectangular objects. In the case of *Gorilla,* the characters are enclosed in defined rectangular shapes.
14. Copyright © 1983 Anthony Browne. Double spread 5. Double spread 9. From *Gorilla* by Anthony Browne. Reproduced by permission of Walker Books Ltd, London SE11 5HJ. www.walker.co.uk

illustration, double spread 8, the bars clearly separate the primates from Hannah and Gorilla, who are contemplated by the child through these two characters' eyes. This is an example of vicarious focalization (Painter 2007). Through it, the child considers the RPs from the point of view of the story's protagonists. Browne utilizes the technique of focalization masterfully to achieve a great sense of identification and connection between the characters of the imaginary world and the young reader.

Hannah is also associated with this idea of imprisonment since, on two occasions, she is depicted behind bars; the bars of the stairs that lead to her room and the bars of her bed (double spread 4). This feature intensifies Hannah's feeling of confinement within her house, where she fails to establish engagement and interaction with her father. The pictures where Hannah is depicted with the gorilla on their way to the zoo are also framed, but the illustrator does not use frames within frames in these. They are only utilized when Hannah is portrayed within the interior settings of the house. The idea of liberty and excitement seems to be represented by an association with the outside world, while the idea of imprisonment is essentially related to house boundaries. As Nikolajeva (2010: 37) points out: 'Frames or absence of frames is a powerful artistic device to convey a symbolic imprisonment and subsequent liberation.'

Concerning salience, the illustrator clearly subordinates all the visual elements to the three main characters in the story: Hannah, her father, and especially, the gorilla. The salience given to these characters is achieved, in part, by their human-like characteristics.[15] Independently of their human and animal nature, the three characters adopt human poses and show human feelings, thus increasing the identification and involvement of the potential readers of the book with the characters of fiction depicted in the illustrations. The prominence given to Gorilla is obtained by the use of metonymies and visual focalizations that present him from Hannah's visual perspective as a large, powerful primate. This fact is made clear when the toy gorilla becomes real and makes contact through his gaze with Hannah, who observes the primate lying down in bed (double spread 6). Browne utilizes a visual metonymy to represent Hannah (Forceville 2009). Hannah is represented through the mound that forms her feet under bedding, a part for the female character in its totality. In turn, by depicting the animal as a huge primate,

15. Human beings generally tend to give more attention to human beings than other non-human participants.

the artist makes the power of the enormous gorilla over Hannah evident and emphasizes the visual contact established between the two characters, the girl and the substitute father.

In the final illustrations, the father, represented in long shots, is the one who is given most prominence due to having the same size as Gorilla and he even has some characteristics typically associated with the primate, like hairy hands or a banana coming out of the back pocket of his trousers. Thus, the size of the RPs as a way of creating salience pervades the whole story. Salience is also achieved by placing the main characters in the foreground and in the centre of the compositions. On double spread 12 where Hannah and the gorilla are dancing on the lawn, they are set in this position and surrounded by another two pairs of dancing gorillas. These last pairs have less importance in the illustration and so are located in the background. Hannah and the gorilla are always placed in the foreground, therefore they have greater salience than the rest of the elements in the landscape, which are in the background.

Finally, the use of colour is another characteristic of compositional meaning, which is relevant to this analysis. In this story, colour fundamentally serves to help the child identify who the main characters are, as they are depicted in saturated and lively colours. Therefore, while the two main characters, Hannah and Gorilla, receive the greatest saturation and contrast of colours (essentially reds, browns and beige), the rest of the elements located in the background (kitchen furniture, pictures, landscape visualized from the front door of the house, the city's buildings in the illustration in which Hannah and Gorilla go to the zoo, the city of New York in the film and the spectators themselves, the pair of dancing gorillas) are characterized by the absence of colour contrast and by a lower colour tone. The salience given to Hannah and the gorilla through the use of colour supports their status as the protagonists of the tale. In addition, in the penultimate illustration, the red colour of Hannah's father's jumper increases his salience as protagonist. At this point, he starts to act like a real father making his presence in Hannah's life evident. Thus, colour allows the illustrator to give more prominence to the main characters of the tale than other secondary elements present in the plot.

The second function of colour in *Gorilla* is to connect or separate the main characters both within a single illustration or across whole sequences. At the beginning of *Gorilla*, for example, the red of Hannah's jumper is contrasted with the blues associated with her father, expressing their lack of contact. However, at the end of the book when father and daughter connect, the reds of their garments match one another. In double spreads 1, 2 and 3, the father and Hannah are associated with environments and colours of dark tones with little saturation. When the father is reading the newspaper in the kitchen, when he walks towards the office or when he is working at a desk, he is dominated by grey, brown, beige and black tones, colours that accentuate the grey world he inhabits. These grey tones change to lively reds and blues in double spread 14, practically at the end of the tale, when the father invites Hannah to go to the zoo.

5.2.4 The interplay of images and words

Following the theoretical frameworks of SFG and Visual Social Semiotics, my aim has been to identify the verbal and visual choices made by Browne to convey textual and compositional meanings in the picture book, *Gorilla*. Now, the attention is focused on the way verbal and visual modalities are combined to create textual and compositional meaning. The analysis of the interplay of images and words at textual level is carried out by comparing the verbal and visual semiotic resources chosen by the writer and the illustrator to make the information flow of the story progress and highlight the most relevant parts of the tale.

The textual analysis reveals that there is an association between the point of departure of the clause as message and the three main characters in the story, Hannah, her father, and the gorilla. The intended readership of the tale, nine year-olds and under, determines the thematic and topical patterning of the verbiage, perfectly organized in simple thematic structures and topical sequences. These textual patterns seem to have a clear correspondence with the visual components shown in the pictures in the story as the illustrator clearly gives the three main characters, Hannah, her father and the gorilla, more space and importance than the other pictorial elements. Next to them, the primates of the zoo are also visual elements that particularly capture the child's attention, especially those depicted in double spread 9, two close-ups that reflect the orangutan and chimpanzee's sadness inside their cages.

The size of the RPs is used as a way of creating salience. The main characters in the story are given special status by placing them in the centre of the composition. In addition, the illustrator clearly subordinates all the visual elements to Hannah, the gorilla and her father, constantly located in the foreground. This visual pattern also has a clear correspondence with the textual component as there is a predominance of constant and linear thematic progressions. By using the constant thematic organization, the main characters are usually located in the initial slot of the clause so that the young child does not lose the thread of the plot. Similar to this finding, when comparing newspaper sports commentaries with other genres, Ghadessy (1995a, b) also finds that the most frequent themes are related to temporal location elements and mainly to major text participants. The constant theme, if employed in many clauses, runs the risk of making the text somewhat static and tedious, even for the young child. Given the age of the audience, the repeated use of this progression achieves its objective of making the story easy to follow.

The linear thematic model (Daneš, 1974) has also been identified. This second textual pattern creates movement in the narrative as the main characters are located in alternate thematic positions. This is also reflected to some extent by the visual component since Hannah, her father and Gorilla appear alternately in the illustrations of the picture book. Hannah is the character who appears the most, many times in the company of Gorilla. A few times she is also accompanied by her father and the primates in the zoo. These alternate settings give a dynamic character to the tale and introduce temporal and causal relations.

The study of the images and their relationship with the text clearly reveals that the two modes, the verbal and the visual, complement one another so that the tale is easy to understand, and in turn, attractive to the young child. The verbal and visual choices made by Browne regarding textual and compositional meaning help the child to identify the main characters in the story and follow the development of their actions. Hannah and the gorilla are given special prominence both in the verbiage, as they tend to occupy the thematic slots of the clause, and in the visual mode, where they are usually placed in the positions of most visual prominence.

The use of framing and colour techniques also make the complementary relationship between pictures and text in this picture book evident. The idea of disconnection that is established between Hannah and her real father by the absence of visual contact and the presence of framing lines between them contrasts with the visual engagement which is kept between Hannah and her stand-in father, the gorilla. From a purely textual/compositional perspective, these aspects are essentially reflected in the visual mode by means of framing and colour contrast and saturation. The verbal component of the tale does also reflect, to a certain extent, this contrast. While Hannah and the gorilla together sometimes occupy the thematic slot of the clause as co-actors of the same process, Hannah and her father do not usually appear together in this position or fulfil a similar function. This emphasizes the sense of companionship that characterizes the relationship between Hannah and the gorilla, and in contrast, assigns an idea of isolation and lack of contact to the relationship maintained by Hannah and her father. Thus, both modalities combine as interdependent components to achieve the same contrastive meanings: companionship versus isolation. The strength given to this contrast would probably have been missed if the text were just a monomodal artefact. Thus, the synergy of verbal and visual components contributes to the development of the story by creating a different and more comprehensive or broader meaning than that achieved by the use of one modality in isolation.

6 Processing reality: The synergy between image and text at representational level. The age factor

In Chapters 3, 4 and 5 the theoretical tools used to study the representational, interpersonal and textual meanings of the sample texts have been explained and exemplified by exploring the picture books *The Very Hungry Caterpillar*, *Where the Wild Things Are* and *Gorilla* respectively. At this point, in Chapter 6 I aim at analysing the verbal and visual intermodal relations of all nine picture books selected for study within a representational perspective. First, in section 6.1 I proceed to studying how the authors, who sometimes also double as illustrators, represent the narrative world in the verbal mode by identifying and counting the processes of the tales and their transitive or intransitive nature. Second, in section 6.2 I determine the extent to which the processes, with their participants and circumstances in the verbal component, are also reflected in the illustrations. In the third section of this chapter, I deal with the kind of intersemiosis that is established between verbal and visual semiotic modes to construct the fictional world narrated in the stories. Essentially, I attempt to answer the following question: are the illustrations a mere reflection of the information that the text expresses, or, on the contrary, are their components essential in the development of the plot? The study of the representational meanings in language and the illustrations shows how the visual and verbal modes work together to transmit the message writers and illustrators wish to convey. To illustrate these facts I comment on the more representative verbal and visual fragments of some of the picture books intended for the different age groups explored in this book. Finally, in section 6.4 I analyse how the age factor may determine the use of the verbal and visual strategies available to writers and illustrators to express representational meaning.

6.1 The representation of reality in language

As shown in Table 6.1, the representation of the narrated events in language is conveyed mainly through material and relational processes. In fact, 49.3% of the processes identified in the sample texts are material and 23.6% are relational. Material processes, which are the most predominant of all types, make reference to the actions in which the main characters are involved. The picture books *Granpa* and *The Rainbow Fish* can be used as evidence to exemplify this fact.

Table 6.1: Types of textual processes

Process type	*Absolute values*	*Values in percentages*
Material	280	49.3
Mental	67	11.8
Verbal	54	9.5
Relational	134	23.6
Behavioural	27	4.8
Existential	6	1.1
Total	568	100%

In *Granpa,* a picture book intended for children in the pre-operational stage, most of the processes identified are material and they convey a feeling of activity and movement. They specifically contribute to the development of the plot by telling the child about the actions carried out by Granpa and his granddaughter while they are together in different situations of their daily lives: sometimes they are planting seeds in the greenhouse (double spread 1) or singing a song (double spread 2).[1] Other times, the main characters go to

1. On the recto of double spread 2 grandfather and granddaughter are also found singing together, an action process, and surrounded by toys. Here the little girl is dressed up as a nurse, which is also an indication of the illness that is advancing in the story. In the next two pages, we begin to notice that the elements connected to the illness increase: the toys themselves become sick, appearing covered with little white sheets.

the beach (double spread 7), and the little girl plays in the sand while Granpa sunbathes (double spread 8). In addition, the narrative also flashbacks to Grandpa's youth. The character appears rolling wooden hoops and skipping down hills with his friends, Harry and Florence, when he was a child (double spread 11), and he also fishes with his granddaughter in a lake (double spread 10). These material processes either refer to moments shared in the present or actions that invoke the grandfather's past life. From this point on, also through two material processes (*come out* and *play*), the narrator of the story intervenes to announce the present illness of the old man without any explicit mention of the sickness itself: 'Granpa can't come out to play today' (double spread 12). This moment does not seem to be taken to heart by the little girl, who continues to make plans for the future, again through the use of the material process *go*: 'Tomorrow shall we go to Africa, [...]?' (double spread 13). Two new double spreads, without text, mark the final point in the story: Granpa's death. I will refer back to these and other previously mentioned episodes expressed by the visual mode later. As shown in the examples given, material processes are typically associated with animate agents, doers of verbal actions, essentially Granpa and his granddaughter.

There is also a predominance of material processes over the other types in *The Rainbow Fish*, aimed at 7–9 year-old children. In this case, they make reference to the actions carried out by the little fish to get one of the glittering scales of the Rainbow Fish, as well as the actions of the main character until he finally becomes aware of the compensations of sharing. For example, in excerpt 1, almost all the processes are material. The verb *bubble* is a material process as it answers the questions, what did he do? In turn, *come over* is also classified as material, as it answers the question, what happened to the fish? The only exception is *thanks*, which here is clearly a formula, rather than having *thank* as verb:

1. [...] the Rainbow Fish pulled out the smallest scale and gave it to the little fish. 'Thank you! Thank you very much!' The little blue fish bubbled playfully, as he tucked the shiny scale in among his blue ones. A rather peculiar feeling came over the Rainbow Fish. (*The Rainbow Fish*, Pfister [1992] 2010)

Regarding relational processes, they reach 23.6% of the tokens identified and principally fulfil an attributive and descriptive function (Halliday 2004) in the sample texts. In *Dear Zoo*, for example, relational processes and their qualities make reference to the unsuitability of the animals sent to the child: the elephant was described as too big, the giraffe as too tall, the lion as too fierce, the camel as too grumpy, the snake as too scary, the monkey as too naughty and the frog as too jumpy. Only the final dispatch is the perfect pet. In this picture book, the only relational process identified is *be*. Due to its descriptive nature, a higher variety and presence of relational processes at this stage of cognitive development might have led to detailed descriptions and digressions that could have slowed down the development of the plot. As Lluch (2003) and Moya and Ávila (2009) state, picture books, as tales, belong to the narrative text type and are principally characterized by a concise presentation of the main characters, a basic account of the development of the action and a brief account of the final outcome.

In *Where the Wild Things Are*, a tale intended for children in the second stage of cognitive development, relational processes also fulfil a descriptive function and are utilized by the author to refer to Max's emotions and the wild things' feelings. Max is described as lonely at the end of the story; he is also called the wildest thing among all monsters when he has a tantrum. In addition, his supper is described as hot, symbolizing the warmth and affection he is provided with at home. As for the wild things, they are related to the attribute of being *frightened* after Max has tamed them by staring into their eyes. The most frequent relational process identified is still *be* and it fulfils both a descriptive (was lonely) and a locative function (to be where the wild things are) (Halliday, 2004). Excerpt 2 provides some examples of other relational processes found in the tale. In it, there are three cases that deserve further comment, specifically the verbs *call* and *make*. Although *call* and *make* are not prototypical relational processes, they have been analysed as such. *Call* in 'He called him the most wild thing of all' is an intensive relational process, sub-classified as *assignment, projection* by Halliday (2004: 283). In turn, *make* in 'and made him king of all wild things' has also been analysed, in line with Halliday (2004: 238), as a *relational, intensive, assignment, neutral process.*

2. [...] and they (the wild things) were frightened and called him the most wild thing of all and made (the creatures, the parentheses are mine) him king of all wild things [...] And Max the king of all wild thing was lonely and wanted to be where someone loved him best of all. [...] so he gave up being king of where the wild things are [...] and sailed back [...] into the night of his very own room where he found his supper waiting for him and it was still hot. (*Where the Wild Things Are*, Sendak [1963] 2000)

The utilization of relational processes with a descriptive function is also notable in the tales written for children in the concrete operations stage. *The Rainbow Fish* is evidence of this. As shown in extract 3, although *be* is still the prototypical relational verb used in the clauses of tales written for 7–9 year-old children, the variety of verbs with a relational nature extends considerably and writers also use processes such as *feel, become, call,* etc. to fulfil a descriptive or identifying function. Note that *feel* is relational in extract 3 (Halliday 2004: 238). However, in extract 4 *feel* requires a different interpretation since it functions as a mental process rather than a relational one. The intensive relationship that was created between he (the Rainbow Fish) and the element, the light touch of the fin, is missing here, where *feel* expresses perception:

3. And the more he gave away, the more delighted he became. ... he at last felt at home among the other fish. Finally the Rainbow Fish had only one shining scale left. His most prized possessions had been given away, yet he was very happy. (*The Rainbow Fish,* Pfister [1992] 2010).
4. Suddenly he felt the light touch of a fin. The little blue fish was back! (*The Rainbow Fish,* Pfister [1992] 2010)

Together with material and relational processes, the presence of mental processes in the sample texts, 11.8% of the tokens identified, plays a key role in the representation of the narrative world. The analysis of transitivity in *Guess How Much I Love you* (aimed at 3–6 year-old children), for example, shows that most of the processes identified are essentially mental and material (33.3% and 27.3% of the tokens identified respectively). Four mental processes (*guess, think, love, wish*) have been recurrently identified and they usually express cognition (*guess, think*) and desire (*love, wish*). The high frequency of mental processes in this tale, especially those expressing desideration, is due to the affectionate nature of a story in which two hares, father and son, compete in an attempt to show how much they love each other: 'I love you all the way up to my toes' (double spread 5). Similarly, in *Gorilla,* a picture book intended for children in the concrete operations stage of cognitive development, the 13 mental processes identified represent the sources of cognition (*think, wonder,...*), desire (*love, like, want,...*) and perception (*see*) for the reality that is being described. The use of mental processes in *Gorilla,* especially those expressing desideration and perception, is determined by the affectionate nature of a tale in which a girl, Hannah, who feels ignored by her real father, is longing to see a real gorilla. Verbs such as *love, like* and *see* make reference to the protagonist's emotional state of loneliness and deep desires: Hannah loves gorillas and wants to see them in the zoo. In fact, in her dreams the toy gorilla she is given as a birthday present becomes real and acts as a substitute father who really cares for her and makes her dreams come true.

From a quantitative perspective the presence of the verbal, behavioural and existential processes is less important than the types of processes previously referred to, as they respectively only reach 9.5%, 4.8% and 1.1% respectively of the token identified in the sample texts. Verbal processes are missing in the tales of the sensory-motor stage but they are utilized by writers in the stories written for children in the other two stages of cognitive development. In *The Rainbow Fish* 12 verbal processes by means of which the narrator reproduces the exact words uttered by the main characters have been counted. *Say* is the most common here. As can be seen in extracts 5 and 6, verbal processes contribute to reflect the direct interactions that are established between the Rainbow Fish and other secondary characters, a starfish and an octopus, when the protagonist of the story becomes aware of the disadvantages of not sharing his beautiful scales with the other creatures in the ocean. Through verbal processes the exact words uttered by the characters in important moments of the development of the story are introduced in direct speech, giving immediacy and dynamism to the tale.

5. One day he (Rainbow Fish) poured out his troubles to the starfish. 'I really am beautiful. Why doesn't anybody like me?' 'I can't answer that for you,' said the starfish. (*The Rainbow Fish*, Pfister [1992] 2010)
6. 'I have been waiting for you,' said the octopus with a deep voice. The waves have told me your story. (*The Rainbow Fish*, Pfister [1992] 2010)

Like verbal processes, behavioural processes have only been identified in the tales written for children in the pre-operational and concrete-operational stages of cognitive development. Processes such as *look* and *watch* may serve as examples of behavioural processes used in *Gorilla* to reflect states of conscious perception represented as forms of behaviour. They show the importance of the utilisation of perception verbs in this tale. Hannah is said to watch programmes on gorillas on television alone when she is ignored by her father and to look at her real father when he finally invites her to visit the zoo and spend time together. Other processes such as *sleep, whisper, smile* and *nod* express physiological and psychological behaviour; they also show that Hannah and the gorilla are engaged in processes that create a sense of interactive contact between them: '"Time for home?" asked the gorilla. Hannah nodded, a bit sleepy' (double spread 12). This contrasts with the lack of engagement that is typically maintained between Hannah and her real father throughout the initial and middle stages of the story. This aspect will be further developed later.

As for existential processes, they have been found in the tales intended for young readers in the three stages of cognitive development. However, their presence is kept to a minimum. In *The Tale of Peter Rabbit*, for instance, only two existential processes have been located in the clauses of the story, one of which in the first double spread introduces the characters in the discursive scene. This process follows the prototypical model of traditional tales: 'Once upon a time there were four little Rabbits [...].' The second existential process, found in the 22nd double spread, evinces the conflict by showing how Peter attempts to escape from Mr McGregor's property, where he is trapped: '[...] and there was no room for a fat little rabbit to squeeze underneath.'

With regards to the transitivity features of these processes, they are used both in transitive and intransitive relationships in the sense that they may involve only one or more participants. At the beginning of *The Rainbow Fish*, when the main character does not want to share his scales with anyone else, most of the processes are intransitive and reflect the Rainbow Fish's loneliness. He rejects the invitation to play with the other fish and the suggestion to share his beautiful scales. Little by little he needs to get in contact with a big octopus to find out why no one else in the ocean likes him, despite his great beauty. When at the end of the story he becomes aware of the advantages of sharing, he joins the other fish. As shown in extract 7, more transitive processes are then used by the writer to convey the idea of sharing and being part of a community:

7. But if you go beyond the coral reef to a deep cave you will find the wise octopus. Maybe she can help you [...] 'I have been waiting for you,' said the octopus with a deep voice. 'The waves have told me your story. This is my advice. Give a glittering scale to each of the other fish [...] I just want one little scale.' The Rainbow fish wavered. Only one very very small shimmering scale, he thought. Well, maybe I wouldn't miss just one. Carefully the Rainbow Fish pulled out the smallest scale and gave it to the little fish [...] The Rainbow Fish shared his scales left and right [...] Finally, the Rainbow Fish had only one shining scale left. His most prized possessions had been given away, yet he was happy. (*The Rainbow Fish*, Pfister [1992] 2010)

Similarly, in *Gorilla* half of the processes identified are used in an intransitive relationship in the sense that they involve only one participant carrying a specific action. Certainly, this does not seem to offer a significant quantitative difference in relation to the transitivity features of processes used here. However, the use of transitive and intransitive relations plays a key role in the representation of reality if we consider the characters involved in the tale and their relation to the processes to which they are associated. An important aspect should be distinguished in this respect. While the relationship established between Hannah and the gorilla is usually realized by transitive relations in which the two participants are involved as co-actors in many of the actions narrated (excerpt 8 sets a good example), the relationship between Hannah and her father is mainly defined by intransitive and copular verbs, especially in the initial and medial stages of the story when there is a lack of contact and communication between the two characters (see excerpt 9). Even in intransitive verbs where only one participant predominates, the use of the third person plural pronoun (they) involves the participation of both characters, Hannah and the gorilla, in the same process (see fragment 10). These facts reflect a contrast between the relationships that are set up between Hannah and her real and substitute fathers. Hannah and the gorilla often act as co-actors of the same process and this gives their relationship a sense companionship. Hannah and her real father, however, are typically involved in intransitive processes which denote isolation and lack of interaction. They either read or work on their own and almost never do anything together.

8. [...] 'Don't be frightened, Hannah,' said the gorilla, 'I won't hurt you. I just wondered if you would like to go to the zoo' [...] and he gently lifted her up [...] The gorilla took Hannah to see the orangutan, and a chimpanzee. (*Gorilla*, Browne [1983] 2002)

9. He went to work every day before Hannah went to school, and in the evening he worked at home. '[...] I'm busy. Maybe tomorrow.' But the next day he was always too busy. (*Gorilla*, Browne [1983] 2002)

10. Afterwards **they** walked down the street together [...] They danced on the lawn [...]. (*Gorilla*, Browne [1983] 2002)

The examples given show that the utilization of transitive and intransitive processes also play an important role in the conveyance of representational meaning. In the next section I will discuss the extent to which these transitive/intransitive relations are also reflected in the visual mode and the way verbal and visual modalities complement each other to construct the fictional world where the main characters are involved. In this way, we may better comprehend whether the RPs depicted in the visual mode are also typically involved in transactional or nontransactional relations where only one or more visual entities are engaged in a particular action or event.

Finally, I will refer to the circumstantial information transmitted in the verbal mode. As stated in Chapter 3, in SFG processes and participants are ascribed to specific circumstances. In the tales intended for the youngest readers, circumstances of place and time are limited in number and no adjuncts of manner have been found. However, in the tales aimed at older children, the amount and variety of circumstantial information increases considerably. In *Dear Zoo,* for example, a tale intended for children in the first stage of cognitive development, there are no adjuncts of place and time to specify the location and the temporal frame in which the story is developed. In *Granpa,* however, adjuncts of time sometimes take the reader to the grandfather's past (When I was a boy); others bring the reader closer to the present moment lived by the characters (today). The future is also indicated by temporal subordinate clauses (When we get to the beach, when I finish this lolly) or by adverbs of time (tomorrow). Place adjuncts are kept to a minimum in the verbal component (down the street), since they are reflected in the visual mode. Grandfather and granddaughter plant seeds in the greenhouse of their home, drink tea in the kitchen of the house, sunbathe and play on a beach of yellow sand, play outside the main entrance of the house, fish together in the lake, watch TV in the dining room, etc ... These environments tend to be represented metonymically in the illustrations (Forceville 2009), whereby a part of an object makes reference to the whole. In this matter the kitchen is represented by a table with plates and cups and a couple of chairs. Finally, manner adjuncts (like arrows), as in '[...] Harry, Florence and I used to come down that hill like little arrows' (spread 20), are rarely used and do not tend to have a direct reflection in the visual mode either. All the aspects already dealt with here in relation to the verbal mode will now be analysed in the visual mode in section 6.2.

6.2 The representation of reality in the visual mode

Following Kress and van Leeuwen's approach to images (2006), in this section I study the correlation between the textual and visual components of the sample texts by comparing the circumstantial participant-process configuration of the verbal component with the corresponding RPs, visual processes and settings shown in the pictures. This comparison serves to determine the types of interaction that the visual and verbal elements exhibit individually in the nine picture books selected for analysis. As reflected in Table 6.2, there is a predominance of embedded images over the other types (64.2% of the tokens identified), as most of the illustrations combine both action and reaction processes. In turn, the presence of action processes is also notable, offering a rate of 27.4% of the cases counted. The frequency of reaction images decreases to 5.4%. Finally, conceptual images only reach 3% of the tokens identified in the illustrations of the nine picture books. Let's analyse now how the choice of these specific visual processes affects the representation of the fictional world in the picture books created for the children of the sensory-motor, pre-operational and concrete operations stages of cognitive development. To do this, I will comment on the most relevant visual passages of the nine picture books.

Table 6.2: Types of visual processes

Categories	*Absolute values*	*Values in percentage*
Action	46	27.4
Reaction	9	5.4
Speech	0	0
Conceptual	5	3
Embedded	108	64.2
Total	168	100

Where's Spot?, a picture book aimed at children up to 2 years old, may be referred to as proof of the high presence of embedded images in the sample texts. In fact, most of the images identified in this tale are embedded and combine both action and reaction processes in the same illustration. As stated in Chapter 3, in reaction images, the RP(s) are carrying out an action and, in turn, looking at each other, at the viewer or somewhere within an image. Evidence of an embedded narrative process in *Where's Spot?* is to be found in double spread 3, in which Sally, Spot's mother, is seen walking and looking for him (narrative processes).[2] The vector of motion is formed

2. http://www.amazon.com/%C2%BFD%C3%B3nde-est%C3%A1-Spot-Eric-Hill/dp/0140557768#reader_0140557768 (pages 7-8; accessed 30 November 2013).

by Sally's body, her tail is up and her legs indicate a walking motion. She is also directing her gaze to an old clock (reaction process, where a snake is hidden. Thus, both action and reaction images are used in this illustration to represent reality, a pattern which is recurrently adopted throughout the whole tale and most of the picture books analysed here. The processes of reaction identified are just shown in the pictures without being necessarily referred to in words. This lack of correspondence between verbal and visual semiotic modes reveals that words and illustrations complement each other to represent the narrative world. In *Where's Spot?* the visual component seems to create the action and movement that the verbal mode lacks, giving the tale the dynamic character that is essential to keep the young child's attention alive. While in the verbal mode, as can be seen in double spread 3, there is only a relational process, *be*, which is static and descriptive, in the illustrations, the visual processes identified are narrative and generate actions and movement.

The presence of embedded images increases in the tales intended for the children in the other two stages of cognitive development. In

Figure 6.1: Embedded image. Big Nutbrown Hare's love for his son.[3]

3. Text © 1994 Sam McBratney. Illustrations © 1994 Anita Jeram. Double spread 5. From *Guess How Much I Love You* written by Sam McBratney, illustrated by Anita Jeram. Reproduced by permission of Walker Books Ltd, London SE11 5HJ www.walker.co.uk

Guess How Much I Love You, a tale aimed at 3–6-year-old children, 83.3% of the processes counted involve action and reaction images. The narrative is essentially established by the actions carried out by Big Nutbrown Hare and Little Nutbrown Hare to show how much they love each other. In addition, the directions marked by the characters' gazes at one another act as vectors that contribute to the representation of reality as they consolidate the kinship between father and son. The vectors are formed principally by the hares' appendages and some components of the landscape. The embedded images are created when the animals gaze at each other and use their limbs to show how much they love each other. This is the case of Figure 6.1, where the extended arms of Big Nutbrown Hare represent how much he loves his son, as is also told in the verbal part of the picture book.

Animal characters are frequently utilized in children's picture books. The animals are typically transformed into anthropomorphic beings with human attributes and motivation, as they are often able to speak, show feelings and even wear garments. Most of these aspects are reflected in *Guess How Much I Love You,* where the main characters are able to speak, think and essentially empathize through mental processes (love) in verbal language and action processes in the visual mode. Even the title of the tale 'Guess how much I love you' or the clause, 'I wish I had ...', represents the presence of human sentiments in this story. The depiction of the picture book protagonists as animals gives the creator the freedom to eliminate various issues that are otherwise essential in an assessment of a character, as for example age, gender and social status. In this way, any reader – be it child or adult – can identify with the characters depicted (Moya and Pinar 2008).

Similarly, in *The Rainbow Fish,* a tale aimed at children in the concrete operations stage, there is also a predominance of embedded images (83.3% of the cases counted) over action images, which represent 16.7% of the tokens identified. The characters appear in motion, swimming in the ocean. The action images are created thanks to the movement vectors that show the fish's bodies, fins, and tails. These are usually combined with reaction processes, which are achieved by the looks exchanged by the inhabitants that populate the ocean. Figure 6.2 illustrates the moment when the Rainbow Fish gives away one of his scales to the small blue fish. Both fish stand in front of one another, staring intensely into each other's eyes (reaction). One of the big fish's fins, functioning as an arm and hand, is ready to hand the small fish one of his glittering scales. In turn, the small fish reaches out his front fin to receive his gift (action).

Figure 6.2: Action and reaction image. Sharing a glimmering scale.[4]

The use of embedded images in this picture book plays an essential role in constructing the moral behind the story. At the beginning, when the Rainbow Fish selfishly prides himself of his rare beauty, there is no eye-contact between the Rainbow Fish and the other creatures in the ocean. However, once he follows the octopus' advice and gives in to generosity, the use of images which involve eye contact between the animals in the ocean increases. By the end of the tale, at which point the Rainbow Fish has truly embraced selflessness, the use of bidirectional reaction processes contributes to create the idea that sharing brings happiness with it. The Rainbow Fish's greed leaves him alone and unhappy. However, after sharing his most prized possession, he feels good about himself and, most importantly, he makes others happy, too. Pfister does not offer a political message as some critics have claimed, accusing him of promoting communism and criticizing the vanity of capitalism. Boortz (2007: 65–70) argues that the tale 'aims towards human beings who are still at their most impressionable age [...]' and 'too many American parents have no idea just what kind of message they're imparting [...]'. Others, as the author himself stated in an interview, consider that it is essentially a tale that shows children the positive things about sharing and friendship.

4. Text and Illustrations © 1992 by North-South Books Inc. Double spread 10. From *The Rainbow Fish* by Marcus Pfister. Reproduced by permission of NorthSüd.

As previously stated, action images also play a key role in the conveyance of experience in the sample texts. They represent 27.4% of the cases counted (see Table 6.2). Unlike embedded images, they do not involve crossing gazes between the participants in a visual composition, but they sometimes bring dynamism to the stories by depicting the actions in which the main characters are involved. *Dear Zoo*, a tale aimed at 0–2 year-old children, may serve to exemplify this fact. In this picture book the action and dynamic images used by the illustrator contrast with the static nature that is reflected in language, where there is a predominance of relational processes, essentially *be*, over the other types: 'He (the lion) was too fierce! I sent him back.' In double spread 3 the action image is formed by the vector that shows the movement of the lion in his cage. The lion is adopting a posture as if it was walking: one of its paws is higher than the other; its tale is lifted, its mouth is open and it is sticking out its tongue. In addition, although in the images there is only one participant depicted, the interactive character of the tale adds movement to the story. Notice that the tale is structured in such a way that it invites a call-response pattern of reading, whereupon the adult reads one part and the child actively replies by identifying the animal delivered by the zoo. In this way, the action achieved by the narrative images, is to a certain extent, emphasized and complemented by the child's participation. The utilization of suspense points encourages the child-reader to find the information that is omitted in the verbiage by lifting up the flaps of the packing boxes where the animals are dispatched. Regarding reaction images, they only reach 5.4% of the visual processes identified in the sample texts. As has been demonstrated before, this low percentage is, to a certain extent, determined by the fact that they are typically used in combination with action processes and, therefore, it turns out to be difficult to identify an image which involves a reaction process by itself.

Conceptual images reach 3% of the tokens counted and have been found only in the picture book *Granpa*. Even though narrative images are frequently the most predominant in children's books, this story's undertaking of such an abstract subject as the death of a grandparent requires a strategic use of five conceptual images on the part of the illustrator. Some of them are classificational; others, however, are associated with symbolic values (symbolic images). Classificational images bring different RPs together showing that they have something in common as is the case with the verso of the second double spread where some garden tools are piled on top of a counter and arranged according to a clear compositional symmetry. Similarly, in the verso of double spread 12, objects related to the grandfather's illness (hot water bottle, thermometer, medicines, etc.) are shown to the reader through a classificational image. Other images are analytical in the sense that they show what participants or objects mentioned in the story are like, as is the case in the first illustration, in which the textual component announces: 'And how's my little girl?' Although essentially narrative (the girl is running towards her granddad with open arms while the old man smiles at her and awaits her sitting in his armchair), this illustration also offers conceptual connotations, since the main characters are described to us, and shown to us, displaying their physical appearance. The illustration contains narrative processes realized by vectors of motion such as the protagonist's arms and legs. In turn, the conceptual nature of the image comes from physical and emotional attributes which bring the old man and the little girl to life. Lastly, Figure 6.3 provides an example of a symbolic image, associated with Granpa's death. The armchair where the grandfather usually sat now appears with green and white lines, vacant, while the little girl stares at it from the verso of the illustration. The table next to the armchair is also empty. Reaction and conceptual symbolic images combine in this double spread to announce that Granpa has passed away. The vacant armchair, therefore, symbolizes death in this illustration. No words seem to be necessary to reflect this concept in this picture book.

Figure 6.3: Granpa has passed away.[5]

5. Text and Illustrations © 1984 John Burningham. Double spread 14. From *Granpa* by John Burningham, published by Jonathan Cape. Reprinted by permission of The Random House Group Limited.

As in language, the visual processes of the illustrations are also associated with specific participants. In fact, most of the visual processes identified in the sample texts, 75.6% of the tokens analysed, are involved in a transactional relationship where there are a minimum of two visual participants carrying out a particular action. Although in *Granpa,* for example, most of the verbs identified in the verbal component are intransitive and copular (72.5% of the cases counted), in the visual mode there is a predominance of transactional processes, which reach the rate of 74.1% of the tokens identified. In fact, the majority of the illustrations contain Granpa and his granddaughter involved in a narrative process of action or reaction. This emphasizes the close relationship that is established between the little girl and her granddad until he passes away. Only nine plates have been found in which there was no transactional relation between Granpa and his granddaughter. Sometimes they are conceptual images, which playfully portray objects related to the protagonists of the story. A paradigmatic example is the contrast marked by the old man's medicines, which foreshadow his illness, and his toys, which nostalgically mirror his past (double spreads 9 and 12).

Similarly, in *Gorilla,* most of the visual processes identified are also transactional (82.7%) and involve more than one participant in the same narrative image. Hannah and the gorilla tend to be engaged in transactional action processes which express affection as when they fly towards the zoo (double spread 7), hug one another (double spreads 8 and 10), walk holding hands on the way back home (double spread 11), dance together on the lawn (double spread 12), or kiss each other to say good night (double spread 13). In addition, in this picture book the use of bidirectional reaction processes plays a key role in the construction of the two opposing worlds where Hannah is involved. In these bidirectional reaction processes Hannah acts as the reactor and the gorilla as the phenomenon which establishes eye contact with the other represented participant. This reaction link gives a sense of companionship to the relationship between Hannah and her substitute father. However, the images where Hannah and her real father are depicted together are usually unidirectional and show a lack of eye contact between the two RPs. Although Hannah makes various attempts to interact with her father, he never makes eye contact with his daughter. In fact, in none of the scenes (even at the end when the text says that Hannah is looking at him) is there any bidirectionality to the reaction process (see Figure 6.4). Here the text announces that Hannah is looking at her father, but the image shows that she is just looking down at a picture she is holding of a gorilla. The use of unidirectional processes emphasizes the idea of loneliness felt by the girl because her father is obsessed with work. It seems evident that the use of unidirectionality and bidirectionality in reaction processes contributes greatly to the creation of meaning in this picture book as a whole: the real father cannot be reached and the eye contact is necessarily transferred to a substitute father, the gorilla. In this sense, I share Lewis's statement (2006: 122) when he affirms that in *Gorilla,* although the words tell us about the actions done by the characters, the picture book is more concerned with looking and watching than with doing.

So, it seems that aspects related to transactionality or bidirectionality contribute greatly to the construction of personal relationships. While nontransactional relations are utilized to express lack of contact and isolation, transactional relations emphasize the idea of contact and companionship that creates strong links between the different characters in a story. The utilization of unidirectional versus bidirectional processes may also help to emphasize the solitude versus the rich social and personal contacts that can be established between the fictional characters of the tales.

Finally, as is the case with verbal mode, visual processes and their participants are also ascribed to a specific setting in the illustrations. In the picture books created for children in the three stages of cognitive development analysed in this book, the images usually contribute more than the words themselves to the construction of location. *Where the Wild*

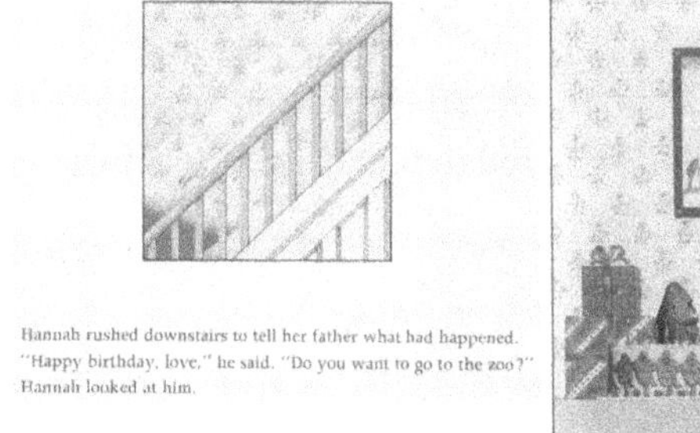

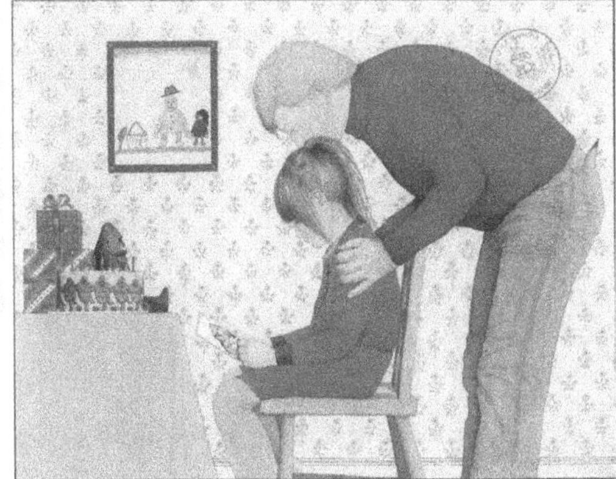

Figure 6.4: Hannah looked at him.[6]

6. Copyright © 1983 Anthony Browne. Double spread 14. From GORILLA by Anthony Browne. Reproduced by permission of Walker Books Ltd, London SE11 5HJ. www.walker.co.uk

Things Are (3–6 year olds) sets a good example, as the elements that form its setting offer information which is relevant for the development of the plot. In double spreads 4 and 5 the text announces that a forest grows in Max's room. The visual component shows the specificities of this forest, full of trees and vegetation, and illuminated by moonlight. The transformation of Max's room into a luxuriant forest leads the young child to the world of dreams and fantasy. In fact, the shifts of setting in this picture book, from Max's interior room to exterior locations (a lush forest, the sea, wild land) and the return home mark the boundaries between the world of reality and security, on the one hand, and the world of magic and excitement, on the other, that the protagonist in the story experiments after the quarrel with his mother. In wild land Max feels free to let his emotions come out and behaves like a wild creature. Once his tantrum vanishes, he comes back to reality and the boundaries of his room reappear.

Circumstantial information of time and manner does not tend to have a direct reflection in the visual mode. Although time adjuncts are not usually reflected in an explicit manner in the visual component, sometimes, however, when these are associated with relevant aspects in the plot development or actions of greater narrative tension, they are explicitly specified in both semiotic modes. In fact, as the action is essentially developed at night time, the moon, which symbolizes the world of dreams and imagination, is frequently depicted in the visual mode, explicitly reiterating the temporal frame which is mentioned in verbal language. Other temporal adjuncts, which make reference to longer periods of time (over the year and in and out of weeks), however, are not echoed in the visual mode. The way circumstantial information and setting are constructed in picture books is further developed in the next section of this chapter.

6.3 Intersemiosis of verbal and visual components at representational level

Having identified the main verbal and visual strategies used by writers and illustrators of picture books to represent the narrative reality, it is essential to analyse the meaning potential that is born of the co-deployment of verbal and visual modes in the sample texts. In Chapter 3, following mainly Unsworth (2006), reference has been made to the main types of intermodal relationships that can be established between words and images in picture books. Together with connection, Unsworth (2006) distinguishes two main types of intersemiosis at representational level: ideational concurrence and ideational complementarity, each one with its different sub-classifications.

In line with the age factor adopted in this study, it seems logical to start from the premise that both verbal and visual semiotic modes offer similar information in the tales created for the youngest children. Initially, it seems logical to predict that in the tales intended for children in the pre-operational stage (from 0 to 2 years of age), the images will most likely be a faithful echo of the meanings transmitted in the verbal component. Images will probably be subservient to language in an attempt to help the child decode the written message. However, in the tales intended for older children, the illustrations will not be a symmetrical reflection of the information that the text transmits; they will probably be essential components in the development of the story. The answer to this premise will reveal the kind of intersemiosis that is established at the representational level between verbal and visual semiotic modes in the picture books intended for the children of the three stages of cognitive development dealt with in this study.

Let's start with the tales of the sensory-motor stage and the way their verbal and visual modalities cooperate to convey experience. As the three tales aimed at 0–2-year-old children follow a similar pattern concerning the synergy of verbal and visual components to create representational meaning, I will comment and exemplify these aspects by referring to the picture book, *Where's Spot?* by Hill. Because of the age range of the target readers, we may initially be inclined to think that images and texts will function at a symmetrical level. However, the relation that exists between text and image is essentially complementary, as both semiotic modes complement each other in order to offer a complete representation of the narrative world to the child-viewer, who, with the help of a mediator, most likely his parents, grandparents, or teachers, will participate, in a more or less active manner, in the development of the story. In *Where's Spot?* the text is really simple, almost limited to the question referencing the whereabouts of Spot. The illustrations and their flaps are converted therefore into essential components for the transmission of information, since, without them, the storyline would be brought to a standstill. For example, after the question 'Is he under the stairs?' the young reader, helped by Sally's sense of smell, who points out the place that must be explored with her head, is invited to open the door under the stairs and find out that it is not Spot there, but another dog. Towards the end of the story, the narrator, or perhaps Sally, announces that the main character is under a rug. This time an interrogative structure is not used, but two declarative sentences: 'There's Spot. He's under the rug.' However, the sighting turns out to be erroneous, for when the rug is lifted, the child discovers that Spot is not there either, but a tortoise, only depicted in the visual mode. This animal in turn directs us towards another possible hiding place: 'Try the basket', where we finally find the protagonist, in an illustration completely lacking text. The illustration depicts Sally focusing her attention and running towards the basket where Spot is hiding. The verbal component of the preceding double spread, *Try the basket*, anticipates the visual narrative processes that are depicted in this illustration: Sally is running (action) and ready to look inside the basket (reaction). These aspects create relationships of complementarity between words and images in this picture book.[7] The different animals hidden inside the house are not mentioned in the text, but are only depicted in the illustrations. The illustrations, then, offer relevant information for the plot that is not mentioned in the verbal mode: the hidden animals in the different parts of the house systematically inform Sally that Spot, the true protagonist, is not in the referenced place and the search must go on. All in all, text and image are essential to forge a true understanding of the content of this tale.

The ideational complementary intersemiosis found in the tales created for very young readers becomes even more evident in the tales intended for children in the pre-operational and concrete-operations stages of cognitive development. I will exemplify this fact by referring to some passages of the picture books, *Where the Wild Things Are, Granpa* and *Gorilla.* In *Where the Wild Things Are* the co-deployment of texts and images becomes essential to understand significant passages of the plot, as all the double spreads that consist of both words and illustrations offer information that is missing in one of the two semiotic modes, be it the verbal or the visual. The complementarity of this picture book intended for children between 3 and 6 years of age offers examples of both augmentation and divergence. Sometimes the pictures clarify the meaning of words by adding visual information, as is the case in double spreads 1 and 2. Max is not making mere mischief as the

7. The tale offers a lot of learning opportunities structured around helping Sally find Spot. Children aged from 0–2 years can learn the names of household objects and furniture (door, clock, piano, stairs, wardrobe, bed, box, rug, basket), some prepositions of place (behind, inside, in, under), the names of different animals, the names of colours, etc.

text announces, but still his behaviour is pretty annoying: he is hammering a nail into the wall to pitch a tent and threatening his dog in his wolf disguise with a fork in his hand. The material process, *made mischief*, cannot be fully understood without the pictures. This material process is explicitly reflected in the visual mode, which enhances and specifies the kind of misbehaviour made by the protagonist in the story. Words and images become both essential resources to fill the gap and take over the narrative

In other occasions, the verbiage limits the possible interpretations the reader may make of the images which, in turn, offer an alternative and divergent perspective. Evidence of this type of intersemiosis is in the different perspective that the illustrator offers to the child-reader with reference to the frightening nature of the wild things. Despite the terrifying events described in the verbal mode, the illustrations show that the monsters are controllable and funny, even friendly. Some of them resemble lions with horns and big claws, others are more humanlike. Without images, *Where the Wild Things Are* would more convincingly qualify as a horror story. Max threatens to eat up his mother: 'I'LL EAT YOU UP!' (double spread 3) and the monsters do terrifying things: 'And when he came to the place where the wild things are they roared their terrible roars and gnashed their terrible teeth and rolled their terrible eyes and showed their terrible claws [...]' (double spread 9). However, the pictures soften the events narrated in verbal language and suggest that the wild things are relatively adorable rather than alarming. Thus, the verbal component and Sendak's artwork complement one another seamlessly, so that they offer complementary information and create, as Nodelman (1988: 227) points out, 'a delicious ambiguity'. Illustrators often offer more information that seems to be necessary for conveying the meaning of an accompanying text. However, this additional information is not superfluous in the picture book at hand. The wild creatures are probably products of Max's imagination and, therefore, they are as horrendous as the protagonist wants them to be (Nodelman 1989). As Nodelman (1988: 221) also states, 'by limiting each other, words and pictures together take on a meaning that neither possesses without the other'.

Narrative processes are associated with RPs that tend to have visual support, mainly those that play a determining role in the development of the plot, in this case Max and the wild things. Max's mother, however, is explicitly mentioned in the verbal mode, but she does not have a direct echo in the illustrations. The description of Max's argument with his mother is only referred to in the words of the first double spreads of the picture book:

'his mother called him "WILD THING!" and Max said "I'LL EAT YOU UP!" [...]'. The quarrel between mother and son is never reflected in the visual mode, probably because the presence of the adult figure in the pictures would have distracted the child's attention from Max's feelings and, perhaps would have made the mother too much of a relevant or central figure. The protagonists of children's tales tend to be children of the same age as their potential readers. Adults, therefore, usually play a secondary role in the development of the plot. Max's mother never appears in the visual mode and is only represented in the last double spread, indirectly, by some food tokens associated with her (a glass of milk, a piece of cake and a bowl of soup), which show the concept of unconditional motherly love. In agreement with Moebius (1986: 146), 'the best picture books can portray intangible and invisible ideas and concepts such as love, responsibility, ideas that escape easy definition in pictures or words'. In the second double spread there is another RP, a dog, which is not mentioned at all in the verbal mode. Thus, the main participants, those that construct the narrative, are represented both verbally and visually. However, secondary participants, which play a minor role in the narrative plot, are only referred in one of the two semiotic modes, be it the verbal or the visual.

As is often the case in picture books, in *Where the Wild Things Are* the setting is essentially constructed in the visual mode. There is no explicit reference either to the physical features of the wild things or to the place where their actions are developed in the verbal component. Consequently, the pictures contribute more than the words themselves to the construction of location. In this sense, the transformation of the main character's bedroom into a forest is original and is evidence of the complementarity that exists between words and images in this tale. The visual mode adds specificity to the change anticipated in the text through the participant *a forest* and the material process *grow*.[8] The boundaries of Max's room turn progressively into an unlimited thick forest full of trees and plants. The transformation of Max's room depicted exclusively in the visual mode takes the child away from reality and leads him to the world of imagination and sub-consciousness. The moonlight creates the mystery typically associated with the world of dreams where Max is totally free to express his emotions and behave wildly.

8. http://www.trazosdetinta.com/wp-content/uploads/2009/10/Maurice-Sendak18.png (accessed November 2013).

Another clear example of the prominent role given to the visual mode to construct the setting of the stories is found in *Granpa*. In this tale, intended for children in the pre-operational stage of cognitive development, the greater richness of the visual mode to express circumstantial information is shown in aspects related to the passage of time. The verbiage does not make reference to any season in particular. However, the images reflect different seasonal periods: In the first double spread, for example, Granpa and his granddaughter are planting seeds, suggesting it is spring time. The summer is reproduced in double spread 7 when the characters walk towards the sea. Autumn is reflected in the yellow leaves of the tree that is located by the river where Granpa and the little girl are trying to catch a fish (double spread 10). Finally, winter is also shown is the next double spread, the eleventh, where Granpa seems to have some difficulty in walking over the snow.

Finally, in *Where the Wild Things Are* there is also a series of wordless illustrations in which Max and the monsters compulsively dance the *wild rumpus*, a metaphor of Max's desire to follow his instinct and primary impulses.[9] In terms of technique, Sendak uses a coloured pen and ink pictures in muted colours. No words are required here to transmit the message to the young child. Max behaves like a wild thing and his tantrum is shown in its highest point. The last page, however, consists only of written language: 'and it was still hot'. After his adventure in wild land, Max comes back to the reality of everyday life where he is provided with the love and affection a child needs. These two passages which consist of images or words alone emphasize the complementary nature of the verbal and visual modes in this picture book. The hypnotic rhythm of the clauses of the text is perfectly complemented with the illustrations in pen and muted colours.

The complexity of the events narrated in the tales for children in the concrete operations stage of cognitive development also favours the use of ideational complementary relations. In *Gorilla*, for example, the intersemiosis established between words and images varies throughout the different illustrations. Sometimes, images and words provide an instantiation of each other, offering similar information and reiterating the content transmitted by each modality. In the first double spread, for example, the first paragraph specifies that Hannah loves and reads books about gorillas and that she also draws pictures of gorillas. The illustration, in turn, faithfully reflects

9. Double spread 12 is an example. See http://www.trazosdetinta.com/wp-content/uploads/2009/10/Maurice-Sendak26.png (accessed 30 November 2013).

these mental and material processes by showing a girl, Hannah, reading a picture book on gorillas while she is sitting on the floor and located under a drawing of a gorilla hanging on the wall. In this case, the verbal and the visual modalities are similar in ideational meaning and the inference required by the child-reader to understand the relationship established between them is minimal. The similarity in meaning also implies certain equivalence in the participant-process configuration of the reality represented via verbal and visual elements.

In other cases, both modes provide different but complementary information, maintaining the child's attention alive through the narrative plot. Through complementary and more indirect interactions the reader's attention and the narrative tension are kept alive since images and words contribute differently to the story line; either the images enhance the meaning of the words, or the latter expand the meaning transmitted by the visual component. A clear example of this is the passage in which the text breaks off and does not specify what really happens (see Figure 5.2). The narrator's words: 'In the night something amazing happened', cannot be understood without the pictures; they become both essential resources to fill the gap and take over the narrative to show how the story develops. This shift of narrative course from words to images takes places during the toy gorilla's transformation. Without the illustration, the viewer cannot decipher the meaning of what has really happened: the toy gorilla becomes a real primate in Hannah's dreams. Thus, in this case the visual mode conveys specificity to the information that is expressed verbally and provides the missing part, which is essential to the development of the plot. At the same time, the images introduce the shift from the everyday reality in Hannah's life to fantasy and excitement. In addition, in this double spread, the words announce that Hannah throws the toy gorilla into a corner with her other toys. But the illustrations show just the final result, that is, the toy gorilla located in the position that the text specifies. However, the action of throwing is not drawn in the pictures. So, the result of the material process, throw, is directly echoed in the illustration but not referred to in verbal language. This emphasizes the complementarity used by Browne to convey the fictional word narrated in the story.

Another good example of *complementarity* and *indirect coherence* is shown in double spread 3, where the text states that Hannah and her father never did anything together. The relationship between the text and the images on the recto can only be understood through making the inference that Hannah is watching television and eating alone as a consequence of her father's lack of time and his devotion to work. The image represents Hannah's isolation and loneliness. This example makes evident that the synergy of verbal and visual components results in new meanings that emerge from the combination of the two modalities: Hannah is watching television alone because her father is too busy to dedicate some of his time to her. The portrayal that is made of the father in this illustration is even more negative than that conveyed by each modality on its own (Gill 2002).

Another example of complementarity between words and images can be identified in the use of reaction images, which involve the exchanging of eye lines between the represented participants in an illustration. Reaction processes are not usually echoed in the verbal component through the use of mental processes of perception, but just shown in the pictures without being necessarily referred to in the words written by the narrator of the tale. In *Gorilla* they are essentially constructed depending on the crossing gazes between the characters of the tale, especially Hannah and the gorilla. As has been previously stated in section 6.2, this reaction link gives a sense of companionship to the relationship that is kept between Hannah and her substitute father, which contrasts with the lack of visual contact that is kept between the girl protagonist and her real father. The idea of companionship versus lack of contact is made more evident in the visual mode than in verbal language.

The complementarity of words and images can also be observed in the representation of circumstantial or locative information in the sample texts. As is frequently the case in picture books, with their limited scope of verbal text, verbal descriptions of setting are frequently absent or negligible. The illustrator can in an instant communicate information about the characters' physical appearance and setting, which would otherwise take a long time to narrate verbally. Consequently, the images contribute more than the words themselves to the construction of location. Although this is a characteristic that all the tales share, regardless of the age group for which they are created, the amount of details that construct the setting of picture books marks a difference between the tales intended for the youngest readers and the tales created for the other two age groups. In the tales aimed at children in the sensory-motor stage, the setting is kept to a minimum and the characters are usually depicted without any setting apart from the elements referred to in the verbal component. In *Dear Zoo,* for example, the animals sent by the zoo are shown in their cages without any extra detail that may distract the attention of the child from the main idea around which the plot is developed. Similarly, in *Where's Spot?* the background is also kept to a minimum: an armchair in the first illustration, a coat stand next to a door in the second double spread, a chair next to an old clock in the third double spread, a piano stool in the fourth, a telephone and a vase with flowers on a small table in the fifth illustration, nothing but the wardrobe referred in the text in the sixth double spread, a lamp on the wall in the seventh image, no background elements from the eighth to the tenth illustrations (where only the objects mentioned in the verbiage are reflected in the visual mode) and just Sally and Spot's food containers in the last double spread. The simple background with which the characters are provided is always the interior part of the house where the protagonist and his mother live. The scarce cognitive development of the toddlers for whom the tale is intended seems to determine the simplicity, and in turn beauty, of the illustrations. They just contain the elements which are essential for the transmission of meaning and for the representation of the narrative events.

However, in the tales intended for readers in the pre-operational and concrete operations developmental stages, background information increases considerably. In *Gorilla*, for example, many details of the interior and exterior parts of Hannah's house are depicted in the illustrations. The recto of double spread 7 sets a good example. In it the gorilla takes Hannah up swinging through the trees towards the zoo. The city of New York, which is not referred to in the verbal mode, appears at the background and is coloured in black tones. A white moon and an orange cat that is spooked at the unlikely sight of the branch-swinging characters complement the visual elements that surround Hannah and the gorilla. Regarding the interior details of Hannah's house, they are rich and are used to create intertextuality (Genette 1989), since the posters and framed paintings hung on the walls function as referential elements to previous literary works. In children's literature, the function of intertextuality is to initiate the young reader in artistic referents of significant socio-cultural import, in an effort perhaps to begin to develop the child's aesthetic sensibilities. An analysis of picture books' visual intertextuality reveals authors' inclination to portray artistic masterpieces. They usually make reference to renowned artists, who are known by adults, although not necessarily by young readers (Hanán-Díaz, 1998: 19), or to shared images of the popular culture imaginarium. Examples of this include the frequent appearance of well-known characters like La Gioconda, King Kong, Charlie Chaplin, a map of Africa, Superman, Che

Guevara, etc. in the pictures that decorate the rooms of Hannah's house. Most of these objects or characters contain gorillas as decorative elements, emphasizing Hannah's love and passion for these animals, and also suggesting the close kinship between humans and their simian cousins. La Gioconda, for example, in double spread 4, or Che Guevara in double spread 12, have gorilla heads.

The multimodal analysis of *Gorilla* confirms that, although some illustrations are a faithful echo of the meanings transmitted by the text, the word/image interaction that is used by Browne to transmit meaning is mainly complementary. Complementary and indirect relationships between words and images help the artist of this picture book to highlight Hannah's loneliness and to create a more negative portrayal of the father in the opening sections of the tale than that achieved by each modality in isolation. Therefore, in picture books, verbal and visual modalities cannot be analysed as separate components, but as interdependent elements which are part of a single multimodal text.

Getting back to the hypothesis formulated at the beginning of this section, contrary to my initial expectations, it seems that even in the tales intended for the youngest readers the relationship between images and words is essentially complementary. The information that the visual mode gives in the tales that form the sample texts is not superfluous, as it provides the essential meaning that is missing in the verbal mode. The use of complementary interanimations in which words and images contribute differently to the story line seems to be a useful technique that is utilized by picture-book artists to make the message of their stories both easily accessible for young children to understand and, in turn, exciting enough to keep them interested.

6.4 The representation of the narrative world and the age factor

To conclude the analysis of the representation of reality, now I examine the extent to which the age factor affects the choices made by writers and illustrators to express representational meaning. First, I identify the types of processes used in the verbal and visual modes of the tales aimed at the children in the sensory-motor, pre-operational and concrete operations stages of cognitive development. A chi-square test is carried out to determine the extent to which the results obtained with respect to representational choices and the age factor are significant and valuable. I conclude this chapter by examining how the participants associated with the linguistic processes are reflected in the visual component of the tales illustrated for the three age groups explored in this study.

As shown in Table 6.3, in all the tales there is an important presence of material processes to represent reality. The average percentage is 49.3% of the total tokens identified. This result increases up to 51.9% in the tales intended for the children in the concrete operations stage and decreases slightly to 48.5% and 44.2%, respectively, in the picture books aimed at children in the sensory-motor and pre-operational stages of cognitive development. It seems evident that the utilization of action processes is essential to convey a feeling of activity and movement in the tales written and illustrated for young readers.

The reality reflected in picture books is not exclusively based on processes of doing and happening. The utilization of relational processes with an identifying and descriptive function is also notable in the tales intended for children of the three stages of cognitive development discussed in this book. The relational process most frequently identified is *be* and it typically fulfils either a descriptive function or an identifying one. However, important differences have been found in this respect. While in the tales aimed at children between 0 and 2 years of age the presence of relational processes is high (47.1%), in the tales of the pre-operational and concrete operations stages of cognitive development this percentage decreases considerably to 20.2% and 20.5% respectively. As the age of the target group increases, the narrative reality becomes more complex, and, consequently, the characters' actions and processes of doing/happening multiply. Nevertheless, in the tales

Table 6.3: Types of processes. The age factor

Process type	*Age group 0–2*		*Age group 3–6*		*Age group 7–9*		*Grand Total*	
	Abs. values	*%*	*Abs. values*	*%*	*Abs. values*	*%*	*Abs. values*	*%*
Material	33	48.5	72	44.2	175	51.9	280	49.3
Mental	2	2.9	29	17.8	36	10.7	67	11.8
Verbal	0	0	18	11	36	10.7	54	9.5
Relational	32	47.1	33	20.2	69	20.5	134	23.6
Behavioural	0	0	10	6.1	17	5	27	4.8
Existential	1	1.5	1	0.6	4	1.2	6	1.1
Total	68	100	163	100	337	100	568	100

aimed at younger readers, the writer also makes a strategic use of relational processes in his creation of the characters, hence yielding to the child's familiarization with them according to their personal qualities or physical aspect (naughty, hungry, grumpy, tall, etc.).

This pattern is reversed when we analyse the frequency of mental processes, which reach an average of 11.8% of the process types counted. In the tales intended for children in the pre-operational stage of cognitive development (3–6 years) the frequency of mental processes is above average and reaches the rate of 17.8% of the cases counted. This percentage decreases only slightly to 10.7% in the tales written for readers in the concrete operations stage. However, the average decreases notably in the tales aimed for the youngest readers, 2.9% of the cases analysed. The tales written for children between 0–2 years of age deal with basic topics related mainly to the actions that the characters are involved in: food and drink, pets, dinner time, etc. However, as the child's age increases, the stories begin to deal with more in-depth themes, such as father-son love, loneliness, obedience, freedom, generosity, feelings, and even death. These aspects require the utilization of mental processes of cognition (guess, think ...), and desire (love, wish ...) in the representation of the reality that is being described. Hence, there is a larger presence of mental processes in the tales aimed for readers in the pre-operational and concrete operations stages of cognitive development than in the tales intended for the youngest readers.

Existential processes are frequently used as openings of traditional tales, essentially fairy tales. However, as shown in section 6.1, their presence is scarce in the picture books of all stages of cognitive development, as all of them are near the average rate of 1.1% of the tokens identified. Finally, the presence of verbal and behavioural processes is less important than the other process types. The analysis carried out reveals that there is a notable difference in this respect between the tales intended for the children in the sensory-motor stage and the picture books created for older children. In fact, while the use of verbal processes is ineffectual in the tales aimed at children between 0 and 2 years of age, their presence increases to 11% and 10.7% in the tales written for children in the pre-operational and concrete operations stages of cognitive development respectively. By means of verbal processes (say, cry, whisper ...), the narrator reproduces the words uttered by the main characters in direct speech in the tales intended for older children, as evidenced in this extract, taken from *Gorilla*: "'Don't be frightened, Hannah," said the gorilla, "I won't hurt you. I just wondered if you'd like to go to the zoo'" (double spread 6). This strategy is not employed in the picture books aimed at the youngest readers, where the events are expressed directly without reproducing the sources from where they come from (either the narrator or one of characters in the story): 'Is he under the bed' (*Where's Spot*? double spread 7). Similarly, while the presence of behavioural processes is inexistent in the picture books written for the youngest children, their frequency increases to 6.1% and 5% in the picture books for the pre-operational and concrete operations stages. Although they are less frequent in number than material, mental, verbal and relational processes, verbs such as listen, laugh, smile, look, etc. are also used in the tales intended for older children to represent the outer manifestations of inner aspects of the main character's experience.

At this point, I have considered it relevant to provide a chi-square analysis using SPSS in order to prove whether the absolute frequencies collected above are statistically significant and, in turn, to measure the extent of the association between process types, either verbal or visual, and the three age groups that constitute the object of our analysis. Before reporting the results of the chi-square analysis, an important limitation of the test needs to be explained. The test is inaccurate if the expected value in any cell of a 2 × 2 table, or in more than 20% of cells in a larger table, falls below 5. As the frequency of use of existential processes is low and their expected values are below 5, these have not been included within the chi-square analysis. After eliminating these, there is only one cell (6.7% of all the cells) within the behavioural process category whose expected value is less than 5 (3.5). Therefore, the results of the chi-square test are valid for establishing the association between textual processes and the age factor. As can be seen from Table 6.4, the value of the chi square is significant at the $p = 0.001$ level.

The contingency table demonstrates that the degree of deviation from the null hypothesis of no association varies somewhat in some aspects from one developmental period to another. Comparing the observed values of frequency with those which would be expected if there were no association between frequency of process types and developmental stage, it would seem that the tales aimed at children between 0 and 2 years of age produce more relational processes (32) than was expected (16). However, the tales intended for children of ages from 3–9 use fewer relational processes than would be expected from no association between this linguistic variable and the stage of cognitive development. In fact, the expected counts for relational processes are 38.6 in the tales intended for 3–6-year-old children

Table 6.4: Textual processes. Age group crosstabulation

Processes		*Age*			*Total*
		0–2	*3–6*	*7–9*	
Behavioural	Count	0	10	17	27
	Expected count	3.2	7.8	16	27
Material	Count	33	72	175	280
	Expected count	33.4	80.7	165.9	280
Mental	Count	2	29	36	67
	Expected count	8	19.3	39.7	67
Relational	Count	32	33	69	134
	Expected count	16	38.6	79.4	134
Verbal	Count	0	18	36	54
	Expected count	6.4	15.6	32	54
Total	Count	67	162	333	562
	Expected count	67	162	333	562

$\chi^2 = 40.623^a$, df = 8, $p = 0.001$

a. 1 cell (6.7%) has expected count less than 5. The minimum expected count is 3.22.

and 79.4 in the tales created for 7–9 year-olds, and the observed frequencies amount to 33 and 69 for the tales written for children in the second and third stages respectively. The characters of tales written for 0–2 year-olds need to be described according to their basic qualities in order to facilitate the young child's identification of them. Relational processes followed by descriptive attributes are principally used in these cases to describe and typify the characters.

In addition, as is also shown in Table 6.4, there are clearly differences in the use of mental processes in the tales intended for the youngest readers (0–2 years of age) and the picture books created for the children in the pre-operational stage of cognitive development. The tales intended at 0–2 year-olds produce fewer mental processes than expected on the basis of no association between developmental stage and process types. The use of these processes is clearly shown to be more relevant in the stories of the second developmental stages than in the first. In fact, the expected count for mental processes is 8 for the tales of the 0–2 year-period and 19.3 for those aimed at 3–6 year-old children, and the observed frequencies account for 2 for the tales intended for the youngest readers and 29 for the picture books written for the children in the second age group respectively. Although with a lower frequency than expected, the use of mental processes is also notable in the tales intended for children in the third stage of cognitive development, where the expected count is 39.7 and the observed count only reaches 36. Through mental processes the writer tackles emotional or conflictive topics that are not dealt with in the tales intended for youngest children.

In the case of verbal and behavioural processes some differences have been identified, as the frequency of these processes in the sample texts has turned out to be null in the tales intended for the children in the sensory-motor stage. However, these processes are used in the picture books created for children in the second and the third developmental stages. In fact, the expected count for verbal processes in the pre-operational and concrete operations stages is 15.6 and 32 respectively, and the observed frequencies account for 18 and 36. With regard to behavioural processes, the expected count in the pre-operational and concrete operations stages is 7.8 and 16 respectively, and the observed frequencies reach 10 and 17. Through verbal and behavioural processes, writers of picture books either introduce more complex structures in indirect speech or reflect some inner aspects of the main characters' experience.

Finally, concerning the use of material processes, the statistical backup reveals that the degree of deviation from the null hypothesis of no association between cognitive stage and the frequency of material processes varies clearly from one developmental phase to another in the sample texts. The literary works for 0–2 year olds produce just about what would be anticipated as the expected frequency of material processes is 33.4 and the observed count reaches 33. However, the tales intended for 3–6 year-olds produce fewer material processes (72) than expected (80.7). Similarly, the expected count for the use of processes of doing and happening is 165.9 for the tales created for readers in the concrete operations stage, and the observed frequencies reach 175. The higher complexity of the plot of the tales written for the oldest children leads the writer to use more material processes to represent the narrative reality. Material processes give the tales the dynamic character which is necessary to draw the children's attention towards the most interesting events in which the main characters are involved.

Having analysed the process types in the verbal component and statistically tested their relevance, I will deal with the types of visual processes which are used by the illustrator to represent reality. As is shown in Table 6.5, embedded images, involving action and reaction, are the most predominant of all types of visual processes. However, their frequency is above average in the picture books intended for the 3–6 year-olds (71.4%) and slightly below average for the children in the sensory-motor stage (53.3%) and the concrete operations developmental stage (62.7%). Later, through the use of a chi-square test it will be determined whether these differences are statistically significant. It seems that in correspondence with the use of material and mental processes of perception in verbal language, illustrators construct the narrative reality through images that involve both vectors of motion and eye lines. These show, as has been previously exemplified, both the actions carried out by the characters of tales and the eye contacts that are established between them.

Together with embedded images, the presence of action processes is also notable and they reach an average rate of 27.4% of the cases counted. However, the data reveal that there are differences in this respect between the different age groups. The tales intended for the children in the concrete operations stage are above average (30.7%) while the picture books intended for the children in the pre-operational stage of cognitive development are below average and only reach 17.5% of the tokens analysed. The major difference is found in the tales illustrated for the children in the sensory-motor stage, which reach the rate of 40% of the tokens identified. It seems that the tales intended for the youngest readers construct, to a great extent, reality through the use of action processes. This corresponds directly with the high utilization of material processes in the verbal component.

The utilization of reaction images is less important in the tales illustrated for the three age groups studied here. They represent 5.4 % of the cases identified and there are no differences in frequency between the tales aimed for the sensory-motor and concrete operations stages. Their frequency, however, seems to be lower in the tales created for the children in the

Table 6.5: Types of visual processes. The age factor

Process type	*Age group 0-2*		*Age group 3-6*		*Age group 7-9*		*Grand Total*	
	Abs. values	*%*	*Abs. values*	*%*	*Abs. values*	*%*	*Abs. values*	*%*
Action	12	40	11	17.5	23	30.7	46	27.4
Reaction	2	6.7	2	3.2	5	6.7	9	5.4
Speech	0	0	0	0	0	0	0	0
Conceptual	0	0	5	7.9	0	0	5	3
Embedded	16	53.3	45	71.4	47	62.7	108	64.2
Total	30	100	63	100	75	100	168	100

pre-operational stage of cognitive development. The lower frequency of reaction images in the sample texts does not imply, however, that their use is not essential to create an idea of companionship or lack of contact between characters. Tales such as *Gorilla* or *The Rainbow Fish* are evidence of this. In fact, while the frequency of reaction images is low if we consider them in isolation, their presence is notable in all the tales, since they play a key role in the construction of embedded images which combine both action and reaction processes in the same illustration.

Finally, the frequency of conceptual images is the lowest of all and they only reach 3% of the tokens analysed. They are missing in the tales of the sensory-motor and concrete operations stages of cognitive development. Only in *Granpa,* a tale intended for children in the pre-operation stage, are they used to deal with the topic of death. Conceptual images do not involve vectors of motion or eye lines and they tend to be associated, at least this is the case of *Granpa*, with symbolic values and concepts.

As for the statistical significance of visual processes in the sample text, the chi-square test in Table 6.6 shows that the results are not valid as there are six cells (50%) that have expected counts of less than 5. This is mainly due to the low utilization of conceptual and reaction processes in all the tales that form the sample texts. Therefore, there is no point in statistically comparing the expected frequencies and the observed counts of visual processes and their possible association with the age factor discussed in this section.

Table 6.6: Visual processes. Age group crosstabulation

Visual processes		*Age*			*Total*
		0–2	*3–6*	*7–9*	
Action	Count	12	11	23	46
	Expected count	8.2	17.3	20.5	46
Conceptual	Count	0	5	0	5
	Expected count	0.9	1.9	2.2	5
Embedded	Count	16	45	47	108
	Expected count	19.3	40.5	48.2	108
Reaction	Count	2	2	5	9
	Expected count	1.6	3.4	4	9
Total	Count	30	63	75	168
	Expected count	30	63	75	168

$\chi^2 = 14.625^a$, df = 6, $p = 0.023$

a. 6 cells (50.0%) have expected count less than 5. The minimum expected count is 0.89.

At this point I will examine how the age factor may influence the visual representation of the participants referred to in the verbal component of the picture books. In multimodal Systemic Functional Linguistics, the processes, either verbal or visual, are associated with participants, which are also reflected somehow in the verbal and visual modes. The main participants, restricted in number, are always referred to in both the verbiage and the illustrations of the picture books. All of the stories, regardless of the age group for which they were created, tend to revolve around two, or a maximum of three characters, one of them being the participant that becomes more prominent in the story. If there are more characters (the number can sometimes increase up to eight), these are clearly secondary and are used to create the narrative thread without depriving the main character from his or her protagonism. However, the way they are represented varies as the age of the readers increases. While the characters in the stories directed towards children between 0 and 6 years old are usually represented in their bodily totality, with all their distinguishing features made visible, in the books for children in the concrete operations stage, the use of visual metonyms (Forceville 2009) to represent both the main and secondary characters becomes a tool with a great narrative value.

The tales created for the youngest readers focus essentially on one participant around whom all the actions are developed. A little and hungry caterpillar is the only character of the picture book written and illustrated by Eric Carle. In turn, Spot, the main character in *Where's Spot?*, is surrounded by other secondary characters, such as his mother, Sally, and all the animals (a big bear, a snake, a hippopotamus, a lion, a monkey, an alligator, three birds, and a tortoise) which appear in the different double spreads of the tale to show that Spot is not in the location referred to in the verbal mode and the illustrations: behind the door, inside a clock, inside a piano, under the stairs, in a wardrobe, under the bed, in a box and under a rug. Similarly, in *Dear Zoo* the main character is the child who writes a letter to the zoo to send him a pet. The people from the zoo also acquire certain relevance as they send different animals (an elephant, a giraffe, a lion, a camel, a snake, a monkey, and a frog), all wrong choices, which are recurrently rejected until they finally send the perfect gift. The animals sent are the secondary characters that contribute to create the story. Regardless of the number of participants involved in the tales of the sensory-motor stage, the characters are represented in their totality in all the illustrations, so that the child can appreciate their different parts and can easily identify them through their basic features. This is also a characteristic of the tales intended for children aimed at young readers between 3 and 6 years old. In *Where the Wild Things Are* Max is the main character, together with the wild monsters. Both Max and the monsters are represented through full-body images. *Guess How Much I Love You* is constructed around two characters, each one sharing the same prominent role. In all the illustrations Big Nutbrown Hare and Little Nutbrown Hare show their bodies in different positions and postures in order to prove how much they love each other. The same goes for *Granpa,* where the two main characters are illustrated in their entirety.

The tales for children in the concrete operations stage of cognitive development are also constructed around a small number of characters. In *Gorilla,* the main character, Hannah, shares a prominent role with her father and the gorilla of her dreams; there are also other secondary characters, an orang-utan and a chimpanzee, who reveal feelings of sadness and lack of freedom caused by their captivity. In *The Rainbow Fish,* a selfish fish with sparkling silver scales is the main character. A little fish, other fish in the ocean and an octopus act as secondary characters and help to round off the plot of this story. Finally, in *The Tale of Peter Rabbit,* indisputably, Peter and Mr McGregor are the two main characters. Peter's sisters, Flopsy, Mopsy and Cotton-tail, his mother, his dead father, a mouse, some sparrows and a cat help to construct the adventures in which Peter is involved until he finally escapes from Mr McGregor's fields. In these tales, the characters are sometimes depicted metonymically since one of their parts is used to refer to them in their totality.

Before showing some examples, taken from *The Tale of Peter Rabbit,* I will briefly discuss the concept of visual metonymy, coined by Forceville (2009), who is aware of the semiotic potential of this trope to convey meaning.[10] Renowned cognitive linguists as Barcelona (2000) and Taylor (2002) have analysed metonymy in verbal manifestations of language. However, Forceville (2009) has studied the potential of metonymy in multimodal discourses like advertising and film. He considers that metonymy fulfils a referential function

10. Two fundamental tropes within cognitive linguistics are metaphor and metonym, defined as phenomena of thought used to conceptualize reality by means of the relationships that are established between a source and a target domain. As Forceville (2009) states, these tropes can also occur in other semiotic representations beyond verbal modes. In this way, within modality studies, the concepts of visual metaphors and metonyms have been introduced, giving way to tropes of a non-verbal nature.

as it involves a cognitive process by means of which we use an entity to stand for another that belongs to the same conceptual domain. He explains the necessity of dealing with non-verbal tropes as follows:

> If, as Lakoff and Johnson famously claim, 'the essence of metaphor is understanding and experiencing one kind of thing in terms of another' (1980, p. 5), it is inevitably that scholars investigate other modes/modalities than language alone. (Forceville, 2010b: 57)

In his several works on multimodal tropes, Forceville (1996, 2006 2009, 2010b) has emphasized repeatedly that visual tropes may function differently depending on the genre in which they are used. Therefore, it is important for the theorization of visual metonymies to consider their occurrence in a variety of genres and analyse how these create meaning in specific contexts. Specifically, in this section, I aim to explore the occurrence of visual metonymies in a picture book in order to study how it may contribute to children's understanding of visual narratives. Visual metonymies generally manipulate the child's attention towards some important aspects of the plot. As Forceville (2009: 58) states: 'the choice of metonymic source makes salient one or more aspects of the target that otherwise would not, or not as clearly, have been noticeable, and thereby makes accessible the target under a specific perspective [...].' The use of a metonymy often implies a change in salience or perspective.[11]

Although Forceville distinguishes different types of metonyms, the most common is that in which one part stands for the whole, as is the case with the tales that form the sample texts. This is precisely what happens in some illustrations of *The Tale of Peter Rabbit*. The first metonymy is identified in the initial illustration of the story and it fulfils the discourse function of introducing the main character to the reader, making a specific feature of Peter's personality evident. Here the rabbits are located near the tree trunk where they live. Mrs Rabbit, the mother of the litter, directs her gaze directly at the viewer, inviting him into the story and introducing her children as the verbal language also does through a there-construction:

11. Adopting a different perspective, Painter *et al.* (2013: 61) also refer to the meaning potential of metonymic representations and distinguish between complete and metonymic depictions of characters within their system of character manifestation. The depiction of a character is complete when there is a full-body representation that includes a facial referent. The depiction is, however, metonymic, if only part of the character's body, a shadow or a silhouette is drawn.

'ONCE UPON A TIME there were four little Rabbits, and their names were – Flopsy, Mopsy, Cotton-tail and Peter.'[12] In the illustration Peter is represented through a visual metonymy: Peter's tail is metonymic for Peter. The trope *tail* for *Peter* draws the reader's attention in a special way, since the text announces that the litter is formed by four rabbits and only three heads can be appreciated. The picture clearly reflects that the main character's sisters, Flopsy, Mopsy and Cotton-tail, do not share the same personality as him. Peter seems to be absorbed in his own world and reveals a different attitude as he does not show his head to the viewer; only his backside can be seen. Thus, the visual component seems to anticipate the rebel nature of the main character, who later trespasses Mr McGregor's garden, not heeding his mother's advice.

Another interesting metonymy, the ears of the rabbit as an allusion of Peter, is found in double spread 19. The illustration reflects that Mr McGregor and Peter are in the shed and the farmer is trying to capture him. Peter is hidden in a watering can. Only his ears can be seen. Presumably the part-whole metonymy suggests the idea that Peter is scared and, as he is aware of the risk he is running, he is trying to hide from Mr McGregor. Earlier in the story, his mother appears reminding him of his father's fatal fate when he was caught by the farmer and turned into a rabbit pie: 'Your father had an accident there; he was put in a pie by Mrs McGregor' (double spread 3). In addition, this metonymic representation puts the child-viewer in a position of dominance as he knows more about what is going on than either Peter or Mr McGregor. The enemy of the rabbit, Mr McGregor, is the only party who does not know where the protagonist is hidden (Moya 2010, 2013). Through this metonymy, Potter manages to put the child-viewer on the protagonist's side, since the main character involves him directly in the plot. In this way, Potter encourages the reader to identify with the defenceless rabbit and to empathize with him in his survival instinct to escape from his predator. This picture book was initially intended for children of the English middle class in the Victorian era. This period was characterized by strict and conservative manners in court and in children's education. In line with the moralizing literature addressed to children that Potter was familiar with,

12. Note that in the verbal component the names of the four little rabbits are displaced towards the left from Flopsy to Peter, so that the viewer can easily identify Peter with the rabbit whose rear end is seen in the illustration, represented through a metonymy.

the author, who also doubles as illustrator, probably followed the ideological requirements of the Victorian period. And, indeed, some moralistic values predominate in the verbal narrative: whilst Peter's sisters behave properly and, consequently, they are rewarded at the end of the tale with a nice supper, Peter, after having disobeyed his mother, is almost killed by Mr McGregor and ends up with a stomach-ache. However, the tale seems to be more than a story in which a character has exposed himself to a risky situation by disobeying his mother's advice. As has been observed in critical literature (Scott, 2001: 29; Carpenter, 1989: 279), Potter's voice seems to be that of a rebel in defence of liberty and natural instinct (Moya 2010). What the author may not be able to express in words is reflected in the visual component of the story. Despite Peter's disobedience, Potter's visual techniques encourage the reader's siding with the helpless, vulnerable rabbit and with his need to escape. Therefore, the narrative function of this second metonymy is to encourage the child's empathy towards the main character in the story.

Finally, double spread 20 is evidence of another metonymy, also used by Potter to further the child-viewer's participation as the protagonist's accomplice.[13] The large foot of Mr McGregor is just about to step on the little rabbit. Once again there is a metonymy that reflects a part (Mr McGregor's boot) for a whole (the old man), while at the same time intensifying the narrative tension and the immediacy of the threat. Peter is about to be stepped on by his aggressor near a small window, also reflected metonymically. The fact that Mr McGregor is reflected through metonymy gives a greater sense of tension in the plot, as the young reader can contemplate how close the protagonist is to being trapped by the adult. If Mr McGregor had been represented completely, the image, without a doubt, would offer less narrative tension and the danger would be less imminent. In turn, the part-whole metonymy, boot for Mr McGregor, is probably used by Potter to dehumanize the old man, who is depicted more as an entity of destruction than as a human being. The studs on the sole of Mr McGregor's boot contribute to representing the farmer as a dangerous man who is utterly devoid of human feelings. So, contrary to the idea of Painter *et al.* that 'a depiction of a character showing recognizable facial features would be described as instantiating more meaning than a depiction solely of the character's arm', (2013: 134) in the examples given above, metonymic

13. http://www.cybercrayon.net/readingroom/books/bp-peterrabbit/peterrabbit-09.html (accessed 30 November 2013).

representations seem to instantiate more meaning than the complete depiction of a character (Mr McGregor, in this case) would have expressed if he had been represented entirely.

Visual metonymies of the type *a part for the whole* are essentially used in the three tales of the concrete operations stage of cognitive development for two main reasons: first, to create narrative tension and emphasize some stages of the story and, second, to facilitate the identification of the fictional characters to the young child.[14] This trope has only been found in the tales of the concrete operations stage, where children have enough cognitive capacity to identify the main characters of the stories without necessarily being depicted in their entirety. The illustrator of picture books intended for younger children, however, prefers to represent their characters entirely for the reasons stated above.

The utilization of visual metonymies may also fulfil another function as they encourage the interaction of the child-viewer with the adult in various ways. Probably the kind of metonymic depiction used in *The Tale of Peter Rabbit* may lead to questions such as: where is Peter in this picture?, what is this (shoe) on the right side of the picture, and whose is it?, etc. In this way, the child will be socialized into the reading experience and will adopt an active role in the understanding of visual language. In addition, by being involved in this linguistic experience, the child reinforces his apprenticeship into the dialogic nature of language, where the mutual completion of utterances plays an important role. Thus, the pictures in children's tales do not serve to merely illustrate the stories, as they do in books for older readers, but to involve the child-viewer in dialogic interaction with the adult (Moya, 2013).

In this chapter I have dealt with the verbal and visual strategies that are available to the picture book's writers and illustrators for their envisioning of narrative reality. I have also analysed how the verbal and visual semiotic modes complement each other in different ways to express representational meaning in picture books intended for children in different stages of cognitive development. This analysis, however, would be incomplete without considering the tools available to the picture books' creators to establish interaction with their young readers and, in turn, to create coherent wholes of communication. These two aspects will be studied in Chapters 7 and 8 of this book.

14. For further information about the utilization and discourse functions of visual metonymies in tales intended for children in the concrete operations stage of cognitive development, see Moya (2013).

7 Interpersonal verbal and visual interdependence in the sample texts

This chapter aims to analyse the verbal and visual choices available for writers and illustrators to generate interaction between the different characters involved in the nine picture books selected for analysis, and also between these characters and the child-reader. The chapter is divided into four parts. In the first two sections I examine how writers and illustrators create interaction between the child-reader and the characters of fiction through language and through images. First, the mood structures and the expressions of modality used by writers to establish interaction are identified. Second, the relations of contact, distance and perspective in the visual component are explored and compared with the information that the verbal mode offers regarding interpersonal features. In the third section, I examine the extent to which verbal and visual modes complement each other in the creation of engagement in the nine picture books under analysis. The results are exemplified with extracts taken from the tales aimed at the different age groups that form the sample texts. Finally, the chapter concludes with an analysis of how the age factor may influence the interpersonal and interactive strategies used by writers and artists of picture books created for children in different age groups. The association between the age factor and types of verbal and/or visual strategies is tested statistically though a chi-square analysis using SPSS.

7.1 The creation of interaction through language

I will start this section by identifying the type of mood structures used by writers of picture books to construct their stories and establish interaction between the main characters and the young child. As can be seen in Table 7.1, most clauses are declarative throughout and reach 88.9% of the cases counted. Thus, as was advanced in Chapter 4, it seems that in the verbal component there is little that is of stylistic importance which is interpersonal and signalled through the grammar, as declarative mood structures do not necessarily induce a lot of engagement. The explanation for this lies in the fact that, while the utilization of imperative and interrogative modes tends to interrupt the thread of the story, declaratives generally contribute directly to the continuity of the plot and present information as fact.

Table 7.1: Mood structures

Categories	*Absolute values*	*Values in percentages*
Declarative	384	88.9
Imperative	21	4.8
Interrogative	27	6.3
Total	432	100

In *The Very Hungry Caterpillar*, a tale intended for 0–2 year-old children, for example, through declarative mood structures, Carle narrates the evolution of the caterpillar, from its birth when it was an egg attached to a leaf up to its conversion into a butterfly, going through different states, through which it eats all the food it finds in its path. The tale contains neither interrogative nor imperative clauses, which may have created engagement between the RPs referred to in the verbal component or between the writer and the young child. In addition, no modal adjuncts have been identified. Excerpt 1 is a clear example of the syntactic and structural patterns that are predominant in the tales that form the sample texts:

1. Now he was not hungry any more – and he wasn't a little caterpillar any more. He was a big, fat caterpillar. He built a small house, called a cocoon, around himself. He stayed inside for more than two weeks. Then he nibbled a hole in the cocoon, pushed his way out and [...] he was a beautiful butterfly! (*The Very Hungry Caterpillar*, Carle [1969] 2002)

Sometimes the declarative clauses identified in the tales act as exclamations at the discourse level. Among other picture books, *The Very Hungry Caterpillar* and *Gorilla* are evidence of this. Indicated as such by an exclamation mark, they are signals to adults reading aloud to children that writers are highlighting key passages in the narrative plots. Specifically in *Gorilla* they are used by Browne to highlight how important gorillas are in the life of the story's protagonist. In double spread 4 through an exclamation, 'The night before her birthday, Hannah went to bed tingling with excitement – she had asked her father for a gorilla!', Browne makes Hannah's interest in gorillas known. In double spread 8, another exclamation, also related to the primates, is used: '(There are) so many gorillas!'. Through it the writer emphasizes the great number of gorillas that Hannah and her companion could see at the zoo, a fact that seems to frighten her at first. At first glance, the content expressed by them does not seem to be relevant to the development of the narrative plot; rather the author gives the world related to the gorillas some special importance by using the exclamation mark. Note that when Browne was a boy he wanted a real trumpet for his birthday, but he got a plastic one instead. His picture book, *Gorilla*, is partly based on that disappointing experience. Hannah is also disappointed when she finds out that the present she is given for her birthday is a toy gorilla, as she was longing to see a real one. Similarly, in *The Very Hungry Caterpillar* two of the declarative clauses identified act as exclamations: 'That night he had a stomach ache!' (double spread 8) and '[...] he was a beautiful butterfly!' (double spread 11). These make reference to two crucial moments of the narrative drama. The night that the caterpillar had a bad stomach ache was the time that he ate the most, a total of nine different food items that helped him to grow and to convert into an adult caterpillar, capable of constructing himself his own cocoon. The end of the story focuses on the transformation of the caterpillar into a beautiful butterfly, an event that is narrated through a declarative sentence with an exclamative punctuation.

The presence of interrogative and imperative mood structures is less notable in the tales that form the sample texts. The former reach the rate of 6.3% of the tokens identified. The percentage of the latter is even lower as imperative structures reach just 4.8% of the cases counted. Although the utilization of interrogatives is low, there are two tales where their presence particularly stands out, *Where's Spot?* (0–2 year-old children) and *Granpa* (3–6 year-old children). In *Where's Spot?* most clauses are interrogative throughout and reach 66.7% of the cases counted. Interrogatives demand rather than give information and, therefore, their presence slows down the development of the plot. However, by using them the narrator interacts with the young child who, accompanied by Sally, Spot's mother, participates actively in the adventure of tracking down Spot around the house. Out of eight interrogatives, seven are *wh*-interrogatives and there is only one yes-no structure. However, all of them act, at the speech-functional level, as questions: 'Where can he be?' and 'Is he behind the door' (double spreads 1 and 2) provide good examples. Even the title of the book, *Where's Spot?*, is interrogative in mood. Owing to the young age of the children for whom the tale is intended, it seems that the writer has preferred to guarantee the interaction between the characters in the tale and the child-reader to develop a lineal plot. This way, the writer creates engagement with the young child, as this latter is directly involved in the development of the story: Spot's search.

Granpa also contains nine interrogative clauses (44.6% of the token identified), which forge engagement between the characters in the story. Through them the writer creates the dialogist structure of the tale, which is essentially based on the conversation established between Granpa and his granddaughter. The first interrogative clause in the initial page, 'And how's my little girl?', is uttered by Granpa and fulfils an introductory function as it presents the main characters in the story. The image that corresponds to this mood structure complements the launch of the protagonists into the narrative discourse. The other eight interrogative clauses are, however, uttered by the little girl. They imitate a conversation that can be maintained between an adult and a child in real life. Children tend to ask a lot of questions while adults have to adopt a passive role and provide the answers requested by their young interlocutors. As shown in excerpts 2–8, through these questions the young child becomes familiar with the topics that are sequentially introduced in the story and with the different situations that the little girl and her grandfather are involved in: the greenhouse where they are planting seeds and where the first reference is made to the word Heaven, a topic somehow related to death (excerpt 2), the house where they took shelter from the rain (excerpt 3), the beach, where the little girl wants to stay forever while she is playing in the yellow sand and eating lollies (excerpts 4 and 5), outside the entrance of the house, where Granpa is jumping rope while his granddaughter reminds him of his past as a young child (excerpt 6), a lake where they try to fish for something for supper (excerpt 7) and, finally, the living-room of Granpa's house where they watch television while the little girl, unaware of Granpa's illness, makes a plan to start an imaginary trip to Africa (excerpt 8).

2. There wouldn't be room for all the little seeds to grow. *Do worms go to Heaven?* (*Granpa*, Burningham [1984] 2003)
3. Noah knew that the ark was not far from land when he saw the dove carrying the olive branch. *Could we float away in this house, Granpa?* (*Granpa*, Burningham [1984] 2003)
4. *When we get to the beach can we stay there forever?* Yes, but we must go back to our tea at four o'clock. (*Granpa*, Burningham [1984] 2003)
5. *When I finish this lolly can we get some more? I need the sticks to make things.* (*Granpa*, Burningham [1984] 2003)
6. When I was a boy we used to roll our wooden hoops down the street after school. *Were you once a baby as well, Granpa?* (*Granpa*, Burningham [1984] 2003)
7. If I catch a fish we can cook it for supper. *What if you catch a whale, Granpa?* (*Granpa*, Burningham [1984] 2003)
8. *Tomorrow shall we go to Africa, and you can be the captain?* (*Granpa*, Burningham [1984] 2003)

As shown in these excerpts, typography[1] contributes directly to the interactive and textual organization of the tale, as it denotes who is speaking without necessarily making the character explicit. The difference in font and typeface establishes a boundary between the words uttered by the grandfather and the narrator, represented in script writing, and the words uttered by the little girl, represented in italics and with a certain curvature. The latter are also typically associated with softness and femininity. By using different typefaces, the worlds of the two main characters in the story are reflected in such a way that they are given their own identities. In spite of their different fonts, the two worlds are joined together to create the dialogue structure of the narrative and show how at certain points within the story the lives of the two characters are parallel. Thus, typography fulfils a double function in this tale: (i) it marks the question–answer interaction

1. Typography can fulfil representational, interpersonal and textual functions when used in a specific context of communication. Typography can represent ideas (a metallic font can suggest durability, for example), it can also express attitudes (a bold font can be interpreted as a warning). Finally, it can also fulfil a function in textuality as font can create hierarchical informative values within a text and signify similarities and differences between textual elements (Van Leuwen 2006; Machin 2007: 92–93).

established between the protagonists and, in turn, (ii) it gives coherence to the story as the differences in font and typeface also help to establish its structural organization.

Although with scarce frequency, out of 432 mood structures identified in the sample texts, 21 are imperatives, which represent 4.8% of the tokens counted (see Table 7.1). The picture book that contains the largest number of imperatives is *The Rainbow Fish*. Imperative clauses such as the ones reflected in extracts 9–13, all of them in direct speech, reflect the starfish, the other fish and the Rainbow fish's direct words in different narrative important moments and give immediacy to the actions carried out by the main characters in the story. The 11th extract shows the Rainbow Fish's rejection to share his scales with the little blue fish. The rest are invitations to the Rainbow Fish to join the other fish in the ocean and share with them part of his beauty. The main character's awareness of the happiness that sharing things with others brings to his life is marked by the use of an exclamation mark in extract 13.

9. 'Come on, Rainbow Fish,' they would call. 'Come and play with us!' (*The Rainbow Fish*, Pfister [1992] 2010)
10. 'Rainbow Fish,' he called, 'wait for me!' (*The Rainbow Fish*, Pfister [1992] 2010)
11. 'Get away from me!' (*The Rainbow Fish*, Pfister [1992] 2010)
12. This is my advice. 'Give a glittering scale to each of the other fish.' (*The Rainbow Fish*, Pfister [1992] 2010)
13. 'Come and play with us!' (*The Rainbow Fish*, Pfister [1992] 2010)

As stated in chapter 4, the attitudes embodied in a text, realised by the system of modal assessment, are also part of the interpersonal metafunction of language (Halliday 2004: Table 10 (6). However, the presence of modal adjuncts is low in the sample texts, especially in the tales intended for the youngest readers. The expressions of modality tend to be restricted to the use of modal auxiliaries. In *Granpa*, for example, modality is expressed exclusively through modal verbs: could, expressing possibility (could we float away in this house, Granpa?, double spread 4), can, meaning permission (when we get to the beach can we stay there for ever?, double spread 7), must, expressing obligation (yes, but we must go back for our tea at four o'clock, double spread 7), can't, marking the lack of ability to carry out an action and anticipating Granpa's death (Granpa can't come out to play today, double spread 12) and, finally, shall, stating an offer (Tomorrow shall we go to Africa, ...?, double spread 13).

Although also with scarce frequency, other expressions exist in the tales aimed at the older children in the concrete operation stage that carry either some subjectivity or emotional attitude. *Gorilla* offers some examples in this respect. In the third double spread of Browne's picture book the modal adjunct, maybe, in '"Not now. Maybe at the weekend," he would say', expresses probability and reinforces the father's lack of attention to Hannah. The modal adjuncts, *never* and *always* (excerpt 14), expressing usuality, are also used in the opening section of the tale to emphasize Hannah's father's lack of time and obsession with work (Gill 2002):

14. [...] But at the weekend he was always too tired. They never did anything together. (*Gorilla*, Browne [1983] 2002)

While Hannah and the gorilla are always involved in relations that imply positive polarity and success in engagement, Hannah and her father seem to be engaged in relations of negative polarity in which the father fails to fulfil her daughter's desire to spend more time with her. Finally, the most relevant expression from a modal perspective is found in double spread 6: '[...] I just wondered if you'd like to go to the zoo'. The invitation to the zoo is tentative as it introduces a note of hesitation or caution (Lewis 2006). Without the interpersonal grammatical metaphor[2] (Halliday 2004), I just wondered, the invitation would sound stronger. This statement serves as an indirect offer uttered by the gorilla to enquire about Hannah's desires and is another example of the verbal interactions that are established between Hannah and her substitute farther.

All in all, the tales offer information rather than demand it and, therefore, the interaction between the writer/illustrator and the young child basically consists of non-negotiation rather than negotiation of meanings. Although

2. Speech functions such as statement, command and question have both congruent and metaphorical realizations. With metaphorical realizations, the grammar works as a metaphor – as when an interrogative like *Could you open the window?* is used to make a request. One kind of interpersonal metaphor involves a first person present tense and a mental process of cognition such as *I think*. Here, the modal adjunct of probability is construed through the grammar as a clause in which the speaker is made responsible for the assessment (Halliday 2004). For further information about the concept of grammatical metaphor, see Halliday 2004: 592–593 and 634–636.

some interrogative and imperative clauses have been identified in the nine picture books that form the sample texts, their presence is low. The mood choices are mainly restricted to declarative structures and the utilization of modal adjuncts is scarce, especially in the tales aimed at the children in the first two stages of cognitive development. So far, it seems that the narrative voice reflects the events from an objective and distant perspective. In the next section, I shall attempt to determine how the visual elements create interpersonal meanings throughout the picture books by focusing the analysis on the interactive features that Kress and Van Leeuwen (2006) distinguish in their grammar of visual design.

7.2 Generating engagement in the visual mode

Now the aim is to find out whether the illustrations suggest relations of intimacy or, on the contrary, imply a certain level of detachment similar to that expressed in the verbal component through the frequent use of declarative clauses with scarce modality markers. The analysis of the illustrations shown in Table 7.2 sheds light on the visual choices made by the illustrators to create engagement. The aspects that predominate in the majority of the illustrations are offers, middle shots, eye-level angels and oblique shots, with certain exceptions that will be commented on later.

Concerning Image act and gaze, the analysis shows that there is a predominance of offers (95.2%) over demand images, which only count for 4.8% of the cases identified. Through offers, the RPs are presented as

Table 7.2: Interactive features

Categories		*Absolute values*	*Values in percentage*
Image act and gaze	Offer	160	95.2
	Demand	8	4.8
Social distance and intimacy	Close-up	19	11.3
	Middle-shot	132	78.6
	Long-shot	17	10.1
Horizontal angle and involvement	Frontal	41	24.4
	Oblique	127	75.6
Vertical angle and power	High	14	8.3
	Eye-level	150	89.3
	Low	4	2.4

items of information for the child, but do not create an affinity with him. In double spread 9 from *The Very Hungry Caterpillar* there is an offer in which the caterpillar is just eating through a green leaf and walking towards the trunk of a tree on the stem of the leaf that serves him as food. There is no eye contact between the RP in the illustration and the child-reader. The RPs become objects of contemplation for the participants reading the picture book. This is also reflected, in a way, in the verbal component where there are no explicit direct appeals from the narrator to the young reader, as all the clauses are declarative: 'The next day was Sunday again. The caterpillar ate through one nice green leaf, and after that he felt much better.'

Similarly, in *Granpa* (a tale intended for 3–6 year-old children) offers simply inform about the sequence of actions and events referred to in the story without establishing eye contact between the RPs and the young child. The RPs, Granpa and his granddaughter, continually look at each other or at something within the image (the beach, the lake, the actions carried out by the other, etc.) without any demand on the viewer to be involved in their fictional world. On the colourless picture on the verso of double spread 2, for example, the visual reader comes across a scene from the grandfather's childhood showing him singing with other children. On the corresponding coloured page, on the recto, Grandpa and his granddaughter are found singing together surrounded by toys. In this illustration, the little girl is dressed up as a nurse which is an indication of the illness progressing in the story. Granpa is seated in his armchair and holding some of the little girl's toys. Here we begin to notice that the elements connected to Granpa's illness increase; the toys themselves become sick and are covered by small white blankets.

Also in the tales intended for the children in the concrete operations stage, there is a predominance of offers over demand images. In *The Tale of Peter Rabbit*, for example, most of the images reflect the sequence of actions carried out by Peter until he finally manages to escape from Mr McGregor's fields. Sometimes the RPs continually look at each other, crossing their gazes, as is the case with double spread 11 where visual contact is established between Peter and Mr McGregor when they encounter for the first time while the farmer is planting cabbage. On other occasions, the RPs look somewhere within the image or are just walking without looking at a specific point, as when Peter feels sick after eating some lettuce, radishes and French beans and looks for some parsley to alleviate his pain. In these cases, there is no eye contact established with the viewer and, consequently, there is no demand on the child to be involved in any way beyond accepting or rejecting the offers of information made by the illustrator.

The presence of demand images is scarce in the sample texts. Picture books tend to avoid demand or contact images, especially those that tell straightforward stories (Lewis 2006).[3] However, when they are used, they are meaningful in key points of the story, since they create a pause in the action, signalling a change in the narrative structure to make the reader reflect on key points of the story (Painter 2007: 42–43). In *Gorilla*, for example, two demand images have been identified in double spread 9, reproduced here as Figure 5.4. Unlike offers, the function of demand images is to encourage the child-reader's empathy for the two characters depicted, in this case an orangutan and a chimpanzee. Although they are wild creatures, the illustrator gives them humanized features, as they convey feelings and demonstrate certain sadness in their eyes. The pictures clearly convey that both animals, by gazing directly at the viewer, are looking for his support and perhaps imploring him to release them from their cages. These demand images achieve a strong engagement between the RPs and the child, and forge the identification of the latter with the animals (Moya 2011).

With regard to the second feature of interactive meaning, social distance and intimacy, middle-distance shots predominate (78.6% of the tokens identified) over close-ups and long-shots, which only reach 11.3% and 10.1% of the cases counted. The RPs are typically shown with a certain proximity to the child-viewer. All the illustrations of *Dear Zoo* (a tale aimed at 0–3 year-old children), for example, are middle-shots. In them the animals and the crates where they are kept are shown full-length but within the viewer's gaze reach and without much space around them. Similarly, in *Where's Spot?*, also a tale intended for children in the sensory-motor stage, Sally, Spot and the animals that she comes across are shown with a certain proximity to the viewer, which generates involvement between him and the RPs depicted in the tale. Double spread 3, already described, provides a good example of a middle and eye-level shot image, as Sally, the clock and the snake inside it are depicted but are closed to the visual gaze of the child-reader.

The 19 close-ups identified in the sample texts also help to forge the identification between the child-viewer and the RPs. This type of images is essentially found in the tales illustrated for the older children. Four close-ups are used by Browne in *Gorilla*. Two of these are illustrations which show

3. From an opposing perspective, Painter (2007: 42) considers that it is not uncommon to find demand images at the beginning of picture books.

the sad faces of the two primates locked in cages (Figure 5.4). The other two close-ups, double spread 13, show the face of Hannah smiling with Gorilla. All of them communicate the way the RPs feel, and suggest an intimate/personal relationship that produces the effect of close proximity between the RP and the viewer. The viewer can see the wrinkles around the gorilla's eyes, and can even distinguish the tufts of hair on the gorilla. Through close-ups and middle shots, Hannah and the gorilla are sometimes depicted showing their feelings to the child-reader. This, of course, reinforces the interaction created between them and the viewer, as Hannah's and the gorilla's facial expressions are shown clearly and allow their feelings to be revealed. Hannah's father, however, never appears in a close-up or reveals his emotions. This has a correspondence in the verbal text, where Hannah is described as having feelings and sentiments (frightened, happy, etc.) while the father is only associated with the attributes of being busy and tired.

There are also 17 long-shots in the sample texts (10.1% of the cases counted), essentially in the tales intended for the children in the pre-operational and concrete operations stages of cognitive development. In these, characters are depicted filling most of the space from the top to the bottom of the pictures and the reader perceives them from a certain distance. The long shots identified tend to show characters surrounded by the setting in which the actions are carried out. In *Granpa*, a picture book created for 3–6 year-old children, for example, through long-shots, which represent 25.9% of the token analysed, characters are surrounded by the setting in which the actions are carried out, both within the exterior settings (beach, lake, countryside) and the interior rooms of Granpa's house (the living-room, the garden, the kitchen). As Scott (2001) states, exterior settings usually provide a high degree of contextual detail as evidenced in Figure 7.1, where colour reigns both on the recto and the verso of the double spread in a moment of greater intimacy and union between Granpa and his granddaughter. Granpa mistakes the little girl's pretend strawberry flavoured ice cream for chocolate in a colourful surrounding full of details (flowers, trees, houses, toys, etc. ...). Happiness is reborn in this centrefold illustration that shows that Grandpa does not remain stuck on real aspects all the time but joins the imaginary world of the little girl; Granpa follows the act and pretends that he is also having strawberry ice-cream. This shows the profound closeness between the characters throughout the story and the emotional link that exists between them. Similarly, in *The Tale of Peter Rabbit*, intended for 7–9 year-old children, through the long-shots identified (18.8% of the cases counted) the main characters are shown full-length and surrounded by a setting, although they are not necessarily located in the far distance. Some of the long-shots reflect interior settings: the tool-shed where Peter tries to hide himself after his first encounter with the farmer or even the Rabbit family's house in the final three illustrations where some kitchen utensils, the main character's bed and some food can be seen. Others, however, show the characters within the natural exterior background, as is evident in double spreads 26 and 27 when Peter is looking from the wheelbarrow towards the gate and later escaping from Mr McGregor; these two illustrations offer detailed foreground distant views in perspective.

As for the third feature of interactive meaning, horizontal angle and involvement, 75.6% of the angles identified in the sample texts are oblique. Frontal angles total 24.4%% of the tokens counted and they essentially predominate in the tales intended for children in the sensory-motor stage. Unlike oblique angles, which show the participants from the side lines and create a sense of detachment (Kress and van Leeuwen 2006: 134), frontal angles generate involvement with the viewer, as evidenced in the last illustration of *The Very Hungry Caterpillar* and in the fifth double spread of *Gorilla,* the latter represented as Figure 5.2. In the former, the colouring of the caterpillar transformed into a butterfly and shown from a frontal angle draws the attention of the reader in a special way, creating a strong link with him. In the latter, the toy gorilla, who has just been transformed

Figure 7.1: Long-shot. Granpa is playing the little girl's toys.[4]

4. Text and Illustrations © 1984 John Burningham. Double spread 6. From GRANPA by John Burningham, published by Jonathan Cape. Reprinted by permission of The Random House Group Limited.

into a real animal, directs his gaze at Hannah so that his facial expression and his eyes are looking at her. Even the two dolls situated on top of the chest of drawers of the girl's room and the poster of King Kong hanging on the wall are shown from a frontal view. Here, the plane of the represented objects and the plane of the illustrator run parallel (Kress and van Leeuwen 2006: 134). Both frontal and oblique angles are used in *Gorilla*, but when the main characters are introduced into the story, they, Hannah, the gorilla and the father, are depicted from a frontal angle. This way the child-viewer is encouraged to feel involvement with the three of them and become part of their adventures.

Oblique angles overcome in number to frontal angles in the sample texts. The ultimate illustration of *Dear Zoo* provides a good example of an oblique angle. In it, the RP inside the crate is not situated before the viewer, but shown from the side. The child protagonist in the tale finally receives the appropriate pet. This illustration leads the story to an end and emphasizes the suitability of the puppy as a pet. So, a frontal angle would probably have been more appropriate than an oblique view here, as it would have generated much more involvement between the child-reader and the fictional character.

The Rainbow Fish, a tale intended for children in the concrete operations stage, also offers clear examples of oblique angles. Most of the planes of this tale, 66.7% of the cases identified, are oblique, since the main character is usually shown from the side lines. He is involved in his own world, separated from the other fish, and also from the world of the child-viewer. Evidence of this is Figure 7.2 where a little fish tries to approach him to request one of his shimmering scales. Here, the big fish is depicted from an oblique angle, which generates certain distance. The use of oblique angles contributes to create the idea of isolation of the Rainbow Fish when in the initial stages of the story he does not want to share his beauty with his fellows in the ocean. In this picture book there are also four double spreads (6, 7, 8 and 10) where the author uses frontal angles, which generate involvement between the main character and the child-reader. In the sixth double spread, for example, a frontal image shows the encounter of the Rainbow Fish with the octopus, showing its accessibility to the reader and its desire that the Rainbow Fish understands the importance of sharing his prized scales with the others. The use of frontal angles contributes to signal Rainbow Fish's change of attitude. In the intermediate stages of the story the Rainbow Fish wants to form part of the fish community that surrounds him and displays a greater involvement with them. In turn, there is greater contact between the protagonist and the

Figure 7.2: Oblique angle. Approaching the Rainbow Fish.[5]

reader, who seems to be able to be a part of the protagonist's doings. Once the change of attitude takes place, the Rainbow Fish enters in to form part of the group of fish from the ocean and puts his differences aside to become one of the others, feeling a sensation of happiness.

Regarding vertical angle and power, the fourth feature of interactive meaning, 89.3% of the images identified are eye-level angles. These are followed by high angles, which only reach 8.3% of the total tokens. Only do 2.4% of the cases analysed correspond to the category of low angles. Thus, most images in the sample texts are represented from an eye-level angle, which implies that the viewer is at the same level as the main characters, and therefore he feels he can identify with them. All the illustrations of *Dear Zoo*, for example, are eye-level angles and these show the crates and the animals that are kept in them without establishing power statuses between the child-viewer and the RPs. Similarly, in *Guess How Much I Love You*, all the images are represented from an eye-level angle, which implies that the child (and probably the adult) is at the same level as the two hares and therefore feels identified with them and their competition to show how much they love each other. Big and Little NutBrown Hare are seen neither from above nor below and, consequently, there is no power difference established between them

5. Text and illustrations © 1992 by North-South Books Inc. Double spread 3. From *The Rainbow Fish* by Marcus Pfister. Reproduced by permission of NorthSüd.

and the young child. Finally, although with a lower frequency, the utilization of eye level angles is also high in the tales intended for 7–9-year-old children. In *The Rainbow Fish,* for example, eye-level angles contribute to create interaction between the little fish, the Rainbow Fish and the young child, essentially when at the end of the story the fish protagonist has learned the lesson that sharing with others brings happiness and friendship.

The utilization of high and low angles in combination with perspective techniques is a feature exclusive to tales intended for children in the concrete operations stage. In *Gorilla,* for example, high (19.4% of the cases identified) and low angles (12.9% of the tokens counted) are also used to establish interaction between the RPs themselves and between these and the viewer. In *The Tale of Peter Rabbit,* interaction is created through the utilization of eye-level angles (75% of the tokens identified) and high angles, which reach the rate of 25% of the cases analysed. In *Gorilla* it is interesting to note that while Hannah and her father are sometimes depicted from a high angle, the gorilla is the only represented participant that is shown from a low angle, suggesting the power he has over Hannah. Figure 7.3 sets a good example. The gorilla is shown from Hannah's perspective, who is scared when the toy gorilla becomes real and directs his gaze towards her. Here perspective techniques perform a fundamental role in the achievement of engagement and affinity between the RPs and the viewer. The illustrator shows the superiority of the gorilla, depicted as a huge animal, over the little girl. The gorilla is seen from Hannah's eyes as a huge and powerful creature embodying the characteristics of protection that are typically associated with fatherhood. In turn, Hannah is drawn as a small girl with whom the child reader can easily identify. Her small head contrasts with the large head of the gorilla, who is squatting in order to establish visual contact with her while smiling so as not to scare the girl. This prominence given to Gorilla is achieved through the use of low angles, which present the character to the reader from the protagonist's visual perspective as a powerful primate of great size. This prompts the child-viewer's identification with and sympathy for Hannah and her problematic situation (Moya 2011). The use of high angles also plays a role in interaction in the tales of the concrete operations stage. Most of the high angles identified in *The Tale of Peter Rabbit* usually show Peter in trouble lying against the ground, as when he is caught in the net and nearly gives up (double spreads 15–17). In this way, the author successfully manages to make the reader feel compassion for the distraught rabbit and to wish for him not to be trapped by the farmer and to be successful in his escapades.

Hannah was frightened. "Don't be frightened, Hannah," said the gorilla. "I won't hurt you. I just wondered if you'd like to go to the zoo."

The gorilla had such a nice smile that Hannah wasn't afraid. "I'd love to," she said.

They both crept downstairs, and Hannah put on her coat. The gorilla put on her father's hat and coat. "A perfect fit," he whispered.

Figure 7.3: Low angles and perspective techniques. Hannah is scared.[6]

With regard to modality, although there are notable differences between the tales intended for children in the different cognitive stages, the tendency is to combine indicators of high and low modality (Lewis 2006: 164). In *Dear Zoo*, a tale intended for 0–2 year-old children, for example, the illustrations are basic drawings of the visual representations of the RPs. The animals' poses are neither detailed nor naturalistic and they do not reflect lifelike characteristics. Therefore, within the naturalistic criterion, which determines the degree of modality of an image on the basis of its resemblance to reality, the level of modality of the images of *Dear Zoo* is low. If the illustrations would have offered more realistic details, they would have probably distracted the child's attention from the relevant aspects of the story. However, the illustrations, with their easy and basic features, can be clearly identified by the under two-year-old child-reader. In addition, the visual proximity of the pictures to the objects they represent helps young children when they decode the message, especially at such an early age when they are unable to read the verbal graphemes. Indicators of high and low modality are combined in the tales of the pre-operational stage. However, the degree of modality is

6. Copyright © 1983 Anthony Browne. Double spread 6. From *Gorilla* by Anthony Browne. Reproduced by permission of Walker Books Ltd, London SE11 5HJ. www.walker.co.uk

higher in these picture books than in the tales of the previous stage. *Granpa* is evidence of this fact. Burninghan usually shows us Granpa and his granddaughter wonderfully illustrated. The protagonists' movements and poses reflect sometimes real characteristics. Other illustrations, however, have a lower level of modality. The main protagonists are sometimes reflected through simple drawings, similar to those made by young children, as it happens in the recto of double spread 7 when Granpa and the girl are shown walking towards the sea. In the last illustration the baby in the carriage is vaguely depicted; only his smiling face can be appreciated. The little girl is pushing a baby carriage with a dog following along behind. The sun is shining and the countryside is green. The baby is not represented totally in the visual mode, only his smiling face is drawn in reference to him. In spite of this, the illustration fulfils its purpose as it successfully achieves the aim of communicating that life still goes on after the death of a close relative. The utilization of yellow and green colours, which are typically associated with hope and happiness, also support this message. Finally, the tales aimed at children in the concrete operations stage also combine indicators of high and low modality. However, the degree of modality increases in them. Potter, for example, gives Peter qualities belonging to the human world, dressing him and bestowing him with the ability to speak and express feeling. Her illustrations are not photographs, but the protagonist's movements and poses are very detailed and naturalistic, achieving a high level of modality. Double spread 23, for example, reflects lifelike characteristics. Peter is shown with his animal features but also reflecting his human-like nature. He adopts a human pose and expresses human feelings when he cries poised at the door upon not being able to communicate with a mouse that was carrying a pea in her mouth. A tear can even be seen falling from his eye. The text and image combine in perfect harmony here to bring the character closer to the reader. The entire scene communicates human feelings (Scott 1994), contradicting Nodelman's thesis. When comparing the communicative function of words with respect to the images, Nodelman indicates (1988: 173) that the accompanying text is essential in those cases in which the writer intends to transmit emotions. However, the mastery of Potter's illustrations, in part, comes from her ability to transmit not only actions, but also feelings. Peter's human appearance and ability to show feelings clearly connects him with the child-viewer, as the main character of the tale has the same feelings and poses as a human being (Moya 2010).

7.3 The interplay of images and words at interpersonal level

At this point I will reflect on the way words and images inter-relate as interdependent components to create interpersonal meaning. As stated in Chapter 4, Royce (2007: 68–69) distinguishes between two basic types of intersemiotic relations at interpersonal level: *attitudinal congruence* and *attitudinal dissonance*. While the former occurs when both text and illustrations cooperate to construct parallel interpersonal content and a similar kind of attitude, the latter, *attitudinal dissonance*, takes place when the intersemiosis of images and words leads to opposite attitudinal meanings. Royce (2007) also differentiates between positive and negative reinforcement of address. Only when there is an identical form of address in the verbal and visual modes, the reinforcement is defined as positive.

Taking these theoretical premises as the starting point, I will study how images and words are combined intersemiotically to construct engagement and interaction between the characters of the tales and the child-reader. The analysis of the co-deployment of images and words at the interpersonal level reveals that in general terms illustrations contribute more than verbal language to the creation of engagement in all the picture books that form the sample texts, independently of the age group for which they are initially written and illustrated. As stated in the first section of this chapter in the verbal component there is a predominance of declarative clauses, a high use of the third person pronouns (he, they) to refer to the main characters, and a low presence of modal adjuncts. All these features suggest a lack of engagement between the characters referred to in verbal language and the reader. This lack of engagement that the use of declarative clauses and the lack of modal adjuncts generate is somehow compensated in the illustrations by the utilization of middle-shots, eye-level angles and some frontal images, which create interaction and involvement between the characters of fiction and the child-viewer.

Although words and images seem to contribute differently to the establishment of interaction, in the tales intended for the youngest children both modes are combined in a perfect symbiosis to construct a similar kind of attitude. Even in the two tales of the sensory-motor phase where the presence of interrogative or imperative clauses directed towards the reader is non-existent, the utilization of declarative clauses with ellipsed constituents generates interaction between the characters of fiction and the young child. In *Dear Zoo*, for example, out of 26 declarative structures, eight have an omitted element, the animal sent from the zoo (They sent me a/an [...]). The child is, therefore, invited to lift up the flaps of the crates where the animals are kept in order to reveal the identity of the creatures sent by the zoo. In this way images and words complement each other to decode the message transmitted by the illustrator and show a similar kind of attitude and type of engagement with the young child. Without necessarily using interrogative structures or modal adjuncts, the writer creates interaction when he invites the reader to find out in the visual mode the information that the ellipsis hides. In most illustrations the identity of the animals from the zoo can only be revealed by lifting up the flaps of the crates where the pets are kept. In turn, the utilization of middle-shots and eye-level angles in the illustrations contributes to generate engagement between the RPs and the young viewer, as the main characters are depicted in a relatively close position and a similar status level to the viewer. Similarly, in *The Very Hungry Caterpillar*, together with middle-shots and eye-level angles, one demand image and nine frontal shots help to create involvement with the young reader as evidenced in the last illustration of the tale where the caterpillar, transformed into a butterfly, establishes a visual link with the child. The ellipsis of the penultimate clause, 'Then he nibbled a hole in the cocoon, pushed his way out and [...]', is an invitation to the young reader to turn the page and find out what happens at the end of the story. Thus, the use of suspense point in the picture books of *Dear Zoo* and *The Very Hungry Caterpillar* generates a kind of interaction with the child reader similar to that achieved by the utilization of interrogative clauses in the tale of *Where's Spot?* The contact established between the RPs and the child-reader in these tales is also reflected in the visual mode through the use of eye-level angles, middle shots, demands and frontal images.

The parallel kind of attitude found in the tales of the sensory-motor stage sometimes turns into attitudinal dissonance in the picture books aimed at older children. As has been commented in Chapter 4, while in *Where the Wild Things Are* the words describe the monsters Max comes across in wild land as terrifying creatures, the illustrations offer a different kind of attitude and emphasize their friendly and funny features, thereby bringing them closer to the viewer. In addition, as can be seen in excerpt 15, the use of the third person pronoun to refer to them presents the creatures from a distance and objective perspective:

15. [...] and tamed them with the magic trick of staring into all their yellow eyes without blinking once and they were frightened and called him the most wild thing of all and made him king al all wild things. (*Where the Wild Things Are*, Sendak [1963] 2000)

The distant perspective achieved in the verbal mode contrasts with the attitude the illustrator generates through the utilization middle-shots and eye-level angles in the visual component, which show the RPs with certain proximity to the viewer.

Similarly, in *Gorilla*, a tale intended for 7–9 year-old children, the analysis carried out reveals that the verbal component accompanying the pictures does not seem to encourage direct interaction between the RPs and the child-reader. This is essentially due to the absence of direct appeals from the narrator to the young child. In the verbal component there is a predominance of declarative mood structures (93.6%) over imperatives (2.6%) and interrogatives (3.8%). The lack of engagement between the fictional characters and the young child is also reflected, to a certain extent, in the visual mode where there is a predominance of offers and a high number of long-shots. Most illustrations are offers since Hannah, Gorilla and Hannah's father sometimes look at each other or at something within the image (a tree, a newspaper, etc. ...) without directing eye contact towards the child-reader. However, although the utilization of offers and long-shots may imply distance from the viewer, other visual devices related to contact, distance and perspective reveal that the illustrator has made choices which do create affinity with the potential reader (Moya 2011). Some of the visual techniques chosen by Browne (frontal and medium angles, demand images, close-ups and focalizations) are evidence of the engagement that is created between the RPs themselves and between these and the child-viewer in this picture book. The child usually looks at the pictures from a frontal viewpoint, which gives him the feeling of being involved in Hannah's and the primates' worlds. In addition, a notable number of images are represented from an eye-level angle, which implies that the child is at the same level as Hannah and the gorilla, and therefore feels identified with them. These features are reinforced by the utilization of demand images and close-ups, which encourage involvement through direct gazing and, in turn, create an intimate relationship with the viewer (Figure 5.4). Finally, the effect of detachment achieved by the use of long-shots is also diminished by the use of focalization techniques. Perspective techniques are used in the visual mode to present the gorilla as a huge and protective animal that fulfils a proper paternal role (Figure 5.2).

The images depicted by Browne show Hannah's vulnerability and need for her father's presence and dedication. All these aspects could not have been deduced from the analysis of verbal language alone. Thus, in the tale at hand images seem to contribute more than words to the creation of engagement between the RPs and the child-reader and, therefore, they convey a different kind of attitudinal meaning at interpersonal level.

Although images tend to contribute more than words to the construction of engagement in the picture books intended for the older children, this does not imply that sometimes both modes are combined to construct a similar kind of attitude. In *Gorilla*, for example, words and images inter-relate as interdependent components to create interpersonal meaning and make evident the different realities in which Hannah is involved: her lonely and ordinary life near the presence of her father versus the accompanied and exciting life outside the house with the gorilla (Gill 2002; Moya 2011). The utilization of interrogative and imperative structures in the verbal mode, although reduced in number, demonstrates the interactive relationship that is maintained between Hannah and the gorilla. While Hannah and the gorilla engage in direct verbal interaction, in which the gorilla asks a question and Hannah responds showing agreement, the interpersonal exchange that is established between Hannah and her real father is essentially non-reciprocal. When Hannah asks an indirect question via the external narrator, her father tends to ignore the girl's attempt to interact with him or spend time with her: 'When Hannah asked him a question, he would say, "Not now. I'm busy. Maybe tomorrow."' (*Gorilla*, double spread 2). Comparatively, the imperative clauses uttered by the gorilla are proof of the gorilla's attempt to fulfil Hannah's desires and calm her fears: '"Don't be frightened, Hannah," said the Gorilla [...]' (Gorilla, double spread 6). The lack of direct and successful negotiations between Hannah and her real father in the verbal component is also conveyed in the visual mode, which clearly demonstrates the lack of communication that characterizes their relationship. In fact, while in most of the illustrations there is eye contact between Hannah and the gorilla, Hannah is never capable of reaching her father's gaze. This gives their relationship a sense of isolation and loneliness, which contrasts with Hannah and the gorilla's successful interactions.

Therefore, the intersemiosis of images and words in Browne's illustrations makes these facts evident and highlights the differences between the two relationships reflected in the tale. Signs of affection between Hannah and the gorilla are frequently depicted in different double spreads where there is some kind of physical contact between them. In double spread 8, for example, Hannah is embracing the gorilla while he touches her left shoulder when they are in front of the primates at the zoo. Later, in double spread 13, the gorilla is kissing her before saying good-bye. While Hannah and the gorilla interact somehow via verbal and visual modes through direct and indirect interrogative structures, signs of affection and eye contact, the interaction that is established between Hannah and her real father is minimal. Only at the end of the tale, in the last double spread, does the father interact directly with his daughter, inviting her to go to the zoo and fulfilling her true desire. Here the father is depicted embracing Hannah's shoulders and, thus, showing affection to her. In turn, the words accompanying the illustration refer to her father's suggestion to visit the zoo: '"Happy birthday, love," he said. "Do you want to go to the zoo?"' This is the only occasion when the father does not fail in an attempt to make Hannah happy and establishes a direct and successful negotiation with his daughter. On this occasion the verbal and the visual modes express a similar interpersonal meaning and introduce a change of emotional attitude in the father's behaviour towards Hannah. Thus, verbal and visual modalities can also be seen to inter-relate in this tale to emphasize the distance and lack of communication between Hannah and her real father until the final stage of the story. The combination of verbal and non-verbal modes highlights the idea of accompaniment and interaction that is typically associated with Hannah and the gorilla's relationship.

All in all, the combination of images and words in the tales intended for the youngest children serves to reinforce the identification of the reader/ viewer with the main character in the story and express a similar kind of attitude at interpersonal level. The use of interrogative structures, which guarantee an interactive tone, and the utilization of ellipses in the verbal component, encourage the child-reader to see if the main character is hidden in the different locations referred to in the verbal component (*Where's Spot?*) or to turn the page and find out how the story progresses (*Dear Zoo*, *The Very Hungry Caterpillar*). The interactive nature of the verbal component achieved through interrogative clauses and ellipses is also reflected in the visual part, as there is a predominance of frontal, eye-level angles and middle-shots. The attitudinal assonance that typically characterizes the tales intended for 0–2 year-old readers sometimes turns into attitudinal dissonance in the tales aimed at 3–9 year-old children. In them he visual mode seems to contribute in large part to the creation of engagement between the RPs and the child than the verbal component. As previously stated, in the verbal component of the tales of the pre-operational and concrete operations stages there is a predominance of declarative mood structures with scarce modality markers over imperatives and interrogatives. So, as the tales offer information rather than demand it, the interaction between the creator and the young child consists of non-negotiation rather than negotiation of meanings. This lack of interaction is also reflected, to a certain extent, in the visual part, as there is a predominance of offers and long-shots. Offers outweigh demands in number, since there is no direct gaze between the RPs and the viewer. In addition, the illustrations are mainly long shots as the RPs are portrayed full length. However, the utilization of other visual devices such as frontal angles, middle-shots, eye-level angels and focalization techniques reveal that illustrators also make choices which do create affinity with the child. The child reader sometimes looks at the pictures from a frontal viewpoint, which gives him the feeling of being involved in the characters' world. In addition, most illustrations are middle-shots through which the characters are depicted within the reach of the viewers' gaze. Finally, as the characters in the stories are usually seen neither from above nor below, there is also no power difference established between them and the observer. This implies that the child is at the same level as them and therefore feels identified with them.

7.4 Interpersonal meaning and the age factor

The comparison between the choices available to writers and illustrators to convey interpersonal meaning in the tales of each stage of cognitive development reveals the extent to which age is a key factor in the inter-semiosis of verbal and visual modes in the sample texts. As can be seen in Table 7.3, independently of the age groups for which the picture books are intended, most of the mood structures identified are declarative throughout. Although the presence of interrogative and imperative clauses is lower in the sample texts, the analysis demonstrates that there are some slight differences between the tales aimed at the children in different age groups. In fact, while imperative clauses reach the lowest rate in the tales created for the youngest readers (1.5% of the token analysed), their presence increases slightly in the tales intended for 3–6-year-old children and for the readers in the concrete operations stage, where they reach 4.8% and 5.9% of the tokens counted respectively. Like questions, commands create engagement between the characters of fiction. In *Guess How Much I Love You*, for example, there is only one imperative clause, which gives the title to the tale, but it generates the interaction that is created between Big and Little Nutbrown Hares to show how much they love each other. Although indirectly, the use of the imperative clause, 'Guess how much I love you', also spawns interaction between Little Nutbrown Hare and the child-reader, who will probably identify with the little character and will join him in the competition against Big Nutbrown Hare, the adult, to show how much he can love his father.

In the case of interrogatives, the pattern observed is the opposite to that followed by imperatives as the former reach the highest rate in the tales written and illustrated for the youngest readers (12.3% of the cases analysed). Their presence, however, decreases considerable to 8.9% and even 4% in the tales intended for the children in the pre-operational and concrete operations phases of cognitive development. When used, interrogative clauses help to forge and define the type of engagement that is established between the characters in the stories. In *Gorilla*, for example, only three direct interrogative clauses have been identified. The first two interrogative clauses, 'What would you like to do now?' (double spread 10) and '(is it) time for home?' (double spread 12), uttered by the gorilla, establish a contrast between the paternal attitude and the primate's. As has been previously stated, while Hannah's father seems to ignore his daughter for lack of time, Gorilla has the girl's wishes in mind and enquires both directly and indirectly about her desires. Hannah, in turn, shows a positive attitude to the gorilla's suggestions and makes her desires explicit: '"I'd love to (go to the zoo)," she said' (double spread 6). Another direct interrogative clause does not appear until double spread 14, practically at the end of the tale: 'Do you want to go to the zoo?', this time emitted by her father. It is a question that does not require an explicit response. Hannah, at last, is invited to visit the zoo, which makes her truly happy. This interrogative structure

Table 7.3: Mood structures. The age factor

Categories	*Age group 0–2*		*Age group 3–6*		*Age group 7–9*		*Grand total*	
	Abs. values	*%*	*Abs. values*	*%*	*Abs. values*	*%*	*Abs. values*	*%*
Declarative	56	86.2	100	95.2	228	90.1	384	88.9
Imperative	1	1.5	5	4.8	15	5.9	21	4.8
Interrogative	8	12.3	9	8.6	10	4	27	6.3
Total	65	100	114	100	253	100	432	100

acts as a counter-expectancy to the lack of interaction that characterizes the relationship between Hannah and her real father during the opening and medial stages of the story (Gill 2002).

With regard to modality markers, certainly their use is scarce in the sample texts. However, some differences have also been identified in this respect between the tales intended for the youngest children and those written for older readers. In the tales aimed at 0–6 year-old children the expressions of modality seem to be restricted to the use of modal verbs and attitudinal lexis. In *Dear Zoo*, for example, the declarative clauses used by Campell to emphasize the unsuitability of the animals sent from the zoo contain attitudinal lexis to express evaluative meaning. All the animals except the last delivery are described in a negative way: *too tall, too fierce, too grumpy, too scary, too naughty,* and *too jumpy*. Only the last parcel seems to be the appropriate pet for the child and is finally kept: 'He was perfect!' (Double spread 8). However, in the tales intended for the children in the concrete operations phase the expressions of modality, although also scarce, increase slightly and the writer's attitudes to the content of communication are made more explicit. In *The Tale of Peter Rabbit*, for example, attitudinal lexis within nominal group and copular structures is used by Potter to express evaluative meaning and to establish a boundary between the protagonist's and his sisters' behaviour. Within a lexico-grammatical framework, Peter's sisters are described as *good little rabbits* while Peter is typically associated with the qualities *naughty* and *frightened*. In fact, he is the one that disobeys his mother's recommendations and trespasses in Mr McGregor's garden. In addition, in the second double spread the modal verb *may* expresses permission given by the person in authority, Mrs Rabbit: 'you may go into the fields or down the lane', after which a prohibition is introduced, which restricts the protagonist's freedom. In the 23rd double spread the modal verb *could* refers to the mouse's lack of ability to give information about the location of the gate that leads to the exit of McGregor's property ('[...] but she [an old mouse] had such a large pea in her mouth that she could not answer'). The most relevant expressions from a modal perspective are found in extract 16 and are realized by the modal adjunct, *unfortunately*, and the interpersonal metaphor, *I think*, which together reveal Potter's attitude to Peter's entrapment in the gooseberry net (Moya 2010). Interpersonal metaphors have only been identified in the tales written for 7–9 year-old readers:

16. After losing them, he ran on four legs and went faster, so that I think he might have got away altogether if he had not unfortunately run into a gooseberry net, and got caught by the large buttons on his jacket. It was a blue jacket with brass buttons, quite new. (*The Tale of Peter Rabbit*, Potter [1902] 2002)

The interpersonal metaphor, *I think*, the modal verb, *might*, expressing factual possibility, and essentially the modal adjunct, *unfortunately*, show Potter's stance in favour of Peter. The fact that the little rabbit runs into a gooseberry net where he was trapped is described by the writer as unfortunate. In this specific case, Potter seems to support the flight of the protagonist, placing the reader of the tale on his side. Following this line, the author leads the reader to identify with the defenceless rabbit and to wish for his escape from his oppressor. This clearly seems to be in opposition of the Victorian philosophy where children were supposed to be punished if they did not follow the rules imposed by their elders. Carpenter (1989: 279), Scott (2001: 29) and Moya 2010: 137–139), among others, support this idea and state that the tone used by Potter to describe the protagonist's disobedience raises the question of where she is on the side of conventionalism or on the side of freedom and natural instinct.

At this point, I consider it relevant to provide a chi-square analysis using SPSS in order to prove whether the absolute values reached before are statistically significant and, in turn, to measure the extent of the correspondence between mood structures and the three age groups for which the picture books studied here are initially intended.[7] The chi-square analysis provided in Table 7.4 demonstrates that the degree of deviation from the null hypothesis of no association between variables varies somewhat in some aspects from one developmental period to another. Comparing the observed values of frequency with the values which would be expected if there were no association between frequency of clause types and developmental stage,

7. As the expected value of imperative clauses is below 5 in the tales written for the youngest children, they have not been included within the chi-square analysis. After eliminating imperative clauses, there is only one cell (16.7%) within the interrogative mood structure category whose expected value is less than 5 (4.2). So, the results of the chi-square test are valid to establish the association between declarative and interrogative mood structures and the age factor. In turn, the association between these two linguistic variables and the age factor is significant since the value of the chi-square test is below 0.05 at 0.042.

Table 7.4: Mood structures. Age group crosstabulation

Mood Structures		*Age*			*Total*
		0–	*3–6*	*7–9*	
Declarative	Count	56	100	228	384
	Expected count	59.8	101.8	222.4	384.0
Interrogative	Count	8	9	10	27
	Expected count	4.2	7.2	15.6	27.0
Total	Count	64	109	238	411
	Expected count	64.0	109.0	238.0	411.0
$\chi^2 = 6.347$, df = 2, $p = 0.042$					

it would seem that the tales intended for 0–2 and 3–6 year-old children use fewer declarative clauses than would be expected. In fact, the expected counts for declaratives are 59.8 and 101.8 in the tales intended for 0-2 and 3-6 year-olds and the observed frequencies account for 56 and 100 respectively. However, the picture books intended for 7–9 year-old readers produce more declarative clauses (228) than would be expected (222.4) if there were no association between this linguistic variable and the age factor.

In the case of interrogative clauses, the statistical data reveal that the tales intended for 0–2 and 3–6 year-old children use more questions than would be expected if there were no association made between this linguistic variable and the stage of cognitive development. In fact, the expected counts for interrogatives are 4.2 and 7.2 in the tales intended for children in the sensory-motor and pre-operational stages of cognitive development and the observed values account for 8 and 9 respectively. In contrast, the tales aimed at children between 7 and 9 years of age produce fewer interrogative clauses than was initially expected. In fact, while the expected count of interrogatives for the tales aimed at 7–9 children is 15.6, observed values reach only 10. Through the use of interrogative clauses, the writer encourages interaction between the youngest children and the characters of the tales included in the sensory-motor and pre-operational stages of cognitive development.

Now that I have analysed the influence that age may have on the choice of mood structures in the verbal component, I shall attempt to determine how the visual strategies used by illustrators may also be determined by the age factor. A chi-square test is also carried out to find out whether these differences are statistically significant. With regard to the category of image act and gaze, as is shown in Table 7.5 in all the tales analysed there is clearly a predominance of offers over demand images, independently of the age group for which a picture book is initially intended. Consequently, the presence of demand images establishing eye contact between the characters of fiction and the young child is low in the sample texts. However, contact images are relatively more frequently used in the tales of the sensory-motor phase (10% of the cases counted) and concrete operations stage (5.3%) than in the picture books intended for 3–6 year-old children, where they just reach 1.6% of the tokens identified.

As for social distance and intimacy some differences have been identified in the tales intended for children in the three stages of cognitive development analysed here. In fact, although middle-shots predominate over close-ups and long-shots, the presence of the former becomes essentially notable in the tales illustrated for the youngest children, where 100% of the shots identified correspond to this category. These generate a certain social relationship between the RPs and the young child. However, the rate of middle-shots decreases considerably to 81% and 68% in the tales of pre-operational and concrete operations stages respectively, where long-shots and close-ups are also utilized by the illustrator to present the characters to the young child. In turn, while the presence of close-ups is clearly important in the tales aimed at 7–9 year-old children (22.7% of the cases counted), these are non-existent or scarcely used in the tales illustrated for 0–2 and 3–7 year-old viewers. The utilization of long-shots reaches the highest rate in the tales intended for children in the pre-operational stage (15.8% of the tokens identified). The

Table 7.5: Interactive features in the illustrations

Categories		*Age group 0–2*		*Age group 3–6*		*Age group 7–9*		*Total*	
		Abs. values	*%*	*Abs. values*	*%*	*Abs. values*	*%*	*Abs. values*	*%*
Image act and gaze	Offer	27	90	62	98.4	71	94.7	160	95.2
	Demand	3	10	1	1.6	4	5.3	8	4.8
Social distance and intimacy	Close-up	0	0	2	3.2	17	22.7	19	11.3
	Middle-shot	30	100	51	81	51	68	132	78.6
	Long-shot	0	0	10	15.8	7	9.3	17	10.1
Horizontal angle and involvement	Frontal	10	33.3	8	12.7	23	30.7	41	24.4
	Oblique	20	66.7	55	87.3	52	69.3	127	75.6
Vertical angle and power	High	0	0	0	0	14	18.7	14	8.3
	Eye-level	30	100	63	100	57	76	150	89.3
	Low	0	0	0	0	4	5.3	14	2.4

percentage decreases to 9.3% in the tales created for 7–9 year-old children. Finally they are non-existent in the tales intended for the youngest readers.

In terms of horizontal angle and involvement there are no important differences between the two variables analysed, frontal and oblique angles, as in all the tales, independently of the age factor, there is a predominance of oblique over frontal angles. However, the tales illustrated for children in the pre-operational phase contain a lesser number of frontal images (12.7%) than the picture books aimed at children between 0–2 and 7–9 years of age, where they reach the rate of 33.3% and 30.7% of the tokens identified in the sample texts. As stated in Chapter 4, images shown from a frontal perspective present the RPs within the viewer's reach generating engagement and inviting the young child to become part of the characters' adventures. Finally, regarding vertical angle and power, the differences among the tales intended for children in different age groups are notable. While eye-level angles reach the rate of 100% of the tokens analysed in the tales aimed at children between 0–2 and 3–6 years of age, their presence decreases to 76% in the tales illustrated for the oldest children. This implies that the utilization of high and low angles is an exclusive feature of the picture books created for the children in the concrete-operations phase, where they reach 18.7% and 5.3% of the cases identified respectively. In these tales high and low angles are used to show either the advantageous positions or the adverse conditions in which the RPs may be involved in the different stages of the story. As has been previously commented, *The Tale of Peter Rabbit* and *Gorilla* are clear evidence of this. Peter, for example, is depicted from a high angle in double spread 16 when he is trapped in a gooseberry net and gives himself up for lost. The toy gorilla of Hannah's dreams is depicted from a low angle in double spread 5 when he transforms into a real primate in order to emphasize his large size and thereby minimize the protagonist's power.

As I did in the case of mood structures, now I also consider it relevant to provide a chi-square analysis using SPSS in order to prove whether the results just commented upon are statistically significant and measure the extent of the correspondence between the four visual interactive features distinguished in Kress and van Leeuwen's grammar and the age factor. However, the results of three of the interactive features of the interpersonal metafunction: image act and gaze (Table 7.6), social distance and intimacy (Table 7.7) and, finally, vertical angle and power (Table 7.8), are not valid as there are between 2 and 4 cells that have expected counts of less than 5. This is mainly due to the low utilization of demand images and low angles

Table 7.6: Image act and gaze. Age group crosstabulation

Image act and gaze		*Age*			*Total*
		0–2	*3–6*	*7–9*	
Demand	Count	3	1	4	8
	Expected count	1.4	3	3.6	8
Offer	Count	27	61	71	159
	Expected count	28.6	59	71.4	159
Total	Count	30	62	75	167
	Expected count	30	62	75	167

$\chi^2 = 3.206$a, df = 2, $p = 0.201$

a. 3 cells (50.0%) have expected count less than 5. The minimum expected count is 1.44.

Table 7.7: Social distance and intimacy. Age group crosstabulation

Social distance and intimacy		*Age*			*Total*
		0–2	*3–6*	*7–9*	
Close-up	Count	0	2	17	19
	Expected count	3.4	7.1	8.5	19
Long-shot	Count	0	10	7	17
	Expected count	3.0	6.4	7.6	17
Middle-shot	Count	30	51	51	132
	Expected count	23.6	49.5	58.9	132
Total	Count	30	63	75	168
	Expected count	30	63	75	168

$\chi^2 = 23.641$a, df = 4, $p = 0.000$

a. 2 cells (22.2%) have expected count less than 5. The minimum expected count is 3.04

Table 7.8: Vertical angle and power. Age group crosstabulation

Vertical angle and power		*Age*			*Total*
		0–2	*3–6*	*7–9*	
Eye-level	Count	30	63	57	150
	Expected count	26.8	56.3	67	150
High	Count	0	0	14	14
	Expected count	2.5	5.3	6.3	14
Low	Count	0	0	4	4
	Expected count	0.7	1.5	1.8	4
Total	Count	30	63	75	168
	Expected count	30	63	75	168

$\chi^2 = 24.998$a, df = 4, $p = 0.000$

a. 4 cells (44.4%) have expected count less than 5. The minimum expected count is .71.

in the illustrated tales for all age groups, and close-ups and long-shots in the tales intended for 0–2 year-olds. As the tests are not valid, there is no point in comparing the expected frequencies and the observed counts of these variables and their possible association with the age factor discussed in this section.

Concerning horizontal angle and involvement, as shown in Table 7.9, no cells have an expected count of less than 5. The minimum expected count is 7.3 and the value of chi-square is 0.023. Therefore, the results related to the association between frontal and oblique angles and the age factor are both valid and statistically significant. The association between frontal angles and the age factor is more relevant in the tales intended for the youngest and oldest children than in those written for 3–6 year-olds. Frontal angles facilitate the very young child's (0–2 year-olds') identification with the characters of the stories and, in turn, attract the attention of 7–9 year-olds towards specific aspects of the plot in the tales included within the concrete-operations stage of cognitive development. In fact, the expected values of frontal images in the tales for 0–2 and 7–9 year-olds are 7.3 and 18.3 and the observed values reach 10 and 23 respectively. However, the association between frontal angles and the tales written for 3–6 year-old readers is less relevant (eight observed values) than expected (15.4). In the case of oblique angles, which are the most predominant in the tales of the three age groups studied here, the association between this category and the age factor is more relevant in the tales intended for 3–6 year-old children than in those written for 0–2 and 7–9 year-olds. In fact, the expected value of these in the tales included within the pre-operational stage is 47.6, and the observed frequency accounts for 55, while the tales aimed at 0–2 and 7–9 year-old children generate fewer oblique angles (20 and 52 respectively) than was expected (22.7 and 56.7).

Table 7.9: Horizontal angle and involvement. Age group crosstabulation

Horizontal angle and involvement		*Age*			*Total*
		0–2	*3–6*	*7–9*	
Frontal	Count	10	8	23	41
	Expected count	7.3	15.4	18.3	41
Oblique	Count	20	55	52	127
	Expected count	22.7	47.6	56.7	127
Total	Count	30	63	75	168
	Expected count	30	63	75	168

$\chi^2 = 7.570$, df = 2, $p = 0.023$

With regard to modality, as has been stated in section 7.2, although the general tendency is to combine indicators of high and low modality, the analysis of the tales show that the degree of modality is higher the greater the age of the children for whom the tales are intended. This way, the tales aimed at the oldest children show a higher degree of modality than those aimed at youngest readers. In the latter the characters are depicted without great detail and according to their basic features. The elephant of the first double spread of *Dear Zoo* provides an example. Its tail is just drawn with a curved stroke. Its head, trunk, ears and feet are represented through the use of grey colour and simple linear strokes, similar to children's pencil drawings. In the picture books illustrated for older children, however, the representation of the protagonist's movements and poses is very detailed and naturalistic, reflecting lifelike characteristics. In double spread 9 of *Gorilla*, included as Figure 5.4, Browne shows us two primates, wonderfully illustrated. The protagonists' heads and gazes are very detailed, reflecting real characteristics. In fact, the colour saturation, the illumination, and the colour modulation of the illustrations in the tale are in many cases similar to the levels used in colour photographs. This does not necessarily imply that the level of modality of the illustrations of the tales intended for 7–9 year-old children is always high. Sometimes illustrators reflect the RPs in these tales in a more abstract way. In the 14th double spread of *Gorilla*, for example, when Hannah is rushing downstairs to tell her father what happened during the night, Hannah's robe represents the protagonist. This metonymic representation succeeds at achieving a sense of speed, supported by the material process *rush*, referred to in the verbal component. Children at this stage have developed their cognitive abilities enough to understand the meaning of more abstract representations. The use of this visual technique is exclusively found in the tales aimed at the oldest children and is, therefore, non-existent or scarce in the tales intended for younger children. Browne most certainly presents the animal characters in more detail than the two human protagonists. The father, above all, is vaguely depicted, especially in the scenes in which he is focused on work, either going to work or working at home at his desk (double spread 2). Even in the illustration where he is reading the newspaper, the colours used to depict the father and the boxes of cereals are less saturated than would be expected in a naturalistic representation. Hannah, on the other hand, is depicted in a more natural way. This visual strategy highlights even further the distance that is established between Hannah and her father in the initial stages of the story and, in turn, contributes to the creation of a link between the girl protagonist and the child-viewer.

The utilization of focalization techniques is different in the tales illustrated for 0–2-year-old children and those intended for older visual readers. While in the former the use of vicarious focalization techniques is non-existent, in the picture books aimed at older children, these seem to perform a role in the achievement of engagement and affinity between the RPs and the viewer. As pointed out in Chapter 4, through indirect focalization the viewer contemplates the RPs from the perspective of another character in the story. *The Tale of Peter Rabbit* provides us with excellent examples of focalization to create engagement between the RPs and the viewer. In double spread 11, for example, when Peter and Mr McGregor meet each other for the first time, the farmer is focalized through Peter's gaze. In this way, the illustrator shows the superiority of the old man over the main character in the story. The viewer is positioned behind Peter's back and sees through his eyes or from a perspective close to it. The scene reveals the power of Mr McGregor, depicted as a big human being. In contrast, the rabbit is drawn as a small creature, with which the child can easily identify.

Double spread 26 is also especially relevant from a focalizing point of view. While the verbal component presents the facts from the narrator's perspective, as the utilization of the third person pronoun, *he*, demonstrates (excerpt 17), the visual component reflects the action carried out by the farmer in the garden through Peter's eyes. The viewer is positioned once again behind Peter's back and sees over his shoulder. It is the first time, just before finding an exit, that the protagonist dominates the situation and contemplates the aggressor with a degree of calmness (Moya 2010):

17. But presently, as nothing happened, he came out, and climbed upon a wheelbarrow, and peeped over. The first thing he saw was Mr McGregor hoeing onions. His back was turned towards Peter, and beyond him was the gate! (*The Tale of Peter Rabbit*, Potter [1902] 2002)

Finally, concerning the intersemiosis of images and words and the age factor, as has been demonstrated in section 7.3 of this chapter, while in the tales aimed at the youngest children both modes seem to cooperate to create a similar kind of attitude, their combination in the tales intended for older readers generate a certain attitudinal dissonance. In *Guess How Much I Love You*, for example, a picture book aimed at 3–6-year-old children, the interaction between young readers and the characters in the story is created essentially by the visual component. The frontal and eye-level angles used by

Jeram personalize the relationship between the child reader and the protagonists, two hares, father and son, involved in an interactive competition to show how much they love each other. In *The Tale of Peter Rabbit*, the high presence of declarative clauses and the low number of modality markers reduce the level of interaction. However, through the utilization of frontal angles, which give the child-reader the sensation of being involved in Peter's deeds, and eye-level angles, which imply that the main character is at the same level as the viewer, the visual component helps more than verbal language to reinforce the identification of the reader with Peter, the rebellious rabbit. So, in the genre of picture books, especially those which are initially written and illustrated for children in the pre-operational and concrete operations stages of cognitive development, images seem to play a more important role than words in creating a bond between the story's characters and the young readers.

8 The interplay of images and words to create textuality

This chapter deals with the way images and words are co-deployed to form coherent messages in the nine picture books selected for analysis. First, by adopting Halliday's Systemic-Functional Grammar, I study how the information is organized in the verbal component so that the tales create a coherent whole (textual metafunction). In this sense, I analyse the character placement in the thematic or rhematic spans of the clause in the sample texts and their global thematic organizations. Second, by applying Kress and van Leeuwen's Visual Social Semiotics approach, the compositional meaning of the picture books is studied in the visual mode, and compared with the information that the analysis of the verbal component reveals. Thus, aspects related to theme and thematic progression (Daneš 1974; Ghadessy 1995a, 1995b; Halliday 2004; Goatly 2008), information value, framing and salience (Kress and van Leeuwen 2006) are examined in both the verbal component and the images. In section 8.3 the combination of text and illustrations in the pages of the tales is explored. Finally, in section 8.4, I attempt to determine the extent to which the age factor may influence the verbal and visual choices made at a textual level. Specifically, I intend to find out whether the distinct developmental stages for which the stories have been created influence the thematic and visual organizations of the tales that form the sample texts. The quantitative data extracted from the empirical study are interpreted in functional terms and proved to be statistically valuable through a chi-square analysis.

8.1 Choices of theme and topic: Thematic organization of the tales

After identifying the typology of themes that most frequently predominate in the verbal component of the tales, their thematic progression is analysed in order to establish their overall textual organization. As is shown in Table 8.1, regarding the typology of simple and multiple themes, the utilization of the simple type is more notable, reaching 63.6% of the cases counted. Evidence of this fact appears in all the tales intended for the children in the sensory-motor, pre-operational and concrete operations stages of cognitive development.

Table 8.1: Simple and multiple themes

Theme	*Absolute values*	*Values in percentages*
Simple theme	314	63.6
Multiple theme	180	36.4
Total	494	100

For example, in *Guess How Much I Love You*, a picture book intended for 3–6-year-old children, the presence of simple themes is greater than the use of multiple themes. The former represent 78.7% of the tokens identified, and are especially used in utterances that make reference to the protagonists, Little and Big Nutbrown Hare, and their attempts to show how much they love each other (see extract 1).

1. I love you as high as I can reach [...] He tumbled upside down and reached up the trunk with his feet. (*Guess How Much I Love You*, McBratney and Jeram [1994] 2006)

Multiple themes reach the rate of 36.4% of the tokens counted and they normally consist of textual and experiential components. *Where the Wild Things Are* provides an example. The frequency of multiple themes (73.9%) overcomes the utilization of simple themes. In this tale, intended for 3–6 year-old children, there are 34 instances of multiple themes, formed by textual (mainly structural conjunctions such as *and, but, so* and *till*) and experiential components. In excerpt 2, *the night, his mother* and *I* are simple themes consisting of a sole ideational component. However, there are two structural themes (*and* and *so*) that precede ideational components (*Max* and *he)* or elided elements (*Max* in 'and made mischief of one kind and another'). The multiple themes identified in the sample texts function as markers of temporal continuity in the narrative structure. The structural conjunction, *and,* in excerpt 3 marks the temporal sequence in which the actions carried out by the wild things take place. First, they roared, then they gnashed their teeth until, finally, they showed their claws. Adverbial clauses such as the one that introduces excerpt 3 are also used to mark the temporal sequence of events narrated in the picture book. In the referred to adverbial clause, *and* and *when* are structural themes, followed by the topical theme *he* which makes reference to the protagonist in the tale, Max, the wildest thing of all. The recurrent use of the conjunction *and* throughout the tale creates a repetitive rhythm and favours the use of syntactic parallelism, which facilitates the young child's understanding of the story. As Nodelman points out (1988: 252), *Where the Wild Things Are* offers 'first a series of kinds of mischief, then a series of kinds of growing, then a series of days and weeks and years, then a variety of the aspects of a wild rumpus'. Later, the same pattern is repeated: once Max arrives to wild land, the wild things misbehave, and there is a series of roars, and a series of days and weeks and years, until Max finally comes back home. This creates a rather informal style, typically adopted by children to communicate ideas and establish the sequence of subsequent actions.

2. The night (theme) Max wore his would suit and 0 (theme) made mischief of one kind and another, his mother (theme) called him 'WILD THING!' and Max (theme) said: 'I' (theme) LL EAT YOU UP!' so he (theme) was sent to bed without eating anything. (*Where the Wild Things Are*, Sendak [1963] 2000)

3. And when he (theme) came to the place where the wild things are they (theme) roared their terrible roars, and (theme) gnashed their terrible teeth and (theme) rolled their terrible eyes and (theme) showed their terrible claws till Max (theme) said: 'BE (theme) still!'. (*Where the Wild Things Are*, Sendak [1963] 2000)

Regarding the marked or unmarked typology of themes (see Table 8.2), most of the themes (81.8%) identified in the sample texts are unmarked, as they tend to be realized by clause constituents that fulfil the syntactic function of subject in either interrogative and declarative mood structures. The use of unmarked prototypical realizations also corresponds with the idea of facilitating the young child's understanding of the plot.

Marked themes only represent 18.2% of the tokens identified in the sample texts. In *The Rainbow Fish*, for example, a tale intended for

Table 8.2: Unmarked and marked themes

Theme	*Absolute values*	*Values in percentages*
Unmarked theme	404	81.8
Marked theme	90	18.2
Total	494	100

7–9-year-old readers, although unmarked themes also overcome marked thematic realizations, the dynamic character of the tale, achieved by the alternation of elements in the thematic slot of the clause, requires the utilization of marked themes (35% of the tokens identified). The introduction of circumstantial information in initial position, which specifies the temporal and spatial frames where the actions carried out by the characters in the story are developed, determines the utilization of non-prototypical themes (excerpt 4). In them, theme and subject do not overlap in the initial slot of the clause. Sometimes adjuncts of manner also start the clauses of the tale (excerpt 5).

4. From then on, no one would have anything to do with the Rainbow Fish. (*The Rainbow Fish*, Pfister [1992] 2010)

5. Carefully the Rainbow Fish pulled out the smallest scale and gave it to the little fish. (*The Rainbow Fish*, Pfister [1992] 2010)

Throughout the selected stories the grammatical function of subject, the textual function of theme, and the pragmatic-discourse function of topic, carried out by the main characters, tend to overlap in the same clause constituent.[1] The analysis of the main character's placement in the thematic and rhematic slots of the clause confirms the tendency of the storywriter to make the topical entities and clausal theme coincide in the picture books that form the sample texts. In fact, theme and topic overlap in 76% of the cases counted (see Table 8.3). By following this strategy, the entities about which information is given are activated from the beginning of the clause, usually in the subject position. Upon locating the characters in the initial position, the author helps the reader follow the story; so from the start the topical entity about which information is transmitted is clearly specified.

1. In the approach adopted here the pragmatic function of topic is considered to be a discourse, cognitive and contextually-referential category, independent of special language-systematic coding, that expresses what the message is about (Cornish, 2004; Moya 2006). Thus, the function of topic is sensitive to both cognitive and pragmatic aspects that go beyond the single correlation of topic with clause-initial position or with any morphological marking. Clausal or local topics, what the clause is primarily about in a specific context of communication, are identified by their referential continuity in the text and by being embodied or subsumed within the discourse topic (van Dijk 1981; Moya 2006). In practical terms, the clausal topics of the tale are prototypically the characters about which information is given at the clause level.

Table 8.3: Theme and topic overlapping

Theme/Topic	*Absolute values*	*Values in percentages*
Theme and topic overlap	379	76.7
Theme and topic do not overlap	115	23.3
Total	494	100

The Tale of Peter Rabbit is clear evidence of this, as theme and topic overlap in 85.8% of the tokens identified. By placing Peter in the initial position, the author helps the reader follow the plot. As can be seen in excerpt 6, Peter becomes the point of departure from which the writer introduces the different actions and in which the character is involved in the different stages of the story:

6. Peter was most dreadfully frightened; he rushed all over the garden; for he had forgotten the way back to the gate. He lost one of his shoes among the cabbages, [A]nd the other shoe among the potatoes. (*The Tale of Peter Rabbit*, Potter [1902] 2002)

However, the theme/topic correspondence is not always so automatic. In all the children's storybooks belonging to the analysed developmental stages, the presence of adverbial components in thematic position is a constant, displacing topical elements towards the rheme of the clause. In this way, the point of departure of the message marks the spatial and temporal framework in which the actions carried out by the main characters are developed. For example, in *The Very Hungry Caterpillar* (aimed at 0–2-year-old children), the days of the week move the topical constituent, typically realized by the pronominal form *he* and the definite expression *the caterpillar*, towards the clausal rheme: 'On Monday he ate through one apple' (double spread 3).[2] In this way the theme coincides with the adverbial group that specifies the temporal frame in which events happen.[3]

2. In the tales analysed there seems to be a preference for proforms over full nominals to refer to a particular character in the story, as the distance between an antecedent and the current mention of the entity is short (usually one sentence) and there is a low level of possible interference from competitors. For further information about accessibility and reference in different genres, see Givón (1983, 1993a and b), Ariel (1990), Chafe (1996) and Moya (2006).
3. Carle's picture books always offer a didactic component along with an entertaining one. In the case of *The Very Hungry Caterpillar*, the child can learn various

This syntactic pattern is recurrent and favours the comprehension of the message on the child's part, since the new information is presented continuously following the same structure: (i) temporal adjunct (day of the week); (ii) main character in rhematic position (the caterpillar); and (iii) the material process (eat) and its affected participant(s) (the delicacies devoured by the caterpillar) in the rhematic slot of the clause. The adversative clause that follows this structure (but he was still hungry) also adopts a recurring syntactic pattern throughout the story: the main character in thematic position, and the relational process with its attribute in the rhematic span of the clause.

Sometimes, as in the case of *The Rainbow Fish*, a tale intended for children in the concrete-operational stage, the location of the topic in the rhematic span of the clause creates expectations and attracts the child's attention to the main character in a special way. In this tale the main topic about which information is given at clause level, *a fish*, is introduced in the rhematic slot of the clause (excerpt 7). Here, the thematic slot is occupied by the adjunct, *a long way out*, which makes reference to the indeterminate location where the fish lives. The minor clause, *not just an ordinary fish, but the most beautiful fish in the entire ocean*, although deprived of a mood element, gives further information about this entity and maintains its continuity in the discourse. A derive theme, *his scales*, further keeps its continuity still and completes the information given about the fish in the introductory paragraph of the tale. However, it is not until the second double spread when the name of the fish is made explicit to the child-reader. He is called by the other fish in the ocean, *Rainbow Fish*.

7. A long way out in the deep blue sea there lived a fish. Not just an ordinary fish, but the most beautiful fish in the entire ocean. His scales were every shade of blue and green and purple, with sparkling scales among them [...] The other fish were amazed at his beauty. They called him Rainbow Fish [...]. (*The Rainbow Fish*, Pfister [1992] 2010)

aspects of life such as science (the metamorphosis from an egg to a caterpillar and from the latter to a butterfly) by reading it. In addition, the story also teaches the names of the days of the week, nutrition (the names of some fruits), and counting up to five. Many of Carle's books also teach other conventional topics, such as telling time in *The Very Grouchy Ladybug* or animal sounds in *The Very Busy Spider.*

Concerning the thematic structure of the tales, an overall view of the thematic progression of the nine picture books analysed confirms that the constant thematic progression is the most predominant of the three main patterns described by Daneš (1974) (Table 8.4). In fact, this thematic scheme reaches 35.4% of the tokens analysed in the sample texts. *Where's Spot?*, a tale intended for very young children, is evidence of this, as part of it (46.2% of the tokens analysed) follows a constant theme progression. As stated in Chapter 5, constant thematic progression is a very appropriate pattern for children's narratives, for in this way, given information is reiterated so that the young child does not lose the thread of the plot.

Table 8.4: Patterns of thematic progression

Thematic progression	*Absolute values*	*Values in percentages*
Constant TP	175	35.4
Linear TP	76	15.4
Derived TP	8	1.6
No TP	235	47.6
Total	494	100

As evidenced in excerpt 8, the participant, Spot, located in theme position, is maintained in a sequence of yes/no interrogative clauses. The answers to these questions are provided by the illustrations, which show the different animals that Sally meets during the adventure of tracing Spot inside the house. Thus, the illustrations complete the information that is missing in the verbal mode. The child can interpret the message as: *no, Spot is not here, but a snake is here,* emphasizing in this way the complementary intersemiosis between the verbal and visual elements. The word, *no,* also forms part of the visual compositions. So, it does not break the constant thematic progression that predominates in some passages of the tale.[4] It is true that the constant

4. In addition, the answer, *no*, is a case of anaphoric ellipsis, where a part of the whole clause is presupposed from the elements that have been referred to in the previous linguistic context. Halliday (2004: 100) considers responses to questions as elliptical clauses, which do not have a thematic structure, as 'they presuppose the whole of the preceding clause'. Therefore, they have not been counted for the purposes of thematicity. As the verbal answer, no, involves the ellipsis of the previous clause (Is he under [...]?), it functions as a mood adjunct of negative polarity in which the rest of the clause is elided.

utilization of this thematic pattern could make the text too static. However, the brevity of the story (hardly nine clauses in length) and the age of the audience (between 0 and 2 years) make the constant thematic model an appropriate tool for helping the child understand the tale.

8. Is he behind the door? ... Is he inside the clock?... Is he in the piano?... Is he under the stairs?... Is he in the wardrobe?... Is he under the bed?... Is he in the box?... (*Where's Spot?*, Hill [1980] 2009)

Daneš' (1974) linear thematic progression is next in frequency and reaches 15.4% of the tokens identified in the sample texts. In *The Rainbow Fish*, a tale written for 7–9-year-old children, through the linear thematic progression Pfister places the two main characters in the story, Rainbow Fish and the little fish (who represents all the fish in the ocean), in the initial and final slots of the clause and creates certain dynamism (see excerpt 9). As the story is basically centred on few characters, this thematic scheme does not cause any difficulty for the child to follow the topical continuity of the characters in the different stages of the story.

9. For a long time he (the Rainbow Fish) watched the little blue fish swim back and forth with his new scale glittering in the water. The little blue fish whizzed through the ocean with his scale flashing, so it didn't take long before the Rainbow Fish was surrounded by the other fish. (*The Rainbow Fish*, Pfister [1992] 2010)

Less notable is the presence of derived thematic progression in the nine picture books selected for analysis, which only reaches 1.6% of the tokens identified. The reason for the low presence of derived themes in favour of constant and linear TPs is that the latter two organize the texts in a way that makes them easier for the young child to understand the thread of the story. Even the linear TP, whose dynamic character might cause certain difficulty for the young child, turns out to be an appropriate structural tool in our picture books since there are few characters around whom the stories are being developed. Only one example of derived TP has been identified in *Dear Zoo*, located specifically in the first double spread: 'I (theme) wrote to the zoo to send me a pet. They (theme) sent me an ...'. The fact that the singular, *the zoo*, is referred to anaphorically as *they* makes it an instance of derived theme; the child must infer that it is *the people at the zoo* who are being referred to. The frequent utilization of derived thematic progressions might have required inferences and associations that would have gone beyond the cognitive ability of young children. In fact, although scarce, the presence of derived thematic schemes turns out to be higher in the tales written for children in the concrete operations stage. In *The Tale of Peter Rabbit*, for example, five tokens of derived theme have been identified. Through some of them, Peter's family is introduced into the story. In excerpt 10 the entities *their names* and *his mother* are sub-themes of the hypertheme, *Peter*, around whom the story is essentially developed.

10. Once upon a time, there were four little rabbits, and their names were Flopsy, Mopsy, Cotton-tail, and Peter [...]. He was so tired that he flopped down upon the nice soft sand on the floor of the rabbit-hole and shut his eyes. His mother was busy cooking; she wondered what she had done with his clothes. It was the second little jacket and pair of shoes that Peter had lost in a fortnight! (*The Tale of Peter Rabbit*, Potter [1902] 2002)

The constant, linear and, to a lesser extent, the derived thematic progressions identified are continually altered throughout the tales that form the sample texts. In fact, as shown in Table 8.4, 47.6% of the tokens analysed do not follow a clear thematic scheme. The reasons are of a different nature. Sometimes the absence of a defined thematic progression is determined by (i) the insertion of different characters alternating in the initial slot of the subsequent clauses. *Dear Zoo* is evidence of this fact. In this tale the linear thematic progression typically used by Campbell is often altered by the recurrent reference made to the different characters in the story: the child protagonist (I), the people at the zoo (they) and the animals dispatched on eight different occasions (he) (excerpt 11). Therefore, although some fragments that follow a constant, derived or linear progression are found, in its totality the tale does not follow a defined thematic pattern due to the alternating nature of the elements that occupy the initial position of the clause. The variation in the informative elements that occupy the initial slot of the clause lends dynamism to the story without adding too much difficulty to the understanding of the plot. In turn, it goes in consonance with the interactive and dialogic structure of the tale:

11. So they (theme, the zoo) sent me a... [Illustration] He (theme, the animal) was too naughty! I (theme, the child protagonist in the story) sent him back. (*Dear Zoo*, Campbell [2007] 1982)

Other times, as is the case of *Guess How Much I Love You*, a picture book written for 3–6 year-old children, the constant and linear thematic patterns utilized by Jeram are often broken by: (ii) the direct appeals by the narrator to the hearer (nothing could be further than the sky); (iii) by the presence of an imperative clause with a mental process in the initial slot of the clause (guess how much I love you); and finally (iv) by the use of circumstantial expressions that refer to the amount of love the characters have for one another (excerpt 12).

12. 'This much,' said Little Nutbrown Hare [...]; 'Hmm, that is a lot,' thought Little Nutbrown Hare; '[...] Oh, that's far,' said Big Nutbrown Hare [...]. (*Guess How Much I Love You*, McBratney and Jeram [1994] 2006)

There are another three reasons why the thematic progressions of the tales are sometimes altered. In *The Rainbow Fish*, for example, a tale created for 7–9-year-old children, the majority of clauses do not follow a thematic progression defined according to Daneš' model (65.5% of the tokens analysed). This is due, in part, (v) to its dialogic nature, which requires the presence of reporting verbs and direct interrogative and imperative structures (see excerpt 13). This fact accentuates the interactive nature that is established between the fictitious characters in the tale and amplifies the variety of elements that can be found in thematic position. The questions used, the imperatives directed towards the protagonist, as well as the rest of the fish that live in the ocean, the alternation of characters or aspects related to them in the discourse scene, etc. augment the variation of the elements in thematic position, and at the same time bring greater dynamics to the narration. In addition, as is shown in excerpt 14, (vi) the use of adjuncts of manner in the initial position moves the topical themes to the rhematic slots of the clause and, in turn, diminishes the possibilities of adhering the textual organization of the tale to any of the thematic progressions identified by Daneš.

13. What good t(theme) were the dazzling, shimmering scales with no one (theme) to admire them? Now he (theme) was the loneliest fish in the entire ocean. One day (theme) he poured out his troubles to the starfish. 'I really am beautiful. Why (theme) doesn't anybody like me' [...] 'Come on (theme), Rainbow Fish,' they (theme) called. 'Come and play (theme) with us!' 'Here (theme) I come,' said (theme) the Rainbow Fish and, happy and a splash (theme), he swam off to join his friends. (*The Rainbow Fish*, Pfister [1992] 2010)

14. Carefully (theme) the Rainbow Fish pulled out the smallest scale and gave it to the little fish. (*The Rainbow Fish*, Pfister [1992] 2010)

Finally, (vii) perhaps the main reason why the constant and linear thematic progressions often used by writers of picture books are interrupted, is concerned with the presence of circumstances of place and essentially time in thematic positions. Sometimes circumstances of place and time, such as *on Tuesday, in the middle of the night, out of the egg* (*The Very Hungry Caterpillar*), *then all around from far away across the world* (*Where the Wild Things Are*), etc., are utilized to mark the spatial frame and temporal sequence of the actions carried out by the main characters. The use of these circumstances preceding the main characters in the initial position of the clause gets rid of any possibility of a defined thematic progression.

In any case, the analysis of the thematic progression of the picture books reveals that the combination of the linear and constant schemes in the same story seems to be a structural pattern commonly used in the tales made for the different developmental stages of cognitive development analysed here. Through them, the main characters occupy the most important positions of the English clause, the beginning and the end, making them accessible to the young child who is still struggling with the difficulties that understanding written code may create.

8.2 Compositional meaning of the illustrations

After having analysed the textual aspects of the nine picture books that form the sample texts, I will now focus the attention of the study on their compositional characteristics in order to find out how the illustrations contribute to their general organization. As stated in Chapter 5, compositional meaning is essentially concerned with the organization of the RPs within an image and it involves features such as the distribution of information, framing and salience.

With regard to the distribution of given and new elements in the tales aimed at 0–2 year-old children, the three picture books included within this age-group follow a prototypical information pattern; given plus new. In this way, while the left part of the illustrations tends to present information that could be considered familiar to the reader (Kress and van Leeuwen 2006), the right-hand side is reserved for the unknown elements. *Dear Zoo* serves as an example to demonstrate this tendency. In the eight double spreads of this picture book, a clearly repetitive information sequence is followed through the verbal and visual elements. In the first double spread, both the verso and the recto introduce new information. The verso of the first page opens with unknown information: 'I wrote to the zoo to send me a pet. They sent me an [...]'. The right hand side of the double spread also offers new elements: (i) an illustration where the animal sent from the zoo can be seen; (ii) a written part that describes its negative characteristics: *He was too big!;* (iii) and the final decision made by the child protagonist to send the animal back.

From the second to the eighth double spread the information pattern followed responds to the prototypical given plus new tendency adopted in the English language. In the aforementioned illustrations the verbal component on the left-hand side presents information that could be considered familiar to the reader (the people at the zoo), already introduced in the first double spread: *So they sent me a [...].* The illustrations on the right-hand side and the verbal elements placed beneath it, however, introduce new information: the different animal sent from the zoo, his unsuitable features and the decision to send him back again: 'He was too grumpy! I sent him back' (double spread 4).[5] Thus, the child will probably perceive the visual material in the way it is presented by the artist, that is, from the given plus new progression represented in western writing cultures as left-page to right-page sequencing. From the second to the last double spread, the same pattern of structure and design is employed since in all of them, the recto, the right-hand side, shows the young child a new animal whose identity has be to be revealed by lifting up the flaps of the crate where it is kept. On the verso, the left-hand side of the double spread, only written language is offered. This repetitive pattern is a constant throughout practically the whole story and guarantees its temporal sequence. See further discussion in section 8.3.

The unmarked information pattern adopted in the tales intended for the youngest children does not necessarily correspond to the tendency identified in the stories illustrated for 3–6-year-old children. In the latter, the distribution of information in the illustrations sometimes adheres to a marked information sequence, since the visual message starts with new information rather than known elements. In *Granpa*, for example, the left-hand sides of the first double spreads contain new information. In the first single spread, Granpa and his granddaughter are introduced into the discourse scene. The little girl is running towards her granddad, who is waiting for her with his

5. http://www.slideshare.net/lisibo/querido-zoo (page 9, accessed 30 November 2013).

Figure 8.1: Singing together.[6]

arms open to embrace her. In the first double spread, the two characters are depicted on the right-hand side while the left-hand side presents some garden tools which introduce the activity which the old man and the little girl are doing; planting seeds in what might be a greenhouse. In Figure 8.1, the left-hand side of the double spread presents once again new informational elements; the little girl's friends who are singing a song 'One man went to mow, went to mow a meadow ...' The right-hand side of this double spread, however, shows Granpa and his granddaughter playing and singing together.

So, the recto (right-hand side) and the verso (left-hand side) of the two single pages and 14 double spreads of this picture book do not seem to follow the given plus new information pattern identified in the tales intended for children in the sensory-motor stage. Rather, they fulfil a different function: to distinguish between the past and the present. The recto tends to be reserved for the illustrations that are somehow connected to Granpa's past and the verso is used to represent the present moments that the old man and the girl protagonist share when they are together until Granpa passes away. Similar cases in which moments from the past are reflected on the left-hand side of the double spreads have been found in 12 other illustrations. However, this general tendency is broken on two occasions. In double spread 13, for example, on the recto Granpa and the girl are watching a cartoon programme on television. This depicts a present moment. The verso, however, does not

6. Text and Illustrations © 1984 John Burningham. Double spread 2. From *Granpa* by John Burningham, published by Jonathan Cape. Reprinted by permission of The Random House Group Limited.

make reference to the past, as could be expected from the general pattern adopted throughout the tale, but to a future plan; 'Tomorrow shall we go to Africa ...?' A ship in motion is depicted in the illustration. In addition, in double spread 10 where the protagonists are involved in the adventure of fishing, both the recto and the verso of the composition make reference to real or imaginary moments of the present time: 'If I catch a fish, we can cook it for supper. What if you catch a whale, Granpa?'

The tales illustrated for 7–9 year-old children do not follow an unmarked given plus new information sequence in the visual component. In *The Rainbow Fish*, for example, although seven illustrations adhere to the prototypical information tendency of given plus new elements, there are also five double spreads that break this unmarked pattern. In double spreads 4–10, the left-hand side is usually occupied by a known entity, the Rainbow Fish, previously introduced in the preceding images of the tale. After him, some new creatures that belong to the maritime world are introduced: the fish that swims away from the Rainbow Fish (double spread 4), the star fish to whom Rainbow Fish pours out his troubles (double spread 5), the octopus that gives advice to the main character (double spreads 6–8), and the little fish again in his second attempt to get a shining scale (double spreads 9 and 10). However, the first illustration, which introduces the main character to the reader, logically offers new information. The second and third double spreads first offer new elements, as their left-hand sides present new characters, which have not been introduced in the first illustration (the other fish in the ocean that were amazed by the beauty of the Rainbow Fish and a little blue fish that dared to ask the Rainbow Fish for one of his shining scales). Following these entities, the Rainbow fish appears on the right hand side of the double spreads, as if he was a new information element. This marked pattern is followed as well in double spreads 11 and 12, on which the left-hand side is occupied by an unknown fish, specifically, the fish of the ocean that are receiving one of the Rainbow Fish's glittering scales. The protagonist here is depicted in the centre of the composition and surrounded by other fish.

Framing is another aspect of the compositional metafunction. As stated in Chapter 5, it allows for two different possibilities; either images spread over the whole composition (thus the only limit is imposed by the space limitations of the page) or the illustration is limited by a frame (which is marked by a line or by white space). According to Kress and van Leeuwen (2006), the absence of frames is an invitation to the viewer to enter the world of the RPs. Frames, however, generate a sense of detachment between the picture and the reader (Moebius, 1986: 141; Nodelman, 1988: 51; Nikolajeva and Scott, 2001: 62). In the tales intended for children in the sensory-motor stage, all the illustrations are unframed and let the viewer see the stories from the inside as if he was a participant in the events being narrated. In *Dear Zoo*, the animals sent to the child protagonist are presented within frames, as they are kept in their different crates. However, the child-reader is given the chance to open the packing boxes by lifting up their different flaps or doors. This allows the animals to be presented as unframed, suggesting certain proximity between them and the child-reader. Every animal that is rejected is closed back in its crate until a new parcel arrives. While the use of frames is an indication of social distance between the RPs and the young child, the absence of frames brings their worlds closer. When the animals arrive and are sent back, they are presented in their framed enclosures. However, once their identities are revealed, they are shown outside frames and close to the viewer.

This tendency is partially broken in the tales illustrated for 3–6 year-old children. In *Granpa* there are no frames. The protagonists offer a story that may belong to the world of reality in which the child belongs. The death of a grandfather, whether we like or not, is a reality we have to face in our daily lives and the absence of frames suggests an invitation to the viewers to become part of the story, or at least to accept the world described in the tale as likely to happen in their own lives. However, in the other two picture books included within this age group, framed illustrations are used to fulfil different functions. Sometimes framing is used to give movement and dynamism to the stories. This is the case of *Guess How Much I Love You*. Most illustrations in this picture book are unframed, which is once more an indication of involvement between the RPs and the young child. The lack of frames creates an intersemiotic compositional cooperation between the visual and verbal modes, which mesh with each other and give the tale a sense of visual and written unity. However, in some illustrations, of which Figure 8.2 below is the most representative, Little Nutbrown Hare is surrounded by a series of circular enclosures, generally with a tint of blue. These undefined circular shapes generate certain detachment, but essentially they show the main character involvement in a series of actions, which give dynamism to the tale. The use of different illustrations in the same double spread speeds up the rhythm of the narration as different actions are depicted within the same visual composition. Little Nutbrown Hare is represented alone hopping up and down, depicting movement in a simultaneous succession.

This sequence of pictures shows moments, that are disjunctive in time but perceived as belonging together, in a clearly defined order (Nikolajeva and Scott 2001; 140). In this case, the exemplification of Big and Little Nutbrown Hares' love is not made through body parts alone, as it was the case in the previous illustrations, but with the whole body. Little Nutbrown Hare is represented visually as are the material processes, hop and bounce. However, the meaning of *as high as I can hop* cannot be deduced from the text alone; the illustration exemplifies and clarifies the extension of the jump, establishing in this way a complementary relationship with the text. Thus, the pictures complete the gaps left by the verbal component.

Other times framing, or rather, the lack of framing, is utilized to introduce the reader to the world of dreams and fantasy. In *Where the Wild Things Are* the framed illustrations identified at the beginning and end of the tale when Max is located in the confines of his room mark the boundary between reality and the magic he lives in when he becomes a wild monster. When Max enters into wild land, he lets his wild instincts come out and there is no need to limit his freedom. Then, the illustrations are unframed. Only when he decides to come back home and leave the wild things, does

Figure 8.2: Little Nutbrown Hare is bouncing up and down.[7]

7. Text © 1994 Sam McBratney. Illustrations © 1994 Anita Jeram. Double spread 8. From *Guess How Much I Love You* written by Sam McBratney, illustrated by Anita Jeram. Reproduced by permission of Walker Books Ltd, London SE11 5HJ www.walker.co.uk

the illustrator use frames once again to mark the boundaries of Max's room and let the reader know that the protagonist has come back to reality.

Finally, the use of framing is accentuated even further in the tales intended for children in the concrete operations stage, where framed illustrations are essentially utilized to convey an idea of disconnection between the RPs and the young child. Although only one illustration has been identified in *The Rainbow Fish* in which the main character is surrounded by dim, circular enclosures, in the other two tales included within this stage, *The Tale of Peter Rabbit* and *Gorilla,* almost all the illustrations are enclosed either in rectangular shapes or in well-established lined frames. In the case of *Gorilla,* there are even two double spreads where Browne uses double frames to emphasize the sadness of the gorillas and the chimpanzees at the zoo, probably caused by their lack of freedom. They are depicted within their cages and behind bars. Figure 8.3 provides a good example of double framing. Together with the thickly drawn square that frame the composition, the bars that separate the apes from Hannah and the gorilla create another enclosure that moves the animals even further away from the viewer's gaze.

Regarding salience, the third feature of the compositional metafunction, in all the tales that form the sample texts, illustrators use size, colour contrast and saturation, sharpness of focus and foreground locations to give the main characters more prominence than secondary participants, who are always

Figure 8.3: Hannah and the gorilla at the zoo.[8]

8. Copyright © 1983 Anthony Browne. Double spread 8. From *Gorilla* by Anthony Browne. Reproduced by permission of Walker Books Ltd, London SE11 5HJ. www.walker.co.uk

subservient to the former and placed in less relevant positions. However, a difference has been found in this respect between the tales intended for the youngest readers and those illustrated for 3–9 year-old children, where the number of details, which construct the setting, increase considerably. In *Dear Zoo,* a tale intended for children in the sensory-motor stage, for example, there are no visual elements in the background. Therefore, the animals and their packing boxes are the only visual participants that receive prominence. They are placed in the centre of the right hand side of the double spreads. The crates receive the greatest saturation and contrast of colours, essentially reds, browns, greens, yellows and oranges. The rest of the double spreads are characterized by the absence of colour, in white, which separates the verbal from the visual components.

In the tales intended for children in the pre-operational and concrete-operations stages, the main characters are also placed in the foreground rather than in the background, which is occupied by the secondary elements that form the setting. Like the tales aimed at children in the sensory-motor stage, the salience given to the RPs is achieved by the use of colour and size techniques, as they are usually illustrated in more vivid colours and with a larger size than the elements in the background. In *Guess How Much I Love You,* a picture book aimed at 3–6 year-old readers, for example, the size of the hares in relation to the landscape is nearly human and sometimes disproportionate. The size of the hares tends to be the same as that of the trees, which are depicted as mature. In Figure 8.4, the height of the hares seems to be exactly the same as that of the tree depicted. The tree and the hares, representing a strong diagonal line, create vectors and a sense of parallelism between both participants. Both the animals and the tree imply movement. The hares are depicted in a stronger brown colour than the tree. In this way, the reader's attention is focused on the hares rather than on the tree. Both hares are always placed in the foreground; they have greater salience than the rest of the elements in the landscape, which are always in the background. Apart from locative circumstances relating to the natural world, such as hills, rivers, butterflies, mushrooms, and large trees, the visual elements, which in particular capture the child's attention, are without doubt the two hares, father and son and their brown colour (especially the father, who stands out for his almost human size and large ears).

Despite the prominence given to the main characters in this picture book, the elements of the background are also depicted in detail and fulfil a more important function in the development of the plot than in the tales

Figure 8.4: The Hares and the tree.[9]

of the sensory-motor stage, where secondary elements are practically missing. In fact, in this picture book, the elements of the background are also used, together with the parts of the hares' body, to quantify love. From the tenth illustration onwards the body becomes unimportant in regard to the transmission of feelings. Rather, from now on, other elements, such as the landscape, the river, the path, the hills and the moon, are taken into account to describe the hares' love for each other. Consequently, the visual elements add to the verbal, since we can also see small houses, trees, roads and a few bushes, not just the river and the hills mentioned verbally by the main characters. The change of alternate settings in this tale gives a dynamic character to the narrative and, in turn, introduces temporal and causal relations. When Little Nut Brown Hare feels sleepy at the end of the story, the green colour that accompanies most of the initial and medial illustrations fades and gives way to dark colours, which suggest that the day is over and it is time to go to bed. The moon depicted on top of the visual composition also contributes to announce the passage from day to night.

Similarly, in *The Rainbow Fish*, a tale intended for children in the concrete-operations stage, size, colour contrast and saturation and the

9. Text © 1994 Sam McBratney. Illustrations © 1994 Anita Jeram. Double spread 7. From *Guess How Much I Love You* written by Sam McBratney, illustrated by Anita Jeram. Reproduced by permission of Walker Books Ltd, London SE11 5HJ www.walker.co.uk

location of the main character in the foreground of the visual compositions give Rainbow Fish more prominence than the rest of the fish that live in the ocean and other elements that form the setting. As can be seen in Figure 8.5, Rainbow Fish's sparkling and shimmering scales make him the most beautiful creature in the ocean. Size, colour contrast and saturation (glittering scales) are used to give the Rainbow Fish the salience his role as main character requires. In the first illustration, the vivid and varied colours of the Rainbow Fish contrast with the pale colour of the ocean, which is made up of duller and less striking tones. From the second to the fourth illustration, the protagonist's richness of colour makes him stand out from the rest of the fish that admire the beauty of his scales, all of whom are enveloped in grey tones similar to the tones in the background, the marine plants and the marine floor. In the fifth illustration, where the Rainbow Fish encounters a starfish, the colour contrast and tone of both animals stand out from the marine background that surrounds them. Here, the main character's importance is obtained visually by his greater size. On the contrary, in illustrations

Figure 8.5: Rainbow Fish and its sparkling scales.[10]

10. Text and Illustrations © 1992 by North-South Books Inc. Double spread 2. From *The Rainbow Fish* by Marcus Pfister. Reproduced by permission of NorthSüd.

6 and 7, a new animal, an octopus of great dimensions, captures the viewer's attention due to its great size. The size of the octopus gives this character a special prominence. In fact, the text announces that the Rainbow Fish needs his advice to solve his problem: all of the fish move away from him when he gets close to them. In spite of the octopus' great size, the importance of the Rainbow fish is still evident in the visual composition, given his colour contrast and saturation. In fact, in illustration 8, the Rainbow Fish once more acquires the maximum prominence, setting him apart from the bluish ink that metonymically represents the octopus. Also, the octopus disappears immediately after having advised the Rainbow Fish to give one of his scales to every fish in the ocean. In the following illustrations (9-12), size, colour contrast and saturation all play a key role in the assignation of prominence to the main character, generally focalized and located in the foreground of all the images.

Although all these compositional features contribute to give the Rainbow Fish the status of protagonist in the story, colour is, without doubt, the feature that is most utilized by Pfister to emphasize his beauty, already announced from the first double spread in the verbal component (see except 7). However, and this makes a difference between the tales intended for 0–6-year-old children and the tales illustrated for 7–9-year-old readers, colour also plays an additional role in the picture books intended for children in the concrete-operations stage of cognitive development. In these, colour is also used to establish either links or lack of contact between characters. *The Rainbow Fish* provides a good example of the double function of colour in the picture books intended for the oldest readers. At the beginning of the tale Rainbow Fish's shimmering scales make him stand out over the other creatures in the ocean and establish a contrast between him and his neighbours. However, after hearing the advice of the big octopus, the Rainbow Fish learns to share his beautiful scales with the rest of the fish and is finally admitted as a member of the marine community. The Rainbow Fish loses his colour contrast and saturation and goes on to acquire a similar prominence to the rest of the fish in the ocean. The colour in the final illustrations (see Figure 8.6 as an example) continues to play a determinant function as it creates links between the Rainbow Fish and the other secondary characters. The Rainbow Fish is like the rest of the fish and is invited to play with them. He can now stop feeling alone after having shared his beauty with the rest of his fellow fish. Also, now, one of the fish stands out for its yellow colour with respect to the others. This detail creates a link between him and the

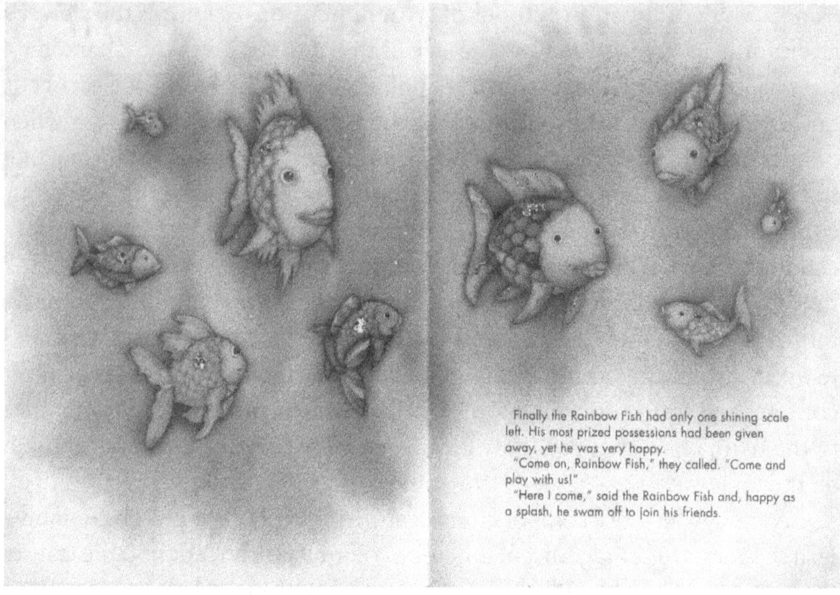

Figure 8.6: Sharing shimmering scales with the other fish.[11]

Rainbow Fish, who now has some shiny scales and prominent, yellow lips. The yellow colour of the lips of the Rainbow Fish matches with the colour of the body of the yellow fish. Perhaps our protagonist has not just found a group of friends, but love as well.

8.3 The synergy of images and words at textual level

In sections 8.1 and 8.2 I have dealt with the thematic organization and informational progression of the nine tales that form the sample texts and also aspects related to information value, framing and salience in the illustrations. Now the co-deployment of words and illustrations to convey textual meaning will be explored. The comparison of the strategies used by the illustrator with the corresponding verbal choices made by the writer of the stories will shed light on the way visual and verbal resources contribute to the overall coherence of the tales. In line with Kress and van Leeuwen

11. Text and Illustrations © 1992 by North-South Books Inc. Double spread 12. From *The Rainbow Fish* by Marcus Pfister. Reproduced by permission of NorthSüd.

(2006) and Royce (2007), in this section I will analyse the main principles of meaning potential within the textual metafunction that are relevant to the study of the combination of verbal and non-verbal modes in multimodal artefacts. Essentially, aspects related to the information value, framing and salience of images are considered and compared with the textual organization of the picture books that form the sample texts. As Royce (2007: 73) points out, the verbal and visual components on the page need to be arranged in such a way that they convey a sense of unity and cooperation to the overall message transmitted to the reader.

The study of the images and their relationship with the text clearly reveals that in the tales intended for the youngest readers (0–2-year-old children) text and illustrations complement each other so that the tales are easy to understand, and in turn, attractive to the young child. The verbal and visual choices made by writers and illustrators regarding textual and compositional meaning help the child to identify the main characters in the stories and follow the development of their actions. Verbal and visual modes are co-deployed in such a way that they create an overall effect of compositional intersemiotic complementarity (Royce 2007: 103), as the two modes blend with each other in order to give special prominence to the main characters in the stories. The textual analysis of *Dear Zoo* reveals that there is a complete association between the point of departure of the clause as message, the theme, and the three main characters in the story, the child-protagonist (*I*), his friends at the zoo (*they*), and the animals dispatched from the zoo. The early age of the children for whom the tale is intended determines its thematic and topical patterning, mainly organized in simple and linear thematic structures. These textual patterns, which prompt the utilization of syntactic parallelism and recurrent structures, can only be achieved thanks to the intersemiosis of verbal and visual elements. The gaps of the rhematic slots of the clauses located on the verso of the double spreads (So they sent me a [...]) are filled in by the RPs depicted in the visual mode, which provide the missing information. This is how the visual mode contextualizes the verbal part, adding newness and definitiveness to the story. So, words and images contribute differently to the overall organization of the tale. The shift of the narrative course from words (they sent me a/an [...].) to images (the animals themselves depicted in the illustrations) takes place every time a new animal is sent from the zoo and makes a perfect symbiosis to facilitate the understanding of the plot by the very young child. Unable to recognize the written graphemes, he can find out the identity of the animals sent by the zoo from the illustrations. In addition, the missing information in verbal language and the necessity to find it in the visual mode encourages the child to establish a dialogic interaction with the adult. The role of the young child is to turn the multimodal text into a dialogic linguistic experience with two participants; the caregiver who reads the story and the child himself, who has to visualize and identify the different animals dispatched from the zoo (Moya 2011).

Thus, the animals from the zoo are given special prominence both in the verbal language, where they are omitted by the use of suspense points in rhematic position, and in the visual mode, where they and their crates are given the greater prominence through colour contrast and saturation. In turn, the adoption of an unmarked information pattern in the visual mode (given plus new) contributes to making the understanding of the plot easy for the young child (see section 8.2). Children under two find some difficulty in decoding written information but tend to be sophisticated readers of visual texts. At this age, it is easier for a young child to understand a written passage if it is also visualized.

Broadly speaking, the textual patterns found in the tales intended for the children in the sensory-motor stage also seem to be adopted in the textual organization of the picture books aimed at children in the pre-operational stage of cognitive development. Theme and topic overlapping and the utilization of constant thematic progression contribute to place the main characters in the initial slot of the clause. In turn, these textual patterns seem to have a correspondence with the visual organization of the tales, as through the use of colour, size and focalization techniques the main characters are given more space and prominence than the other pictorial elements. Thus, the main characters tend to be located in thematic position in the verbal mode and, in turn, are usually depicted in vivid and saturated colours, large size and in foreground positions in the visual mode. The picture book, *Granpa,* provides a good example. As stated in section 8.1, the textual analysis of this picture book, intended for 3-6 year-old children, reveals that there is an association between the point of departure of the clause as message and the two characters in the story, Granpa and the little girl, frequently located in the thematic slot of the clause (93.8% of the cases counted). This textual scheme relates to the visual components shown in the pictures as the illustrator clearly gives the two main characters more space and importance than the other secondary pictorial elements such as the girl's toys, Granpa's childhood friends, the interiors of the house, and even the exterior backgrounds. The main characters in the story are also given special status by placing them in or around the centre of the illustrations.

The pattern of constant theme contributes to the creation of a static style that, while facilitating the comprehension of the message, does not need to be maintained for long periods of time in a text. This would be tedious for the reader and would produce a stagnant sensation regarding the transmission of information (Eggins 1994). In fact, the constant thematic progressions identified are not maintained for a long period. They are often interrupted by the different informative elements that are sequentially introduced into the narrative discourse (worms, one man, I, Noah, we, that, this (ice cream), Harry, Florence and I, etc. ...). The alternation of elements in the thematic and rhematic slots of the clause contributes to creating a dynamic style, which is also reflected in the visual mode, since the illustrations in *Granpa* do not follow the given plus new progression pattern seen in the tales aimed at children in the sensory-motor stage. As stated in section 8.2, the verso, or left-hand part, of the page, in black and white, usually embodies unfamiliar information for the viewer, frequently connected with Granpa's past. Meanwhile, the illustrations on the recto of the double spreads, in colour, tend to offer information that corresponds to the present or imaginary moments shared by the old man and his granddaughter. Colour and typography mark these two different periods of time, thereby helping the young child to decode the content and come to terms with the dialogic structure of the tale.

The analysis of the images and their relationship with the text reveals that the verbal and visual choices made by Birmingham regarding textual and compositional meaning help the child identify the main characters in the story and follow the development of their actions. The protagonists are given special prominence both in the verbal mode, as they tend to occupy the thematic slots of the clause and to follow constant thematic progressions, and also in the visual mode, where they are usually placed in the positions of most visual prominence. In addition, the study of the images and their relationship with the text clearly shows that both modes, the verbal and the visual, help to avoid monotony in an attempt to make the tale attractive to the young child. The use of linear thematic progressions and the utilization of a marked information pattern in the illustrations help to achieve this aim.

Finally, in the tales intended for 7–9-year-old children, the textual and compositional patterns adopted present a certain similarity with those used in the picture books intended for 3–6-year-old children. In fact, the textual analysis reveals that there is also a strong association between the main characters in the stories and the thematic slot of the clause (76.7% of the tokens identified follow this thematic pattern). In addition, the utilization of constant and linear thematic progressions helps to locate the main characters in the initial and final positions of the clause, facilitating the child's understanding of the plot. These textual patterns seem to have a correspondence in the visual mode, where the RPs tend to be located in the positions of most visual prominence, usually in the foreground and around the centre of the visual compositions. The size of the RPs is also used here as a way of creating salience.

The Tale of Peter Rabbit provides a good example to illustrate the intersemiosis of textual and compositional features of picture books intended for children in the concrete-operations stage of cognitive development. Peter, the main character, tends to be located in the thematic slot of the clause, a pattern that is also achieved through the high utilization of constant thematic progressions throughout the tale. Theme and topic overlap in 85.8% of the cases identified, and the constant thematic progression reaches 50.4% of the tokens analysed. In addition, thanks to the use of linear thematic progressions (which reach 14.2% of the items counted), other important characters, such as Mr McGregor, and to a lesser extent, Peter's sisters, also occupy the thematic positions of the clause. In except 15, for example, when Peter meets Mr McGregor for the first time, the farmer is introduced in the final slot of the clause. Later, the old man is taken as a theme of the following clause since he is the character that dominates this narrative stage and starts the conflict. These textual patterns seem to have a correspondence in the visual mode, as Potter gives Peter and Mr McGregor more visual prominence than the other characters in the tale through the use of size, focalization techniques and the their placement in the centre and foreground of the compositions.

15. But round the end of a cucumber frame, whom should he meet but Mr McGregor! Mr McGregor was on his hands and knees planting out young cabbages, but he jumped up and ran after Peter, waving a rake and calling out, 'Stop thief!' (*The Tale of Peter Rabbit*, Potter [1902] 2002)

Unlike other secondary characters, Peter tends to be located in the foreground and in the centre of the illustrations and is usually represented in a bigger size. In addition, Peter is present in 28 out of the 32 illustrations that make up the tale. His sisters, however, are only depicted in 10 illustrations, essentially at the beginning of the story and in the final four pictures.

In illustrations 29 and 30 they appear almost shaded in the background. In the last two illustrations the three sisters become more prominent when they look at her mother while she is cooking their rewarding supper: bread, milk and blackberries. Peter especially comes to prominence when he is involved in dangerous situations. In them, he is depicted in the foreground and with saturated colours. A clear example is double spread 20, when the farmer, Mr McGregor, is about to step on him after he escapes from the window of the tool-shed where he had hidden himself. The second major figure of this picture book, Mr McGregor, appears in only eight illustrations and, unlike Peter, he tends to be located in the background where he receives a lesser visual prominence. Double spreads 26, 27 and 28 are evidence of this. Before escaping, Peter can see the old man while he is hoeing onions in the 26th illustration. Peter is located in the foreground and gives his back to the child-viewer. Mr McGregor, however, seen from Peter's perspective, is depicted further away from the visual reach of the reader. Similarly, in illustration 27, when Peter finally manages to escape from Mr McGregor's garden, the old man is located in the background and only his diffused silhouette can be appreciated. However, Peter is depicted in the foreground, and at relatively close distance to the viewer. Finally, in illustration 28, the farmer can scarcely be seen behind the scarecrow he has made to frighten the birds.

Size is also used as a tool to give prominence to a specific character in the different stages of the plot and to mark the difference in importance between Peter and Mr McGregor. Let us now compare illustrations 10 and 11. In the 10th illustration Peter is depicted in the foreground and with great size. The blue colour of his jacket also helps to highlight his importance in the visual composition. Behind him some plants and a sparrow are depicted in less saturated colours. However, in illustration 11, when Peter encounters Mr McGregor for the first time and the conflict starts, Peter's size decreases considerably, especially compared to Mr McGregor's size (which is shown in the background). Peter becomes smaller when he faces his enemy. Thus, the illustrator manages to show the weakness of the main character and brings him closer to the child-reader, facilitating his identification with the rabbit.

Finally, regarding the distribution of information in the verbal and visual components of the tale, as Peter tends to be located in the initial slot of the clause, the tendency in the verbal component is to start with given information and terminate with new information at the end. This pattern, however, is not necessarily adopted in the visual mode. The restriction of space in the illustrations of the tale allows Potter to show just the characters that carry out an action in a specific moment of the plot. In double spread 15, for example, Peter is trapped in a gooseberry net; he is lying on the floor, surrounded by the net. There are no other visual components through which the reader could distinguish between given and new elements or the left and right hand sides of the double spreads. Note that, according to Kress and van Leeuwen (2006) while the known elements tend to be placed on the left-hand side of the visual composition, the new information is typically located on the right-hand side. Therefore, the information pattern in the illustrations of *The Tale of Peter Rabbit* seems to respond to the temporal and logical sequence of events rather than to the purely informational values distinguished by Kress and van Leeuwen (2006).

Despite this lack of correlation between verbal and visual modes as far as the distribution of information is concerned, the study of the images and their relationship with the text clearly reveals that in the picture books aimed at 7–9-year-old children the two modes, the verbal and the visual, also complement one another in a perfect symbiosis. The main characters are given special prominence both in the verbal mode, as they tend to occupy the thematic slots of the clause, and in the visual mode, where they are usually placed in the positions of most visual prominence. The major complexity of the plots forces writers and illustrators to use verbal and visual techniques to make the understanding of the messages that the tales convey more accessible to the young child.

8.4 Thematicity, composition and the age factor

The aim of this final section is to determine the extent to which the age factor may influence the thematic and compositional patterns of the picture books that form the sample texts. First, I will compare the thematic organization of the picture books intended for children in each of the three stages of cognitive development. Later, aspects related to visual compositionality are analysed in the illustrations of the stories included in the three age groups. The comparison between the thematic and compositional strategies used by writers and illustrators to form coherent wholes of communication in the tales intended for children in the sensory-motor, pre-operational and concrete operations stages will reveal how the age factor influences the way verbal and visual components are combined in picture books to convey textual meaning. A chi-square analysis using SPSS is carried out in order to determine whether the differences found in distribution are statistically significant.

The analysis of the thematic scheme of the tales reveals that the picture books intended for children of the three age groups studied here follow a similar thematic organization. In fact, on the whole, simple and unmarked themes overcome multiple and marked themes. As can be seen in Table 8.5, the frequency of simple themes reaches 61.8%, 59.7% and 65.9% of the tokens identified in the tales written for 0–2, 3–6 and 7–9-year-old children, respectively. The utilization of multiple themes, although also similar in the tales intended for the three age groups studied here, seems to be slightly higher in the tales intended for 0–2 year-old children (38.2% of the cases counted) and 3–6 year-old children (40.3%) than in the tales destined for children in the concrete operations stage, where the percentage of multiple themes (34.1%) is below the average of 36.4%.

Table 8.5: Simple and multiple themes: Age distribution

Theme	*Age group 0–2*		*Age group 3–6*		*Age group 7–9*		*Grand total*	
	Abs. values	*%*	*Abs. values*	*%*	*Abs. values*	*%*	*Abs. values*	*%*
Simple theme	42	61.8	83	59.7	189	65.9	314	63.6
Multiple theme	26	38.2	56	40.3	98	34.1	180	36.4
Total	68	100	139	100	287	100	494	100

Similarly, the use of unmarked themes is the prototypical pattern followed by the writers of all the tales analysed in this study and seems to be independent of the age for which the stories are initially intended. As Table 8.6 reveals, unmarked themes average more than 81% of the cases analysed in all the picture books that form the sample texts. Meanwhile, the use of marked themes does not reach 19% of the cases counted in any of the tales included within the three stages of cognitive development. All this coincides with the idea of making a message that will be easy for the young reader to understand, as the high presence of simple and unmarked themes generates simple syntactic structures to construct the plot of the stories. Only in the tales intended for 3–6-year-old children does the utilization of marked themes decreases slightly as their frequency is below average and reaches 16.5% of the tokens identified.

Table 8.6: Unmarked and marked themes: Age distribution

Theme	*Age group 0–2*		*Age group 3–6*		*Age group 7–9*		*Grand total*	
	Abs. values	*%*	*Abs. values*	*%*	*Abs. values*	*%*	*Abs. values*	*%*
Umarked theme	55	80.9	116	83.5	233	81.2	404	81.8
Marked theme	13	19.1	23	16.5	54	18.8	90	18.2
Total	68	100	139	100	287	100	494	100

The chi-square tests carried out below with regard to the use of simple/multiple and marked/unmarked themes demonstrate that the associations that may exist between the thematic patterns adopted by children's writers and the age factor are not statistically significant. As shown in Tables 8.7 and 8.8, the probability associated with the chi square value is above 0.05 in both the simple and multiple (0.442) and the marked and unmarked chi-square

Table 8.7: Simple and multiple themes: Age group crosstabulation

Theme		*Age*			*Total*
		0–2	*3–6*	*7–9*	
Simple	Count	42	83	189	314
	Expected count	43.2	88.4	182.4	314
Multiple	Count	26	56	98	180
	Expected count	24.8	50.6	104.6	180
Total	Count	68	139	287	494
	Expected count	68	139	287	494
$\chi^{22} = 1.635$, df = 2, $p = 0.442$					

Table 8.8: Marked and unmarked themes. Age group crosstabulation

Theme		*Age*			*Total*
		0–2	*3–6*	*7–9*	
Marked	Count	13	23	54	90
	Expected count	12.4	25.3	52.3	90
Unmarked	Count	55	116	233	404
	Expected count	55.6	113.7	234.7	404
Total	Count	68	139	287	494
	Expected count	68	139	287	494
$\chi^2 = .366$, df = 2, $p = 0.833$					

tests (0.833). So, there is no association between the thematic strategies used by picture books' writers and the three age group categories analysed here. For this reason, in these cases there is no point in comparing the observed distributions of data with those expected on the basis of the null hypothesis of no association between variables.

Now I will compare the theme-topic overlapping in all the tales included in each age group in order to ascertain if the age factor determines the placement of the characters (about which the plot is constructed) in the thematic or rhematic slots of the clause. As shown in Table 8.9, in the selected stories the characters that carry out the main actions are considered to be topical elements and tend to be placed in the thematic positions of the clause. More than 76% of the analysed cases of the sample texts follow this general tendency. Upon locating the characters in initial position, the author facilitates protagonist identification from the beginning of the story so that from the start, the topical entity about which information is transmitted is clearly specified.

Theme/topic correspondence is slightly more evident in the tales written for children who are in the sensory-motor stage and pre-operational stages of cognitive development than in the tales meant for the oldest children. In the first two age groups (0–2 and 3–6 year-old children), theme/topic overlapping reaches 77.9% and 80.6% of the cases identified, respectively. Finally, in the tales related to the concrete operations stage, the topical components continue to appear mainly in initial position, although there is a minor descent in the frequency of characters located in the thematic span of the clause. In fact, in the literary works of the concrete operations stage, theme/topic correlation diminishes to 74.6%, the lowest percentage found in this respect. In these tales, the cases where the main characters are located in the rhematic slot of the cause increase to 25.4%, almost two points

Table 8.9: Theme and topic overlapping: Age distribution

Theme	*Age group 0–2*		*Age group 3–6*		*Age group 7–9*		*Grand total*	
	Abs. values	*%*	*Abs. values*	*%*	*Abs. values*	*%*	*Abs. values*	*%*
Theme and topic overlap	53	77.9	112	80.6	214	74.6	379	76.7
Theme and topic do not overlap	15	22.1	27	19.4	73	25.4	115	23.3
Total	68	100	139	100	287	100	494	100

higher than the average percentage found in the sample texts (23.3%). On the whole, the scarce cognitive capacity and inexperience with storybooks of the child in these stages make it necessary for the author to plant in his or her mind who the protagonist is from the start.

However, the correlation between theme and topic is not always so automatic. As stated in section 8.1, the utilization of adjuncts of time in the thematic slot of the clause is a constant in the tales that form the sample texts, regardless of the cognitive stage for which they are initially intended. However, some differences have been found in this respect. While in the tales written for 0–2 and 3–6 year-old children *then* and *later* are the adverbials typically employed to demonstrate to the reader or listener that the actions happen one after another, in the children's storybooks related to the concrete operations stage, the adjuncts of time located in thematic position increase in variety and precision and introduce temporal and spatial details missing in previous stages. Adjuncts suh as *the night before her birthday* or *in the middle of the night* (Gorilla) specify the time in which the action occurs with greater detail and are not just generics like *later* or *then,* which are more characteristic of the tales of the first developmental stages to show the logical sequence of events. Although the tales continue with hardly any leaps of time, the stories last longer and contain more temporal information. Adjuncts of time, realized by subordinate time clauses, can also be identified in the stories of the concrete operations stage, as is seen in extract 16 taken from *The Tale of Peter Rabbit*:

16. After losing them, he (topic) ran on four legs and went faster, so that I think he might have got away altogether if he had not unfortunately run into a gooseberry net, and got caught by the large button on his jacket. (*The Tale of Peter Rabbit,* Potter [1902] 2002)

In this way, the message's point of departure sometimes coincides with the temporal coordinates in which the action is developed and the appearance of the character or topical component is postponed until the rhematic positions. These temporal constructions present greater complexity and, therefore, are not used in the literary works of the sensory-motor stage. However, they are sparsely incorporated in the tales of the pre-operational stage and increase progressively in those of the concrete operations stage.

The appearance of adjuncts of manner (see excerpt 5) and place (see excerpt 15) is more limited in the clausal theme, through which the author enriches the text by specifying where and how the actions are carried out. Some cases have been identified in the tales intended for 7–9 year-old children. This is evidence of the greater expressive richness that children of advanced ages demand. Here, the author does not limit him or herself to only telling what the characters do and when, as in the tales of the sensory-motor and pre-operational stages, but rather offers new expressive nuances.

At this point, I consider it relevant to provide a chi-square analysis using SPSS in order to measure the extent of the correspondence between theme/topic overlapping and developmental stage in the clauses of the sample texts. The chi-square analysis provided in Table 8.10 reveals that there are no significant differences between theme and topic overlapping and the age factor. The probability associated with the chi square value (0.375) is above 0.05, which makes the chi-square test non-significant. Regardless of the degree of cognitive and linguistic maturity of the listeners or readers, the stories belonging to the three different developmental stages do not show any significant variations in relation to theme-topic overlapping. Therefore, so far age does not seem to play a key role in the determination of the thematic strategies used in picture books intended for young readers. The specific characteristics of the genre seem to condition, to a great extent, the linguistic strategies used by writers of picture books to organize information in a coherent way, independent of the cognitive stage for which the stories are created.

The goal now is to relate the notion of thematic progression in children's storybooks, as formulated in Daneš' framework, to different phases in children's cognitive development, as manifested in stories written for children of different ages. The constant thematic progression model is, as can be seen in Table 8.11, the most utilized in the stories of all developmental periods, reaching 35.4% of the identified cases in the sample texts. However, its frequency is lower in the tales intended for 0–2-year old children (26.5%

Table 8.10: Theme and topic overlapping: Age group crosstabulation

Theme and topic overlap			*Age group*			*Total*
			0–2	*3–6*	*7–9*	
Overlap	No	Count	15	27	73	115
		Expected count	15.8	32.4	66.8	115
	Yes	Count	53	112	214	379
		Expected count	52.2	106.6	220.2	379
Total		Count	68	139	287	494
		Expected count	68	139	287	494

$\chi^2 = 1.960$, df = 2, $p = 0.375$

of the tokens counted) than in the picture books written for older children. In the stories intended for children in the pre-operational period (3–6-year-old children), the percentage is higher at 39.6%. This figure decreases to 35.5% in the picture books written for 7–9-year-old children. As the plots become more complex and the age of the children for whom the tales are intended increases, the frequency of constant themes also increases, perhaps in an attempt to make the understanding of the tales easier for the young readers. By using constant thematic organization, the characters are often located in the initial position throughout a series of clauses so that the information is introduced in a predictable and easily decipherable way.

Although in the picture books written for the youngest children the constant theme is still the most frequent type of thematic progression seen, the utilization of linear thematic schemes is also important in the overall organization of these stories. In part, this is due to the high use of basic adjuncts of time in the initial position of the clause (*then, later, on Monday,* etc.), which mark the temporal sequence of the story. These expressions organize the sequence of events in the stories destined for children, but tend to break the sequences of constant theme progression where the main characters are located in the initial slot of the clause. As shown in section 8.1, *The Very Hungry Caterpillar* provides a clear example of this fact. In addition, as the stories written for the youngest children are brief and constructed with, on average, seven to ten clauses in length, the storywriter for children aged 0 to 2 years resorts to using the linear thematic progression model (14.7% of the tokens analysed). This contributes to the stories' dynamic character and helps avoid textual monotony. These linear thematic chains give the tales a sense of dynamics as they allow writers to place the main entities about which information is transmitted in alternative thematic and rhematic

Table 8.11: Patterns of thematic progression: Age distribution

Thematic progression	*Age group 0–2*		*Age group 3–6*		*Age group 7–9*		*Grand Total*	
	Abs. values	*%*	*Abs. values*	*%*	*Abs. values*	*%*	*Abs. values*	*%*
Constant TP	18	26.5	55	39.6	102	35.5	175	35.4
Linear TP	10	14.7	16	11.5	50	17.4	76	15.4
Derived TP	1	1.5	0	0	7	2.4	8	1.6
No TP	39	57.4	68	48.9	128	44.6	235	47.6
Total	68	100	139	100	287	100	494	100

positions. On the contrary, the constant theme, if employed in many clauses, runs the risk of making the text somewhat tedious, even for a young child.

The linear thematic model, although still less frequently used than the constant thematic progression in the sample texts (15.4% of the tokens identified), reaches the highest percentage in the stories of the concrete operations stage at 17.4%. This percentage decreases to 14.7% in the stories written for 0–2-year-old children and to 11.5% in the tales aimed at 3–6-year-old readers. In the tales of the concrete operations stage, the linear thematic pattern reaches the highest percentage. The character's continual entrances onto, and exits from the narrative scene, and the necessary reactivation of those participants that have momentarily lost their topical status characterize the storybooks of this stage. In this context, the linear pattern is much more fitting, as it favours the alternating of characters in the clausal theme. The linear thematic progression reaches the lowest percentage in the tales written for children in the sensory-motor stage (11.5% of the tokens identified). Although this thematic scheme is also used in these stories, the constant thematic progression is still the most frequent thematic pattern identified in them. The stories intended for 3–6-year-old children deal with more complex topics (death, love, fantasy) than the tales destined for the youngest children, which give information about simple topics (pets, animals, food, etc.). Thus, the constant thematic pattern seems to be an appropriate model to locate the main characters in the initial slot of the clause through a sequence of clauses and facilitate the understanding of the plot to the child under six years of age.

The utilization of derived thematic progressions is less notable in the sample texts and reaches an average of 1.6% of the cases identified. However, its presence also varies considerably in the tales intended for the different age groups analysed here. The frequency of derived thematic progression reaches its highest point in the tales of the concrete operations stage at 2.4%. The percentage value of this thematic progression declines to 1.5% in the stories for 0–2 year-old children and is non-existent in the tales written for children in the pre-operational stage. No doubt, derived thematic progressions require inferences that may be difficult to understand for 0–6-year-old children. However, derived patterns, although their utilization is low, seem to be more appropriate for the tales destined for the oldest children.

Finally, the analysis of the thematic progression of the children's picture books studied reveals that they do not seem to lend themselves easily to the basic patterns of progression as distinguished by Daneš. Above all, the global faithfulness of texts to these patterns is obviously lower in the tales included within the first age range than that observed in the picture books of the second and third stages (see Table 8.11 above). In the stories intended for 0–2-year-old children, the utilization of clause constituents that can be located in the thematic part of the clause broadens considerably, especially in regard to adjuncts of time, which mark the temporal sequence of the actions and events carried out in the story. In fact, while 57.4% of the tokens identified in the tales intended for the children in the sensory-motor stage do not adapt to any of Daneš' (1974) thematic progressions, this percentage decreases to 48.9% and 44.6% in the picture books written for 3–6 and 7–9 year-old children, respectively. In any case, it should be noted that in the literary works of all the developmental stages analysed, the linear and constant progression patterns are the most utilized, while the use of the derived or other more complex combinations could complicate the structural organization of the story and would be less appropriate for the youngest children.

The contingency table provided in Table 8.12 demonstrates that, there are clearly significant differences in proportions across the variables as a whole. The probability associated with the chi square value (0.01) is below 0.05, which makes the chi-square test significant.[12] This means that, if we compare the observed distributions of data with those expected on the

Table 8.12: Thematic progression: Age group crosstabulation

Thematic Progression		*Age*			*Total*
		0–2	*3–6*	*7–9*	
Constant	Count	18	55	102	175
	Expected count	32.1	66.6	76.2	175
Linear	Count	10	16	50	76
	Expected count	14	28.9	33.1	76
No TP	Count	39	68	7	114
	Expected count	20.9	43.4	49.7	114
Total	Count	67	139	159	365
	Expected count	67	139	159	365
$\chi^2 = 98.661$, df = 4, $p = 0.001$					

12. It has not been possible to include the figures for derived progression, since two of the expected frequencies fall below 5, which invalidates the analysis. I have therefore done the test with constant, linear and no TP only.

basis of the null hypothesis between variables, particular associations can be identified between thematic progression and the age factor. Therefore, there are significant differences in the utilization of thematic progression schemes across the picture books intended for the children in the three age groups distinguished in this study.

Tales aimed at 7–9-year-old children produce more constant thematic progression than expected on the basis of no association between the developmental stage and Daneš' Thematic Progression types. The utilization of constant thematic progression is shown to be more relevant in the stories of the third developmental stage than in the picture books included within the first two developmental stages. In fact, the expected count for constant patterns is 76.2 for the tales of the 7–9-year-old group, and the observed frequencies account for 102. However, the statistical evidence reveals that literary works for 0–2 and 3–6 year-olds produce less constant thematic progression than would be expected since the expected frequencies account for 32.1 and 66.6 respectively, and the observed values just reach 18 and 55.

In addition, the picture books written for 7–9-year-olds also produce more linear models than expected. In fact, the expected count for linear thematic progression is 33.1 and the observed value increases to 50. The opposite tendency has been found in the tales destined for 0–2 and 3–6 year-olds, where the expected frequencies of linear thematic progression account for 14 and 28.9 respectively, and the observed values just reach 10 and 16. As has been previously pointed out, the picture books written for the 7–9-year-olds contain more topical entities or characters who constantly enter and leave the narrative scene. They need to be reactivated continuously when they reach prominence in the plot. This fact leads the writer to use linear and constant thematic progressions which favour the alternation of characters in initial and final positions of the clause and, in turn, facilitate the understanding of the message to the young child.

Furthermore, the storybooks intended for 7–9 year-olds produce fewer cases of no thematic progression than expected. In fact, in the tales intended for the readers of the concrete operations stage, the expected count for the lack of thematic progression is 49.7 and the observed frequencies account for only seven. However, the tales written for 0–2 and 3–6-year-old children follow the opposite tendency, since in them the expected counts (20.9 and 43.4) are lower than the observed values for the lack of thematic progression: 39 and 68. Therefore, the tales destined for young readers (0–6 year-olds) do not seem to adapt themselves so easily to the types of thematic schemes as distinguished by Daneš as the tales written for 7–9-year-old children. Thus, the degree of deviation from the null hypothesis of no association between cognitive stage and thematic progression varies from the tales of the third developmental phase (7–9-year-old children) to those intended for 0–6-year-old children.

With regard to the compositional organization of the tales that form the sample texts, the aspects related to information value, framing and salience seem to reveal important differences between the tales included in the three age groups studied in this book. In the case of information value, age seems to be the key factor that distinguishes the tales intended for the youngest children (0–2-year-old readers) from those illustrated for older readers (3–9 year-olds). Actually, while the former tend to follow an unmarked given-new distribution of information, the latter do not adhere so easily to this prototypical information pattern. In the tales illustrated for children of 3 years onwards, the recto, or the right-hand side of the double spreads, which is prototypically reserved for the new informational elements, is sometimes filled with participants that represent known or familiar information. The writers of these tales seem to pay less attention to the presentation of information in the prototypical given plus new way. The cognitive capacity of 3–6 and 7–9 year-olds allows them to follow the plot of the stories they read even though the new participants are located on the left-hand side of the double spreads and the given information is placed on the recto of the visual compositions. This marked information sequence brings dynamism to the tales, as it avoids the predictable information patterns that typically characterize the outlines of the tales illustrated for the youngest readers. All these aspects have been dealt with and demonstrated in section 8.2.

As for framing, while the illustrations are unframed in the tales intended for the youngest readers, the use of framing increases considerably in the picture books illustrated for those in the pre-operational and concrete operations stages of cognitive development, reaching the highest use in the latter age group. The illustrator avoids frames in the tales included within the sensory-motor stage so that the children are involved in the actions carried out by the main characters. Although this tendency can also be found in the picture books intended for 3–6-year-old children, the use of framed lines increases considerably in the tales written for this age group. Here framing essentially fulfils the function of establishing a boundary between reality and fiction and also contributes to creating dynamism when the same character is shown in a series of framed illustrations in the same double spread. Finally, the utilization of framing is notable in the tales illustrated for 7–9-year-old children, where most of the illustrations analysed appear in enclosed shapes or lined frames. Although the use of framed lines generates a certain detachment, the viewer seems to be mature enough to still be able to enter into the world of fiction that the illustrator creates in the stories of this stage of cognitive development.

An analysis of salience, the third feature of the compositional metafunction, reveals that in all the tales that form the sample texts the main characters achieve more prominence than secondary participants through the use of colour contrast and saturation and sharpness of focus and size techniques. Indeed, the main characters are usually illustrated in more vivid colours and with a larger size than the elements in the background. However, some differences have been found between the tales included within each of the three age groups analysed in this study. The tales intended for the youngest children focus essentially on the participants around whom the story is created. Background elements are practically non-existent. This way the child's attention is drawn towards the most important visual components of the plot, which are sometimes also referred to in the verbal component. This tendency is broken in the tales illustrated for older readers (3–9-year-old children). In these, as the age of the visual readers for whom the tales are destined increases, the elements that form the setting are bigger in number and are elaborated in more detail. In addition, in the picture books included in the concrete-operations stage, colour plays an additional role that seems to be missing in the tales illustrated for younger readers. Here, apart from giving prominence to the main characters, colour is also used either to establish links or lack of contact between the characters in the stories. *The Rainbow Fish* and *Gorilla* contain clear evidence of this fact. In the latter, for example, only when Hannah's father invites his daughter to visit the gorillas at the zoo is there a connection between both characters. This event is emphasized by the red colour of their garments. This is the only illustration in the whole tale where father and daughter wear the same colours.

Despite the differences found at the textual and compositional level between the tales intended for the three age groups studied in this book, the analysis of the intersemiosis of images and words in picture books reveals that, as multimodal products, images and words complement each other in order to help the young reader identify the main characters and understand the plots of the stories they read. The analysis carried out demonstrates that in the verbal component, the writer of children's stories intended for any age group has a predisposition to introduce the characters from the beginning of the narration in thematic position (76.7% of the cases identified) and to utilize, essentially in the stories intended for 7–9 year-olds, constant and linear thematic progression patterns (35.4% and 15.4% of the topical sequences counted respectively), which favour the appearance of repetitive structures and syntactic parallelism. Character placement in initial position helps the child to more easily identify the topical entities around which the plot is constructed. Theme/topic identification seems to be a useful tool to clarify which character information is offered at each moment of the narration. In addition, the utilization of adjuncts, especially temporal ones, in thematic position sometimes makes the characters or topical entities move towards the rhematic slot of the clause. Through these, the temporal sequence of the actions carried out by the main topical entities is clearly specified.

In turn, in the illustrations, the main characters are also given the greatest prominence through use of size, sharpness of focus and colour contrast and saturation. In addition, the unmarked thematic positions where the main participants are located seem to have a correspondence, essentially in the case of the tales made for the youngest children (0–2 year-olds), with the unmarked information pattern, given plus new, generally adopted in the visual component. This makes the stories easy to understand and attractive enough to entice the young child's attention towards the most relevant information transmitted by the visual language. Both words and images contribute to locate the informational elements in the most relevant position of the clause and the most prominent locations of the visual compositions. This unmarked information pattern is sometimes broken in the tales intended for older readers (6–9-year-old children) as there are also some illustrations where the new information is located in the left-hand side and the known and familiar elements are reserved for the recto of the visual compositions. The illustrator adopts this information scheme in order to generate dynamism and avoid monotony. When the prototypical information pattern is abandoned, the child has to face new informational possibilities. However, this challenge is not necessarily insuperable, as even in the tales intended for children in the concrete-operations stage, the characters about which information is given at the clausal level (which correspond to human participants, or at least humanized participants) are often located in the thematic slot of the clause.

9 Conclusions

In the introduction I stated that the aim of this book was to identify the verbal and visual strategies used by writers and illustrators of children's picture books to convey a representation of reality, to create interaction with child-readers and to form coherent wholes of communication. In addition, the second aim in this book was to determine the extent to which the age of the children for whom the tales were initially written and illustrated might influence the verbal and visual choices made by writers and artists of picture books when designing a story for children. My work as an educator of future pre-school and primary school teachers has led me to choose quality picture books, both in content and technique, so that my own students may analyse and become familiarized with them, and will later use them as teaching tools in their foreign language classes. Certainly I have been able to prove that, for clearly commercial reasons, erroneous and misleading recommendations have been made regarding the target age of the potential readership (as for instance on book covers or in children's sections in bookshops). Strachan (2008: 18) shares this reasoning and affirms that 'age levels when stated on the back of books, in bookshops or even in publisher's briefs can be confusing. [...] Age levels in books are just a general indication and should not be taken as hard and fast rules. Some publishers or bookshops will use the range of 6–9 years, while others specify 7–9 and/or 8–12.' In general, the age range of the target readers is extended so as to increase the number of consumers. Sometimes the selection of picture books is essentially motivated by purely commercial interests. Other more objective criteria such as the cognitive development of the reader and linguistic and visual factors are unfortunately often overlooked, or are not properly considered as the determining factors for the structuring of a reasoned and appropriate selection of stories for children in a specific age group. Although, as Colomer (2005: 16) and Strachan (2008: 176) indicate, the borders of any reading stage are loose and children's books are difficult to be accurately classified by age; the information that is offered to the possible buyer of a visual narrative can lead caregivers, teachers and mediators to make erroneous recommendations in relation to the age period for which a tale is intended.

In addition, adults are usually the ones who choose and buy the tales for their young readers. However, they are not necessarily trained to select the appropriate books for a child to read. Writers and illustrators of children's picture books may be aware of the cognitive level of their potential readers, and are perhaps likely to intuitively take these aspects into account when developing their craft. However, there is no guarantee that their knowledge of these cognitive capacities in any way prevail over their own artistic, creative drive. So, it is not the artists' responsibility to create tales that are adequate for the different cognitive developmental stages of the young readers. This task befalls upon the mediators, parents, teachers, editors and essentially researchers who try to accommodate the works created for children for their reading comprehension level and their cognitive development. What is certain is that, although there are no absolutes or clearly defined lines to classify an illustrated story based on a given age (as the rate of emotional development can vary widely even between children of the same age), young readers need distinct types of stories based on their age, interests, emotional maturity and ability to read and comprehend the world around them.

In the first chapter of this book I referred to classic studies on children's literature that classify tales according to psycholinguistic and cognitive perspectives. Researchers such as Tucker (1984), Townsend (1990), Cerrillo and Yubero (2007), Strachan (2008) and Moya and Ávila (2009) have identified some of the features that typically characterize the literary works intended for children of different age groups. Among them, Cerrillo and Yubero 2007: 287–289) offer a classification of children's books whereupon the topics, language and design are analysed to determine the actual relation between the books and the target readership's age. As stated in Chapter 1, the tales intended for children of normal development in the sensory-motor stage are said to deal with topics which are associated with the children's home, toys and pets. As with contents, the structure of these tales is also simple in the sense that it consists of a brief presentation of the main characters, a quick development of the plot and a final and clear outcome. Basic expressions and short clauses are the two characteristics that define the language utilized in them. In the picture books aimed at children in the pre-operational stage, age range 3–6 years, the range of topics dealt with increases considerably and includes topics such as the home, nature, schools, personified animals and fables and short stories with everyday anecdotes. Their structure is still characterized by its expressive simplicity without digressions or detailed descriptions that could complicate the linear and temporal development of the tale. Regarding format, there is still a predominance of large format designs with coloured illustrations combined with brief, large-print texts. As the amount of language increases with respect to the tales of the previous stage of cognitive development, the utilization of syntactic parallelism and repetitive structures increases considerably. Finally, the stories aimed at children from 7–9 years of age are more complex from both content and structural perspectives. The topics of the tales in the concrete operations stage extend considerably to include the more abstract topics of freedom, obedience, friendship, solitude, fantastic stories and extraordinary legends, etc. Their literary structure is still brief, with clear orientation, quick development of the plot and brief conclusion, but there is much more action. In addition, the language is more complex than in the previous stages and there is a lesser degree of repetition and syntactic parallelism. Although the illustrations still play a key role in the design, verbal language gains relevance in the tales intended for children in this phase.

Along with these other characteristics previously mentioned by other researchers in children's literature, what other aspects of a verbal and visual nature contribute to the creation of picture books so that they are appealing and, at the same time, appropriate for children of a specific age? At this point, after having used the analytical tools provided by SFG and Visual Social Semiotics, I now attempt to reflect the verbal and visual characteristics of picture books aimed at children in the three age groups that have been considered throughout this book. This way, we may better amplify the information provided on the tales' covers, on web pages, commercial brochures and literary reviews. First, in section 9.1, I examine how the age factor may influence the verbal and visual choices made by writers and illustrators to convey reality, create interaction and form coherent texts in the tales intended for the youngest children (0–2 years). Second, in section 9.2, I deal with the representational, interpersonal and textual strategies used by writers and illustrators in the tales aimed at children in the pre-operational stage (3–6 years). Finally, in section 9.3, I examine the way verbal and visual strategies are combined to construct meaning and stimulate the engagement between reader and text (7–9 years). The final aim is to provide teachers and mediators with specific tools that may help them to select the most appropriate material for their young readers. The chapter concludes with some general comments on the potential of picture books to encourage reading among young children.

9.1 The tales created for children in the sensory-motor stage (0–2 years)

At the representational level, the picture books created for 0–2 year-old children are basically constructed via processes of doing and happening, which refer to actions carried out by the protagonists and which contribute dynamism to the narration. It is also noteworthy that the presence of relational processes is equally high in these tales. Relational processes are used by picture-books writers to describe and typify the characters and so facilitate the child's identification of them according to their most prominent features. At this stage of cognitive development, the relational process *be* is the most frequently identified and it fulfils either a descriptive or an identifying function. The sum of the material and relational processes reaches 96.6% of the tokens identified in the tales aimed at the youngest children. It seems evident that, from a linguistic perspective, the author of these stories constructs them based on actions carried out by the characters and on relational processes with a descriptive function. The use of mental processes, however, is not significant in this stage, as demonstrated by the chi-square test presented in Chapter 6. Lastly, the frequency of verbal and behavioural processes is null, which, as will be seen later, contrasts with the stories for older children.

Regarding the processes used in the visual mode, embedded images, which combine action and reaction processes in the same illustration, predominate in the tales written and illustrated for children in all the age groups analysed in this book. They represent 53.3% of the tokens counted in the three tales that belong to the sensory-motor stage. Like processes of doing, embedded images also generate action and reaction, which are created by the presence of vectors of motion and the crossing gazes established between two or more represented participants. Action images involving only vectors of motion are also noteworthy in the tales created for the youngest children. This fact establishes a direct correspondence with the high utilization of material processes in the verbal component. Finally, the occurrence of conceptual images, typically associated with abstract and symbolic concepts, is not present in the tales illustrated for 0–2 year-old children. The topics dealt with in them are simple and revolve around children's daily routines, houses and toys.

The picture books aimed at 0–2 year olds are typically centred on one or two participants around whom all the actions are developed. These tend to be reflected both in the verbal and visual modes, especially the participants that play a leading role in the story. If the number of participants is bigger, there is always one of them who becomes more prominent than the others. When the characters, regardless of their primary or secondary role, are represented in the visual mode, they are depicted entirely, showing all the parts of their bodies without using visual metonymies. This way the young child can identify them through their basic and schematic features. This is also a characteristic typically associated with the tales intended for children in the pre-operational stage of cognitive development. However, as will be specified later, the tales aimed at 7–9-year-old children seem to follow a different pattern in this respect.

As for the intersemiosis of verbal and visual modes to represent the narrative reality, contrary to my initial expectations, words and images offer different but complementary information. Given the simplicity of the plot and form that characterize the tales intended for children between 0 and 2 years old, it seems logical to presume that the co-deployment that is established between the verbal and visual components will be symmetrical. A child under two years of age, who has not yet the capacity to decipher written language, will be able to understand the story with the help of the information provided by the illustrations. However, images are not a faithful echo of the meaning transmitted by the text; on the contrary, they are usually essential components in the development of the stories. The illustrations usually provide part of the information that is missing in the verbal component. Without them, the stories would be brought to a standstill. *Where's Spot?* and *Dear Zoo* are clear evidence of this. The animals hidden in the different locations of the house where Spot and his mother, Sally, live and the animals sent from the zoo to the child protagonist in *Dear Zoo* are depicted in the visual mode without being referred to in words. This shift in narrative path from words to images takes places every time a new animal is sent from the zoo. Other times, as happens in *The Very Hungry Caterpillar*, the pictures add specificity to the represented participants, in this case, the different foods eaten by the caterpillar. In addition, circumstantial information of time is not reflected in the images, but in the verbal mode. As most illustrations lack a setting and background details that can mark the timeline of the story, the temporal background (on Monday, on Tuesday, more than two years, etc.) in which the story is developed is provided exclusively by the verbal component.

With regards to the interpersonal/interactive meaning, in the picture books aimed at the youngest children, most of the modal structures identified in the verbal component are declarative. In fact, in only one story, *Where's Spot?*, have interrogative phrases also been identified, through which interaction between the characters in the story and the young reader is generated. The use of interrogative clauses in this tale ('is he under [the stairs/ the wardrobe,' etc.]?) interrupts, to a certain extent, the natural flow of the story, as each new question encourages the child-reader to see if Spot is hidden in the different locations referred to in the verbal component. Only when the child-reader finds out that the puppy is not in a specific place, does the plot progress and the search continue. The other two stories analysed in this stage, *Dear Zoo* and *The Very Hungry Caterpillar*, however, do not make use of interrogative clauses. The presence of imperative clauses is not significant either as only one has been counted in the three tales. Declarative clauses, the most predominant of all types of structures, contribute directly to the continuity of the narratives and, in turn, encourage interaction with the child, who is invited to look for the missing information in the illustrations. In turn, although in the visual mode there is a predominance of offers and oblique angles (which imply some social distance and the lack of an intimate relationship between the characters of fiction and the viewer), the utilization of eye-level angles and middle shots create affinity with the child. All the images are represented from an eye-level angle, which implies that the child is at the same level as the RPs and therefore identifies with them. In addition, all the images are middle-shots, which suggest the young child's involvement with the RPs, as they are depicted with a certain proximity to the viewer. Finally, although less notable from a quantitative perspective, there are also ten frontal angles and three demand images which also contribute to the engagement between the young child and the characters in the stories. The young reader looks at the pictures from a frontal viewpoint, which gives him the feeling of being involved in the RPs' world. The demand images, in turn, establish eye-contact between the characters of the tales and the child-viewer.

With regard to the interpersonal intersemiosis of verbal and visual modes in the tales aimed at the youngest children, the results of the analysis reveal that both the visual mode and verbal language cooperate to construct parallel interpersonal content and a similar kind of attitude (Royce 2007:

68–69). In fact, even in the two stories from this stage in which there are no interrogative or imperative clauses, the verbal mode, in a way, creates engagement between the RPs and the viewer. In *Dear Zoo*, for example, the verbal invitation to the child (They sent me a [....]) to lift up the flaps and see what is inside contributes greatly to the creation of engagement. Here the identity of the RPs can only be revealed by lifting up the flaps where the animals are hidden or kept. In turn, the meaning that the ellipsis in the second-to-last illustration in *The Very Hungry Caterpillar* portrays (Then he nibbled a hole in a cocoon, pushed his way out and [...]) can only be revealed when you turn the page, and the text, as well as the images, show the transformation of the caterpillar into a beautiful butterfly. Thus, there is congruence in attitudinal terms between the verbal and the visual modes of the tales aimed at the youngest children.

In terms of textual/compositional meaning, the analysis reveals that in the tales intended for children in the sensory-motor stage there is an association between the point of departure of the clause as message (theme) and the main characters in the stories: the child-protagonist (he) and his friends at the zoo (they) in *Dear Zoo*, the caterpillar in *The Very Hungry Caterpillar* and Spot in *Where's Spot?* usually occupy the initial and topical positions of the clause more often than the rhematic slots. The early age of the children for whom the tales are intended determines their thematic patterning, mainly organized in simple, unmarked and constant thematic structures. These textual patterns are occasionally interrupted by the utilization of time and place adjuncts which mark the temporal sequence of the story and the locative framework where the actions carried out by the main characters are developed.

Although the tales do not follow a definite thematic scheme, there is a predominance of constant thematic progressions over linear and derived thematic patterns. By using the constant thematic organization, the characters are often located in an initial position through a series of clauses so that the young child, who cannot yet recognize written words, does not lose the thread of the plot. The constant theme, if employed in many clauses, runs the risk of making the text somewhat static and tedious, even for the young child. Given the age of the audience (under 2), the use of this progression achieves its objective of making the story easy to follow as the child can hear and, in turn, see the events read by the mediator in the different illustrations of the tale.

The theme-topic overlap pattern and the use of constant theme progressions in the verbal mode have a correspondence in the visual semiotic component where the visual participants, their processes and the circumstances associated with them adhere to a 'given plus new' distribution of information. This information pattern facilitates the understanding of the message to the young child. While the verso of the double spreads tends to convey given information related to the main characters, the recto offers the new informative elements of the message. In *The Very Hungry Caterpillar*, for example, the fruits devoured by the tiny animal are located on the verso of the double spreads representing given information while the new food, yet to be tested, tends to be placed in the recto.

Another characteristic of the tales intended for the youngest children is that, as all illustrations are unframed, there is a recurrent invitation to the child-viewer to see the stories from inside. The young child, for instance, can become involved in the actions of the hungry caterpillar, counting the fruits he eats through and, at the same time, feeling, through the sense of touch, the holes that have been made through the core of the foods that the voracious caterpillar finds in his path.

The study of the images and their relationship with the text clearly reveals that both modes, the verbal and the visual, complement each other in order to help the child to identify the main characters in the stories and follow the development of their actions. Verbal and visual modes are co-deployed in such a way that they create an overall effect of compositional complementarity as the two modes blend with each other to give special prominence to the main characters in the stories. In language, the participants tend to be located in the thematic slot of the clause. In turn, in the visual mode, they are given the greater prominence through strong colour saturation and the adoption of an unmarked information pattern.

9.2 Picture books intended for children in the pre-operational stage (3–6 years)

From a representational perspective, like the picture books intended for the youngest children, the tales aimed at children between 3–6 years of age are also constructed through material and relational processes. The former are the most frequently used and reach the rate of 44.2% of the tokens identified. These are followed by relational processes, which represent 20.2% of the process types. If we compare this percentage with that obtained in stories intended for children between 0–2 years of age, the presence of relational processes is much less relevant in the pre-operational stage: from 41,1% in the sensory-motor stage to 20.2% in the stories written for 3–6 year-old children. Therefore, when the plot complexity is augmented, the actions carried out by the characters still continue to basically define the plot of the story. In turn, the presence of the relational processes, typically used to typify the characters, is not as necessary as in the previous stage, possibly due to the greater cognitive development of the child. In addition, while the verb, be, dominates in the stories that are written for younger readers, the variety of relational processes increases in the stories written for children in the second cognitive stage. Verbs such as call, make, etc., start to form part of the lexical assembly of these tales.

Stories in the pre-operational stage further distance themselves from the tales of the previous stage through the use of mental processes. Whereas in the earlier stage such processes are scarce (2.9%), in the pre-operational period they emerge as central concerns for plot development. These stories deal with more emotional and abstract topics, such as love, loneliness, and death. Hence, the use of mental processes, essentially those expressing affection, increases considerably until reaching 17.8% of the tokens identified. *Guess How Much I Love You* is clear evidence of this. Lastly, the use of behavioural and, above all, verbal processes (absent in the previous stage) is a characteristic that differentiates the stories written for each of the stages. Thanks to these verbal processes, more complex clauses are slowly and effectively introduced through reported speech, reflecting the words said by the characters and giving the story more of a conversational feel.

When it comes to the visual processes of the illustrations, the stories of the pre-operational stage resemble those of the preceding stage in that there is a clear predominance of embedded images in which action and reaction processes are combined in the same visual composition. In fact, the percentage of embedded processes in the tales illustrated for children between 3 and 6 years of age is the highest of all, reaching 71.1% of the tokens counted. Together with embedded images, action processes also play an important part in the representation of the reality. Due to the affectionate nature of the tales included in this age group, conceptual images, although smaller in number, are also used to represent abstract concepts such as death, as for example in *Granpa*. These processes, however, are missing in the picture books aimed at children in the sensory-motor and concrete operations stages of cognitive development.

Just as in stories intended for children from 0–2 years of age, the characters in the illustrations of the picture books created for 3–6 year-olds are shown with all the parts depicted and without using visual metonymies. The detail in the visual construction of the characters increases considerably with respect to the previous stage, where they are depicted in a schematic and minimalist drawing style (Painter *et al.* 2013: 31).

Like in the tales of the previous stage, in the picture books created for children in the pre-operational stage, verbal and visual modes are combined in such a way that words and images complement each other to convey a representation of reality. Perhaps the most significant example of such complementarity is *Granpa*. The vacant armchair where the old man used to sit down on is shown empty after he passes away. The text is limited to announcing that Granpa is ill and that he cannot come out to play. Thus images and words specialize in conveying particular meanings, as either the images enhance the meaning of the words, or it is the words which expand upon the meaning transmitted by the visual component. This way one of the modes becomes essential to fill the gap that is missing in the other mode and take over the narrative. In the picture books aimed at children between 3–6 years of age, there are also passages which consist of images or words alone offering complementary information to the development of the plot. In *Where the Wild Things Are*, for example, there are a series of wordless illustrations in which Max and the monsters dance the *wild rumpus*, a metaphor of Max's desire to follow his primary impulses. In addition, the landscape in the picture books included in this stage of cognitive development, which is richer in detail than in the tales intended for the youngest children, is not described by using words. It is only represented through images.

Yet another similarity between the tales of the sensory-motor and pre-operational stages is the emphasis on declarative clauses. In the stories for children between 3 and 6, these account for 95.2% of the tokens identified. The presence of interrogative and imperative structures is less important. The former have been identified exclusively in *Granpa*. Through them, Burningham creates the dialogist structure of the tale, which is essentially based on the conversation between Granpa and his granddaughter. In turn, imperative clauses, although scarce in number, also contribute to create an interactive relationship between the main characters of pre-operational stage tales, specifically Max and the monster in *Where the Wild Things Are* and between Big and Little Nutbrown Hare in *Guess How Much I Love You*. Max, for example, uses imperative clauses to command the wild things to stop dancing, indicating that his tantrum has passed. In addition, the challenge between Big Nutbrown Hare and his son is rooted in the imperative clause that the title to the tale: 'Guess how much I love you'.

While the use of declarative clauses with ellipsed elements helps to create engagement between the characters and the child in the tales intended for 0–2 year-olds, the high presence of declarative clauses and the low utilization of modal adjuncts in the picture books aimed at 3–6 year-olds result in the hampering of an intimate bond between the child and characters in the stories. The high utilization of declarative mood structures in language seems to have a correspondence with the predominance of offers and oblique angles in the visual mode. Most of the illustrations identified are offers where the RPs keep looking at each other or at something within the image without making any demand to the viewer. In addition, most illustrations are oblique angles which present the RPs from the sidelines and generate detachment. Finally, unlike the stories of the previous stage, where all the angles were middle-shots, in the stories intended for children in the pre-operational stage, 15.8% of the tokens identified are long-shots. Through them, the characters are usually portrayed full size. This seems to imply objectivity and some social distance. However, even though the utilization of offers, oblique angles and long-shots may imply distance with the viewer, other devices related to the systems of distance and perspective reveal that the illustrator makes choices which stimulate the affinity between the reader and the characters. All the images in the sample texts are represented from an eye-level angle, which implies that the child reader is at the same level as the protagonists and therefore feels identified with them. In addition, most of the illustrations are middle-shots, which create a certain social relationship between the characters of the tales and the young reader. Sometimes the reader looks at the pictures from a frontal viewpoint (12.7% of the cases counted), which gives her/him the feeling of being involved in the RPs' world. These features are reinforced by the depiction of main participants in the foreground, which brings them closer to the viewer.

Therefore, unlike the stories intended for the youngest readers, the co-deployment of verbal and visual modes in the tales aimed at children between 3-6 years of age generates a certain discrepancy in attitudinal terms (Royce 2007: 68–69). In *Granpa*, for example, the omniscient and distant tone of the narrator becomes fairly evident when announcing, in the third person,

Grandpa's illness ('Granpa can't come out to play today', double spread 12). This marks a stark contrast to the proximity and intimacy brought on by the middle-shot and eye-level image, and in which the character appears resting in his armchair with a blanket over his lap and next to a table full of medications. This dissonance in interactive attitude is emphasized in the stories written and illustrated for children between 7 and 9 years of age and establishes a clear difference between the tales included in the sensory-motor stage and those intended for older readers.

As for modality, indicators of high and low modality are combined in the picture books illustrated for 3–6 year-old children. The representation of the characters in the stories written for children in the pre-operational stage is undoubtedly not as basic as it is in the stories for the previous stage. The characters in the earlier phase are depicted in a schematic way, according to their more basic features. The eyes of the puppy Spot are represented by two dots, just like his whiskers. In the stories included in the pre-operational stage, however, the representation of the characters becomes more detailed. The protagonists' movements and poses in *Granpa* reflect real characteristics and achieve a notable level of modality according to the visual perspective defined by Kress and van Leeuwen (2006). The wild things and the transformation of Max's room into a forest are wonderfully depicted in great detail. Other illustrations, however, still have a lower level of modality. The whale that the grandfather and granddaughter try to fish is vaguely depicted through the lines that give form to its body. This dual play between high and low modality brings the young reader closer to the characters in the story. If the characters are reflected using a high level modality, especially all of the main characters, the child easily feels him or herself reflected in them, as they are the true protagonists of the story and their traits are similar to those of the young reader. The secondary characters, however, are usually reflected through a lesser degree of modality, imitating in part the typical tracings of 3–6 year-olds' drawings.

In terms of textual/compositional meaning, the tales written and illustrated for the children in the pre-operational stage follow a similar pattern to that which is utilized in the stories written for children in the previous stage. Theme and topic overlapping and the utilization of unmarked and constant themes reach the highest percentage in the picture books analysed in this stage. The tales are typically organized in simple, unmarked constant thematic structures where theme and main characters tend to overlap in subject position. Even in the case of multiple themes, which reach the highest percentage in the tales of the pre-operational stage, the components that make up the thematic slot of the clause consist of textual elements (and, so, then, ...) and ideational, topical constituents. Although the constant thematic scheme is the most predominant pattern identified, this is not the only type. As was also the case of the tales written for the youngest children, throughout the stories, at different intervals, the writer also produces sequences of linear thematic progression. These linear thematic chains give the tales a sense of dynamism as they allow writers to place the main entities about which information is given in alternative thematic positions.

These textual patterns, which contribute to locate the main characters in the initial slot of the clause, seem to have a clear correspondence with the visual components, as the illustrator clearly makes the characters stand out within the illustrated space. They are placed in the foreground rather than in the background, which is occupied by the elements that form the setting. The salience given to the RPs is also achieved by the use of colour and size techniques, as they are usually illustrated in more vivid colours and with a larger size than the elements in the background. Thus, in the tales intended for children in the second phase of cognitive development, the verbal and the visual modes also complement one another so that the stories are easy to understand, and in turn, attractive for the young child. The RPs are depicted more prominently in both the verbal mode (their positioning within the thematic slot of the clause) and the visual mode (through the strategic salience of their features, their positioning within and in relation to space, etc.).

Although most illustrations are unframed and invite the viewer to see the stories from inside, some framed visual compositions have also been identified in the three picture books created for readers in the pre-operational stage. In *Where the Wild Things Are* some framed illustrations have been found, essentially in the first and last double spreads of the tale, when Max is depicted within the confines of his room. Once the magic starts and the room is transformed into a wild forest, the boundaries disappear and the illustrations used by Sendak are unframed. Max becomes the king of all wild things and there is no need to limit his freedom. The presence of frames, although scarce, establishes a difference between the visual components of the tales intended for the children in this developmental stage and the picture books illustrated for the youngest children, as in the latter all the illustrations are typically unframed.

In addition, unlike the prototypical information pattern, given plus new, found in the tales aimed at children between 0 and 2 years of age, in the tales intended for children in the current stage, the distribution of information in the visual component tends to follow a marked information sequence. *Where the Wild Things Are* is evidence of this. The first time a wild thing appears is in the left-hand side of the eighth double spread. Meanwhile, Max, who represents information already known to the reader, is depicted in the right-hand side of the visual composition. In the picture book at hand, the typical unmarked information tendency is often altered, since the visual message starts with new information rather than known elements. Thus, the theories described by Kress and van Leeuwen to define the visual and informative organization of multimodal advertising texts do not always appear to adapt to other genres completely, in this case, children's stories. Whatever may be the reason for not following a defined or non-marked informative pattern, the truth is that these alterations help to maintain the child's attention in the plot development, since the changes in the presentation of information bring dynamism to the narration and avoid the predictable outlines that are sometimes so characteristic of children's stories. Lewis (2006) considers that this alteration affects how the characters are represented, and states: 'Anyone attempting to move from right to left can usually be seen to be deliberately interfering with the general movement of characters in the story, to be blocked in some way, to be returning from adventures or to possess a sinister purpose' (Lewis 2006: 113).

9.3 Tales aimed at young readers in the concrete operations stage (7–9 years)

At a representational level, the tales intended for children in the concrete operations stage of cognitive development follow a pattern that is similar to that which is found in the stories aimed at children in the pre-operational stage. Material processes continue to be the most predominant of all types. In fact, their presence reaches the highest percentage of the three age groups studied here (51.9%). The chi-square test carried out in Chapter 6 demonstrates that the association between material processes and the age factor is found to be more relevant in the tales written for 7–9-year-old readers than in the stories intended for younger children. In this third stage, the more complex topics result in an increase of the number of actions carried out by the characters. Consequently, the frequency of processes of doing and happening is also greater. Though of an inferior presence (20.5% of the tokens counted) relational processes have an important function in the representation of reality. At the same time, the variety of verbs of a descriptive nature increases. Along with *be*, which continues to be the most employed relational verb, verbs such as *feel, become, call*, etc. appear more often to describe or identify main and secondary characters. However, the presence of relational processes in the second and third age groups is not as significant as in the stories intended for children from 0-2 years of age, where the description of the characters through their fundamental characteristics is necessary for the young reader to easily identify them. Verbal and behavioural processes are also utilized to convey meaning in the tales intended for children between 7 and 9 years of age, establishing a sharp contrast with stories aimed at younger children, where the percentage in the use of these processes is practically non-existent. Finally, although the association between mental processes and the age factor is less relevant than expected in the tales aimed at 7–9-year-old readers, their presence is still necessary to reflect the main characters' emotional and conflictive aspects.

Regarding visual processes, as is also the case of tales in the two previous stages, embedded images containing vectors of motion and eye lines are the most predominant of all types. These are followed by action processes, which also contribute to generate dynamism. In spite of the complexity of the topics dealt with in these tales, such as solitude, friendship, freedom, obedience, etc., no conceptual images denoting abstract concepts and related to symbolic values have been identified. It seems that the illustrators essentially construct their stories through the actions carried out by characters, as well as through the visual and affective ties established between them.

Unlike the characters in the stories directed towards children between 0 and 6 years old, who are represented entirely, with all their parts clearly depicted, the characters of the tales illustrated for children in the concrete operations stage are sometimes represented through part-whole metonymies. Thus one of their parts (face, head, foot, etc.) is used to refer to them in their totality. Metonymies are used in the three picture books of the concrete operations stage, first to create narrative tension and emphasize some stages of the story and, second, to establish a bond between the fictional characters and the child-viewer. In addition, visual metonymies are also utilized to encourage the child-viewer's interaction with the adult, who may ask questions about the representational meaning of the metonymies in order to find out whether the child understands the message transmitted by the illustrations.

Regarding the co-deployment of verbal and visual modes in the tales intended for 7–9-year-old children, as is also the pattern followed in the stories included in the previous cognitive stages, words and images offer different but complementary information to transmit the message writers and illustrators wish to convey. Images become necessary instruments for the development of the narrative storyline, as they offer information that is missing in the verbal mode. The statement, 'In the night something amazing happened,' taken from *Gorilla*, cannot be understood without the illustrations, which show how the toy gorilla Hannah was given for her birthday becomes real. The images from stories aimed at children in the third stage of cognitive development contain unidirectional or bidirectional reaction processes that generally establish either contact or lack of visual engagement between the RPs. These relationships tend to only be reflected in the visual component without necessarily mentioning in the verbal mode. In this way, the combination of both modes can create more positive or negative portrayals of the characters than those achieved by each modality in isolation. Lastly, the description of characters and the setting where the actions are developed are exclusively reflected in the illustrations, as was the tendency already found in the picture books illustrated for the children in the second stage of cognitive development. In the present stage, the details related to the setting encourages relationships of intertextuality through which the intention is to familiarize the child with other texts or illustrations extracted from other literary works or from the world of classic art. Browne's *Gorilla* is a clear example of this.

In terms of interpersonal/interactive meaning, like in the tales created for children in the other two previous stages of cognitive development, the majority of the clauses identified are also declarative and, consequently, the verbal part does not generally stimulate an interaction between the story characters and the child-viewer. The chi-square test carried out in Chapter 7 demonstrates that the use of declarative clauses, although notable in all the tales that form the sample texts, is clearly shown to be more relevant in the stories for the concrete-operations stage than in the tales intended for younger readers. The increased number of actions in which the characters are involved in the stories written for 7–9 year-olds requires the presence of declarative sentences in order to maintain the plot and offer information in an objective way for the young reader. The opposite pattern is found in the utilization of interrogative clauses. Although smaller in number than declarative clauses, interrogative mood structures are shown to be more relevant in the picture books written for 0–2 and 3–6-year-old children. Interrogatives help to generate interaction between the young child and the characters in the story, engaging young children in the adventures described in the tales.

On the other hand, as seen in the stories analysed in the two previous stages, in the visual component of the picture books illustrated for children between 7 and 9 years of age most of the shots are offers and oblique angles, which imply a lack of interaction and involvement similar to that expressed in the verbal mode through the use of declarative structures with scarce modality markers. In addition, 9.3% of the tokens analysed are long-shots as the characters, except when they are depicted metonymically, are usually portrayed full length, which seems to imply objectivity, some social distance and not an intimate relationship. Certainly, features such as offers, oblique angles and long-shots generate detachment. However, other traits related to distance and perspective (eye-level angles, middle shots and frontal images) reveal an attempt to create some sense of engagement between the fictitious characters and the young reader. Most images are represented from an eye-level angle or shot, generating interaction. Contrary to Kress and van Leeuwen (2006), such interaction is also induced by high and low angles presented in some picture books included within the concrete operations stage. For example, in *The Tale of Peter Rabbit*, Peter is depicted from a high, superior angle just in the crucial moment when he is truly in danger. The angle overtly emphasizes the smallness of the helpless animal, hence conjuring the reader's sense of empathy and compassion towards the vulnerable protagonist. In addition, in *Gorilla*, Hannah is depicted from a low angle when the toy gorilla becomes real, suggesting her fear and powerlessness before the presence of the enormous ape who emerges from the foot of her bed. The use of middle-shots also contributes to create a certain social relationship between the characters of fiction and the young child as the former are shown relatively close to the viewer.

These interactive features are reinforced by the use of four demand images, 23 frontal angles and 17 close-ups. Although of a low frequency, the use of demand images attests to the illustrator's intention to incite a strong engagement between the heroes and the viewers. Interestingly enough, this type of image is rather infrequent in picture books (Lewis 2006), as direct visual contact with the recipient of the tale can interrupt, albeit momentarily, the development of the narrative plot. The 20 frontal angles show the RPs from a frontal viewpoint, which gives the reader the feeling of being involved in the RPs' adventures. Finally, close-ups reach the highest percentage (22.7% of the cases counted) in the tales created for children in the concrete operations stage, a feature which marks an important difference between the stories from this stage and stories intended for younger readers. In addition, the effect of detachment achieved by the utilization of offers and oblique angles is diminished by the use of vicarious focalization techniques, which bring the characters of the story closer to the young reader. For instance, in *The Tale of Peter Rabbit*, indirect focalization techniques are used to present actions which involve the most danger for the protagonist. These actions, conveyed through Peter's eyes, forge in this way the identification between the hero and the reader.

Another difference which, on an interpersonal level, can be established between the stories designed for children between 7 and 9 years of age and those written and illustrated for younger children has to do with their degree of modality. The mastery of the illustrators of the picture books included within the concrete operations phase lies in drawing animals, essentially rabbits and gorillas, and their movements and poses give their illustrations a high level of realism. Undoubtedly, the details of the illustrations of these picture books increase with respect to the drawings in the stories included in previous stages. Browne's gorillas, for example, are able to express sadness in their eyes; the poses of Peter are similar to those adopted by a human, at the same time that they reflect the essential characteristics of a rabbit. The illustrations no longer include mere lineal and colourless strokes that could still be found in some drawings in the stories intended for children in the pre-operational stage. Illustrations in the picture books intended for older children are real masterpieces of art, and reflect the objects depicted with a high level of resemblance to reality, especially if we consider that they are part of stories intended for children.

Lastly, the interpersonal intersemiosis of the picture books intended for children between 7 and 9 years of age reveals that, as also happened in the tales included in the pre-operational stage of cognitive development, the visual mode seems to contribute more to the creation of engagement between the RPs and the child than the verbal component. In fact, verbal and visual modes are co-deployed to construct certain attitudinal dissonance. In *The Tale of Peter Rabbit*, for example, Potter describes the passage when Peter is trying to escape from Mr McGregor by jumping out of a small window with an objective tone, guaranteed by the use of the third narrative person, which emphasizes the remoteness of the action: '[...] The window was too small for Mr McGregor, and he was tired of running after Peter. He went back to his work' (double spread 20). However, the middle and eye-level angle of the image accompanying the text, together with the elements in the foreground that are proximate to the viewer, prompt the engagement between characters and the child-reader, encouraging the latter's involvement and interaction in the story. In the illustration, Mr McGregor is represented through the part-whole metonymy, boot for the old man. The metonymy emphasizes the threat and danger that is upon Peter in this moment of the narration. It seems, hence, that the text and images complement one another to create a dissonance on an interpersonal level. The distance that imposes the use of the third person in the narration contrasts with the interaction and closeness that comes from the middle, nearly close-up, of Mr McGregor's threatening boot. This way, the illustration emphasizes the imminent threat that is upon the little rabbit when he is about to be stomped on by the old man.

Finally, in terms of textual/compositional meaning, the stories intended for children between 7 and 9 years of age also follow a very similar pattern to that adopted by the picture books included in the two previous cognitive stages. In the works created for children in the concrete operations stage, the characters also tend to be located in thematic position. The larger number of participants about whom information is offered at the clausal level makes the plot more difficult for young readers to decode. Therefore, character placement in thematic position helps the child to more easily identify the topical entities around which the plot is constructed. The fact that the chi-square analyses show that the association between thematic strategies and the age factor is not always statistically significant proves that genre plays a key role in the thematic organization of the stories. This seems to support Ghadessy's (1995a, b) finding that thematic organization correlates with genre, and that different genres and registers follow specific thematic developments.

However, significant differences have been found with regard to Daneš' thematic patterns between the tales included in the concrete-operations stage and those intended for 0–6 year-olds. The utilization of constant and linear thematic progressions turn out to be more relevant in the stories of the third developmental stage than in the picture books intended for 0–2 and 3–6-year-old children. In general, the stories do not seem to lend themselves easily to the basic patterns of progression, especially in the case of the tales intended for the youngest children. This is basically due to the high presence of temporal adjuncts located in thematic position to mark and clarify the temporal sequence of the actions. Due to the larger number of participants who continuously gain and lose topic continuity in the stories included within the concrete operations stage, constant and linear thematic schemes play a key role in their overall organization. These favour the alternation of characters in the initial and final position of the clause. In fact, the picture books intended for 7–9 year-olds seem to adapt more easily to the thematic progression distinguished by Daneš than the tales written for younger readers.

In the literary works of all the developmental stages analysed, the lineal and constant progression patterns, which favour the appearance of repetitive structures and syntactic parallelism, are the most utilized, while the use of the derived or other more complex combinations could complicate the structural organization of the stories, which would be less appropriate for the youngest children. In fact, derived thematic progression is scarce in the stories for the younger readers and is completely non-existent in the stories written for the children in the pre-operational stage.

As is also found in the tales intended for children between 0 and 6 years of age, these constant and linear thematic patterns through which the main characters are placed in the most important positions of the clause seem to have a clear correspondence with the visual components, where the RPs are placed in the positions of most visual prominence. The illustrators clearly give the RPs more space and importance than they do to other pictorial elements. The size of the RPs is still used as a way of creating salience. In addition, the main characters, constantly located in the foreground, are provided with special status by placing them in the centre of the composition.

The use of framing and colour strategies establishes a difference between the tales intended for younger readers and those aimed at children in the concrete operations stage. Unlike the tales intended for children between 0 and 6 years of age, in which illustrations are usually unframed, framing in this posterior stage projects a certain distance between the RPs and the young child. *Gorilla* and *The Tale of Peter Rabbit* are clear evidence of this. While in the former the characters are surrounded by sharp, square frames, in the latter they are surrounded by dim, circular enclosures, which suggests that the characters are more likely to feel secure and content than those included in rectangular or square frames.

Colour also plays a key role to give prominence to the most relevant characters in the stories. However, in the tales created for children in the concrete operations stage it is also utilized to emphasize either the engagement or the lack of contact between some of the characters. For example, when at the beginning of *Gorilla* there is no eye contact between Hannah and her father and they are involved in different activities, the red of Hannah's jumper contrasts with the dark blue associated with her father. However, at the end of the story their relationship changes and father and daughter connect with each other when he finally devotes time to her and invites her to go to the zoo. Then the red of their garments matches one another, in clear allusion of the companionship that now binds them.

Finally, regarding the information pattern, the tales created for the children in the concrete operations stage do not seem to follow an unmarked given plus new sequence in the visual component, only found in the tales illustrated for the youngest children. In *The Tale of Peter Rabbit*, for example, text and illustration alternate in both the left and the right-hand sides of the pages, exhibiting an exquisite balance between verbal and visual modes. In double spread 20, when Peter flees from Mr McGregor, the characters are situated in opposite pages. Peter, scurrying through the tool-shed window, is placed on the left-hand side, while the old man occupies the right-hand side, indicating new information. However, in double spread 27, when Peter is about to escape from Mr McGregor's farm, the old man is located on the left-hand side and Peter on the right. Thus, characters move both from the left to the right and the other way round without following a typical information sequence. This 'arrhythmic' display evokes, perhaps in allusion to Peter's own improvised reactions, a sense of lack of direction and confusion.

To sum up, these nine picture books present some similar representational, interpersonal and textual patterns in different developmental stages. The fact that the analyses carried out show that the differences, although existing in absolute and relative values, are not always statistically significant, proves that the genre of the tales plays a key role in their representational, interpersonal and thematic organizations, regardless of the cognitive stage for which the stories are created. Thus, it seems that the representational, interpersonal and thematic configurations of the tales correlate, to a certain extent, with genre, in this case the genre of picture books.

The picture books adapt to specific genre characteristics which determine, to a great extent, their internal configuration and the choices made by the author and illustrator on a representational, interpersonal and textual level. In representational terms, essentially material and relational processes predominate in the verbal component to represent the narrative reality in all the tales that form the sample texts. These are followed in frequency by mental and verbal processes. Regarding the visual processes identified, embedded images are the most predominant of all types. Similarly, relations of complementarity define the intersemiosis that is established between the verbal and the visual modes of all the tales included in the sample texts. In addition, in interpersonal terms, the high presence of declarative sentences in the verbal component seems to be the general pattern of the majority of the stories analysed. Regarding the visual feature of image act and gaze, neither do the differences seem to be notable, since offers predominate over demand images in the picture books of the three cognitive stages. Slight differences have been found in the presence of frontal and oblique angles: oblique angles predominate over frontal angles. The high use of offers in the illustrations reflect the objective tone conjured by declarative sentences. In textual terms all the stories follow a similar pattern: the main characters usually occupy the thematic position of the clause, particularly in all the stories for the first two age groups. At the same time, the typology of themes responds to the categories of simple and unmarked. If marked themes exist, it is essentially due to the presence of temporal and locative adjuncts that mark the sequential and the spatial frame within which the action is developed. Much like in our conclusions, when comparing newspaper sports commentaries with other genres, Ghadessy (1995b) finds that the most frequent themes are related to the major text participants and temporal location elements. Regarding the patterns of thematic progression, the constant theme progression is the most predominant in all the picture books of the three stages of cognitive development, followed by the linear TP, which reaches its highest percentage in the stories aimed at children from 7–9 years of age. In addition, from a compositional perspective, in all the tales the main RPs are depicted with a bigger size than the elements that form the background and are placed in the positions of most visual prominence around the centre and in the foreground of the illustrations.

Although, as I have suggested above, there are common features that are most likely determined by the demands of the genre itself, the analytical results also point to important differences between the stories of the age groups. On a representational level, for example, relevant differences have been identified between distinct age groups. The frequency of behavioural, verbal and mental processes is non-existent or low in the stories aimed at children in the sensory-motor stage, being more relevant than expected in the picture books intended for 3–6 and 7–9 year-old children. This pattern is inverted when we analyse the frequency of relational processes, which is high in the stories intended for younger children and, nevertheless, decreases in the picture books written for children in the pre-operational and concrete operations stages. Finally, the utilization of material processes, although notable in all the tales, turns out to be more significant in those written for 7–9 year-old readers than in the picture books of preceding stages. In the visual component, the results of the analysis show that action processes reach the highest percentage in the stories of the sensory-motor stage. When it comes to the visual representation of the participants, these are usually full-body portrayals in the sensory-motor and pre-operational stages. However, visual metonymies are used in the tales created for the children of the concrete operations stage. In addition, from an interpersonal perspective, the use of imperative sentences increases slightly from the sensory-motor to the concrete operations stage. Interrogative structures, however, decrease slightly but steadily from stories aimed at the youngest children, where they reach 12.3% of the tokens analysed, to the stories intended for older children, where they barely reach 4% of the tokens counted. In the stories aimed at the youngest readers, the interrogative clauses play an important role to create interaction. The chi-square test carried out in Chapter 7 proves that the association between interrogatives and the age factor is more relevant in the tales intended for 0–6 year-olds than in the picture books written for 7–9-year-old readers. The opposite pattern is found in the case of declarative clauses. The association between these and the age factor is more significant in the tales intended for older readers than in those for children in the sensory-motor and pre-operational stages. Regarding the interpersonal characteristics of the visual component, the second interactive category, social distance and intimacy, offers differential features between the stories created for each developmental stage. So, although middle-shots predominate in all the picture books, their presence varies noticeably depending on the age group for which the story is illustrated. While middle-shots reach 100% of the cases identified in tales intended for the youngest children, this frequency progressively decreases to 81% in the picture books for children between 3 and 6 years of age and to 68% in the tales aimed at children in the concrete operations stage. At the same time, the absence of close-ups in stories for the youngest readers or their scarce presence in the picture books included in the second developmental stage contrast with their important presence in stories created for children from 7–9 years of age (22.7% of the tokens analysed). In these, they are used to show the characters' feelings or the difficulties that the protagonist is having or has to overcome. On the other hand, while long-shots reach 15.8% of the tokens identified in the tales for the age group 3–6, their presence is non-existent in the stories created for children between 0 and 3 years of age, where only middle-shots are used to create a certain social relationship between the RPs and the young child. As for vertical angle and power, unlike the stories intended for children in the sensory-motor and pre-operational stages, where no low angles were identified, in the tales of the concrete operations stage 5.3% of the cases counted respond to this category. In turn, high angles, which reach 18.7% of the tokens analysed in the picture books included in the third stage of cognitive development, are also missing in the tales aimed at the children between 0 and 6 years of age. This makes the category of eye-level angles less noteworthy (76%) in the tales aimed at children between 7 and 9 years of age than in the tales created for children between 0 and 6 years, where eye-level angles reach 100% of the tokens counted. Finally, the chi-square test presented in Chapter 7 proves that the tales intended for the youngest and oldest children (0–2 and 7–9 year-olds) produce more frontal angles than expected. However, the opposite pattern is found in the tales illustrated for children in the intermediate stage. With regards to the textual aspect, given the greater number of characters entering and leaving the narrative scene, the tales written for 7–9-year-old readers adapt more easily to the constant and linear thematic patterns distinguished by Daneš. These thematic schemes favour the placement of topical entities in the thematic and rhematic slots of the clause and, consequently, facilitate the children's identification of characters. However, the tales intended for younger readers do not lend themselves so easily to Daneš' thematic progressions. In part, this is due to the utilization of temporal adjuncts in the theme slot of the clause. Finally, in the visual component, framing and colour also reveal differences between the stories. So, while in the stories intended for children between 0 and 6 years of age the illustrations tend to be unframed, the pictures of the tales aimed at children in the concrete operations stage are usually framed. Colour, on the other hand, is handled to make the characters stand out in the tales for the third cognitive stage, at the same time that it signifies upon the connection (or lack thereof) between characters. Finally, while the tales created for the youngest children seem to adapt more easily to the prototypical information pattern, given plus new, the picture books illustrated for the children in the latest stage do not necessarily follow this sequence, given that in them the left-hand side of the double spreads can also contain new information.

Apart from the verbal and visual differences that may exist between tales for different age groups, in picture books text and image come together in perfect expressive symbiosis. In good quality picture books images do not fulfil a secondary function. Together with the text, they become primordial in the construction of the narrative story (Peña 2006: 35; Pelayo 2006: 58). There is an interconnection between the verbal and visual codes so that text and illustrations cannot be understood without the presence of the other.

Even though young readers' capacity to interpret images is surprising, we need a visual grammar to help us make a rigorous analysis of the available mechanisms for constructing meaning through non-verbal semiotic modes. A child is certainly able to interpret images long before learning how to read and decipher the written code. This does not, however, imply that the learning of the visual code does not require any education to be acquired. In order to learn the code, it is essential to work with the mechanisms that visual grammars offer and to equip the child with the tools necessary to manage in everyday life. Due to technological development, every day we are more and more immersed in a world of images and visual items. I have attempted to show how any image, apart from representing reality, whether an abstract or concrete form (representational function), also forms part of a type of communicative interaction with the visual reader of the message (interactive function) and, with or without the text that accompanies it, can also constitute a coherent message (compositional function).

On a representational level, writers and illustrators need to be conscious of the communicative potential that emanates from the combination of the verbal and visual modes in picture books so that text and image offer complementary meanings without exceeding the cognitive limits of child-readers. In turn, at the interpersonal level it is therefore useful for writers and illustrators to master and be familiar with the visual strategies which may be exploited to create interaction between the young reader and the protagonists. The use of frontal images, close-ups, middle and eye-level angles and focalization techniques may contribute to bring the child-reader and the fictional characters much closer together. Through these, the child will find it easier to identify with the protagonists of the visual narrative and to understand the message the author intends to convey. If illustrators manage to generate interaction between tales and their readers by means of visual techniques, they will stir children's interest to read stories aimed at the different stages of their cognitive development.

Lastly, on a textual level, textual and compositional techniques may be used to help the child follow the plot and identify the main characters. Emphasis on the relevance of the characters may come through both in the textual mode, where they will often be placed in the thematic position of the clause, as well as the visual mode, where they can be located in positions of the most informative relevance. On a compositional level, for example, we can train the child to understand the symbolism of colour or the use of framing techniques and how these can help determine the meaning of an image. This way, children will be able to understand tales above and beyond their explicit meaning, generating interpretations that contemplate what is implicit on the surface, but which demand more complex skills in order to be revealed. Fomentation and promotion of reading is, without a doubt, one of the pending tasks of educators and parents of the current generations, where the power of the image and its synergetic combination with the written code may encourage children to enter into the fascinating adventure of reading books.

References

Ariel, Mira (1990) *Accessing Noun-Phrase Antecedents.* London: Routledge.

Astorga, Cristina (2009) The text and image matching: One story, two textualizations. In Eija Ventola and A. Jesús Moya (eds) *The World Told and the World Shown: Multisemiotic Issues,* 124–138. Basingstoke: Palgrave Macmillan.

Ávila, Jesús Ángel (2007) *La progression temática y tópica de narraciones infantiles en lengua inglesa. Un estudio contrastivo [Thematic and Topical Progression of Children's Tales in the English Language. A Contrastive Study].* Unpublished Dissertation. Cuenca: Universidad de Castilla-La Mancha.

Baldry, Anthony (2004) Phase and transition, type and instance: Patterns in media texts as seen through a multimodal concordance. In Kay O'Halloran (ed.) *Multimodal Discourse Analysis: Systemic Functional Perspectives,* 83–108. London: Continuum.

Baldry, Anthony and Paul Thibault (2006) *Multimodal Transcription and Text Analysis: A Multimodal Toolkit and Course Book.* London: Equinox.

Barcelona, Antonio (ed.) (2000) *Metaphor and Metonymy at the Crossroads: A Cognitive Perspective.* Berlin and New York: Mouton de Gruyter.

Barthes, Roland (1977) *Introduction to the Structural Analysis of Narratives: Image-Music-Text.* London: Fontana.

Bateman, John (2008) *Multimodality and Genre: A Foundation for the Systematic Analysis of Multimodal Documents.* Basingstoke: Palgrave Macmillan.

Bateson, Gregory (2000) *Steps to an Ecology of Mind: Collected Essays in Anthropology, Psychiatry, Evolution and Epistemology.* Chicago: IL, Chicago University Press.

Bezemer, Jeff and Gunther Kress (2008) Writing in multimodal texts: A social semiotic account of designs for learning. *Written Communication* 25 (2): 165–195.

Bjorvand Agnes-Margrethe (2010) Do sons inherit the sins of their fathers? An analysis of the picture book Angry Man. In Teresa Colomer, Bettina Kümmerling-Meibauer and Cecilia Silva-Díaz (eds.) *New Directions in Picture Book Research,* 217–232. New York and London: Routledge.

Boortz, Neal (2007) *Somebody's Gotta Say It.* New York: HarperCollins.

Bortolussi, Marisa (1985) *Análisis Teórico del Cuento Infantil [Analysis of Children's Tales].* Madrid: Alhambra.

Bowcher, Wendy L. (2007) A multimodal analysis of good guys and bad guys in Rugby League Week. In Terry D. Royce and Wendy L. Bowcher (eds) *New Directions in the Analysis of Multimodal Discourse*, 239–274. Mahwah, NJ: Lawrence Erlbaum.

Bravo-Villasante, Carmen (1985) *Diccionario de autores de la literatura infantil mundial [Dictionary of World Authors of Children's Literature]*. Madrid: Escuela Española.

Browne, Anthony (2008) *Piggybook*. London: Walter Books.

Butler, Christopher S. (2003) *Structure and Function: A Guide to Three Major Structural–Functional Theories. Part 1: Approaches to the Simplex Clause. Part 2: From Clause to Discourse and Beyond*. Amsterdam and Philadelphia, PA: John Benjamins.

Butler, Christopher S. (2005) Functional approaches to language. In Christopher Butler, María Gómez-González and Susana Doval-Suárez (eds) *The Dynamics of Language Use: Functional and Contrastive Perspectives*, 3–17. Amsterdam and Philadelphia, PA: John Benjamins.

Butler, Christopher S. (2006) Functionalist theories of language. In Keith Brown (ed.) *The Encyclopaedia of Language and Linguistics*, Second Edition: Volume 4, 696–704. Oxford: Elsevier.

Butler, Christopher, S. (2009) Criteria of Adequacy in Functional Linguistics. *Folia Lingüística* 43 (1): 1–66.

Butler, Christopher S. and Francisco Gonzálvez-Garcia (2005) Situating FDG in Functional-Cognitive Space. In J. Lachlan Mackenzie and Maria de los Ángeles Gómez-González (eds) *Studies in Functional Discourse Grammar*, 109–158. Bern: Peter Lang.

Butler, Christopher S. (2011) Functional Linguistics. In Anne McCabe, *An Introduction to Linguistics and Language Studies*, 365–368. London: Equinox.

Bybee, Joan (2010) *Language and Cognition*. Cambridge: Cambridge University Press.

Bybee, Joan (2012) Usage-based theory and exemplar representations of constructions. In Thomas Hoffman and Graeme Trousdale (eds) *The Oxford Handbook of Construction Grammar*, 49–69. Oxford: Oxford University Press.

Carpenter, Humphrey (1989) Excessively impertinent bunnies: The subversive element in Beatrix Potter. In Gillian Avery and Julia Briggs (eds) *Children and their Books: A Celebration of the Work of Iona and Peter Opie*, 271–298. Oxford: Clarendon Press.

Carpenter, Humphrey and Mari Prichard (1984) *The Oxford Companion to Children's Literature*. Oxford: Oxford University Press.

Cerrillo, Pedro (1996) Qué leer y en qué momento [What to Read and When]. In Pedro Cerrillo and Jaime Garcia Padrino (eds) *Hábitos lectores y animación a la lectura [Getting into the Habit of Reading]*, 47–57. Cuenca: Ediciones de la Universidad de Castilla-La Mancha.

Cerrillo, Pedro and Santiago Yubero (2007) Qué leer y en qué momento [What to read and when]. In Pedro Cerrillo and Santiago Yubero (eds) *La formación de mediadores para la promoción de la lectura. Segunda Edición, [Training Specialists in the Promotion of Reading. 2nd Edition]*, 285–293. Cuenca: Servicio de Publicaciones de la Universidad de Castilla-La Mancha.

Chafe, Wallace (1996) Inferring Identifiability and Accessibility. In Thorstein Fretheim and Jeanette K. Gundel (eds) *Referents and Referent Accessibility*, 37–46. Amsterdam: John Benjamins.

Chomsky, Noam (1957) *Syntactic Structures*. Cambridge, MA: MIT Press.

Chomsky, Noam (1965) *Aspects of the Theory of Syntax*. Cambridge, MA: MIT Press.

Chomsky, Noam (1986) *Knowledge of Language: Its Nature, Origins and Use*. New York: Praeger.

Chomsky, Noam (1995) *The Minimalist Program*. Cambridge, MA: MIT Press.

Chomsky, Noam (2005) Three factors in language design. *Linguistic Inquiry* 36 (1): 1–22.

Colomer, Teresa (1998) *La Formación del Lector Literario. Narrativa Infantil y Juvenil Actual [Training Young Readers to Read. Contemporary Children's Literature]*. Madrid: Fundación Sánchez Ruipérez.

Colomer, Teresa (2001) La Selección de Obras de Referencia Histórica [Selecting Works of Historical Reference]. In Pedro Cerrillo and Jaime García Padrino (eds) *La Literatura Infantil en el siglo XXI [Children's Literature in the XXI Century]*, 67–78. Cuenca: Ediciones de la Universidad de Castilla-La Mancha.

Colomer, Teresa (ed.) (2005) *Siete llaves para valorar las historias infantiles [Seven Keys to Assess Children's Tales]*. Salamanca: Fundación Germán Sánchez Ruipérez.

Colomer, Teresa, Bettina Kümmerling-Meibauer and Cecilia Silva-Díaz (eds) (2010) *New Directions in Picture Book Research*. New York and London: Routledge.

Cornish, Francis (2004) Focus of Attention in Discourse. In Lachlan Mackenzie and María Gómez-González (eds) *A New Architecture for Functional Grammar*, 117–150. Berlin and New York: Mouton de Gruyter.

Croft, William (1995) Autonomy and functionalist linguistics, *Language* 71 (3): 490–532.

Croft, William (2001) *Radical Construction Grammar: Syntactic Theory in Typological Perspective*. Oxford: Oxford University Press.

Culicover, Peter W. and Ray Jackendoff (2005) *Simpler Syntax*. Oxford: Oxford University Press.

Culicover, Peter W. and Ray Jackendoff (2006) The simpler syntax hypothesis. *Trends in Cognitive Linguistics* 10 (9): 413–418.

Cullinan, Bernice E. and Diane G. Person (eds) (2001) *The Continuum Encyclopaedia of Children's Literature*. London: Continuum.

Dahle, Gro and Svein Nyhus (2003) *Sinna Mann [Angry Man]*. Oslo: Cappelen.

Daneš, Frantisek (1974) Functional sentence perspective and the organization of the text. In Frantisek Daneš (ed.) *Papers on Functional Sentence Perspective*, 106–128. Prague: Academic.

Díaz, Jesús (2007) El simbolismo en los muros [Symbolism in the Walls]. *Lenguaje y Textos [Language and Text]* 26: 145–160.

Dik, Simon C. (1989) *The Theory of Functional Grammar. Part 1: The Structure of the Clause.* Dordrecht: Foris.

Dik, Simon C (1997a) *The Theory of Functional Grammar. Part 1: The Structure of the Clause.* Kees Hengeveld (ed.) Berlin/New York: Mouton de Gruyter.

Dik, Simon C. (1997b) *The Theory of Functional Grammar, Part 2: Complex and Derived Structures.* Kees Hengeveld (ed.). Berlin/New York: Mouton de Gruyter.

Dillon, Grace (2006) *Writing with Images: Introduction: Image Text Multiples and other Mixed Modes.* Retrieved on 3 May 2013 from http://courses.washington.edu/hypertxt/cgi-bin/book/wordsimages/wordsimages.html

Donaldson, Margaret (1978) *Children's Minds.* London: Fontana Press.

Downing, Angela (1991) An alternative approach to theme: A systemic-functional perspective. *Word* 42 (2): 119–143.

Downing, Angela and Philip Locke (2006) *English Grammar. A University Course. Second Edition.* London and New York: Routledge.

Eco, Umberto (1979) *The Role of the Reader: Explorations in the Semiotics of Texts.* Bloomington, IN: Indiana University Press.

Eggins, Suzanne ([1994] 2004) *An Introduction to Systemic Functional Linguistics,* 12th Edition. New York/London: Continuum.

Elleström, Lars (ed.) (2010) *Media Borders, Multimodality and Intermediality.* Basingstoke: Palgrave Macmillan.

Fabb, Nigel (1997) *Linguistics and Literature.* Oxford: Blackwell.

Fairclough, Norman (1995) *Critical Discourse Analysis. The Critical Study of Language.* London: Longman.

Fawcett, Robin P. (2000) A *Theory of Syntax for Systemic Functional Linguistics.* Amsterdam and Philadelphia, PA: John Benjamins.

Fawcett, Robin P. (2008) *Invitation to Sytemic Functional Linguistics through the Cardiff Grammar. An Extension and Simplification of Halliday's Systemic Functional Grammar.* 3rd edition. London: Equinox.

Feaver, William (1977) *When We Were Young: Two Centuries of Children's Book Illustrations.* London: Thames and Hudson.

Firth, Jan R. (1957) *Papers in Linguistics 1934–1951.* London: Oxford University Press.

Foley, William. A. and Robert .D. Van Valin Jr. (1984) *Functional Syntax and Universal Grammar.* Cambridge: Cambridge University Press.

Forceville, Charles (2006) Non-verbal and multimodal metaphor in a cognitive framework. agendas for research. In Gitte Kristiasen, Michel Achard, René Dirven and Francisco Ruiz de Mendoza (eds) *Cognitive Linguistics: Current Applications and Future Perspectives,* 379–402. Berlin and New York: Mouton de Gruyter.

Forceville, Charles (2009) Metonymy in visual and audiovisual discourse. In Eija Ventola and A. Jesús Moya (eds) *The World Told and the World Shown: Multisemiotic Issues,* 56–74. London: Palgrave Macmillan.

Forceville, Charles (2010a) *Review: The Routledge Handbook of Multimodal Analysis.* Retrieved on 10 January 2013 from *Journal of Pragmatics*: http://www.elsevier.com/wps/find/journaldescription.cws_home/505593/description#description

Forceville, Charles (2010b) Why and how study metaphor, metonymy, and other tropes in multimodal discourse? In Rosario Caballero and Maria Jesús Pinar (eds) *Ways and Modes of Human Communication,* 56–76. Cuenca: Ediciones de la Universidad de Castilla-La Mancha.

Forceville, Charles (2011) Review: Elleström, Lars (ed.) (2010) *Media Borders, Multimodality and Intermediality.* Houndmills, Basingstoke: Palgrave Macmillan. *Journal of Pragmatics* 43 (12): 3091–3094.

Fowler, Roger (1986) *Linguistic Criticism.* Oxford: Oxford University Press.

Fox, Barbara (2007) Principles shaping grammatical practices. An exploration. *Discourse Studies* 9 (3): 299–318.

Fries, Peter (1981) On the status of Theme in English: Arguments from discourse. *Forum Linguisticum* 6 (1): 1–38.

Gamble, Nikki. and Sally Yates (2002) *Exploring Children's Literature: Teaching the Language and Reading Fiction.* London: Paul Chapman.

Genette, Gérard (1989) *Palimpsesto. La Literatura en el Segundo Grado [Palimpsest. Literature in the Second Grade].* Madrid: Taurus.

Ghadessy, Mohsen (ed.) (1995a) *Thematic Development in English Texts.* London: Pinter Publisher.

Ghadessy, Mohsen (1995b) Thematic development and its relationship to registers and genres. In Mohsen Ghadessy (ed.) *Thematic Development in English Texts,* 105–128. London: Pinter.

Gibson, James (1977) The theory of Affordances. In Robert Shaw and John Bransford (eds) *Perceiving, Acting, and Knowing.* Hillsdale: NJ: Lawrence Erlbaum Associates.

Gill, Talia (2002) *Visual and Verbal Playmates: An Exploration of Visual and Verbal Modalities in Children's Picture Books.* Unpublished BA (Honours). Department of Linguistics, University of Sydney.

Givón, Talmy (ed.) (1983) *Topic Continuity in Discourse: A Quantitative Cross-language Study.* Amsterdam and Philadelphia, PA: Jonh Benjamins.

Givón, Talmy (1993a) *English Grammar: A Function-Based Introduction.* Vol 1. Amsterdam: John Benjamins.

Givón, Talmy (1993b) *English Grammar: A Function-Based Introduction.* Vol 2. Amsterdam: John Benjamins.

Givón, Talmy (1995) *Functionalism and Grammar.* Amsterdam and Philadelphia, PA: Benjamins.

Givón, Talmy (2001a) *Syntax: An Introduction. Vol. 1* . Amsterdam: John Benjamins.

Givón, Talmy (2001b) *Syntax: An Introduction. Vol. 2.* Amsterdam: John Benjamins.

Goatly, Andrew (2008) *Explorations in Stylistics.* London: Equinox.

Goffman, Erving (1983) The Interaction Order: American Sociological Association, 1982 Presidential Address. *American Sociological Review* 48 (1): 1–17.

Golberg, Adele (1999) *Construction Grammar (A Reader for the LSA Summer Institute).* University of Illinois at Urbana–Champaign.

Golden, Joanne M. (1990) *The Narrative Symbol in Childhood Literature: Explorations in the Construction of Text.* Berlin: Mouton.

Gonzálvez-Garcia, Francisco and Christopher S. Butler (2006) Mapping functional-cognitive space. *Annual Review of Cognitive Linguistics* 4: 39–96.

Graham, Judith (2000) Creativity and picture books. *Reading* 34 (2): 61–67.

Gregory, Michael (1967) Aspects of varieties differentiation. *Journal of Linguistics* 3 (2): 177–197.

Gregory, Michael (1978) *Language and Situation: Language Varieties and their Social Contexts.* London: Routledge and Kegan Paul.

Gregory, Michael (1988) Generic situation and register: A functional view of communication. In J. D. Benson, M. J. Cummings and W. S. Greaves (eds) *Linguistics in a Systematic Perspective,* 301–329. Amsterdam: Benjamins.

Hall, Edward. T. (1992) *An Anthropology of Everyday Life: An Autobiography.* New York: Anchor Books.

Halliday, M. A. K. (1968) Notes on transitivity and theme in English. Part 3. *Journal of Linguistics* 4 (2): 179–215.

Halliday, M. A. K. (1970a) Language structure and language functions. In John Lyons (ed.) *New Horizons in Linguistics,* 140–165. Harmondsworth: Penguin.

Halliday, M. A. K. (1970b) Functional diversity in language as seen from a consideration of modality and mood in English. *Foundations of Language* 6 (3): 322–336.

Halliday, M. A. K. (1978) *Language as Social Semiotic: The Social Interpretation of Language and Meaning.* London: Edward Arnold.

Halliday, M. A. K. (1994 [1985]) *An Introduction to Functional Grammar.* London: Edward Arnold.

Halliday, M. A. K. (2004) *An Introduction to Functional Grammar.* Third Edition. Revised by Christian M. I. M. Matthiessen. London: Edward Arnold.

Halliday, M. A. K. and Christian Mathiessen (1999) *Constructing Experience through Meaning: A Language-Based Approach to Cognition.* London and New York: Cassell.

Halliday, M. A. K. and Ruqaiya Hasan. (1985/1989) *Language, Context, and Text: Aspects of Language in a Social-Semiotics Perspective.* Geelong, Victoria: Deakin University Press. Republished 1989, Oxford: Oxford University Press.

Hanán Díaz, Fanuel (1998) Códigos Perdidos: Recuperando Imágenes en los Libros Ilustrados. [Lost Codes: Recovering Images in Picture Books] *Relalij,* Julio/Diciembre 8*:* 18–23.

Hanán Díaz, Fanuel (2007) *Leer y mirar el libro álbum: ¿un género en construcción? [Reading and Seeing Picture Books. A Developing Genre]* Bogotá: Grupo Norma.

Hazard, Paul (1964) *Los Libros, los Niños y los Hombres [Books, Children and Men]*. Barcelona: Juventud.

Hengeveld, Kees and J. Lachlan Mackenzie (2006) Functional Discourse Grammar. In Keith Brown (ed.) *The Encyclopaedia of Language and Linguistics*. Second Edition, 668–676. Oxford: Elsevier.

Hengeveld, Kess and J. Lachlan Mackenzie (2008) *Functional Discourse Grammar. A Typologically-based Theory of Language Structure*. Oxford: Oxford University Press.

Hengeveld, Kees and J. Lachlan Mackenzie (2009) Functional Discourse Grammar. In Bernd Heine and Heiko Narrog (eds) *The Oxford Handbook of Linguistic Analysis*, 367–400. Oxford: Oxford University Press.

Hoperabundo, Anna and EijaVentola (2009) Multisemiotic marketing and advertising: Globalization versus localization and the media. In Eija Ventola and A. Jesús Moya (eds) *The World Told and the Wold Shown: Multisemiotic Issues*, 183–206. London: Palgrave Macmillan.

Hopper, Paul. J. (1987) Emergent Grammar. *Proceedings of Berkerly Linguistics Society* 13: 139–157.

Hopper, Paul J. (1998) Emergent Grammar. In Michael Tomasello (ed.) *The New Psychology of Language: Cognitive and Functional Approaches to Language Structure*, 155–175. Mahwah, NJ: Lawrence Erlbaum.

Hopper, Paul J. (1988) Emergent Grammar and the A Priori Grammar Constraint. In Deborah Tannen (ed.) *Linguistics in Context: Connecting Observation and Understanding*. 117–134. Norwood, NJ: Ablex.

Hopper, Paul J. and Sandra A. Thompson (1980) Transitivity in grammar and discourse. *Language* 56 (2): 251–299.

Hopper, Paul J. and Sandra A. Thompson (1993) Language universals, discourse pragmatics, and semantics. *Language Sciences* 15 (4): 357–376.

Hopper, Paul and Sandra A. Thompson (2008) Projectability and clause combining in interaction. In Laury, Ritva (ed.) *Crosslinguistic Studies of Clause Combining: the Multifunctionality of Conjunctions*, 99–124. Amsterdam: John Benjamins.

Hunt, Peter (1991) *Criticism and Children's Literature*. Oxford: Basil Blackwell.

Hunt, Peter (ed.) (2004) *International Companion Encyclopaedia of Children's Literature. Second Edition. Volume I.* London: Routledge.

Hürlimann, Bettina (1968) *Tres Siglos de Literatura Infantil Europea [Three Centuries of European Children's Literature]*. Barcelona: Juventud.

Jackendoff, Ray (2007) A whole lot of challenges for linguistics. *Journal of English Linguistics* 35 (3): 253–262.

Jenks, Chris (1995) *Visual Culture*. London: Routledge.

Jewitt, Carey (ed.) (2009a) *The Routledge Handbook of Multimodal Analysis*. London and New York: Routledge.

Jewitt, Carey (2009b) An introduction to multimodality. In Carey Jewitt (ed.) *The Routledge Handbook of Multimodal Analysis,* 14–27. London and New York: Routledge.

Jewitt, Carey (2009c) Different approaches to multimodality. In Carey Jewitt (ed.) *The Routledge Handbook of Multimodal Analysis,* 28–39. London and New York: Routledge.

Jones, Rodney (2005) You show me yours, I'll show you mine: The negotiation of shifts from textual to visual modes in computer mediated interaction among gay men. *Visual Communication* 4 (1): 69–92.

Jones, Rodney (2009) Technology and sites of display. In Carey Jewitt (ed.) *The Routledge Handbook of Multimodal Analysis,* 114–126. London and New York: Routledge.

Jordan, Alice (1973) Children's classics. In Virginia Haviland (ed.). *Children and Literature. Views and Reviews,* 38–43. London: The Bodley Head.

Knox, John S (2009) Phd dissertation. *On Online Newspaper Home Pages: A Social-Semiotic Perspective.* University of Sydney.

Kress. Günther (1997) Visual and verbal modes of representation in electronically mediated communication: the potentials of new forms of text. In Ilana Snyder (ed.) *Page to Screen: Taking Literacy into the Electronic Era,* 53–79. Sydney: Allen and Unwin.

Kress, Günter (2000) Design and transformation: New theories of meaning. In Bill Cope and Mary Kalantzis (eds) *Multiliteracies: Learning Literacy and the Design of Social Futures,* 153–61. Melbourne: Macmillan.

Kress, Günther (2003a) Genres and the multimodal production of 'Scientificness'. In Carey Jewitt and Gunther Kress (eds) *Multimodal Literacy,* 173–86. New York: Peter Lang.

Kress, Günther (2003b) *Literacy in the New Media Age.* London: Routledge.

Kress, Günther (2009) What is mode? In Carey Jewitt (ed.) *The Routledge Handbook of Multimodal Analysis,* 54–67. London and New York: Routledge.

Kress, Günther (2010) Multimodality. A *Social Semiotic Approach to Contemporary Communication.* London and New York: Routledge.

Kress, Günther and Theo van Leeuwen (2001) *Multimodal Discourse. The Modes and Media of Contemporary Communication.* London: Arnold.

Kress, Günther and Theo van Leeuwen (2002) Colour as a semiotic mode: Notes for grammar of colour. *Visual Communication* 1 (3): 343–368.

Kress, Günther and Theo van Leeuwen (2006 [1996]) *Reading Images. The Grammar of Visual Design.* London: Routledge.

Kuno, Susumu (1980) Functional Syntax. In E. A. Moravcsik and J. R. Wirth (eds) *Current Approaches to Syntax,* 117–135. New York: Academic Press.

Lakoff, George and Mark Johnson (1980) *Metaphors We Live By.* Chicago, IL: University of Chicago Press.

Lemke, Jay (1998a) Introduction: Language and other semiotic systems in education. *Linguistics and Education* 10 (3): 245–246.
Lemke, Jay (1998b) Multiplying meaning: Visual and verbal semiotics in scientific texts. In Jim Martin and R. Veel (eds) *Reading Science: Critical and Functional Perspectives on Discourses of Science,* 87–113. London: Routledge.
Lemke, Jay (2000) Opening up closure: Semiotics across scales. In Jerry L. R. Chandler and Gertrudis Van de Vijver (eds) *Closure: Emergent Organizations and their Dynamics.* Vol. 901, 100–111. New York: Annals of the New York Academy of Sciences.
Lemke, Jay (2002) Travels in hypermodality. *Visual Communication 1 (3):* 199–325.
Lewis, David (2006 [2001]) *Reading Contemporary Picture Books. Picturing Text.* London: Routledge.
Light, P. H, Dorothea N. Buckingham and A. H. Robbins (1979*)* Conservational Task as an Interactional Setting. *British Journal of Educational Psychology* 49 (3): 304 –310.
Lim Fei, Victor (2004) Developing an integrative multi-semiotic model. In Kay O'Halloran (ed.) *Multimodal Discourse Analysis. Systemic Functional Perspectives,* 220–247. London/New York: Continuum.
Lim Fei, Victor (2007) The visual semantics stratum: Making meaning in sequential images. In Terry D. Royce and Wendy L. Bowcher (eds) *New Directions in the Analysis of Multimodal Discourse,* 195–214. Mahwah: Lawrence Erlbaum.
LLuch, Gema (2003) *Cómo analizamos relatos infantiles y juveniles [How to Analyse children's Stories].* Bogotá: Norma.
Machin, David (2007) *Introduction to Multimodal Analysis.* London: Hodder Arnold.
Machin, David (2009) Multimodality and the theories of the visual. In Carey Jewitt (ed.) *The Routledge Handbook of Multimodal Analysis,* 181–190. London and New York: Routledge.
Malinowski, Bronislaw (1923) *The Problem of Meaning in Primitive Languages. Supplement to C. K. Ogden and I. A. Richards. The Meaning of Meaning.* London: Routledge and Kogan Paul.
Malinowski, Bronislaw (1935) *Coral Gardens and their Magic,* Vol. 2. London: George, Allen and Unwin.
Martin, Jim (1992) *English Text: System and Structure.* Amsterdam and Philadelphia, PA: John Benjamins.
Martin, Jim (2001) Giving the game away: Explicitness, diversity and genre-based literacy in Australia. In R. de Cilla, H. J. Krumm and R. Wodak (eds) *Functional Il/Literacy,* 155–174. Vienna: Verlag der Osterreichischen Akadamie der Wissenschaften.
Martin, Jim (2008) Intermodal reconciliation: Men in arms. In Len Unsworth (ed.) *New Literacies and the English Curriculum: Multimodal Perspectives,* 112–148. London: Continuum.

Martin, Jim and David Rose (2007 [2003]) *Working with Discourse: Meaning beyond the Clause*. Second Edition. London: Continuum.

Martin, Jim and David Rose (2008) *Genre Relations. Mapping Culture*. London: Equinox.

Martin, Jim R. and Peter White (2005) *The Language of Evaluation, Appraisal in English*. London and New York: Palgrave Macmillan.

Martinec, Radan and Andrew Salway (2005) A system for image-text relations in new (and old) media. *Visual Communication 4 (3)*: 337–371.

Martínez-Cabeza, Miguel Ángel (2002) *The Study of Language beyond the Sentence. From Text Grammar to Discourse Analysis*. Granada: Comares.

Matthiessen, Christian (2007) The multimodal page: A systemic functional exploration. In Terry Royce and Wendy Bowcher (eds) *New Directions in the Analysis of Multimodal Discourse*, 1–62. London: Lawrence Erlbaum.

Matthiessen, Christian (2009) Multisemiosis and context-based register typology: Registerial variation in the complementarity of semiotic systems. In Eija Ventola and A. Jesús Moya. *The World Told and the World Shown: Multisemiotic Issues*, 11–38. London: Palgrave Macmillan.

McCloud, Scott (1994) *Understanding Comics: The Invisible Art*. New York: Harper Collins.

Mendikoetxea, Amaya (2011) Formal linguistics. In Anne McCabe *An Introduction to Linguistics and Language Studies*, 362–365. London: Equinox.

Moebius, William (1986) Introduction to picture books codes. *Word and Image* 2 (2): 141–158.

Moya, A. Jesús (2005) The assignment of topical status in FDG: A textual analysis. In J. Lachlan Mackenzie and María de los Ángeles Gómez-González (eds) *Studies in Functional Discourse Grammar. Linguistic Insights. Studies in Language and Communication*, 195–226. Berlin: Peter Lang.

Moya, A. Jesús (2006) The continuity of topics in journal and travel texts: A discourse functional perspective. *Functions of Language* 13 (1): 37–76.

Moya, A. Jesús (2010) A multimodal analysis of *The Tale of Peter Rabbit* within the interpersonal metafunction. *ATLANTIS* 32 (1): 123–140.

Moya, A. Jesús (2011) Engaging readers through language and pictures. A case study. *Journal of Pragmatics* 43 (12): 2982–2991.

Moya, A. Jesús (2013) Visual metonymy in children's picture books. In Maria J. Pinar (ed.) *Multimodality and Cognitive Linguistics. Special Issue of Review of Cognitive Linguistics* 11 (2): 336–352.

Moya, A. Jesús and Jesús A. Ávila (2009) Thematic progression of chilldren's stories as related to different stages of cognitive development. *Text and Talk* 29 (6): 755–774.

Moya, A. Jesús and Mª Jesús Pinar (2008) Compositional, interpersonal and representational meanings in a children's narrative. A multimodal discourse analysis. *Journal of Pragmatics* 40 (9): 1601–1619.

Moya, A. Jesús and Mª Jesús Pinar (2009) On Interaction of image and verbal text in a picture book. A multimodal and systemic functional study. In Eija Ventola and A. Jesús Moya (eds) *The World Told and the World Shown: Multisemiotic Issues,* 107–123. London: Palgrave Macmillan.

Nichols, Johanna (1984) Functional theories of grammar. *Annual Review of Anthopology,* 13: 97–117.

Nikolajeva, Maria (2010) Interpretative codes and implied readers of children's picturebooks. In Teresa Colomer, Bettina Kümmerling-Meibauer and Cecilia Silva-Díaz (eds) *New Directions in Picture book Research,* 27–40. New York and London: Routledge.

Nikolajeva, Maria and Carole Scott (2000) The dynamics of picture books communication. *Children's Literature in Education* 31 (4): 225–239.

Nikolajeva, Maria and Carole Scott (2001) *How Picture Books Work.* New York and London: Garland Publishing.

Nodelman, Perry (1988) *Words about Pictures: The Narrative Art of Children's Picture Books.* Athens, GA: The University of Georgia Press.

Nodelman, Perry (1989) Decoding the images. How picture books work. In Peter Hunt (ed.) *Understanding Children's Literature,* 129–139. London and New York: Routledge.

Norris, Sigrid (2004) *Analysing Multimodal Interaction. A Methodological Framework.* New York and London: Routledge.

Norris, Sigrid (2009) Modal density and modal configurations: Multimodal actions. In Carey Jewitt (ed.) *The Routledge Handbook of Multimodal Analysis,* 78–90. London and New York: Routledge.

Norris, Sigrid and Rodney Jones (eds) (2005) *Discourse in Action: Introducing Mediated Discourse Analysis.* London: Routledge.

O'Halloran, Kay (1999) Interdependence, interaction and metaphor in multisemiotic texts. *Social Semiotics* 9 (3): 317–354.

O'Halloran, Kay (2000) Classroom discourse in mathematics: A multi-semiotic analysis. *Linguistics and Education* 10 (3): 359–388.

O'Halloran, Kay (2003) Intersemiosis in mathematics and science: Grammatical metaphor and semiotic metaphor. In Anne Marie Simon-Vandenbergen, Miriam Taverniers and Louise Rabelli (eds) *Grammatical Metaphor: Views from Systemic-Functional Linguistics,* 337–365. Amsterdam: John Benjamins.

O'Halloran, Kay (ed.) (2004) *Multimodal Discourse Analysis. Systemic Functional Perspectives.* London and New York: Continuum.

O'Halloran, Kay (ed.) (2005) *Mathematical Discourse: Language, Symbolism and Visual Images.* London: Continuum.

O'Halloran, Kay (2007) Systemic Functional Multimodal Discourse Analysis (SF-MDA) approach to mathematics, grammar and literacy. In Anne McCabe, Mick O'Donnell and Rachel Whittaker (eds) *Advances in Language and Education,* 77–102. London: Continuum.

O'Halloran, Kay (2008) Systemic Functional Discourse Analysis (SF-MDA): constructing ideational meaning using language and visual imagery. *Visual Communication* 7 (4): 443–475.

O'Halloran, Kay (2009) Historical changes in the semiotic landscape: From calculation to computation. In Carey Jewitt (ed.) *The Routledge Handbook of Multimodal Analysis*, 97–113. London and New York: Routledge.

O'Halloran, L. Kay and Bradley Smith (2011) Multimodal Text Analysis. Retrieved on 3 May 2013 from http://multimodal-analysis-lab.org/_docs/encyclopedia/01-Multimodal_Text_Analysis-O'Halloran_and_Smith.pdf

O'Toole, Michael (1994) *The Language of Displayed Art*. London: Liecester University Press.

O'Toole, Michael (1999) *Engaging with Art. A New Way of Looking at Paintings*. Perth: Murdoch University.

O'Toole, Michael (2004) Opera Ludentes: The Sydney Opera House at work and play. In Kay O'Halloran (ed.) *Multimodal Discourse Analysis*, 11–27. London: Continuum.

O'Toole, Michael (2011) *The Language of Displayed Art*. London: Routledge.

Painter, Claire (2007) Children's picture book narratives: Reading sequences of images. In Anne McCabe, Mick O'Donnell and Rachel Whittaker (eds) *Advances in Language and Education*, 40–59. London: Continuum.

Painter, Claire Jim Martin and Len Unsworth (2013) *Reading Visual Narratives. Image Analysis of Children's Picture Books*. Sheffield and Bristol, CT: Equinox.

Pelayo, Alex (2006) *Herramientas de la ilustración para crear significado [Visual Strategies to Create Meaning]*. In CRA (Centro de Recursos para el Aprendizaje) [Learning Resources Centre] (ed.). *Ver para leer: acercándonos al libro album [Seeing to Read. Approaching Picture Books]*, 54–65. Chile: Unidad de Currículum y Evaluación (Curriculum and Assessment Unit)/Centro de Recursos para el Aprendizaje [Learning Resources Centre]. Ministerio de Educación.

Peña, Manuel (2006) *El libro álbum, un objeto cultural [Picture Books as Cultural Objects]*. In CRA (Centro de Recursos para el Aprendizaje). [Learning Resources Centre] (ed.). *Ver para leer: acercándonos al libro album [Seeing to Read. Approaching Picture Books]*. 34–39. Chile: Unidad de Currículum y Evaluación (Curriculum and Assessment Unit)/Centro de Recursos para el Aprendizaje [Learning Resources Centre]. Ministerio de Educación.

Piaget, Jean (1981) *Psicología y pedagogía [Psychology and Pedagogy]* (8ª edición). Barcelona: Ariel.

Piaget, Jean (1984) *La Representación del Mundo del Niño [The Child's Conception of the Word]*. (6 Edición). Madrid: Morata.

Prince, Ellen. F. (1978) A comparison of Wh-clefts and It-clefts in discourse. *Language* 54 (4): 883–906.

Prince, Ellen F. (1981) Toward a taxonomy of given-new information. In Peter Cole (ed.) *Radical Pragmatics*, 223–255. New York: Academic Press.

Reynolds, Kimberly (ed.) (2005) *Modern Children's Literature: An Introduction*. London: Palgrave Macmillan.

Royce, Terry D. (2007) Intersemiotic complementarity: A framework for Multimodal Discourse Analysis. In Terry D. Royce and Wendy L. Bowcher (eds) *New Directions in the Analysis of Multimodal Discourse*, 63–110. Mahwah: Lawrence Erlbaum.

Schwarcz, Joseph (1982) *Ways of the Illustrator: Visual Communication in Children's Literature*. Chicago, IL: American Library Association.

Silva-Díaz, Cecilia (2006) *La función de la imagen en el álbum [The Function of Picture Books]*. In *Ver para leer: acercándonos al libro album [Seeing to Read. Approaching Picture Books]*, 42–53. Santiago de Chile: Unidad de Currículum y Evaluación (Curriculum and Assessment Unit)/Centro de Recursos para el Aprendizaje [Learning Resources Centre]. Ministerio de Educación.

Scollon, Ron (1998) Reading as social interaction: The empirical grounding of reading. *Semiotica* 118 (3–4): 281–294.

Scollon, Ron (2001) *Mediated Discourse. The Nexus of Practice*. London: Routledge.

Scollon, Ron and, Scollon Suzie Wong (2003) *Discourse in Place: Language in the Material World*. New York: Routledge.

Scollon, Ron and Scollon, Suzie Wong (2009) Multimodality and language: A retrospective and prospective view. In Carey Jewitt (ed.) *The Routledge Handbook of Multimodal Analysis*, 170–180. London and New York: Routledge.

Scott, Carole (2001) An unusual hero: Perspective and point of view in *The Tale of Peter Rabbit*. In Margaret Mackey (ed.) *Beatrix Potter's Peter Rabbit: A Children's Classic at 100*, 19–30. Lanham, MC: Scarecrow.

Sikorska, Magdalena (2005) The stories illustrations tell: The creative illustrating strategy in the pictures by Beatrix Potter and Janosch. *New Review of Children's Literature and Librarianship* 11 (1): 1–14.

Sipe, Lawrence (2008) *Storytime: Young Children's Literary Understanding in the Classroom*. New York: Teachers College Press.

Sipe, Lawrence (2012) Revisiting the relationship between text and pictures. *Children's Literature in Education* 43 (1): 4–21.

Soriano, Marc (1995) *La Literatura para Niños y Jóvenes: Guía de Exploración de sus Grandes Temas [Children's Literature: A Guide to Critical Themes]*. Buenos Aires: Colihue.

Spitz, Ellen (1999) *Inside Picture Books*. New Haven, CT: Yale University Press.

Strachan, Linda (2009) *Writing for Children*. London: AC Black Publishers.

Stengling, Maree (2009) Space and communication in exhibitions: Unravelling the nexus. In Carey Jewitt (ed.) *The Routledge Handbook of Multimodal Analysis*, 272–283. London and New York: Routledge.

Stevenson, Deborah (1998) Narrative in picture books or, the paper that should have had slides. In Betsy Hearne, Janice del Negro, C. Jenkins and Deborah Stevenson (eds) *Story: From Fireplace to Cyberspace*: 66–77. Urbana, IL: The Board of Trustees of the University of Illinois.

Sunderland, Jane (2011) *Language, Gender and Children's Fiction*. London: Continuum.

Taylor, Judy (1987) *Beatrix Potter and Peter Rabbit*. London: F. Warne and Co.

Taylor, Judy (2002) Category extension by metonymy and metaphor. In René Driven and Ralf Pörings (eds) *Metaphor and Metonymy in Comparison and Contrast*, 323–334. Berlin and New York: Mouton de Gruyter.

Thompson Geoff and Peter Muntigl (2008) Systemic Functional Linguistics: An interpersonal perspective. In Antos Gerd and Eija Ventola (eds) *Handbook of Interpersonal Communication*, 77–106. Berlin and New York: Mouton de Gruyter.

Townsend, John Rowe (1990) Standards of criticism for children's literature. In Peter Hunt (ed.) *Children's Literature: The Development of Criticism*, 57–70. London: Routledge.

Townsend, John Rowe (1983) *Written for Children*. London: Penguin.

Tucker, Nicholas (1984) *The Child and the Book: A Psychological and Literary Exploration*. Cambridge: Cambridge University Press.

Tucker, Nicholas (2002a) *The Rough Guide to Children's Books 0–5 Years*. London: Rough Guides.

Tucker, Nicholas (2002b) *The Rough Guide to Children's Books 5–11 Years*. London: Rough Guides.

Unsworth, Len (2006) Towards a metalanguage for multiliteracies education: Describing the meaning-making resources of language-image interaction. *English Teaching, Practice and Critique* 5 (1): 55–76.

Unsworth, Len (2008a) Explicating inter-modal meaning-making in media and literary texts: Towards a metalanguage of image/text relations. In Andrew Burn and Cal Durrant (eds) *Media Teaching: Language, Audience, Production*, 48–80. London: AATE-NATE and Wakefield Press.

Unsworth, Len (2008b) Multiliteracies and metalanguage: Describing image/text relations as a resource for negotiating multimodal texts. In Donald J. Leu, Julie Corio, Michele Knobel and Colin Lankshear (ed.) *Handbook of Research on New Literacies*, 377–405. Mahwah, NJ: Erlbaum.

Unsworth, Len and Chris Cléirigh (2009) Multimodality and reading: The construction of meaning through image-text interaction. In Carey Jewitt (ed.) *The Routledge Handbook of Multimodal Analysis*, 151–164. London and New York: Routledge.

Van Dijk, Teun (1981) Sentence topic and discourse topic. In Teun van Dijk *Studies in the Pragmatics of Discourse*, 177–193. La Haya: Mouton Publishers.

Van Leeuwen, Theo (2005a) *Introducing Social Semiotics*. London: Routledge.

Van Leeuwen, Theo (2005b) Typographic meaning. *Visual Communication* 4 (2): 138–143.

Van Leeuwen, Theo (2009) Parametric systems: The case of voice quality. In Carey Jewitt (ed.) *The Routledge Handbook of Multimodal Analysis*, 68–77. London and New York: Routledge.

Van Leeuwen, Theo (2011) *The Language of Colour: An Introduction*. London: Routledge.

Van Valin, Robert D., Jr. (1995) Role and reference grammar. In Jef Verschueren, Jan-Ola Östman and Jan Blommaert (eds) *Handbook of Pragmatics*, 461–469. Manual. Amsterdam and Philadelphia, PA: Benjamins.

Van Valin, Robert, D., Jr. (2000) Functional linguistics. In Mark Aronoff and Janie Rees (eds) *The Handbook of Linguistics*, 319–336. Oxford: Blackwell.

Van Valin, Robert D., Jr. (2005) *Exploring the Syntax-Semantics Interface*. Cambridge: Cambridge University Press.

Van Valin, Robert D., Jr and Randy J. LaPolla (1997) *Syntax: Structure, Meaning and Function*. Cambridge: Cambridge University Press.

Ventola, Eija, Charles Cassily and Martin Kaltenbacher (2004) *Perspectives on Multimodality*. Amsterdam: John Benjamins.

Ventola, Eija and A. Jesús Moya (eds) (2009) *The Word Told and the World Shown: Multisemiotic Issues*. London: Palgrave Macmillan.

Virilio, Paul (1994) *The Vision Machine*. Indianapolis, IN: Indiana University Press.

Vygotsky, Lev (1978) *El Desarrollo de los Procesos Psicológicos Superiores [The Development of Higher Mental Functions]*. Barcelona: Crítica.

Zaparaín Fernando and Luis Daniel González (2010) *Cruce de caminos. Álbumes ilustrados: construcción y lectura. [A Crossroads. Picture Books: Construction and Reading]*. Cuenca and Valladolid: Editions of the University of Castilla-La Mancha and the University of Valladolid.

Picture books

Browne, Anthony (2002 [1983]) *Gorilla*. London: Walter Books.

Burningham, John (2003 [1984]) *Granpa*. London: Red Fox.

Campbell, Rod (2007 [1982]) *Dear Zoo*. Malaysia: Macmillan.

Carle, Eric (2002 [1969]) *The Very Hungry Caterpillar*. China: Puffin.

Hill, Eric (2009 [1980]) *Where's Spot?* London: Penguin.

McBratney, Sam and Anita Jeram (2006 [1994]) *Guess How Much I Love You*. London: Walker Books

Pfister, Marcus (2010 [1992]) *The Rainbow Fish*. Hong Kong: NorthSouth.

Potter, Beatrix (2002 [1902]) The Tale of Peter Rabbit, 1902. In Beatrix Potter *The Complete Tales. The Original and Authorized Edition by Frederick Warne*, 9–20. London: Penguin.

Sendak, Maurice (2007 [1963]) *Where the Wild Things Are*. London: Red Fox.

Index

www.ingramcontent.com/pod-product-compliance
Lightning Source LLC
LaVergne TN
LVHW010443080826
844660LV00026B/1207
* 9 7 8 1 9 0 8 0 4 9 7 8 0 *